Interagency Fratricide

Policy Failures in the Persian Gulf and Bosnia

Vicki J. Rast
Major, USAF

Air University Press
Maxwell AFB, AL 36112-6615

June 2004

Air University Library Cataloging Data

Rast, Vicki J., 1966-
    Interagency fratricide : policy failures in the Persian Gulf and Bosnia / Vicki J.
Rast.
        p. : ill. ; cm.
    Includes bibliographical references and index.
    ISBN 1-58566-126-0
    1. War—Termination. 2. United States—Government policy—Decision making.
3. Civil-military relations—United States. 4. Military art and science—Decision making. 5. Administrative agencies—United States. 6. Public administration—Decision
making. I. Title.
    341.66—dc22

Disclaimer

Air University Press
131 West Shumacher Avenue
Maxwell AFB AL 36112–6615
http://aupress.maxwell.af.mil

Where there is no vision, the people perish.
Proverbs 29:18 (KJV)

For all who have dedicated their lives
to the pursuit of security . . .
especially those who have made the ultimate sacrifice.

Contents

PART I
Framing the Problem

PART II
Analysis and Findings

PART III
Conflict Termination Policy Development

Illustrations

Figure

Tables

Foreword

Leaders face enigmatic challenges within our increasingly complex world of international affairs. Foremost among them for the US government is determining how senior officials—policy makers and military commanders—can harness effectively the friction inherent to the interagency policy-making process, doing so in ways that advance US national security during interventions into conflicts and wars. Specifically, leaders and decision makers at every level must understand the roles they play in generating and sustaining interagency conflict that detracts from the nation's capacity to develop sound conflict termination policy, thereby impairing our ability to analyze crises, envision desired end states, formulate termination criteria, and execute termination strategies. To address this issue, we must first understand the sources of that friction, identifying its causes and consequences across the policy-making arena.

Interagency Fratricide: Policy Failures in the Persian Gulf and Bosnia provides a comprehensive analysis of the factors that affected both interagency processes and policy outcomes during the Persian Gulf War (1990–91) and the early stages of the Bosnia crisis (1993–95). Going one-on-one with members of Washington's policy elite who were involved directly in these two cases, the author demonstrates that the US government's approach to termination policy proved fragmented and personality driven. She systematically presents evidence to support the study's conclusion, revealing that the nature of the gap between diplomats and war fighters will consistently produce policies that bring about cease-fire in the form of war termination, but fail to address the underlying causes and conditions that generated conflict (and, potentially, war). These issues must be resolved if the US government hopes to improve the social and political conditions of those embroiled in conflict while at the same time bolstering a security posture favorable to US interests in the aftermath of intervention. The three sections of this work thematically present the interagency process, the analysis and its findings, and implications for future termination policy development endeavors.

This book is the first of its kind. It integrates the real-world experiences of post–Cold War diplomats and war fighters, demonstrating that *both* need to think in more far-reaching terms regarding the development of conflict termination policy and the interagency's role therein. As Carl von Clausewitz says, this type of intellectual endeavor must be undertaken "before the first shot is fired." To accomplish this feat, policy makers must cast aside their institutional and individual personalities to determine what is best for those on whose behalf the United States intervenes—especially when the armed forces are called upon to act in the service of our country. I commend this work to you as a necessary first step in understanding interagency policy making. It's up to you to bridge the gaps between diplomats and war fighters toward creating effective conflict termination policy in the future.

RONALD R. FOGLEMAN
General, USAF, Retired

About the Author

Maj Vicki J. Rast is a 1988 graduate of the United States Air Force Academy. She received a master's degree in public administration from Troy State University, Troy, Alabama, in 1992. An F-16 aircraft maintenance officer, she served in Southwest Asia during the Persian Gulf War and in Saudi Arabia during Operation Southern Watch. A distinguished graduate of both the US Air Force Squadron Officer School and the US Air Command and Staff College, she earned her PhD in conflict analysis and resolution from the Institute for Conflict Analysis and Resolution, George Mason University, Fairfax, Virginia, in 1999. Her publications include "Coalitions: The Challenge of Effective Command and Control in Support of the Air Campaign"; "National Fragmentation, Ethnicity, and the New World Order"; "The Iraq-Kuwait Crisis: Structural Deprivation Leads to Revolution"; *Intervention Design in Conflict Analysis and Resolution: Theory, Practice, and Research* (coeditor); and "Conflict Termination in the Persian Gulf War: Policy Failure Sustains Conflict." Major Rast served previously as assistant professor of national security studies, Air University; she is currently associate professor of political science, USAF Academy.

Acknowledgments

My deepest appreciation goes first to the 135 participants who shared their lives with me by providing their perspectives on the ways Washington really makes policy (see app. A). Without exception, these professionals each treated me as a colleague and spoke candidly. I hope the conclusions presented here do justice to their ideas and to their continued commitment to establishing security around the world.

Many people encouraged me and provided intellectual stimulation throughout the development of this project. Others offered conceptual critiques, created networking opportunities, provided resources, rendered feedback on preliminary conclusions, served as outside readers, and contributed limitless support. To these friends and colleagues I owe great appreciation: Dr. Russell O. Cadman, Gen Michael P. C. Carns, Gen Ralph E. Eberhart, Maury Enright, Gen Ronald R. Fogleman, Lt Gen John W. Rosa Jr., Col Stephen C. German, J. Wesley Jeffries, Ambassador Jacques Paul Klein, Susie B. Matthews, Dr. Susan Allen Nan, Brig Gen Gary L. North, Prof. Richard Rubenstein, Mara Lyn Schoeny, Gen and Mrs. John Shalikashvili (USA), Col Tim and Mrs. Jody Vining, Dr. Susan Woodward, and my colleagues at the Institute for Conflict Analysis and Resolution.

I remain deeply indebted to the US Air Force and Air University for providing the chance to expand my perspective, my potential, and my horizons. On a very personal level, Col John Warden, USAF, retired; Lt Col Larry Weaver (PhD), USAF, retired; and Maj Ronald Mitchell, USAF, retired, created this opportunity to broaden my mind, my understanding, and my life. I thank them as my professional mentors and also as my friends. Upon my arrival in Washington, D.C., Col Alan Gropman (PhD), USAF, retired, took me under his wing, providing access to critical resources, shaping my intellect, and networking me with "all the right people." He served as my safety net and confidant, encouraging me through it all! I appreciate the relationships I have shared with these professionals. Thank you.

I am also indebted to the members of my dissertation committee. These four men remained dedicated to my intellectual development throughout this process. I am particularly indebted to Dr. Christopher Mitchell for his creativity and for providing the nurturing environment that convinced me this work *could* be done under extremely restrictive working conditions. Dr. Daniel Druckman provided the methodological rigor this research required; I remain grateful to him for enhancing my capacity to frame complex problems from multiple perspectives. Dr. Harold Gortner (and his wife Sylvia) provided the glue that held me together throughout this process, keeping me both sane and focused. I will not live long enough to repay them. Finally, in addition to creating this opportunity, Dr. Larry Weaver encouraged me at every step in the process and convinced me this research *should* be done.

Tracy Ann Breneman-Penas and Larissa Fast became my steadfast colleagues and remained my closest friends throughout the duration of this study. They came through (again!) for me at the end of this long journey by reading the entire manuscript. Likewise, Lt Col Paul Moscarelli and Lt Col Dave Eiting, USAF, retired, promoted this work and provided keen insight regarding its publication. Lt Col Chris Cain (PhD) edited the final manuscript. Mr. Preston Bryant, Dr. Richard Bailey, Ms. Debbie Banker, Ms. Joan Dawson, and Mr. Steve Garst, along with the entire AU Press team, made my dream a reality—words never can express fully the depths of my gratitude! While the errors contained herein remain mine alone, the commitment of these people to excellence shows through this product. I could not have completed this book without them.

Finally, to my family I owe . . . everything. My parents and best friends, Charles and Marlene Besecker, provide a nurturing environment that continues to embrace me with love. The lessons they taught me long ago enabled me to complete this endeavor. I remain eternally grateful. And, last on this list but *first in my life* is my husband, Marcus Rast. His unassailable devotion helped me maintain my relationship with God and enabled me to put everything in His hands during these trial-filled years. Marcus also served as my research assistant, proofreader, caretaker . . . and supported me in other ways too numerous to mention here. Absent his unconditional love and selfless dedication, this project would still be on the drawing board. Thank you for making my dream a reality, honey—*you complete me and I will always love you!*

Introduction

Decision makers do not make choices as unitary actors. This study examines interagency conflicts within the US government's decision-making processes in cases of coercive intervention and the manner in which such conflicts affect policies regarding termination and withdrawal. Specifically, it also examines conflict termination policies regarding the second Persian Gulf War and the Bosnia conflict.

Graham Allison and Morton Halperin's ideas provide the foundation for identifying the players and contextual factors that regulate decision making. To operationalize the study's theoretical perspectives, this framework develops six interrelated signed digraph models. Using a multimethod approach, the study collects and analyzes quantitative and qualitative data from informed respondents. The quantitative analysis illuminates relationships that affect interagency conflict; the qualitative analysis identifies themes that respondents perceived as most important in developing interagency policy. These seven macros and their supporting micro themes are then organized in terms of their capacity to influence the ways in which (1) *dynamic themes* influence interagency dynamics, (2) *contextual parameters* framing the policy process shape interagency dynamics and substantive outcomes, and (3) *cross-cutting effects* influence both dynamic themes and contextual elements. The themes are then used to investigate the development of termination policy in the Persian Gulf and Bosnia.

In the final analysis, the gap between diplomats and war fighters dominates an interagency process likely to produce a policy that brings about *war termination* in the form of cease-fire. However, it almost inevitably fails to achieve *conflict termination* in the form of sustainable peace. This outcome results largely from interagency conflict that emanates from five key factors:

1. defects in leadership,
2. the absence of strategic vision,
3. dissimilar organization cultures,
4. disparate worldviews, and

5. the absence of an integrated interagency planning mechanism.

These factors impede the effective development of crisis analysis, end-state vision, termination criteria, and termination strategy. With these findings noted at the outset, a few words regarding the presentation of ideas will help guide you through the study's three interrelated sections.

Interagency Fratricide at a Glance

Part I frames the nature of interagency policy making within a "less than rational" political environment. To demonstrate the overwhelming influence that rational choice theory has had upon conceptions of foreign policy decision making, this discussion critiques the rational actor model for its inability to incorporate all facets of human choice. This marked examination shows precisely why people—both as individuals and particularly when called upon to act as a group—cannot make decisions according to this utility-maximizing approach. Yet, this section confirms that such an approach has dominated both theorists' and practitioners' approaches to conflict termination, a conclusion illustrated through the most widely accepted models of conflict termination. Given that groups cannot adhere to the tenets of rational choice theory in practice, the author invokes Allison's bureaucratic politics model to capture the dynamics of the national security policy-making system as it exists in reality. From this theoretical foundation, a research methodology is presented to bridge the gap between the theory and practice of national security decision making.

Part II analyzes the evidence and presents three major classifications of findings. Using the term *dynamic themes* as the first category, the work depicts the influence leadership, negotiation, and domestic politics have upon the interagency process. *Contextual parameters*, the second category, further circumscribes the interagency process. Specifically, the analysis demonstrates the ways in which strategic vision and planning processes, in conjunction with desires to protect institutional equities, affect interagency dynamics and policy outcomes. This discussion concludes with an analysis of two factors that have *crosscutting effects* on policy process inputs and outcomes as it focuses on the ways in which role and mission ambiguity and the media influence the interagency process.

The final section, Part III, presents the implications these interagency findings hold for termination policy development. Gaining insight from the Persian Gulf War and the crisis in Bosnia, the evidence shows that while the interagency process is designed to bridge the gaps across the US government's executive branch in theory, in practice the elements identified within *dynamic themes, contextual parameters,* and *crosscutting effects* adversely affect decision makers' abilities to develop conflict termination policy for the crisis at hand. These two cases provide evidence that the interagency process demands both intellectual and structural overhaul if it is to fulfill its original, and much needed, purpose.

As a final note, quoted material comes directly from the interview transcripts that support this research. Where possible, this research frames quotations in terms of the individual's level within the interagency process, departmental affiliation, and the case with which he or she is associated. Although the names of all 135 informants are included in appendix A, I have taken great care to preserve their anonymity with regard to specific comments—I hope I have done them justice.

PART I

Framing the Problem

Chapter 1

Conflict Termination within a Bureaucratic Environment

If the decision to end a war were simply to spring from a rational calculation about gains and losses for the nation as a whole, it should be no harder to get out of a war than to get into one.

—Fred Charles Iklé

As the web of international relations becomes increasingly complex within the context of globalization, any government acting as an external intervenor will encounter challenges that require intervention and conflict termination policies. Yet, researchers and practitioners have performed only limited critical analysis regarding the ways intraparty dynamics shape intervention policy development in general and conflict termination policy development in specific. An overabundance of research regarding intraparty and group dynamics appears within the organization theory, organizational and group behavior, and group dynamics literatures.[1] While these fields have dominated scholarly discourse regarding group behavior, none of these areas adequately addresses the internal relationships that structure governmental intervention policy development. Conversely, the conflict resolution field encompasses an extensive body of literature regarding third-party intervention, albeit from foci that do not evaluate deliberately the relationships between intraparty dynamics and policy development. The lack of analysis regarding the linkage between group decision-making processes and conflict termination policy development presents a significant gap that must be bridged if intervenors—both official government-sponsored agencies and unofficial private entities—are to facilitate conflict termination policy development as a practical step toward conflict resolution and, ultimately, conflict transformation.

Toward achieving that goal, this book analyzes how conflict within and across US government (USG) agencies (the

3

interagency[2]) affects the creation and promulgation of intervention and conflict termination policies that include (a) effective crisis analysis, (b) a vision for the desired end state, (c) conflict termination criteria, and (d) a strategy to bring about conflict termination for complex international crises. Hence, this study aims to achieve four interrelated goals:

1. Enhance understanding of conflict termination and its relationship to war termination, conflict settlement, conflict resolution, and conflict transformation;

2. Establish a framework for conflict termination policy development in accordance with the four elements outlined above;

3. Analyze critically the policy processes that shaped conflict termination policy for the second Persian Gulf War (1990–91[3]) and the Bosnia crisis that led to the Dayton Accords (1993–95); and

4. Demonstrate the implications of developing conflict termination policy via an interagency process rife with all the advantages and disadvantages attendant to bureaucratic decision making.

Figure 1 focuses the study by illustrating that international crises include parties in conflict—adversaries and stakeholders. These stakeholders include "allies" or "partners" and the USG. The circle around the USG acknowledges that other actors influence policy development but indicates that this work focuses upon the USG policy process in "virtual" isolation from the other actors. Figure 1 likewise communicates that the *crisis* catalyzes policy development and, hence, interagency conflict across the agencies within the policy process.

Once a crisis attracts USG attention, members of the executive branch interagency process, in concert with other interested parties—both official and unofficial—begin analyzing the problem to formulate a strategy to address the crisis.[4] These decision makers generate an interagency policy that communicates the US government's official position regarding the crisis. The question for this crisis policy cycle then becomes: "If the policy achieves war termination, does it then begin to establish the conditions for conflict termination that lead to a

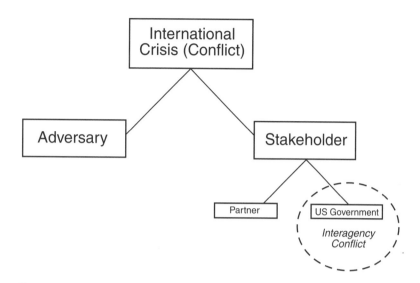

Figure 1. International Crisis: Aligning the Parties in Conflict

better state of peace (defined as either a sustainable peace or an acceptable level of instability), or does this policy become the catalyst for continued or future conflict?" In this manner, figure 2 captures the focal points of this work.

To begin grounding this research in the literature, it is appropriate to acknowledge that this approach investigates I. William Zartman's question regarding the potential efficacy of negotiation as a decision-making process.[5] In so doing, it bridges existing gaps between the bureaucratic politics, decision theory, negotiation, and conflict resolution literatures. A conceptual framework based upon theories that illuminate understanding of negotiation practices, the bureaucratic politics model of decision making, and conflict termination policy guide this study.

Interagency Decision Making via Negotiation

This book explores two aspects of decision making and links them to conflict termination. First, it investigates the US government's policy-making process by identifying the sources of potential interagency conflict within the bureaucratic decision-making arena. Second, it analyzes the effects of choices that

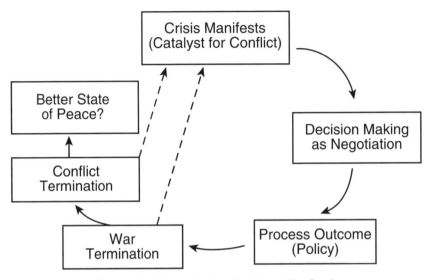

Figure 2. Crisis Policy-Making Life Cycle

underpin strategy development and traces those effects to the US government's development of conflict termination policy for its interventions into the Persian Gulf (1990–91) and Bosnia (1993–95). Once these areas are analyzed, this study then identifies the most influential factors in developing the outcome (i.e., the intervention policy and termination strategy) and maps them relationally to discern their influence on the conflict termination policy development process. A brief explanation of intraparty negotiation as a decision-making process effectively identifies the linkages within this conceptual framework.

Zartman maintains that negotiation represents a mode of decision making that can reconcile two (or more) conflicting points of view into a single decision.[6] In light of this perspective, the interagency decision-making process involves some aspects of negotiation within a bounded context. Within the US national policy-making arena, the bureaucratic model of decision making provides the overarching contextual parameters while intraparty multilateral negotiation provides the mechanism for policy development. Consequently, the effects of conflict within *the interagency process* must be evaluated according to (1) the context of the crisis' environment and (2) the dynamics of the bureaucratic politics model of decision making. Together, these shape the nature of the multilateral negotiations between relevant actors.

Scholars and analysts within the fields of public administration and organization theory have gone to great lengths to develop our understanding of the nature of bureaucracy. From the earliest descriptive works of Max Weber through the efforts of James March and Herbert Simon, the bureaucratic environment has been described as one of unrivaled complexity.[7] Important for this study, however, are the specific contextual factors that shape the application of the bureaucratic decision-making model within the USG.

The foregoing description of the political environment highlights the necessity of considering the influence contextual factors have upon the selection of a theoretical frame for decision making. When looking at US security policy development, one can rapidly discern that Washington's multifaceted context requires the application of a model that captures the nature of the process as it actually occurs *in practice*. This research assumes the most relevant model is the bureaucratic politics model, not the rational actor model.[8] To validate this selection, a brief comparison of the two conceptual frameworks is required.

The bureaucratic decision-making model recognizes that government is comprised of multiple actors with various degrees and sources of influence or power.[9] These actors operate within a bureaucratic structure of sometimes-competing ideologies and policy preferences. Political scientists John Spanier and Eric Uslaner contend "policy-making in these circumstances involves attempts to reconcile the policy preferences of the various 'players' with their different perceptions and interests."[10] Through a process of compromise and mutual adjustment, actors make decisions that integrate their conflicting policy preferences, irrespective of the policy's ability to maximize a particular intervention's potential effectiveness. Alternatively, the rational actor model attempts to prescribe decision choices based upon potential effectiveness rather than upon a suboptimal compromise outcome.

The rational actor model focuses upon the development of policies that can achieve effectively a stated purpose.[11] In this sense, the government is viewed as a unitary actor, an assumption that most probably accounts for its dominance in the study of international relations and policy development.[12] Specifically, Spanier and Uslaner posit this model "assumes that decision-makers will (1) select the objectives and values that a given policy is supposed to achieve and maximize, (2) consider the various alternative means to achieve these purposes, (3) calculate the likely consequences of each alternative course, and (4) choose the course most likely to attain the objectives originally selected."[13] This brief description of the two dominant decision-making frameworks highlights the disagreement that exists regarding their historical and prospective applications. This variance in perspective stems in part from the nature of the decision-making environment.

The theory that undergirds Western understanding of the bureaucratic model recognizes the dynamics between relevant actors. It does not provide, however, keen insight into the process used to frame those interactions within the governmental infrastructure. To develop such insight, we must recognize that the decisions resulting from this model's application emerge as products of an extremely complex multilateral negotiation. As such, we must understand the relevant actors before we can attempt to analyze the process.

The Actors

Identifying relevant actors in a situation as complex as the US national security policy-making process presents a formidable task. Within this analysis, the research examines official decision makers, influential actors, and contextual factors. The paragraphs that follow briefly describe these actors; each is explored in depth in chapter 4.[14]

Official decision makers are those actors who are involved in the formal decision-making process by virtue of their "official" governmental position. Influential in the formulation of national security policy are the National Security Council (NSC) and the US Congress (fig. 3). The National Security Act of 1947 created the NSC (and the NSC system and its staff) "to advise the President with respect to the integration of domestic, foreign, and military policies relating to the national security so as to enable the military services and the other Departments and

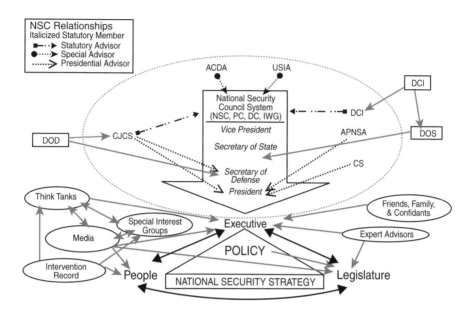

Figure 3. NSC Policy-Making Structure: Decision Making as Negotiation

agencies of the government to cooperate more effectively in matters involving the national security."[15]

Since its purpose includes providing advice on issues that span domestic and international arenas, its membership includes the highest-level decision makers within the federal government. Specifically, the NSC is comprised of the president, the vice president, the secretary of state, and the secretary of defense.[16] While other actors shape the overall decision-making process within the NSC system, it is sufficient at this juncture to introduce the primary actors and to note that the agency originated from a recognition—in the wake of the United States's World War II experience—that the security policy process should be institutionalized to guarantee the participation of those decision makers most responsible—constitutionally speaking—for national security policy. However, the NSC does not operate as the sole decision-making agency; the US Congress also plays a significant role in policy development.

The Congress influences the policy process through multiple channels. However, two dominate: (1) the power to declare war and, conversely, (2) the capacity to enact legislation limiting the use of force. First, and perhaps most fundamentally, the Congress is the only branch of the USG authorized to "declare war" by virtue of the powers prescribed by the Constitution of the United States.[17] The checks and balances built into the relationship between the executive and legislative branches offer opportunities for debate, compromise, and systematic policy development. Paradoxically, the president serves as commander in chief of the armed forces but does not possess the authority to "make war." The ambiguity surrounding the relationship between making war and being responsible for all military conduct created a relationship devoid of its theoretical basis. Throughout history, the executive operated at the margins regarding constitutional interpretation while congressional critics claimed that the executive continually usurped congressional power regarding the use of force. This belief, coupled with a desire to reassert itself on the national level, prompted the Congress to use its second source of power: the ability to constrain the use of force through legislation. The 1973 Congress enacted via joint resolution the War Powers Resolution.

Donald Snow and Eugene Brown contend the War Powers Resolution "represented a dramatic milestone in the reassertion of congressional prerogatives in international affairs."[18] In its present form, it requires the president to "consult with [the] Congress before committing armed forces to hostilities."[19] As has been demonstrated since its adoption, significant ambiguity continues to shape implementation of this requirement. In an effort to clarify any potential misunderstanding of the consultation requirement, the Congress included a reporting provision to augment the consultation role.

As a second requirement, the president must "report to the Congress within 48 hours any time US armed forces are dispatched (1) 'into hostilities or into situations where imminent involvement in hostilities is clearly indicated by the circumstances,' (2) into foreign territory while 'equipped for combat,' or (3) 'in numbers which substantially enlarge United States Armed Forces equipped for combat already located in a foreign nation.'"[20]

As for the first provision, both the president and the Congress have interpreted this requirement expediently; it functions as an elastic barrier in the national security decision-making process. While the first two requirements necessitate that the Congress remains an active player in the security policy arena, it is the third legal tenet that achieves particular import for analyzing conflict termination policy development.

The most important section of the War Powers Resolution for this study is Section 5, the provision outlining the termination of hostilities and the withdrawal of US personnel.[21] Should the first two measures prove insufficient for providing express legislative approval regarding the development and implementation of foreign policy, this provision would correct the shortfall in two ways. First, while the president maintains the latitude to employ force as the commander in chief, the executive can do so only for a 60-day period. If at the end of the 60-day window the Congress has not declared war or has not authorized *explicitly* the continued deployment (either by continuing resolution or by extending presidential authority for a specified period), the president is without legal authority to continue the deployment.[22] Congressional inaction requires the president to withdraw deployed forces. Most important here is the implication that an explicit requirement exists for the development of a termination plan (and hence, an "exit strategy") in cases wherein the Congress *has not* declared war. The significance of this requirement will emerge throughout the analysis of the relationship between the interagency's policy development process and its ability to promulgate conflict termination policy.

While the NSC's statutory members (president, vice president, and secretaries of state and defense) and the Congress emerge as the dominant "official players" within the policy development arena, they operate within a bureaucratic environment that consists of many unofficial, yet powerfully influential, actors. These actors play momentous roles in framing vital issues related to intervention decisions.

The environment that bounds the policy-making arena remains rich with actors who influence the policy process in myriad ways. Whether framing the principal issues, providing information to other actors (both official and unofficial), or possessing the ability to influence individual decision makers, these actors can individually and collectively exert enormous pressures upon the bureaucratic process. In fact, the very nature of the bureaucratic process provides these actors leverage at the highest levels of government. These actors can be categorized according to their relative positions within the global arena as having influence along a shifting continuum, ranging from major to peripheral effect.

Actors who possess foremost influence are those official government agencies (beyond those previously mentioned as official decision makers) that exert pressure upon the NSC system; they are personified by the principals and deputies within the cabinet-level departments. Those exerting peripheral influence on the official policy process include nongovernmental organizations, private and/or voluntary organizations, the media, and academic institutions.[23] Identifying these actors as they relate to specific crises would prove impossible. However, four highly influential a priori actors emerge as preeminent in any crisis: the media, think tanks, "expert" advisors, and the public.

The structure of the multilateral negotiation begins to take shape as the policy preferences (i.e., political choices) of these actors conflict within a complex web of intricate relationships. These two aggregates (i.e., the official decision makers and influential actors) possess the capacity to incorporate vast numbers of independent actors who are recognized as dominant players within the interagency process. However, room must be created for those elements not considered traditional players within an otherwise personified process.

Policies or goals serve as contextual factors that impinge upon bureaucratic decision-making processes. For example, economic development goals—as contextual factors encompassing multifaceted yet nonaggregated memberships—could be considered a contextual element that exerts an inordinate capacity to shape foreign and security policy decisions. Consequently, policy makers must consider such elements along with other relevant contextual factors when analyzing the overall policy-making process. To enhance analytic validity, great care must be taken to identify these components through an inductive exploratory process to ensure they are characterized in light of their relationship to the process as a whole. With a cursory understanding of the players, we can now begin to outline the second major component of this part of the study by developing a joint understanding of the multilateral negotiation process.

The Process

The negotiation literature remains one of the most richly developed components of its parent field, conflict resolution. In looking to the theoretical literature that frames the study of negotiation, particularly fitting for this research is Zartman's policy analysis approach, one that "views negotiation as a learning process in which the parties react to each other's concession behavior[s]."[24] Whether this perspective serves as the theoretical frame for the analysis of this policy-making process remains to be seen, but it begins to shed light on one approach to framing the overall process.

The richness of the literature presents a significant challenge for the development of any research design in that it addresses multiple dimensions of negotiation processes, structures, and outcomes.[25] Yet, as meaningful as this understanding is, it has been developed largely by analyzing interactions between two actors.[26] As a result, Zartman calls for research to increase our understanding of the dynamics of this complex negotiation process across multiple actors.[27]

While this study examines bureaucratic decision making by framing the process in terms of a multilateral negotiation, the specific elements of analysis have not yet been determined beyond the dependent conceptual focus (i.e., conflict termination policy). The study identifies independent and intervening factors as the product of an extensive literature review (see chap. 5). With this caveat in mind, it is important to acknowledge from the outset that this approach moves beyond a "purely inductive" inquiry, exploring several relationships of particular interest.

First, this analysis develops an understanding of the roles *philosophy* and *ideology* play in shaping the organizational attitudes of those agencies involved in the negotiation process. It explores the ways in which this attitudinal perspective shapes the specific behaviors of the individual negotiators once embroiled in policy negotiations. As a second area of inquiry, the research examines how organizational culture influences the

13

principals' negotiating behaviors, as well as that of the other agency members involved in the negotiation.[28] Specifically, it addresses the ways in which principals view themselves and how those perspectives shape their images of out-groups. In doing so, the research explores the role organizational culture plays in sustaining perceptions of in-group/out-group dynamics and investigates the overall influence this dynamic has upon the multilateral interagency negotiating process. Third, the research investigates the relationship between crisis context and how the interagency negotiation process evolves. In other words, does the nature of the crisis shape the roles played by the principals? How does it frame their analytic processes and negotiating behaviors?

This overview by no means identifies every aspect of the negotiation process explored herein. It does, however, provide a starting point that, when taken in conjunction with an extensive literature review, identifies elements that can be measured and analyzed in light of the specific aspects of the policy-making process. Once explored, this work evaluates the policy outcome in light of its ability to achieve conflict termination.

The Efficacy of the Policy-Making Process

While the notion of conflict termination is not new, it remains a relatively understudied concept in terms of empirical research. Much of what has been written looks to cost-benefit modeling as the prominent answer to the question of why conflicts end.[29] Those perspectives contain significant variations surrounding other critical matters, including whether the termination policy addressed the conflict's underlying causes, the anticipated duration of the termination, and the conditions that produced the actual termination.[30] Much like the notion of leadership, it has sometimes been epitomized as the "I'll know it when I see it" phenomenon.

Within the complex conflict systems that normally characterize international conflict, this "know it when I see it" phenomenon results largely from the level of control the bureaucracy exercises when making such determinations. As a result, an actor's definition of conflict termination extends from one's official position within the decision-making process. Further, this position initially is framed and constantly reframed by the theoretical perspective that shapes the attitudes and behaviors the position demands in the moment. Hence, I propose that the factors governing the ability to negotiate successfully within the bureaucratic model *shape* actors' perspectives regarding the conditions necessary to terminate conflict. While this is an interesting prospect, and one this research develops further, a growing interest in conflict termination studies has generated multiple, sometimes conflicting, perspectives. The literature surveyed in chapter 3 outlines prominent ideas regarding conflict termination.[31] As with any other field of inquiry, the various perspectives on conflict termination ultimately reflect different approaches to understanding the critical aspects of conflict dynamics.

Richard Barringer's work captures a core perspective. This analyst defines *termination* in a limited sense as the "posthostilities phase, in which organized hostilities are terminated by all parties to the dispute, although the dispute is as yet unresolved and is perceived in military terms by at least one party and could generate renewed hostilities either immediately or after a prolonged period of cease-fire and renewed preparations for combat."[32]

In evaluating this perspective, one immediately recognizes that conflict termination focuses upon instances of war. Yet, war is a specific form of interaction that exists within the broader conflict spectrum. Hence, this definition represents an appropriate starting point for this work and remains valid as we investigate the influence of intraparty conflict on conflict termination policy development.

The critical focus of this research is multifaceted. First, it explores the ways in which interagency conflict (i.e., intraparty conflict within the USG bureaucracy) influences the development of conflict termination policy. As such, it analyzes the interagency's ability to analyze the crisis and develop a desired end state, conflict termination criteria, and a strategy through the process of a multilateral negotiation based within bureaucratic environment. Second, using comparative methodology, it analyzes conflict termination policy in light of two case studies.

It explores the relationship between interagency conflict and the US government's capacity to develop policy with a particular focus on generating criteria to secure the effective termination of international crises as a step toward sustainable peace or, as a minimum, acceptable levels of instability.

The outcome of multilateral negotiation constitutes a policy directive that should focus fundamentally on reestablishing peace through terminating the conflict. An inherent assumption for any intervention strategy is that it should achieve its stated objectives through the most expedient and least costly means available—again by conveying the influence of the rational actor model as it applies to the *outcome* of the process. Thus, the first level of analysis focuses specifically upon the dynamics of the policy process intended to produce a conflict termination strategy. It explores the role interagency negotiations and interagency conflict play in defining conflict termination and in identifying and selecting termination criteria. Relatedly, it investigates the intervenor's mechanisms for evaluating the efficacy of conflict termination criteria, as well as its criteria for evaluating the sustainability of conflict termination. It also identifies actors who exert dominant influence on developing the decisions that frame conflict termination and illuminates the reasons for their dominance. This perspective serves as the bridge for the final aim of this research: conceptualizing a new theoretical framework for thinking about and analyzing conflict termination policy development within a politicized bureaucratic arena. In other words, this second thrust attempts to bridge the gap between the theoretical aspects of an intervention policy that focuses on conflict termination and its practical ability to develop conflict termination criteria in light of the real-world context that frames the conflict system and policy choices.

In summary, this work analyzes the influence interagency conflict has upon the US government's capacity to develop termination policy that could serve as a prerequisite for the resolution of a particular international conflict. The emphasis here is on the dynamics of the *policy-making process* as they shape termination policy, not on the actual achievement of a "successful" termination "on the ground" in terms of post hoc policy implementation analysis.[33] The research approaches the challenge by examining the relationship between the nature and level of interagency conflict and the US government's capacity to produce conflict termination policy. It does so through a two-level approach. First, it views the policy-making process as a multilateral negotiation involving three primary aggregates: official decision-makers, influential actors, and contextual factors. Looking through the bureaucratic politics lens, it analyzes the relationship between this multilateral negotiation process and the generation of termination policy that can achieve (potentially) effective conflict termination. As an initial step toward enhancing our understanding of the relationship between these critical factors, it analyzes the theoretical and practical aspects of the conflict termination policy development process that produce conflict within the USG bureaucracy. Probing deeper, it evaluates the intervention policy-making process by identifying the ways in which the decision-making process frames specific aspects of termination policy in light of their potential to "terminate" conflict when considering the causes and conditions that promoted the original conflict. The book explores the relationship between USG interagency conflict and conflict termination policy development to identify the factors that shape the intervention and termination policy development process. To provide an additional measure of structure to this approach, a brief overview of subsequent chapters is now appropriate.

Outline of the Study

Following the conceptualization of the research problem in this segment, chapter 2 develops the theoretical underpinning of rational choice theory, the prevailing approach to decision making. Demonstrating how this theory informed the rational actor model's development, this discussion critiques the approach, highlighting its inability to account effectively for all dimensions of decision making—whether at the individual or group level. However, as noted in chapter 3, despite these "recognized" shortcomings, this theoretical perspective informs the accepted conflict termination models that guide our thinking, discourse, and policy process. Arguing that a more complex understanding of group choice is required, chapter 4 begins constructing a new comprehension of decision making within a highly politicized bureaucratic environment. Building upon the works of Graham Allison and Morton Halperin, it begins to frame the policy-making environment by identifying the relevant national security policy actors.[34] Extending this bridge, chapter 5 details the conceptualization of the research problem and its requisite formalization by creating multiple signed digraph models that hypothesize relations regarding interagency dynamics. In preparation for this empirical analysis, it discusses the quantitative data collection and analysis method, as well as the data's limitations. It outlines the quantitative analysis and employs Spearman rank-order correlation coefficients to depict the statistically significant relationships via six modified signed digraph models. This discussion details the quantitative findings that serve as the organizing rationale for the qualitative analyses presented in chapters 6–8. To demonstrate the effects of interagency conflict upon conflict termination policy development, chapter 9 applies the quantitative and qualitative findings to two historical cases. By using the Persian Gulf War and the Bosnia crisis as examples, this discussion illuminates ways in which interagency conflict influenced crisis analysis development, framed the vision for the desired end state, affected termination criteria selection, and circumscribed the formulation of termination strategy. Finally, chapter 10 addresses the three research questions that framed this study:

1. What factors create or intensify interagency conflict within the USG during conflict termination policy development?
2. How does "decision making by negotiation" shape policy choices within the USG crisis policy-making arena?
3. In what ways does interagency conflict influence the US government's capacity to develop conflict termination policy for international conflicts?

The conclusions help develop a general framework for understanding interagency conflict and its effects on policy development. In the future, policy makers and analysts can apply this understanding across group decision-making activities, irrespective of actor or issue specificity.

This section purposefully oversimplifies the methodology the research employs as well as the nature of the theoretical and practical issues it discusses. However, it does provide a window into the overarching approach this work employs. The findings of this research will hold far-reaching implications for ways to conceptualize conflict termination policy development for complex contingencies that demand an interagency approach to policy development and implementation.

Implications

The findings of this research begin to bridge the gaps among several diverse theoretical perspectives regarding the influence interagency conflict has upon the US government's decision-making process when involved in protracted violent conflict—specifically, the ability to develop conflict termination policy for international crises. It integrates prominent concepts from several fields into a single interdisciplinary approach to the major problems facing the evolving conflict resolution field as well as the practical aspects of conflict intervention. Unlike prior research, it describes in rich detail the ways in which decisions made within a bureaucratic environment through the process of multilateral negotiation frame the US government's ability to terminate international conflict in light of real-world conditions that shape conflict systems. Given the assumption that the United States will retain its role as a leader among third-party intervenors, the results of this study could lay the foundation for future structural or doctrinal changes across the US government's interagency process. It may also, for the first time, identify the potential influence that bureaucratic decision making has upon the US government's ability to act as a lead agent in global social change; that is, the outcome of third-party interventions should lead to the creation of a "better state of peace."[35] In related fashion, the study begins to address questions regarding the potential of the policy development process to shape, either positively or negatively, the conflict situation. It identifies the most effective process for developing conflict termination strategy and its critical indicators of likely effectiveness. Consequently, it has the potential to address the influence "decision making by negotiation" has upon the creation of policy that supports the public interest.[36] Most importantly, this study helps develop a more thorough understanding of the process used to craft conflict termination policy. The results may in fact move us one step closer toward achieving conflict resolution in situations of deep-rooted, protracted social conflict.[37] Chapter 2 begins this process by exploring the foremost theoretical conception of decision making: rational choice theory.

Notes

1. In the organization theory literature see also Harold F. Gortner, Julianne Mahler, and Jeanne Bell Nicholson, *Organization Theory: A Public Perspective* (Pacific Grove, Calif.: Brooks/Cole Publishing Co., 1989); see also and Jay M. Shafritz and J. Steven Ott, eds., *Classics of Organization Theory*, 2d, Revised and Expanded ed. (Chicago: The Dorsey Press, 1987). In the organizational and group behavior literature see also J. Steven Ott, *The Organizational Culture Perspective* (Chicago: The Dorsey Press, 1989); see also J. Steven Ott, ed., *Classic Readings in Organizational Behavior* (Pacific Grove, Calif.: Brooks/Cole Publishing Co., 1989); see also Edgar H. Schein, "Defining Organizational Culture," in *Classics of Organization Theory*, ed. J. M. Shafritz and J. S. Ott (Pacific Grove, Calif.: Brooks/Cole Publishing Co., 1987); see also Edgar H. Schein, "Group and Intergroup Relationships," in *Classic Readings in Organizational Behavior*, ed. J. S. Ott (Pacific Grove, Calif.: Brooks/Cole Publishing Co., 1989); see also Edgar H. Schein, *Organizational Culture and Leadership* (San Francisco: Jossey-Bass Publishers, 1992). Finally, in the group dynamics literatures see Scott T. Allison, Leila T. Worth, and Melissa W. Campbell King, "Group Decisions as Social Inference Heuristics," *Journal of Personality and Social Psychology* 58, no. 5 (1990): 801–11; Kenneth Bettenhausen and J. Keith Murnighan, "The Emergence of Norms in Competitive Decision-Making Groups," *Administrative Science Quarterly* 30, no. 3 (1985): 350–72; Jack S. Levy, "Prospect Theory, Rational Choice, and International Relations," *International Studies Quarterly* 41, no. 1 (1997): 87–112; Todd J. Maurer and Robert G. Lord, "An Exploration of Cognitive Demands in Group Interaction as a Moderator of Information Processing Variables in Perceptions of Leadership," *Journal of Applied Social Psychology* 21, no. 10 (1991): 821–39; Jeffrey T. Polzer, "Intergroup Negotiations: The Effects of Negotiating Teams," *Journal of Conflict Resolution* 40, no. 4 (1996): 678–98; Johannes A. Zuber, Helmut W. Crott, and Joachim Werner, "Choice Shift and Group Polarization: An Analysis of

the Status of Arguments and Social Decision Schemes," *Journal of Personality and Social Psychology* 62, no. 1 (1992): 50–61.

2. Donald Snow and Eugene Brown advise that this is the label given to the overall policy coordination process. Throughout this research, it applies to the USG interagency process. See also Donald M. Snow and Eugene Brown, *Puzzle Palaces and Foggy Bottom: US Foreign and Defense Policy-Making in the 1990s* (New York: St. Martin's Press, 1994).

3. "First Persian Gulf War" refers to the Iran-Iraq War, 1980–1988; "Persian Gulf War" or "Gulf War" refers to the 1990–1991 crisis.

4. As the findings indicate in the section on "Crisis Analysis" in chapter 9, crisis definition remains the crucial element in the policy-making process. At this juncture, it is important to note that this diagram assumes the USG has made the initial decision to begin the crisis analysis process.

5. I. William Zartman, "Negotiation as a Joint Decision-Making Process," *Journal of Conflict Resolution* 21, no. 4 (1977): 619–38.

6. See also Harold F. Gortner, Julianne Mahler, and Jeanne Bell Nicholson, *Organization Theory: A Public Perspective*, 2d ed. (Fort Worth: Harcourt Brace College Publishers, 1997); and see also Zartman, "Negotiation."

7. See also James G. March and Herbert A. Simon, "Theories of Bureaucracy," in *Classics of Organization Theory*, ed. Jay M. Shafritz and J. Steven Ott (Pacific Grove, Calif.: Brooks/Cole Publishing Co., 1978); and see also Max Weber, "Bureaucracy," in *Classics of Organization Theory*, ed. J. M. Shafritz and J. S. Ott (Pacific Grove, Calif.: Brooks/Cole Publishing Co., 1987).

8. See also Graham T. Allison, *Essence of Decision: Explaining the Cuban Missile Crisis* (Boston: Little, Brown and Co., 1971); Renato Raul Boschi and Eli Diniz Cerqueira, "The Bureaucracy, Its Clientele and Power Relations: A Theoretical Model," *Dados* 17 (1978): 97–116; Angela M. Bowey, "Approaches to Organization Theory," *Social Science Information/Information sur les Sciences Sociales* 11, no. 6 (1972): 109–28; R. B. Jain, "Politicization of Bureaucracy: A Framework for Measurement," *Res Publica* 16, no. 2 (1974): 279–302; Barbara J. Robins, "Policy Outputs and Bureaucracy: The Roles of Need, Demand, and Agency Structure," *Urban Affairs Quarterly* 18, no. 4 (1983): 485–509; Norman C. Thomas, "The Presidency and Policy Studies," *Policy Studies Journal* 9, no. 7 (1981): 1072–82; and Antonio Ugalde, "A Decision Model for the Study of Public Bureaucracies," *Policy Sciences* 4, no. 1 (1973): 75–84.

9. See also Allison, *Essence of Decision*; see also Boschi and Cerqueira, "The Bureaucracy"; Michael G. O'Loughlin, "What Is Bureaucratic Accountability and How Can We Measure It?" *Administration and Society* 22, no. 3 (1990): 275–302; and Alan Ned Sabrosky, James Clay Thompson, and Karen A. McPherson, "Organized Anarchies: Military Bureaucracy in the 1980s," *Journal of Applied Behavioral Science* 18, no. 2 (1982): 137–53.

10. See also Lincoln P. Bloomfield, *The Foreign Policy Process: A Modern Primer* (Englewood Cliffs, N.J.: Prentice-Hall, Inc., 1982); and John Spanier and Eric M. Uslaner, *How American Foreign Policy Is Made* (New York and Washington, D.C.: Praeger Publishers, 1974), 105.

11. See also Allison, *Essence of Decision*; and see also Morton H. Halperin and Graham T. Allison, "Bureaucratic Politics: A Paradigm and Some Policy Implications," in *Theory and Policy in International Relations*, ed. Raymond Tanter and Richard H. Ullman (Princeton, N.J.: Princeton University Press, 1974).

12. See also Bloomfield, *The Foreign Policy Process*; and see also Spanier and Uslaner, *How American Foreign Policy Is Made*.

13. Spanier and Uslaner, *How American Foreign Policy Is Made*, 103.

14. This depiction represents the author's view of the static process based upon the structural relations prescribed by US statutes (regarding official decision makers) and a priori assumptions (regarding all other actors and contextual factors).

15. *National Security Act of 1947*, title 50, sec. 402 (2 January 2001), online, Internet, 25 July 2000, available from http://uscode.house.gov/use.htm.

16. Chapter 4 discusses additional members, including the statutory and special advisors. This section merely familiarizes the reader with the two primary actors and their bases of authority.

17. See also Article 1, Section 8, in Richard G. Stevens, *The Declaration of Independence and the Constitution of the United States of America* (Washington, D.C.: National Defense University Press, 1995).

18. Snow and Brown, *Puzzle Palaces and Foggy Bottom*, 157.

19. Ibid., 163.

20. Ibid.

21. Ibid.

22. Ibid. Note that a 30-day extension is provided for the safe withdrawal and redeployment of troops. Thus, the president is granted a total of 90 days within which to secure congressional support for his actions.

23. For an in-depth explanation of the multiple "tracks" that influence policy making, see also Louise Diamond and John McDonald, *Multi-Track Diplomacy: A Systems Approach to Peace*, 3d ed. (West Hartford, Conn.: Kumarian Press, Inc., 1996).

24. See also Paul R. Pillar, *Negotiating Peace: War Termination as a Bargaining Process* (Princeton, N.J.: Princeton University Press, 1983); and see also Zartman, "Negotiation."

25. Some of the more relevant categories of literature include (1) *negotiating behaviors:* M. I. Friedman and W. E. Jacka, "The Negative Effect of Group Cohesiveness on Intergroup Negotiation," *Journal of Social Issues* 225 (1975): 181–94; see also Dean Pruitt, *Negotiation Behavior* (New York: Academic Press, 1981); see also Dean G. Pruitt, "Strategy in Negotiation," in *International Negotiation: Analysis, Approaches, Issues*, ed. V. Kremenyuk (San Francisco: Jossey-Bass, 1991); see also Dean G. Pruitt and Peter J. Carnevale, *Negotiation in Social Conflict*, ed. Tony Manstead, *Mapping Social Psychology Series* (Pacific Grove, Calif.: Brooks/Cole Publishing, 1993); see also James A. Wall, *Negotiation, Theory and Practice* (Glenview, Ill.: Scott, Foresman, 1985); and see also I. William Zartman, "The Structure of Negotiation," in *International Negotiation: Analysis, Approaches, Issues*, ed. Viktor

Aleksandrovich Kremeniuk (San Francisco: Jossey-Bass, 1991); (2) *factors shaping negotiation:* Daniel Druckman, "Determinants of Compromising Behavior in Negotiation: A Meta-Analysis," *Journal of Conflict Resolution* 38, no. 3 (1994): 507–56; Daniel Druckman, "Situational Levers of Position Change: Further Explorations," *Annals of the American Academy of Political and Social Science* 542 (November 1995): 61–80; Ole Elgstrom, "National Culture and International Negotiations," *Cooperation and Conflict* 29, no. 3 (1994): 289–301; Robert J. Janosik, "Rethinking the Culture-Negotiation Link," *Negotiation Journal* 3, no. 4 (1987): 385–95; Zvi Levy, "Negotiating Positive Identity in a Group Care Community: Reclaiming Uprooted Youth," *Child and Youth Services* 16, no. 2 (1993): xv–123; John A. Parnell and Ben L. Kedia, "The Impact of National Culture on Negotiating Behaviors across Borders," *International Journal of Value Based Management* 9, no. 1 (1996): 45–61; see also Jeffrey Z. Rubin, Dean G. Pruitt, and Sung Hee Kim, *Social Conflict: Escalation, Stalemate, and Settlement,* 2d ed. (New York: McGraw-Hill, Inc., 1994); and see also Ralph H. Turner, "Unanswered Questions in the Convergence between Structuralist and Interactionist Role Theories," (Los Angeles: University of California Press, 1982); (3) the *relationship between process and outcomes:* Jack Bilmes, "Negotiation and Compromise: A Microanalysis of a Discussion in the United States Federal Trade Commission" (Honolulu: University of Hawaii, 1994); Daniel Druckman and Robert Mahoney, "Processes and Consequences of International Negotiations," *Journal of Social Issues* 33, no. 1 (1977): 60–87; Paul F. Gerhart, "Determinants of Bargaining Outcomes in Local Government Labor Negotiations," *Industrial and Labor Relations Review* 29, no. 3 (1976): 331–51; C. R. Mitchell, "Classifying Conflicts: Asymmetry and Resolution," *Annals of the American Academy of Political and Social Science* 518 (November 1991): 23–38; I. William Zartman, "Decision Support and Negotiation Research: A Researcher's Perspective," *Theory and Decision* 34 (1993): 345–51; and see also Zartman, "The Structure of Negotiation"; and (4) the *sustainability of outcomes based upon process:* Marina Ajdukovic, "Psychosocial Aspects of Nonviolent Resolution of Conflicts; Psihosocijalni Aspekti Nenasilnog Rjesavanja Sukoba," *Drustvena Istrazivanja* 4, no. 1 (15) (1995): 49–55; Nimet Beriker and Daniel Druckman, "Simulating the Lausanne Peace Negotiations, 1922–1923: Power Asymmetries in Bargaining," *Simulation and Gaming* 27, no. 2 (1996): 162–83; see also Gerhart, "Determinants of Bargaining Outcomes in Local Government Labor Negotiations"; see also Hrach Gregorian, *Congressional-Executive Relations and Foreign Policymaking in the Post–Vietnam Period: Case Studies of Congressional Influence* (Waltham, Mass.: Brandeis University, Department of Politics, 1980); see also Levy, "Prospect Theory, Rational Choice, and International Relations"; and John Scanzoni and Deborah D. Godwin, "Negotiation Effectiveness and Acceptable Outcomes," *Social Psychology Quarterly* 53, no. 3 (1990): 239–52.

26. For specific examples of bilateral negotiation processes, see Nimet Beriker and Daniel Druckman, "Models of Responsiveness: The Lausanne Peace Negotiations (1922–1923)," *Journal of Social Psychology* 131, no. 2

(1991): 297–300; Beriker and Druckman, "Simulating the Lausanne Peace Negotiations, 1922–1923: Power Asymmetries in Bargaining"; Laszlo Bruszt and George K. Horvath, "1989: The Negotiated Revolution in Hungary," *Social Research* 57, no. 2 (1990): 365–87; Ole Elgstrom, "Norms, Culture, and Cognitive Patterns in Foreign Aid Negotiations," *Negotiation Journal* 6, no. 2 (1990): 147–59; Johan Kaufmann, "The Middle East Peace Process: A New Case of Conference Diplomacy," *Peace and Change* 18, no. 3 (1993): 290–306; and J. P. Perry Robinson, "The Negotiations on Chemical-Warfare Arms Control," *Arms Control* 1, no. 1 (1980): 30–52. Additionally, while a scant literature does address multilateral negotiation, it rarely incorporates a robust understanding of the processes' relationship to conflict termination or resolution. See, for example, Vicki L. Golich, "A Multilateral Negotiations Challenge: International Management of the Communications Commons," *Journal of Applied Behavioral Science* 27, no. 2 (1991): 228–50; Charles Heckscher, "Multilateral Negotiation and the Future of American Labor," *Negotiation Journal* 2, no. 2 (1986): 141–54; and see also Raimo Vayrynen, ed., *New Directions in Conflict Theory: Conflict Resolution and Conflict Transformation* (Newbury Park, Calif.: Sage Publications, Inc., 1991).

27. See also Zartman, "Negotiation as a Joint Decision-Making Process."

28. *Principals* refers to voting, decision-making NSC members (i.e., the president, vice president, the secretaries of state and defense), and statutory advisors (e.g., the director of Central Intelligence and the chairman of the Joint Chiefs of Staff). Chapter 4 explains these actors in detail.

29. See also Bruce C. Bade, *War Termination: Why Don't We Plan for It?* (Washington, D.C.: National War College, 1994); see also Joseph A. Engelbrecht Jr., "War Termination: Why Does a State Decide to Stop Fighting? (World War II, Anglo-Boer War, Japan, Great Britain)" (PhD diss., Columbia University, 1992); and Christopher R. Mitchell, "Ending Conflicts and Wars: Judgement, Rationality and Entrapment," *International Social Science Journal* 43, no. 1:127 (1991): 35–55.

30. Paul Seabury and Angelo Codevilla use these frames to describe war termination in terms of three forms of peace: peace of cultural conquest, peace of the prison, and peace of the dead. See also Paul Seabury and Angelo Codevilla, *War: Ends and Means* (New York: Basic Books, 1989).

31. See also Sam Allotey et al., *Planning and Execution of Conflict Termination* (Maxwell AFB, Ala.: Air Command and Staff College, 1995); Stephen J. Cimbala, "C2 and War Termination," *Signal* 43 (1988): 73–78; see also Stephen J. Cimbala, "The Endgame and War," in *Conflict Termination and Military Strategy: Coercion, Persuasion, and War*, ed. S. J. Cimbala, *Studies in International Security Affairs and Military Strategy* (Boulder, Colo.: Westview Press, 1987); see also Stephen J. Cimbala, *U.S. Military Strategy and the Cold War Endgame* (Ilford, Essex, England: F. Cass, 1995); see also Stephen J. Cimbala, ed., *Strategic War Termination* (New York: Praeger Publishers, 1986); see also Stephen J. Cimbala and Sidney R. Waldman, ed., *Controlling and Ending Conflict: Issues before and after the Cold War* (New York: Greenwood Press, 1992); see also Stephen J. Cimbala and Keith A.

Dunn, *Conflict Termination and Military Strategy: Coercion, Persuasion, and War* (Boulder, Colo.: Westview Press, 1987); see also Bruce B. G. Clarke, *Conflict Termination: A Rational Model* (Carlisle Barracks, Pa.: US Army War College, 1992); Bruce B. G. Clarke, "Conflict Termination: What Does It Mean to Win?" *Military Review* 72 (1992): 85–86; see also Mitchell, "Classifying Conflicts: Asymmetry and Resolution"; see also C. R. Mitchell, *The Structure of International Conflict* (New York: St. Martin's Press, 1981); see also Mitchell, "Ending Conflicts and Wars: Judgement, Rationality and Entrapment"; Christopher R. Mitchell and Michael Nicholson, "Rational Models and the Ending of Wars," *Journal of Conflict Resolution* 27 (1983): 495–520; Lewis A. Coser, "The Termination of Conflict," *Conflict Resolution* V, no. 4 (1961): 347–53; see also Ernest F. Estes, *Conflict Termination in Crisis Management* (Maxwell AFB, Ala.: Air Command and Staff College, 1973); see also D. V. Johnson, *Impact of the Media on National Security Policy Decision Making* (Carlisle Barracks, Pa.: US Army War College, Strategic Studies Institute, 1994); Michael R. Rampy, "Endgame: Conflict Termination and Post–Conflict Activities," *Military Review* 72 (1992): 42–54; see also James E. Toth, *Conflict Termination: Considerations for Development of National Strategy* (Maxwell AFB, Ala.: Air War College, 1978); and see also Walter Wojdakowski, *Conflict Termination: Integrating the Elements of Power in Today's Changing World* (Carlisle Barracks, Pa.: US Army War College, 1993).

32. See also Richard E. Barringer, with the collaboration of Robert K. Ramers, *War: Patterns of Conflict* (Cambridge, Mass.: The MIT Press, 1972).

33. Although a noble goal and worthy endeavor, this research makes *no attempt* to evaluate the termination policy itself relative to the myriad conditions that affect policy implementation once the physical intervention has occurred and the fog and friction that accompany such actions impinge upon the "best laid plans of mice and men."

34. See also Graham T. Allison, "Conceptual Models and the Cuban Missile Crisis," in *International Relations: Contemporary Theory and Practice*, ed. G. A. Lopez and M. S. Stohl (Washington, D.C.: CQ Press, 1989); see also Allison, *Essence of Decision;* and see also Halperin and Allison, "Bureaucratic Politics: A Paradigm and Some Policy Implications."

35. See also Fred Charles Iklé, *Every War Must End* (New York: Columbia University Press, 1991); and see also Sir Basil Henry Liddell Hart, *Strategy* (New York: Praeger, 1954).

36. Oran R. Young, "Intermediaries: Additional Thoughts on Third Parties," *Conflict Resolution* 16, no. 1 (1972): 52–73.

37. See also Louis Kriesberg, *International Conflict Resolution: The US-USSR and Middle East Cases* (New Haven, Conn.: Yale University Press, 1992).

Chapter 2

Rational Choice Theory:
Individual and Group Choice

Policymaking is . . . a process of "conflict and consensus-building."
— Graham T. Allison

An extensive and expanding body of literature attempts to describe, explain, and predict the ways in which individuals and groups make decisions. This research spans multiple fields, including "communication, economics, engineering, management, political science, psychology, social psychology, and sociology."[1] Increasingly, interest in individual and group decision-making processes has begun to pervade conflict resolution studies. An understanding of decision-making processes holds import for all levels of conflict analysis, but is particularly critical when the decisions and the efforts to implement them overwhelmingly influence one's very existence—socially, politically, economically, informationally, and militarily.

Collectively, these multidisciplinary and interdisciplinary inquiries highlight theoretical understandings that have become widely accepted rationales for human choice behaviors. The ensuing discussion surveys two such rationales that hold significant import for the conflict termination policy development process—rational choice theory and the bureaucratic politics model of decision making. Despite ideas to the contrary,[2] this research concludes that the bureaucratic approach characterizes interventionist policy development, *especially during crises*. This bureaucratic approach portends grave consequences for the development of conflict termination policy's four elements (crisis analysis, desired end state, termination criteria, and termination strategy).

The complexity of the decision-making process obscures the application of the bureaucratic approach. Consequently, the *process* enjoined to generate policy decisions (the bureaucratic model as the framework for decision making) has been confused

27

with the *outcomes* (the policy vision, objectives, and strategies that parallel the framework of the rational actor approach). Before delving into specific models, it is necessary to provide a brief theoretical rationale to explain how most decision makers select a preferred framework.

Decision-Making Approaches: Units of Analysis as Delimiters

Five dominant schools of thought have captured multiple perspectives on the study of decision making: (1) rational choice theory, (2) the "individual differences perspective," (3) satisficing, (4) the organizational (or structural) approach, and (5) the bureaucratic politics approach.[3] Note that various authors classify these categories differently, based primarily upon personal preferences and educational perspectives.[4] One distinguishing component of these five schools of thought is their focus on differing units of analysis: They examine either individual or group decision making. Focusing on the unit of analysis as the crucial delimiter, approaches to decision making align with one of two perspectives contingent upon their focus on *unitary actor* or *group* processes. In this manner, studies of choice relate naturally to either the behavioral (i.e., individual) or the organizational (i.e., group) paradigm.[5] All others emerge as natural extensions of these two categorizations.[6]

The ensuing discussion outlines the origins and assumptions of the rational actor model and its central theory—rational choice theory. Once outlined, the analysis evaluates its fundamental assumptions to reveal the model's inherent flaws as a preliminary step toward demonstrating rational choice theory's inapplicability for group decision making. This perspective on group decision making is explored further to stress the rational actor model's failure to enhance our understanding of collective choice processes and outcomes. Because of the inherent limitations of the rational choice model, the bureaucratic politics model emerges as a viable alternative that describes and explains the influence group-specific phenomena have upon collective decision making. Finally, the interaction of the two models illustrates the need for research that focuses upon the contextual elements that influence conflict termination policy making within the US government.

Rational Choice Theory

Known more broadly by its conceptualization as the rational actor model, rational choice theory remains the dominant normative theory of human decision making across many of the social sciences.[7] Despite the ongoing and multifaceted criticisms this perspective has endured, Jack Levy, a preeminent political scientist, contends "rational choice has become the most influential paradigm in international relations and political science over the last decade."[8] Consequently, we must look deeper into its origins to comprehend fully the rationale behind its conception and its application to human choice.

The theory of rational choice is one of the oldest and best-developed theories of choice.[9] Within the field of economics, it has served as a foundational concept for understanding individual decision making, serving as the standard by which decisions are evaluated.[10] By focusing on the logic of optimal choice, the rational perspective attempts to prescribe the normative ways in which people *should* make decisions when operating within the guidelines of individual self-interest.[11] Within this paradigm, individuals strive to maximize personal utility.[12] Relatedly, organizations strive to maximize profits.[13] It is this self-interested, profit-maximizing perspective that sustains the basis of the rational actor approach. To understand the ways in which this perspective shapes decision making, we must explore its assumptions as they relate to its motivations for selection.

Ideas regarding utility and profit maximization for individuals and organizations are based upon the ability to compute mathematically "subjective expected-utility" (SEU).[14] In lay terms, SEU models imply an acute ability to calculate or, as in game theory, to order preferences for outcomes based upon (a) *probabilities* for a particular course of action, prospects which are then treated as being individually subjective, and (b) *worth*, an economic measure of individual utility.[15] Such computations require decision contexts to conform to the following assumptions:

29

(1) the decision maker knows his or her goals, (2) unlimited and complete information is available, (3) no cognitive limitations constrain the decision maker, (4) no limitations exist regarding time or costs, and (5) the decision maker possesses the capacity to quantify alternatives—in terms of value and risk separately—in such a way that one dominates all others.[16] Applied to unitary actor decision making, Michael Nicholson insists that "the basic principle of rationality which is assumed is that the actor has a clear idea of what he (or she) wants, and pursues it in the most efficient way possible. In effect, rationality is defined as efficiency. . . . [Because] it is possible for the decision-taker to formulate what he wants . . . preferences between alternatives are expressible in a clear-cut way and remain relatively constant over time."[17]

These assumptions are extended erroneously to organizations so that groups are treated as unitary actors much in the same way the rational actor model deals with individuals. Yet, groups or organizations are not unitary actors; therefore, the fundamental premises of rational choice cannot apply, owing to the multiple interests and objectives of the group members. Hence, George Huber posits that rational choice theory suggests, *"organizational decisions are consequences of organizational units using information in an intendedly rational manner to make choices on behalf of the organization"* (emphasis in original).[18]

On the surface, the assumptions that undergird the rational actor approach appear logically consistent. Indeed, they descriptively would be *rational* except for one macro-level contextual factor: Humans, while operating alone or as members of groups, rarely, if ever, possess the capacity to fulfill the strict requirements of this prescriptive theory. More specifically, the assumptions that place boundaries upon this type of decision-making activity ensure that people can never operationalize fully the conceptual paradigm. Critics repeatedly identify this factor in their in-depth analyses of the rational actor model's limiting factors.

Limitations of the Rational Choice Approach

The literature scrutinizing rational choice theory is as multidisciplinary as the various individuals and organizations that have attempted to discover prescriptive and descriptive approaches to unitary actor and collective choice.[19] Given this discussion's focus regarding the affects of interagency conflict on conflict termination policy development, it is imperative to identify the critiques that relate directly to the model's assumptions to show that even if individuals aspire to make rational decisions, they consistently cannot do so because of innate human factors.[20] Further, it is important to recall that international relations scholars, as well as the populace in general, commonly believe that the USG makes foreign policy decisions via the rational actor model.[21] Hence, assessing the model's assumptions in light of both individuals and groups proves illuminating, confirming that humans cannot effectively employ rational choice theory at *either* the individual *or* group level.

Individuals as Aspiring Rational Actors

Putting aside for the moment the idea that people could indeed purposefully choose to act in a manner that is not rational,[22] by examining the assumptions of rational choice theory independently of one another, we can begin to see why this approach remains flawed as either a descriptive explanation or predictive framework for human decision making. As the impending discussion demonstrates, it can therefore serve only as a normative model.[23]

Decision Makers Know Their Goals

More than any other assumption, this proposition seems to emerge as a sound axiom of individual choice. Indeed, individuals may know their goals *at* a specific time. Rational choice theory presumes, however, that these goals remain static over time or for some period.[24] Further, it implies individuals possess the capability, again through SEU modeling, to differentiate clearly and prioritize these goals. These available choices then become "preference orderings" (discussed in greater depth as the fifth assumption) that can be prioritized easily with no external influence. In turn, these preference orderings represent the relative "'value' or 'utility' of alternative sets of consequences."[25] Subscribing to this process infers that individuals possess the innate ability to establish quantifiable "utility" functions for every aspect of their lives—and that these functions are "complete, transitive, and stable."[26]

Paradoxically, rational choice theory is based upon the macro-level assumption that these utility functions can be measured comparatively across different individuals. In fact, the basis of expected utility within microeconomics accepts that utility functions across independent individuals possess no comparative property.[27] Further, as Geoffrey Brennan contends, it is critical to note that not all desired goals are *desirable*—the ends for a rational actor, based upon the premise of individual utility maximization, may not be normatively *good* in all cases.[28] In this sense, one could posit that Saddam Hussein's 1990 invasion of Kuwait proved rational based upon *his* individual utility function. Based upon a territorial dispute extending from the 1913 British-Ottoman "Draft Convention on the Persian Gulf Area," Iraq attempted to incorporate Kuwait in both 1938 and 1963. Although both attempts proved unsuccessful, they provided a precedent for Hussein's 1990 actions.[29] However, the Kuwaitis would retort that his invasion proved normatively *bad*—both for them and those who subscribe to the provisions of international law and ideas regarding national sovereignty (not to mention human rights ideals), and, eventually, for Hussein himself in conjunction with the Iraqi people.

In light of the above analysis regarding the foundational assumption of rational choice theory and its parent field, microeconomics, the use of the term *irrational* to describe human behavior that does not comport with the preference orderings and utility functions of the "evaluating" individual is theoretically inappropriate in all situations given the basis of rational choice theory itself.[30] The example involving Hussein's invasion of Kuwait, albeit limited within this context, demonstrates that one's assessment of rationality remains bound contextually. When placed within the framework of theory's remaining assumptions—tenets that in many ways synergistically amplify rational choice theory's inability to serve as a predictive theory of human choice—this problem is magnified exponentially.

Unlimited and Complete Information

Information search remains a critical, fundamental element of the decision-making process.[31] Under the rubric of rational choice theory, the individual has the capacity (in terms of time and resources) to access all sources of information and should, therefore, obtain complete information regarding the current situation. However, multiple factors, sometimes interrelated, limit one's ability to access and process information.

Brennan recognizes that rational choice theory demands optimal information gathering and usage.[32] However, questions emerge regarding the meaning of *optimal* when applied to decision making. Does optimal refer primarily to the robustness of the information-gathering effort and then to its interpretation and application? This approach implies linearity, which generates a process that compartmentalizes information until the decision maker knows all relevant information. This notion accentuates related challenges: (a) can individuals effectively compartmentalize information, (b) who identifies the criteria for an exhaustive search,[33] (c) who shapes the criteria for relevancy—and perhaps more important, irrelevancy—and are these criteria inflexible over time,[34] and (d) is there an inherent distinction between knowing all information and having the capacity to *use* it in some meaningful way. What are the criteria for *meaningful* in this sense? Obviously, this line of reasoning can transform itself into an infinitely circular process. It does expose, however, a major flaw intrinsic to rational choice theory. Other concerns emerge regarding this tenet as well, foremost among them relating to compartmentalization, "new" information, and the practical impediments to human prescience and omnipresence.

If an individual effectively compartmentalizes information, what effect would exposure to new information have upon such distillation? While not addressed within rational choice theory, an individual employing this model in its classic form would be compelled to create subprocesses to manage, interpret, and incorporate new information based upon preexisting cognitive maps that resulted from the initial information search.[35] Pushing this argument further, one would have to presume that the presence of new information would alter one's utility functions and, subsequently, one's preference orderings. This being the case, the underlying premise of preference stability is no longer valid.

Relatedly, significant flaws in the theory emerge when assessing the individual's independent ability to know everything and to foresee accurately all the possible consequences of one's choice. Obviously, individuals possess neither of these capabilities. Choices inherently involve risk to self and others and therefore require the individual to order his or her preferences accordingly. As a counter argument, if one could know all possible consequences of one's choice and discovered that the selection of the option that maximized individual utility would most certainly have a catastrophic impact upon others, would one pursue that course of action absent its moral implications? This situation illuminates another of Brennan's critiques: Not all human behavior is so narrowly self-interested.[36] From the evaluative perspective, would one's actions in the hypothetical given above be deemed *rational* in light of the broader negative outcome? In deliberating over this dilemma, reconsider the Iraq-Kuwait example broached earlier. These theoretical stipulations remain constrained by the more practical considerations of information search and processing. This includes, but is not limited to, cognitive and resource constraints as well as one's capacity to quantify alternatives based upon personal goals.

No Cognitive Limitations

The ability to know and use all information (or even any information) is directly conditioned by the capacity to process data and formulate meaningful information: each individual's "cognitive imperfections" affect such processing.[37] Commenting on rational choice theory, Thomas Ulen defines a *cognitive imperfection* as "any property of the mind that causes an individual decision maker to make less than optimal decisions or choices."[38] Ulen divides these imperfections into two classes: (1) hardware problems (i.e., those related to the physiological structure of an individual's brain), and (2) software problems (i.e., those related to an individual's lack of learning or an insufficient experience base). Acting independently or in tandem, these cognitive imperfections limit an individual's capacity to

34

process information "rationally" toward the creation of utility-maximizing preference orderings as they hinder information processing along several dimensions.[39] For our purposes, two psychological processes—cognitive dissonance and judgmental heuristics—emerge as particularly important since they hold relevance for both individual and group decision making.

In 1957, Leon Festinger developed cognitive dissonance theory to help explain the psychological and motivational effects of an individual experiencing simultaneously two cognitive phenomena that did not fit together.[40] "In general," says Festinger, "two cognitions are dissonant with each other if, considering these two cognitions alone, the obverse of one follows from the other."[41] Festinger pushes the potential implications of such dissonance further, insisting that an individual will take positive action to reconcile the differing cognitions to alleviate psychological (and perhaps physical) stress. Ulen maintains this conception holds import for rational choice theory in that it may impair an individual's ability to create and sustain "stable, well-ordered preferences."[42] In this case, Festinger's "positive action" occurs when an individual discounts stress-inducing data in favor of alternative information sets that relieve or, at the very least, do not create psychological discomfort. Hence, cognitive dissonance can serve as a screening mechanism whereby individuals degrade their ability to access and process all information (assuming, of course, limitless information could indeed ever become a practical reality). This phenomenon relates to the second critical process, the application of judgmental heuristics.

Beginning with the groundbreaking work of Amos Tversky and Daniel Kahneman, authorities within cognitive psychology (and other disciplines) continue to refine explanations that support the use of heuristics.[43] Known in lay terms as "rules of thumb," the application of heuristics indicates that individuals do not comply in all instances with the assumptions of rational choice theory in that their "internal logic bears little resemblance to the rules of probability."[44] Instead, they rely upon their ability to recall information from memory along three interrelated dimensions: (1) availability, (2) representativeness, and (3) anchoring and adjustment. These dimensions influence one's capacity to process information, especially in times of crisis and greatly enhanced stress.[45] Beginning with availability, each of these requires a brief overview to demonstrate how they influence information processing.

The *availability* heuristic relates to one's recall or memory capacity in the sense that frequency and probability (in the form of recency or familiarity) bias one's perception of current events.[46] Issues that are preeminent in one's memory dominate decoding of real-time experiences. Ulen cites as one example the tendency of people to believe that New York City experiences more murders than suicides each year when in fact the opposite is true. He contends this phenomenon is "explainable by the fact that murders receive much more publicity than do suicides and are, therefore, much more in people's memory than is information about suicide."[47] Additionally, past events that are more salient than current events can cause an individual to perceive that immediate experiences mirror prior events.[48] The past event's significance, as it resonates with a present state of mind, overpowers an individual's real-time cognitive situation, distorting reality retrospectively toward the prior experience. In this manner, salience can limit an individual's ability to process information based upon the current situation, thereby narrowing one's feasible courses of action when making choices based upon the present situation and its future consequences. Closely related to the phenomenon of availability is that of representativeness.

According to Mary Zey, *representativeness* causes people to "act as if stereotypes are more common than they actually are."[49] Individuals classify information based upon its similarity with past information and its relevant category (this too relates to the compartmentalization discussion presented earlier). This heuristic's inherent danger, as it relates to decision making, or any other human activity for that matter, is that such compartmentalization may cause individuals to overlook data's anomalous properties, ones that necessitate further inquiry or multiple categorization. Such approaches promote stereotyping as they fail to incorporate evidence contrary to one's past experience. Taken together, these elements influence the selection of one's anchoring point as well as one's ability to adjust this referent once established.

As with the foregoing heuristics, selection of an *anchoring point* remains contingent upon one's ability to gather and process information. In essence, an anchoring point is an individual's initial impression of a situation.[50] This initial value may emerge as a component of problem formulation or "it may be the result of a partial computation. In either case, adjustments are typically insufficient . . . [because] different starting points yield different estimates, which are biased toward the initial values."[51] Therefore, any *adjustment* made in connection with a less than optimal starting point—especially in the absence of information that realigns the anchoring point—most probably will generate a skewed outcome over successive iterations of information processing. Pushing this idea further assumes that one knows the optimal starting point or even that one exists—but does it? Multidimensional cognitive processes, anchoring, and adjustment simultaneously influence the previous heuristics in that the salience of a particular anchoring point can further distort availability and representativeness by excluding known relevant information.[52]

These two potential cognitive limitations, whether manifest as "hardware" or "software" problems, indicate that there are instances wherein one may not act rationally according to the precepts of rational choice theory. Instead, cognitive dissonance and judgmental heuristics, in concert with various other bias-generating mechanisms, limit a person's ability to gather and process information. While these represent a few of the internal constraints on the individual, external factors further curb one's ability to employ the rational actor model.

No Resource Constraints

Only within a utopian world could one operate inside a boundless, infinitely limitless environment. Since such a world does not exist, decision makers must adapt information gathering and processing efforts to the contextual bounds that define their operational parameters. This said, individuals typically face multiple, interrelated resource constraints, including those related to time restrictions and financial standing.

Unlike most other aspects of human existence (e.g., power, financial prowess, material possessions, or opportunity), time stands alone as a fixed quantity—there are only 24 hours in each day, and the clock cannot be turned backward or, indeed, halted to *create* more time. While recognizing the antithesis Albert Einstein proposed,[53] for the purposes of our discussion, time remains a "fixed" quantity. Putting a practical face on this issue demonstrates that while deadlines can be extended to provide additional time to make a choice, one's ability to preclude other activities from impinging upon that extension remains severely limited by the complexities of the globalized world within which we now live. When looking at the foreign policy development process, this axiom becomes more than problematic.

The classic rational actor model presumes that time does not create internal (or external) pressures that drive an individual toward a particular course of action. Rather, people make choices based upon personal utility maximization—irrespective of other factors such as time constraints. Practical experience, however, teaches us that time is indeed a limited commodity and, as such, must be used judiciously when making decisions. Note also the argument that time is also a cost, calculated in terms of dollars as well as opportunity. Just as the aphorism contends that "time is money," a natural corollary paralleling the limits of time is one's financial resource base.

Most individuals live within a bounded financial world, one wherein—ironically—subjective measures of utility appropriately serve as the basis for purely economic decisions.[54] Hence, if an individual gains more pleasure from reading as opposed to watching a movie, all other things being equal, a person who acts "rationally" would purchase a book in place of attending the theater. In this sense, it may be that rational choice theory can begin to predict decision outcomes if all other theoretical precepts endure. However, rational choice theory holds that individuals are able to maximize utility without considering the realistic bounds of their financially constrained world—resource constraints, therefore, do not impel individuals to choose particular courses of action. Nor is the individual's ability to gather and process information limited in any way because of impending, perhaps escalating, costs.

Clearly, propositions suggesting that time and cost constraints are "nonissues" within the realm of decision making remain invalid. As we attempt to apply theory to practice, we realize that personal, repetitive experience dictates that neither time nor resources exist unconstrained by their environments. Further, experience makes evident that these are identified before many other limiting factors as restrictions on choice, particularly when the "feasibility" test is applied to particular courses of action to "cut away" options that are too costly (in terms of time and/or resources). The foregoing factors interact synergistically to hinder the decision maker's capacity to prioritize alternatives based upon computable numerical weights.

Capacity to Quantify Alternatives

Proceeding from the perspective that an individual can quantifiably assess, or at least order consistently, every aspect of his or her life presents a challenge even for the most mathematically inclined, not to mention those who possess an average capacity to engage complex mathematical formulae. In light of the foregoing discussion, it appears that the capacity to formulate equations to compute utility is not the major limiting factor of the "rational actor" approach. In situations where individuals are not mathematically gifted, it does, however, influence one's decision-making process by increasing the likelihood that an individual who is deficient in computational ability will rely more heavily upon judgmental heuristics and a limited information search to frame alternative choices. Herbert Simon captures the essence of the problem in his critique of rational choice theory: "In the real world we usually do not have a choice between satisfactory and optimal solutions, for we only rarely have a method of finding the optimum. . . . We cannot, within practicable computational limits, generate all the admissible alternatives and compare their relative merits. Nor can we recognize the best alternative, even if we are fortunate enough to generate it early, until we have seen all of them. We satisfice by looking for alternatives in such a way that we can generally find an acceptable one after only moderate search."[55]   This perspective serves as the basis for

Simon's *satisficing* model of decision making.[56] Harold Gortner, Julianne Mahler, and Jeanne Bell Nicholson contend "satisficing takes the perspective of a single decision maker or a unified group and holds that the first alternative encountered that meets or exceeds the decision maker's minimum expectations or demands will be chosen."[57] Inherent in Simon's critique are implicit references that weaken two other assumptions of rational choice theory, specifically information search and resource constraints.

Simon's reference to a moderate search indicates that time and resource constraints (namely, financial costs) naturally limit the extent of one's information search. Discussed at great length earlier within the section on resource constraints, such limitations force individuals to establish and prioritize criteria that prevent them from conducting exhaustive searches. Others support this position as well, stating that it would be impractical to conduct such a comprehensive search.[58] Helmut Jungermann insists that "with finite time and resources available, it is not rational to spend infinite effort on the exploration of all potential consequences of all options. Rather, the decision costs are weighted against the potential benefits resulting from the application of a decision strategy, and this may lead to violations of SEU model rationality."[59] Consequently, when measured against the opportunity costs of time and support, an exhaustive search can deplete resources that could be used to analyze other issues, making such frivolous behavior less than rational. John O'Neill's work highlights one final, related critique that relates to an individual's ability to compute quantifiable measures for alternatives.

O'Neill posits that this assumption implies that individuals have no differences in preference orderings and that their measures of subjective expected utility remain identical.[60] It follows, then, that this assumption requires a "single unit of measurement, capable of ranking all objects and states of affairs from 'best' to 'worst' . . . it requires even more: a common unit of value of which the best option will possess the greatest amount."[61] He takes the argument further, stating that "there has to be a particular single property that all objects and states of affairs possess, and that this property is considered to be the source of their value."[62] In developing this idea of "value-monism," O'Neill suggests that rational choice theory prescribes that all aspects of life can be compared across a single scale. Consequently, earning a dollar, buying a house, giving birth to a child, saving another person's life, and dying should all, according to the premise put forth by rational choice theory, possess some "single property" that enables a decision maker to rank order them in a mutually exclusive fashion along a single continuum. Experience teaches us that not all objects or states of affairs possess an inherent exchange component wherein one can be substituted for another. Referring to the examples offered earlier, one can more than reasonably say that the intrinsic values associated with earning a dollar versus that of saving another's life are so qualitatively different that placing them along a single continuum would appear nonrational at best, ludicrous at worst. In this manner, O'Neill contends some values are not "reducible to others, nor to some other common value . . . there is no privileged canonical description for the purpose of an overarching evaluation which could rank all such areas against each other."[63]

Collectively, the limitations of rational choice theory assumptions quickly lead one to conclude that the "rational actor" approach to decision making can serve only as a normative guide for individual decision making. One has to ask, however, if this can ever occur in reality if humans simply cannot comply with the tenets of the rational actor model. Surely, the important thing is to find out—empirically—how humans choose. Extending the predictive or descriptive capacity of such a model beyond its normative potential obscures the true nature of the process by which individuals make decisions. As critical as this discussion has been regarding rational choice theory's application to individual choice, the variation between units of analysis makes this critique more exacting when applying the model to groups wherein the conflicting and often competing individual agendas defy the identification of "rational" goals.

Groups as "Less than Rational" Actors

The elements of the critique presented above apply to the group decision maker as well as the individual;[64] after all, groups are composed of multiple individuals. When approaching the nature of decision making in linear fashion, one could accept the premise of image theory as well, noting that decision making begins with the individual and then progresses to a broader context as individuals within a group make decisions and then work with their colleagues to develop a group decision.[65] It is this process of integrating several independent choices toward *one* group decision that further undermines the application of rational choice theory to the group decision-making process. The group process is far from linear, occurring instead as a complex, multilayered, dynamic interaction across multiple individuals.

Specifically, the nature of group dynamics reinforces those rational choice theory limitations that apply to individuals, giving these limitations the potential to produce a multiplier effect at the group level. That said, the properties of groups must be highlighted to demonstrate that rational choice theory remains inherently flawed when applied to decision makers who are not unitary actors. By their very nature, groups are not unitary actors. This erroneous inference, however, has served as the basis for the ongoing application of rational choice theory to organizations and groups. Let me begin by outlining some basic differences between individuals and groups. While these are not necessarily the classic divisions highlighted across the organization theory or organizational behavior disciplines, they capture the essence of the variance between individuals and groups that makes the application of rational choice theory inappropriate within any collective choice setting.[66]

Collective Value Dissensus: A Mandate for Intragroup Negotiation

Mary Zey is correct in her assessment that "value is subjective because it is defined as individual preferences and therefore varies from individual to individual."[67] The subjectivity of values produces goals that represent the desires and needs of the individual.[68] A challenge emerges within the group setting when these differing values and goals are encoded across diverse individual cognitive maps that produce different interpretations even though actors experience events at the same time and within the same contextual environment.[69] Evaluated within the group decision-making environment, divergent cognitive maps based upon asymmetric values create intragroup conflict surrounding problem definition, information search, course of action development, and selection of alternatives, that is, the actual decision outcome itself. Further, Uriel Rosenthal and Alexander Kousmin contend that decision makers may hold differing opinions regarding "appropriate implementation strategies."[70] Ian Morley insists that the process by which some form of consensus is reached is one of the defining factors of group decision making.[71] This process, according to Colin Eden's analysis regarding strategy development as a social process, has to be one of negotiation and intraorganizational bargaining.[72]

Pushing this idea further, Zey highlights Anselm Strauss's work on negotiation,[73] in conjunction with Samuel Bacharach and Edward Lawler's research on power within organizations,[74] to illustrate that within a group setting, a process of exchange shapes decisions over time. James March and Zur Shapira contend that the nature of this exchange synergistically ensures that organizational decisions are not congruous with those made by any one individual, and, indeed, choices may reflect little semblance of the well-ordered preference and utility functions demanded by rational choice theory.[75] In this manner, the practice of group decision making may depart from a utility maximization focus should the negotiation process facilitate an exchange wherein individuals move from their initial individual choices toward a more agreeable—yet not necessarily utility or profit maximizing—alternative course of action.

Recognizing that individuals within groups possess a variety of values, goals, and ideas, one begins to distinguish that decisions made within group settings represent a different type of outcome. This consensually developed "political resultant"[76] is influenced in many ways since it represents the negotiated choice of a bargaining process that is shaped by an organizational dynamic bound by interdependence and social learning.[77]

Social Interaction and Organizational Culture

A second major difference between individual and group decision strategies emanates from the idea that the process is indeed a negotiation.[78] Unlike purely rational unitary actor decision making, the negotiation process is a social interaction characterized by the interdependence of actors who have some commitment to one another as well as to the organization. The values and symbols that characterize the organizational culture define these commitments.[79]

Acknowledging the power of values and symbols, Mariam Thalos critiques rational decision theory through the lens of the social interactionist. In an insightful and philosophical approach, Thalos debunks the perspective that "rational decision-makers are autonomous entities—answering only to their own beliefs and desires."[80] In their empirical study on the structure and content of human decision making, Scott Allison, Anna Marie Jordan, and Carole Yeatts corroborate Thalos's ideas.[81] These researchers discovered that group decision making is indeed a social process, one that involves other people either directly or indirectly.[82] Paralleling Abraham Maslow's "belongingness and social interaction" needs, this connection with others can dampen the desire for individuals within groups to maximize their individual utility as the more salient goal becomes maintaining social relationships in the face of hard choices and reciprocal interdependence. Yet, the idea of maintaining relationships is not the only contextual constraint on individual choice. Depending upon one's goals, loyalty to the organization may supersede interpersonal allegiance as an individual strives to maintain cognitive congruence within a demanding organizational environment.

Studies within the fields of management, psychology, organizational behavior, and related disciplines have gone to great lengths to explain and predict the influence that organizational culture has upon human behavior.[83] The "property of groups of people and not individuals," Daniel Druckman insists organizational cultures influence the attitudes, emotions, and behaviors of members through indirect, often implicit, means.[84] While the "precise linkages between culture and performance have not been documented,"[85] experience and observation lead us to believe that organizational culture does indeed play a pivotal role in shaping collective decision processes through the accepted structuration of the group's social milieu, including its organizational structure, informal processes, and norms.[86] From this perspective, an awareness of organizational culture can facilitate understanding "subcultural dynamics within organizations."[87] Such understanding should enhance our ability to comprehend more keenly the nature of "decision making as negotiation" within groups as it occurs across intraorganizational coalitions that are based upon preexisting and newly developing subcultures. Much of the social science literature is beginning to identify social learning as one of the most important processes shaping human behaviors.[88] While not fully developed, the influence social learning has upon shaping organizational cultures and their subcultures, as well as the decision-making processes they employ, is beginning to receive heightened attention. Indeed, as Craig Thomas indicates, social learning shapes the sustainability and durability of organizational culture as "the members of an epistemic community have similar normative values, believe in the same causal relationships, and have a common methodology for validating knowledge, all of which shape their formulation of best management practices."[89]

In light of March and Simon's proposition that "decision-making is an arena for symbolic action,"[90] one can begin to see the confluence of values, goals, and organizational culture as this union influences decision-making processes within complex groups. Within an organizational context, utility-maximizing precepts may fall short of meeting the individual's or group's need to negotiate a compromise choice. Ironically, Kenneth Arrow attempts to validate the tenets of rational choice theory within this setting by insisting that rationality is a useful concept only if grounded within the "social context within which it is embedded."[91] He would, therefore, agree with the findings of Scott Allison and others. Yet, in light of the requirements of rational choice theory, this form of agreement confirms the inability of individuals to act in a purely rational fashion at any point in time. Humans can never escape the social contexts that frame their sense of reality and, therefore, their choice of preference. Indeed, it is the process of cognitive framing that shapes human perceptions of the problem—perceptions that enable them to act "rationally" within this frame—and the potential courses of action they can employ to create a favorable outcome. Consequently, the research surrounding cognitive framing accentuates one of the most critical deficiencies of the rational actor approach.

Framing—Reference Points, Risk, and Preference Orderings

More than any other phenomenon, the act of framing a situation—both consciously and unconsciously—establishes the starting point for all decision-making activities and continuously molds the process throughout its entirety. In their seminal work on framing decisions and the psychology of choice, Tversky and Kahneman conclude "the framing of an action sometimes affects the actual experience of its outcomes."[92] Two schools of thought form the basis for current ideas regarding framing.[93] The first school, the sociological and social psychological stream, refers specifically to the works of G. Bateson and Erving Goffman.[94] They critique this perspective by stating that it is overly broad because it takes account of the "actor's perception of both the social context and its social demands."[95] As the second stream, these authors identify the cognitive psychological and decision research arenas. Highlighting the efforts of M. Minsky, E. B. Hunt, and Kahneman and Tversky,[96] and Lee Roy Beach and others posit that this approach is overly narrow, "concentrating on the ways in which specific characteristics of problems influence how they are interpreted by the problem solver and how these interpretations determine the means by which he or she attempts to solve the problems."[97] Whether one adopts the perspective of the sociologist or the cognitive psychologist, the effects of framing shape decision making in at least three fundamental and interrelated ways: They influence the selection of reference points, attitudes toward risk, and the ordering of preferences.

Relying heavily upon the research of Tversky and Kahneman, Levy points out that the idea of "reference dependence is particularly important because people treat gains and losses differently—they overvalue losses relative to comparable gains."[98] Although he is specifically addressing reference dependence as the central assumption of prospect theory, Levy's idea is logically applicable because prospect theory is a refinement of rational choice theory under conditions of a boundedly rational unitary actor.[99] Levy indicates that individuals are customarily "risk-averse with respect to gains and risk-acceptant with respect to losses" and would therefore order preferences taking risk factors into account.[100] As a natural extension, Levy maintains that "the asymmetry of gains and losses and the role of the reference point in defining these distinct domains, the identification, or framing, of the reference point can have a critical effect on choice. A change in frame can result in a change in preferences (preference reversal) even if the values and probabilities associated with outcomes remain the same."[101] Noting that people perceive a difference in potential outcomes based upon the way in which risk is framed, Levy uses a medical treatment as an example to make his point, saying "it makes a difference whether a particular treatment has a 90 percent survival rate or a 10 percent mortality rate."[102]

The critical connection between the framing of reference points, risk, and preferences is best captured in March and Shapira's postulate that "rational models see decisions as being made by the evaluation of alternatives in terms of their future consequences for prior preferences."[103] Based upon the research presented herein, one could reasonably predict that the framing of a decision issue in parallel with a reference point entailing high risk—ranked as the most rational choice according to preference orderings—would most likely be disregarded in favor of one with reduced anticipated risk. In so doing, the decision maker would act in a nonutility-maximizing fashion, thereby failing to uphold the requirements of rational choice theory. Alternatively, the decision maker could reframe the situation, an act that would also violate rational choice theory since efforts to do so would necessarily presuppose a limited information search in the face of increased risk.

In looking at the aggregative effect of the challenges inherent to issue framing at the group level, it quickly becomes apparent that situations requiring collective decisions within any group or organizational setting comprised of multiple individuals require the development of a negotiated consensual choice. This course of action will be shaped by such intraorganizational factors as group dynamics, social interaction, and organizational culture. The synergistic effect of these group processes require decision analysts to look beyond rational choice theory toward alternative approaches that enable groups to predict choices accurately based upon effective descriptions and inclusive explanations of human behavior within a particular collective.

Rationale for Alternative Approaches

The majority of the literature cited as evidence in the foregoing critique of rational choice theory indicates that the theory's precepts fail to provide an accurate description, explanation, or prediction of human choice behavior when forced to make decisions either as individuals or groups. The critique then focused specifically upon the unit of analysis issue, insisting that groups do not act as unitary actors within the decision process because "Humans do not always make rational choices."[104] Rather, they must manage through some interactive and iterative process to develop decision alternatives that adequately incorporate the attitudinal and behavioral dynamics specific to each group. A vital challenge inherent to this approach is that this process must create consensus within an environment rife with value conflicts that recurrently manifest themselves at the interpersonal and intergroup levels, both within a single organization and between agencies. Further, ongoing social interaction and the parameters of the organization's culture mandate conformity to decision rules and behavioral guidelines, factors that further impede both the individual's and the group's ability to conform to every rational choice theory tenet. Finally, the process of framing and its relationship with reference points, risk orientations, and preference orderings becomes problematic within the group setting wherein multiple "frames" must be integrated toward a prioritized group utility function. Indeed, Thomas Schelling argues that "in a collectivity there is no unanimous preference" and hence, " 'rational decision' has to be replaced with something like collective choice."[105] With this perspective guiding exploration of the interagency process, the book's remainder

48

advances our understanding regarding Schelling's notion of collective choice and its influence upon conflict termination policy development.

Notes

1. Randy Y. Hirokawa and Dierdre D. Johnston, "Toward a General Theory of Group Decision Making: Development of an Integrated Model," *Small Group Behavior* 20, no. 4 (1989): 500.

2. See also Paul R. Pillar, *Negotiating Peace: War Termination as a Bargaining Process* (Princeton, N.J.: Princeton University Press, 1983); and see also John Spanier and Eric M. Uslaner, *How American Foreign Policy Is Made* (New York & Washington, D.C.: Praeger Publishers, 1974).

3. See also Peter G. Keen and Michael S. Scott Morton, *Decision Support Systems: An Organizational Perspective* (Reading, Mass.: Addison–Wesley Publishing Co., 1978).

4. See also Harold F. Gortner, Julianne Mahler, and Jeanne Bell Nicholson, *Organization Theory: A Public Perspective*, 2d ed. (Fort Worth: Harcourt Brace College Publishers, 1997); Michael I. Harrison and Bruce Phillips, "Strategic Decision Making: An Integrative Explanation," *Research in the Sociology of Organizations* 9 (1991): 319–58; and Paul Charles Nutt, "Some Guides for the Selection of a Decision-Making Strategy," *Technological Forecasting and Social Change* 19, no. 2 (1981): 133–45.

5. See also Baruch Fischhoff, Bernard Goitein, and Zur Shapira, "Subjective Expected Utility: A Model of Decision Making," in *Decision Making under Uncertainty: Cognitive Decision Research, Social Interaction, and Development and Epistemology*, ed. R. W. Scholz (North-Holland, Netherlands: Elsevier Science Publishers B. V., 1983); see also Karl E. Weick, "Rethinking Research on Decision Making," in *Decision Making: An Interdisciplinary Inquiry*, ed. G. R. Ungson and D. N. Braunstein (Boston, Mass.: Kent Publishing Co., 1982); see also Mary Zey, "Criticisms of Rational Choice Models," in *Decision Making: Alternatives to Rational Choice Models*, ed. Mary Zey (Newbury Park: Sage Publications, 1992); and see also Mary Zey, ed., *Decision Making: Alternatives to Rational Choice Models* (Newbury Park: Sage Publications, 1992).

6. From this perspective, the rational actor model serves as the macrotheory for prospect theory. See Daniel Kahneman and Amos Tversky, "Prospect Theory: An Analysis of Decision under Risk," *Econometrica* 47 (1979): 263–91; Jack S. Levy, "Prospect Theory and International Relations: Theoretical Applications and Analytical Problems. Special Issue: Prospect Theory and Political Psychology," *Political Psychology* 13, no. 2 (1992): 283–310; and Jack S. Levy, "Prospect Theory, Rational Choice, and International Relations," *International Studies Quarterly* 41, no. 1 (1997): 87–112. For *satisficing*, see also James G. March and Zur Shapira, "Behavioral Decision Theory and Organizational Decision Theory," in *Decision Making: Alternatives to Rational Choice Models*, ed. Mary Zey (Newbury Park: Sage Publications, 1992); and see also Herbert A. Simon, "A Behavioral Model of

Rational Choice," (1975); and for *incrementalism,* see John Forester, "Bounded Rationality and the Politics of Muddling Through," *Public Administration Review* 44, no. 1 (1984): 23–31; and Charles E. Lindblom, "The Science of 'Muddling through,'" *Public Administration Review* 19 (1959): 79–88. Although the organizational model paralleled the development of the bureaucratic politics model, because it is a multiple-actor model, it is classified with the bureaucratic politics model as a framework for group decision making. See also Graham T. Allison, *Essence of Decision: Explaining the Cuban Missile Crisis* (Boston: Little, Brown and Co., 1971); and see also Richard Cyert and James March, *A Behavioral Theory of the Firm* (Englewood Cliffs, N.J.: Prentice-Hall, 1963).

7. Thomas S. Ulen, "The Theory of Rational Choice, Its Shortcomings, and the Implications for Public Policy Decision Making," *Knowledge: Creation, Diffusion, Utilization* 12, no. 2 (1990): 170–98.

8. Levy, "Prospect Theory, Rational Choice, and International Relations," 87.

9. See also Kenneth J. Arrow, "Rationality of Self and Others in an Economic System," in *Decision Making: Alternatives to Rational Choice Models,* ed. Mary Zey (Newbury Park, Calif.: Sage Publications, 1992); Steve Chan, "Rationality, Bureaucratic Politics and Belief System: Explaining the Chinese Policy Debate, 1964–66," *Journal of Peace Research* 16, no. 4 (1979): 333–47; see also Richard M. Cyert and James G. March, *A Behavioral Theory of the Firm,* 2d ed. (Cambridge, Mass.: Blackwell Publishers, 1992); see also Gortner, Mahler, and Nicholson, *Organization Theory: A Public Perspective;* see also Helmut Jungermann, "The Two Camps on Rationality," in *Decision Making under Uncertainty: Cognitive Decision Research, Social Interaction, and Development and Epistemology,* ed. R. W. Scholz (North-Holland, Netherlands: Elsevier Science Publishers B. V., 1983); see also Keen and Morton, *Decision Support Systems: An Organizational Perspective;* see also Levy, "Prospect Theory, Rational Choice, and International Relations"; see also Thomas C. Schelling, *Choice and Consequence* (Cambridge: Harvard University Press, 1984); and Herbert A. Simon, "Rational Decision Making in Business Organizations," *American Economic Review* 64, no. 4 (1979): 493–513.

10. See also John von Neumann and Oskar Morgenstern, *Theory of Games and Economic Behavior* (Princeton, N.J.: Princeton University Press, 1944).

11. Ibid.

12. Utility is a construct based upon the technical creation of "indifference curves" (i.e., the calculated measure of "the locus of points representing market baskets among which the consumer is indifferent"). In this manner, *utility* is defined within classic microeconomics as "the level of enjoyment or preferences attached by [a] consumer to this market basket." In this sense, the "consumer" is the individual decision maker and the "market basket" represents the alternative choice. While an understanding of these concepts remains critical to grasping the full complexity of rational choice theory, their complete explanation here would require a separate chapter. For an explanation of these ideas, refer to Mansfield, especially chapters 3 and 4. See

also Edwin Mansfield, *Applied Microeconomics* (New York: W. W. Norton & Co., 1994).

13. See also Paul Koopman and Jeroen Pool, "Organizational Decision Making: Models, Contingencies and Strategies," in *Distributed Decision Making: Cognitive Models for Cooperative Work*, ed. Jens Rasmussen, Berndt Brehmer, and Jacques Leplat (Chichester, England: John Wiley & Sons, 1991); and see also Mansfield, *Applied Microeconomics;* and see also Schelling, *Choice and Consequence.*

14. See also Fischhoff, Goitein, and Shapira, "Subjective Expected Utility: A Model of Decision Making"; see also Levy, "Prospect Theory, Rational Choice, and International Relations"; see also Roland W. Scholz, "Introduction to Decision Making under Uncertainty: Cognitive Decision Research, Social Interaction, and Development and Epistemology," in *Decision Making under Uncertainty;* see also Roland W. Scholz, ed., *Decision Making under Uncertainty;* and see also Ulen, "The Theory of Rational Choice." Others cite Bayes' Rule as the basis for rational choice theory, see Max Black, "Making Intelligent Choices: How Useful Is Decision Theory?" *Dialectica* 39, no. 1 (1985): 19–34; and see also Jungermann, "The Two Camps on Rationality." While an in-depth or comparative discussion of this foundational theory in relation to SEU modeling is beyond the scope of this work, suffice it to say they both refer to the maximization of individual utility.

15. See also Fischhoff, Goitein, and Shapira, "Subjective Expected Utility: A Model of Decision Making." Amos Tversky and Daniel Kahneman have conducted experiments that have called the SEU approach into question. See Amos Tversky and Daniel Kahneman, "The Framing of Decisions and the Psychology of Choice," Science 211 (1981): 453–58. Discussed in more length in the ensuing subsection that illuminates the limitations of rational choice theory, these authors identify heuristics that serve as "rules of thumb," mechanisms through which individuals make decisions by means other than the rational actor approach.

16. Jerome H. Black, "The Probability-Choice Perspective in Voter Decision Making Models," *Public Choice* 35, no. 5 (1980): 565–74; R. M. Cyert, H. A. Simon, and D. B. Trow, "Observation of a Business Decision," *The Journal of Business* 29 (1956): 237–48; see also Keen and Morton, *Decision Support Systems: An Organizational Perspective;* see also Koopman and Pool, "Organizational Decision Making: Models, Contingencies and Strategies"; see also Simon, "Rational Decision Making in Business Organizations"; see also Ulen, "The Theory of Rational Choice"; and see also Zey, ed., *Decision Making: Alternatives to Rational Choice Models.*

17. Michael Nicholson, "Negotiation, Agreement and Conflict Resolution: The Role of Rational Approaches and Their Criticism," in *New Directions in Conflict Theory: Conflict Resolution and Conflict Transformation*, ed. Raimo Vayrynen (Newbury Park, Calif.: Sage Publications, Inc., 1991), 58.

18. George P. Huber, "Decision Support Systems: Their Present Nature and Future Applications," in *Decision Making: An Interdisciplinary Inquiry,*

ed. G. R. Ungson and D. N. Braunstein (Boston, Mass.: Kent Publishing Co., 1982), 254.

19. See also, for example, Max Black, "Making Intelligent Choices: How Useful Is Decision Theory?" J. Ferejohn and D. Satz, "Unification, Universalism, and Rational Choice Theory," *Critical Review* 9 (1995): 71–84; see also Jeffrey Friedman, ed., *The Rational Choice Controversy* (New Haven, Conn.: Yale University Press, 1996); see also Donald P. Green and Ian Shapiro, *Pathologies of Rational Choice Theory: A Critique of Applications in Political Science* (New Haven, Conn.: Yale University Press, 1994); see also Ida R. Hoos, *Systems Analysis in Public Policy: A Critique*, 2d ed. (Berkeley, Calif.: University of California Press, 1974); see also Jungermann, "The Two Camps on Rationality"; Eleanor Farrar McGowan, "Rational Fantasies," *Policy Sciences* 7, no. 4 (1976): 439–54; see also K. R. Monroe, ed., *The Economic Approach to Politics: A Critical Reassessment of the Theory of Rational Action* (New York: HarperCollins, 1991); Bernice A. Pescosolido, "Beyond Rational Choice: The Social Dynamics of How People Seek Help," *The American Journal of Sociology* 97, no. 4 (1992): 1096–1138; Larry Samuelson, "Bounded Rationality and Game Theory," *The Quarterly Review of Economics and Finance* 36 (1996): 17–35; see also Donald A. Schon and Martin Rein, *Frame Reflection: Toward the Resolution of Intractable Policy Controversies* (New York: Basic Books, 1994); see also Simon, "Rational Decision Making in Business Organizations"; Mariam Thalos, "Self-Interest, Autonomy, and the Presuppositions of Decision Theory," *American Philosophical Quarterly* 34, no. 2 (1997): 287–300; and see also Zey, ed., *Decision Making: Alternatives to Rational Choice Models*.

20. See also Irving L. Janis, *Crucial Decisions: Leadership in Policymaking and Crisis Management* (New York: Free Press, 1989); see also Ulen, "The Theory of Rational Choice"; Zey, "Criticisms of Rational Choice Models"; see also and Zey, ed., *Decision Making: Alternatives to Rational Choice Models*.

21. See also Pillar, *Negotiating Peace: War Termination as a Bargaining Process;* and Spanier and Uslaner, *How American Foreign Policy Is Made*.

22. See also Jungermann, "The Two Camps on Rationality."

23. See also Zey, "Criticisms of Rational Choice Models."

24. See also Geoffrey Brennan, "What Might Rationality Fail to Do?" in *Decision Making: Alternatives to Rational Choice Models*, ed. Mary Zey (Newbury Park, Calif.: Sage Publications, 1992).

25. See also Allison, *Essence of Decision: Explaining the Cuban Missile Crisis*, 29; and Ulen, "The Theory of Rational Choice."

26. See also Mansfield, *Applied Microeconomics;* and Ulen, "The Theory of Rational Choice," 177.

27. Edwin Mansfield's *Applied Microeconomics* readily admits that individuals assign different values to different market baskets. In this manner, then, individuals prefer one choice to another based upon factors that remain specific to the particular individual. To illustrate, Mansfield points out than an "alcoholic will sometimes trade a valuable item like a watch for an extra drink of whiskey, whereas the president of the Temperance Union will

not give a cent for an extra (presumably the first) dose of Demon Rum." Hence, different individuals assign different value to particular choice alternatives, see Mansfield, *Applied Microeconomics*, 68.

28. Brennan, "What Might Rationality Fail to Do?" 59.

29. See also Lawrence Freedman and Efraim Karsh, *The Gulf Conflict, 1990-1991: Diplomacy and War in the New World Order* (Princeton, N.J.: Princeton University Press, 1993); and see also Vicki J. Rast, "The Iraq-Kuwait Crisis: Structural Deprivation Leads to Revolution," in *Intervention Design in Conflict Analysis and Resolution: Theory, Practice, and Research*, ed. L. A. Fast and V. J. Rast et al. (Fairfax, Va.: Institute for Conflict Analysis and Resolution, George Mason University Press, 1998).

30. See also Black, "Making Intelligent Choices: How Useful Is Decision Theory?"

31. See also James E. Anderson, *Public Policy-Making* (New York: Praeger, 1975); D. W. Bunn, "Policy Analytic Implications for a Theory of Prediction and Decision," *Policy Sciences* 8, no. 2 (1977): 125–34; see also William D. Coplin, *Introduction to International Politics* (Columbus, Ohio: Charles E. Merrill, 1971); see also Charles F. Hermann, "The Knowledge Gap: The Exchange of Information between the Academic and the Foreign Policy Communities" (paper presented at the Annual Political Science Association Meeting, Chicago, Ill., 7–11 September 1971); see also Koopman and Pool, "Organizational Decision Making: Models, Contingencies and Strategies"; see also Harold D. Lasswell, *The Decision Process: Seven Categories of Functional Analysis* (College Park, Md.: Bureau of Governmental Research, 1956); see also March and Shapira, "Behavioral Decision Theory and Organizational Decision Theory"; E. S. Quade, ed., *Analysis for Military Decisions* (Chicago: Rand McNally, 1964); and see also Ulen, "The Theory of Rational Choice."

32. See also Brennan, "What Might Rationality Fail to Do?"

33. See also Gortner, Mahler, and Nicholson, *Organization Theory: A Public Perspective*.

34. Ibid.

35. Jerel A. Rosati, "The Power of Human Cognition in the Study of World Politics," *International Studies Review* 2, no. 3 (2000): 45–75.

36. See also Brennan, "What Might Rationality Fail to Do?"

37. Ulen, "The Theory of Rational Choice," 175.

38. Ibid.

39. See also Simon, "Rational Decision Making in Business Organizations."

40. See also Leon Festinger, *A Theory of Cognitive Dissonance* (Stanford: Stanford University Press, 1957).

41. Leon Festinger, "The Motivating Effect of Cognitive Dissonance," in *Classic Readings in Organizational Behavior*, ed. J. S. Ott (Pacific Grove, Calif.: Brooks/Cole Publishing Co., 1989), 74.

42. Ulen, "The Theory of Rational Choice," 178; and see also Rosati, "The Power of Human Cognition in the Study of World Politics."

43. See also Tversky and Kahneman, "The Framing of Decisions and the Psychology of Choice"; Amos Tversky and Daniel Kahneman, "Judgment under Uncertainty: Heuristics and Biases," *Science* 185, no. 4157 (1974): 1124–31; Amos Tversky and Peter Wakker, "Risk Attitudes and Decision Weights," *Econometrica* 63, no. 6 (1995): 1255–80; Scott T. Allison, Leila T. Worth, and Melissa W. Campbell King, "Group Decisions as Social Inference Heuristics," *Journal of Personality and Social Psychology* 58, no. 5 (1990): 801–11; Jonathan B. Berk, Eric Hughson, and Kirk Vandezande, "The Price Is Right, but are the Bids? An Investigation of Rational Decision Theory," *American Economic Review* 86, no. 4 (1996): 954–70; see also Fischhoff, Goitein, and Shapira, "Subjective Expected Utility: A Model of Decision Making"; see also Keen and Morton, *Decision Support Systems: An Organizational Perspective;* see also March and Shapira, "Behavioral Decision Theory and Organizational Decision Theory"; see also Rosati, "The Power of Human Cognition in the Study of World Politics"; see also Scholz, ed., *Decision Making under Uncertainty: Cognitive Decision Research, Social Interaction, and Development and Epistemology;* see also Ulen, "The Theory of Rational Choice"; Mark van de Vall, "Utilization and Methodology of Applied Social Research: Four Complementary Models," *Journal of Applied Behavioral Science* 11, no. 1 (1975): 14–38; and see also Alan A. Zox, "A Heuristic Typology of Policy Formation within Institutions of Higher Education" (PhD diss., Rutgers University, 1977).

44. Fischhoff, Goitein, and Shapira, "Subjective Expected Utility: A Model of Decision Making," 196.

45. See also Rosati, "The Power of Human Cognition in the Study of World Politics."

46. See also Tversky and Kahneman, "Judgment under Uncertainty: Heuristics and Biases."

47. Ulen, "The Theory of Rational Choice," 182.

48. See also Tversky and Kahneman, "Judgment under Uncertainty: Heuristics and Biases; and see also Zey, ed., *Decision Making: Alternatives to Rational Choice Models.*

49. Zey, "Criticisms of Rational Choice Models," 17.

50. See also Ulen, "The Theory of Rational Choice."

51. Tversky and Kahneman, "Judgment under Uncertainty: Heuristics and Biases," 1128.

52. Ibid. Tversky and Kahneman demonstrate this potential through their "wheel of fortune" experiment. They asked students to estimate the percentage of African nations that were members of the United Nations by spinning a wheel (marked with numbers from zero to 100) and then deciding if the actual membership percentage was higher or lower than that displayed on the wheel. Next, they asked the students to provide numerical estimates for their percentages. The most interesting result of this experiment emerged as the median estimate for those who got a "10" on the wheel was 25; for those with a "65," the median estimate was 65 percent. Obviously, the numbers on the wheel had no relationship to the actual percentage of African nations that were members of the UN. Instead, the subjects allowed

the combined effect of judgmental heuristics to influence their decisions. See also Ulen, "The Theory of Rational Choice."

53. See also Albert Einstein, *Relativity: The Special and the General Theory*, Reprint ed. (New York: Crown Publication, 1995).

54. See also Levy, "Prospect Theory and International Relations: Theoretical Applications and Analytical Problems. Special Issue: Prospect Theory and Political Psychology."

55. Herbert A. Simon, *The Sciences of the Artificial* (Cambridge, Mass.: The MIT Press, 1969), 64.

56. See also James G. March and Herbert A. Simon, *Organizations* (New York: John Wiley, 1958).

57. Harold F. Gortner, Julianne Mahler, and Jeanne Bell Nicholson, *Organization Theory: A Public Perspective* (Pacific Grove, Calif.: Brooks/Cole Publishing Co., 1989), 258; see also David J. Hickson, "Decision-Making at the Top of Organizations," *Annual Review of Sociology* 13 (1987): 165–92; see also Irving L. Janis and Leon Mann, *Decision Making: A Psychological Analysis of Conflict, Choice, and Commitment* (New York: Free Press, 1977); see also Jungermann, "The Two Camps on Rationality"; see also Keen and Morton, *Decision Support Systems: An Organizational Perspective;* and see also March and Shapira, "Behavioral Decision Theory and Organizational Decision Theory."

58. See also Allison, *Essence of Decision: Explaining the Cuban Missile Crisis;* Lindblom, "The Science of 'Muddling through'"; and see also B. Staw, "Motivation from the Bottom Up," in *Psychological Foundations of Organizational Behavior*, ed. B. Staw (Santa Monica, Calif.: Goodyear, 1977).

59. Jungermann, "The Two Camps on Rationality," 71.

60. John O'Neill, "Cost-Benefit Analysis, Rationality and the Plurality of Values," *The Ecologist* 26, no. 3 (1996): 98.

61. Ibid.

62. Ibid.

63. Ibid., 100.

64. See also Mary Zey, "Introduction to Alternative Perspectives: Macroemphasis on Organizations and Institutions," in *Decision Making: Alternatives to Rational Choice Models*, ed. Mary Zey (Newbury Park, Calif.: Sage Publications, 1992).

65. See also Lee Roy Beach et al., "Image Theory: Decision Framing and Decision Liberation," in *Decision-Making and Leadership*, ed. Frank Heller (Cambridge: Cambridge University Press, 1992).

66. See also Hirokawa and Johnston, "Toward a General Theory of Group Decision Making: Development of an Integrated Model."

67. Zey, "Criticisms of Rational Choice Models," 17.

68. See also Janis, *Crucial Decisions: Leadership in Policymaking and Crisis Management.*

69. See also Chan, "Rationality, Bureaucratic Politics and Belief System: Explaining the Chinese Policy Debate, 1964–66"; Michael Handel, "The Yom Kippur War and the Inevitability of Surprise," *International Studies Quarterly* 21 (1977): 461–502; see also Richard Neustadt, *Alliance Politics* (New York:

Wiley, 1980); see also Bruce M. Russett, "Refining Deterrence Theory: The Japanese Attack on Pearl Harbor," in *Theory and Research on the Causes of War*, ed. D. G. Pruitt; and see also R. C. Snyder (Englewood Cliffs, N.J.: Prentice-Hall, 1969); and M. J. Shapiro and G. M. Bonham, "Cognitive Process and Foreign Policy Decision-Making," *International Studies Quarterly* 17 (1973): 147–74.

70. Uriel Rosenthal and Alexander Kousmin, "Crisis and Crisis Management: Toward Comprehensive Government Decision Making," *Journal of Public Administration Research and Theory* 7, no. 2 (1997): 285.

71. See also Ian E. Morley, "Intra-Organizational Bargaining," in *Employment Relations: The Psychology of Influence and Control at Work*, ed. Jean F. Hartley and Geoffrey M. Stephenson (Oxford, United Kingdom: Blackwell, 1992).

72. Colin Eden, "Strategy Development as a Social Process," *Journal of Management Studies* 29, no. 6 (1992): 799–811.

73. See also Anselm Strauss, "Summary, Implications, and Debate," in *Negotiations: Varieties, Contexts, Processes, and Social Order* (San Francisco: Jossey-Bass, 1978).

74. See also Samuel B. Bacharach and Edward J. Lawler, *Power and Politics in Organizations: The Social Psychology of Conflict, Coalitions, and Bargaining* (San Francisco: Jossey-Bass, 1980).

75. See also March and Shapira, "Behavioral Decision Theory and Organizational Decision Theory."

76. Allison, *Essence of Decision: Explaining the Cuban Missile Crisis*, 162.

77. Joseph J. Molnar, "Comparative Organizational Properties and Interorganizational Interdependence," *Sociology and Social Research* 63, no. 1 (1978): 24–48.

78. This premise easily could have been seen in the reverse as well. Social interaction across multiple organizational actors causes individuals to engage in a negotiation process as a means to make decisions. See I. William Zartman, "Decision Support and Negotiation Research: A Researcher's Perspective," *Theory and Decision* 34 (1993): 345–51.

79. See also Pescosolido, "Beyond Rational Choice: The Social Dynamics of How People Seek Help."

80. Thalos, "Self-Interest, Autonomy, and the Presuppositions of Decision Theory," 287.

81. Scott T. Allison, Anna Marie R. Jordan, and Carole E. Yeatts, "A Cluster-Analytic Approach toward Identifying the Structure and Content of Human Decision-Making," *Human Relations* 45, no. 1 (1992): 49–72.

82. Diana Richards, "Is Strategic Decision Making Chaotic?" *Behavioral Science* 35, no. 3 (1990): 219–32.

83. Jennifer A. Chatman and Sigal G. Barsade, "Personality, Organizational Culture, and Cooperation: Evidence from a Business Simulation," *Administrative Science Quarterly* 40 (1995): 423–43; see also Daniel Druckman, "Organizational Culture," in *Enhancing Organizational Performance*, ed. Daniel Druckman, Jerome E. Singer, and Harold Van Cott (Washington, D.C.: Na-

tional Academy Press, 1997); Calvin Morrill, "The Management of Managers: Disputing in an Executive Hierarchy," *Sociological Forum* 4, no. 3 (1989): 387–407; Andrew M. Pettigrew, "On Studying Organizational Cultures," *Administrative Science Quarterly* 24, no. 4 (1979): 570–81; see also Edgar H. Schein, "Defining Organizational Culture," in *Classics of Organization Theory*, ed. J. M. Shafritz and J. S. Ott (Pacific Grove, Calif.: Brooks/Cole Publishing Co., 1987); and see also Edgar H. Schein, "Group and Intergroup Relationships," in *Classic Readings in Organizational Behavior*, ed. J. S. Ott (Pacific Grove, Calif.: Brooks/Cole Publishing Co., 1989).

84. Druckman, "Organizational Culture," 96; and Patrick G. Scott, "Assessing Determinants of Bureaucratic Discretion: An Experiment in Street-Level Decision Making," *Journal of Public Administration Research and Theory* 7, no. 1 (1997): 35–57. For an excellent treatment on the affective-motive component of values as they relate to decision making, see also Amitai Etzioni, "Normative-Affective Factors: Toward a New Decision-Making Model," in *Decision Making: Alternatives to Rational Choice Models*, ed. Mary Zey (Newbury Park, Calif.: Sage Publications, 1992).

85. Druckman, "Organizational Culture," 96.

86. See also Beach et al., "Image Theory: Decision Framing and Decision Liberation"; and Kenneth Bettenhausen and J. Keith Murnighan, "The Emergence of Norms in Competitive Decision-Making Groups," *Administrative Science Quarterly* 30, no. 3 (1985): 350–72.

87. Edgar H. Schein, *Organizational Culture and Leadership* (San Francisco: Jossey-Bass Publishers, 1992), xii.

88. Eytan Avital and Eva Jablonka, "Social Learning and the Evolution of Behaviour," *Animal Behaviour* 48, no. 5 (1994): 1195–99; Sanjeev Goyal and Maarten Janssen, "Can We Rationally Learn to Coordinate?" *Theory and Decision* 40, no. 1 (1996): 29–49; Joan E. Grusec, "Social Learning Theory and Developmental Psychology: The Legacies of Robert Sears and Albert Bandura," *Developmental Psychology* 28, no. 5 (1992): 776–86; J. Richard Harrison and Paul McIntosh, "Using Social Learning Theory to Manage Organizational Performance," *Journal of Managerial Issues* 4, no. 1 (1992): 84–105; Jun Nakazawa et al., "From Social Learning Theory to Social Cognitive Theory: Recent Advances in Bandura's Theory and Related Research," *Japanese Psychological Review* 31, no. 2 (1988): 229–51; Jeffrey L. Okey, "Human Aggression: The Etiology of Individual Differences," *Journal of Humanistic Psychology* 32, no. 1 (1992): 51–64; and Matthew J. Zagumny, "Mentoring as a Tool for Change: A Social Learning Perspective," *Organization Development Journal* 11, no. 4 (1993): 43–48.

89. Craig W. Thomas, "Public Management as Interagency Cooperation: Testing Epistemic Community Theory as the Domestic Level," *Journal of Public Administration Research and Theory* 7, no. 2 (1997): 222. In "Introduction: Epistemic Communities and International Policy Coordination," *International Organization* 46 (1992), Peter Haas defines an *epistemic community* as a network of professionals with recognized expertise and competence in a particular domain and an authoritative claim to policy relevant knowledge within that

domain or issue-area. Although an epistemic community may consist of professionals from a variety of disciplines and backgrounds, they have (1) a shared set of normative and principled beliefs, which provide a value-based rationale for the social action of community members; (2) shared causal beliefs, which are derived from their analysis of practices leading or contributing to a central set of problems in their domain and which then serve as the basis for elucidating the multiple linkages between possible policy actions and desired outcomes; (3) shared notions of validity—that is, intersubjective, internally defined criteria for weighing and validating knowledge in the domain of their expertise; and (4) a common policy enterprise—that is, a set of common practices associated with a set of problems to which their professional competence is directed, presumably out of the conviction that human welfare will be enhanced as a consequence. (p. 3)

90. March and Shapira, "Behavioral Decision Theory and Organizational Decision Theory," 289.

91. Arrow, "Rationality of Self and Others in an Economic System," 63.

92. Tversky and Kahneman, "The Framing of Decisions and the Psychology of Choice," 458.

93. See also Beach et al., "Image Theory: Decision Framing and Decision Liberation."

94. See also G. Bateson, *Steps to an Ecology of Mind* (San Francisco: Chandler, 1972); and Erving Goffman, *Frame Analysis* (Cambridge, Mass.: Harvard University Press, 1974).

95. Beach et al., "Image Theory: Decision Framing and Decision Liberation," 180.

96. See also M. Minsky, *Semantic Information Processing* (Cambridge, Mass.: MIT Press, 1968); see also E. B. Hunt, *Artificial Intelligence* (New York: Academic Press, 1975); and see also Kahneman and Tversky, "Prospect Theory: An Analysis of Decision under Risk."

97. Beach et al., "Image Theory: Decision Framing and Decision Liberation," 180.

98. Levy, "Prospect Theory and International Relations: Theoretical Applications and Analytical Problems. Special Issue: Prospect Theory and Political Psychology," 89.

99. Ibid.

100. Ibid., 90; see also Tversky and Kahneman, "The Framing of Decisions and the Psychology of Choice"; Amos Tversky and Daniel Kahneman, "Loss Aversion in Riskless Choice: A Reference Dependent Model," *Quarterly Journal of Economics* 41 (1991): 1039–61; and see also Tversky and Wakker, "Risk Attitudes and Decision Weights."

101. Levy, "Prospect Theory and International Relations: Theoretical Applications and Analytical Problems. Special Issue: Prospect Theory and Political Psychology," 90.

102. Ibid. Levy cites empirical evidence to support his position, calling attention to laboratory experiments. See also, for example, C. F. Camerer, "Individual Decision Making," in *The Handbook of Experimental Economics,*

ed. J. H. Kagel and A. E. Roth (Princeton, N.J.: Princeton University Press, 1995); D. M. Grether and C. R. Plott, "Economic Theory of Choice and the Preference Reversal Phenomenon," *American Economic Review* 69 (1979): 623–38; see also Kahneman and Tversky, "Prospect Theory: An Analysis of Decision under Risk"; see also A. E. Roth, "Introduction to Experimental Economics," in *The Handbook of Experimental Economics*, ed. J. H. Kagel and A. E. Roth (Princeton, N.J.: Princeton University Press, 1995); P. Slovic and S. Lichtenstein, "Preference Reversals: A Broader Perspective," *American Economic Review* 73 (1983): 596–605; Amos Tversky and Daniel Kahneman, "Rational Choice and the Framing of Decisions," *Journal of Business* 59, no. 4, 2 (1986): S251–S278; and Amos Tversky, Paul Slovic, and Daniel Kahneman, "The Causes of Preference Reversal," *American Economic Review* 80 (1990): 204–17.

103. March and Shapira, "Behavioral Decision Theory and Organizational Decision Theory," 274.

104. Zey, "Criticisms of Rational Choice Models," 17; and see also Allison, *Essence of Decision: Explaining the Cuban Missile Crisis*.

105. Schelling, *Choice and Consequence*, 93.

Chapter 3

Conflict Termination Models

It is always easy to begin a war, but very difficult to stop one, since its beginning and end are not under control of the same man.

—Sallust

Contemporary thinkers and operational planners erroneously conflate the term *war termination* with the terms *conflict termination* and *conflict resolution* and, hence, with peace. Desires to calculate termination decisions according to the tenets of rational choice theory prove responsible, in part, for these flaws in planning and execution. This problem remains pronounced within the USG—the Department of Defense in particular. Media reports and political pundits (e.g., television's "talking heads" and Sunday morning political talk shows such as *Meet the Press*) exacerbate this problem of defining the desired ends by confounding the public's understanding regarding the nature of a conflict and USG's desired ends. In fact, accepted models of termination decision making rely almost exclusively upon the rational actor model and its assumptions regarding unitary actors and quantifiable utility functions.[1] Rigorous analysis, however, condemns this approach for its inability to account for the influence of emotive and psychological factors that are not calculable overtly and thus are not considered in the rational actor model approach. As Jerel Rosati argues, cognitive processes may be the most influential factors in decision making.[2] The omission of these factors from contemporary conflict termination models helps to account for the mismatch between "theory and practice," as USG's decision makers think their intervention policies work toward conflict resolution. In practice, however, implementation of these policies tends to induce war termination only in the form of a cease-fire. Further, conflict termination models of this genre attempt to predict the point at which hostilities will end but fail to link this point to the more important process that attempts to move parties in conflict toward sustainable resolution.

Christopher Mitchell's alternative approaches are examined to illuminate the inherent dangers of the rational actor approach (i.e., the entrapment model), as well as rational actor model's inability to account for forward-looking leaders who presciently step away from immediate utility calculations and focus instead on developing broader understandings of potential future gains (i.e., the enticing opportunity model). Invoking Mitchell's ideas that relate to interagency fragmentation, the rational actor model is critiqued for its failure to recognize the adverse effects that group dynamics hold for termination decision making.

Penned well over 20 years ago, Fred Iklé's dictum regarding the nature of war termination and rational calculations continues to confound those who become embroiled in conflict and war. Iklé says, "If the decision to end a war were simply to spring from a rational calculation about gains and losses for the nation as a whole, it should be no harder to get out of a war than to get into one."[3] Although Iklé sees war as a distinct form of discord, his words hold true for the broader spectrum of conflict as well since "war" is a specialized violent manifestation of conflict. Hence, his ideas remain valid for those who attempt to initiate conflict termination processes.[4] Before discussing models of conflict termination, relevant concepts must be defined to ground the discussion that follows.

Points or Processes?

Effective analysis of the models that currently guide our understanding of conflict termination processes requires that we first define what we mean by conflict termination. In contrast to a widely accepted viewpoint, this work views conflict termination as a process and not merely as the cessation of hostilities.[5] This perspective is sometimes misconstrued, however, as many who think and write about this topic—particularly those within the US Armed Forces—use the term with a focus on the *point in time* at which violent hostilities come to an end (e.g., AFDD 2).[6] More critically, however, this group uses the term *war termination* erroneously, equating the cessation of hostilities with conflict termination, conflict resolution, and peace.[7] The utility of both perspectives remains limited—the first fails to provide an answer to questions regarding what follows the cessation of hostilities, while the second is both theoretically and practically misleading. A more advantageous perspective is one that views conflict termination as a bridge toward a "better state of peace" in terms of creating a more favorable and stable posthostilities environment.[8] In this way, conflict termination is recognized as part of an integrated process toward sustainable conflict resolution and conflict transformation. Figure 4 makes this distinction visible by highlighting the integrative, building-block approach from initial war termination to the higher-order goal of conflict transformation.

As a concept, war termination captures only the cessation of violent hostilities. It does not imply that communication is taking place or that a settlement has been proposed. The time and resources required to achieve war termination remain limited relative to other desired end states. In contrast, conflict settlement infers that war termination has been achieved and

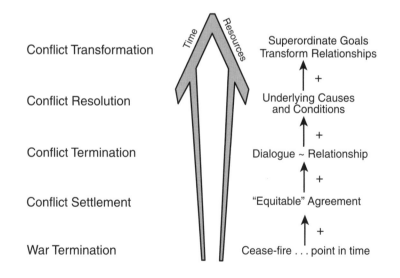

Figure 4. Conceptual Relationships across Termination Concepts

that the parties are working toward securing a "fair and equitable agreement" regarding the issues and exchanges necessary to maintain nonviolent relations.[9] Conflict settlement is a necessary step toward conflict termination—adherence to a mutually acceptable agreement in conjunction with the development of dialogue processes toward resolving the issues in conflict. Once established according to mutually acceptable ground rules, this dialogue serves as the foundation for conflict resolution; that is, a proactive approach to removing the underlying causes and conditions of conflict as parties attempt to reconcile relationships. Finally, through either conflict termination or conflict resolution processes, parties in conflict can achieve conflict transformation as they reframe relationships in positive directions that alleviate the sources of the conflict. Note again, however, that the time and resources this demands are extensive, especially when compared with the relatively limited commitment required to bring about war termination. Although military planners and war fighters tend to focus exclusively upon war termination, other thinkers and practitioners (e.g., Stephen Cimbala, Christopher Mitchell, and Michael Rampy) acknowledge that these conceptual distinctions represent more than nuanced definitions. These distinctions frame strategies as leaders determine the ultimate goal of any approach to ending violent conflict and war. Highlighted below, several authors capture the essence of this dynamic process.

Leading thinkers who regard conflict termination as a process include Cimbala, Mitchell, and, from the US military perspective, Rampy. Cimbala makes the distinction between the termination point and process clear in his study on war: "Termination implies something specific about the ending of war. Termination is the result of intention to limit the scope or duration of the war because that limitation accomplishes some desirable policy objective . . . terminating a war rather than ending it results in some trade-offs which might not appeal to all belligerents. . . . Termination . . . thus implies something premeditated, although perhaps flexibly adapted to time and circumstances."[10] The salient point is that when viewed as part of a decision-making process, conflict termination requires an active decision, or, as a minimum, a series of (limited) decisions, on the part of the belligerents.[11]

Mitchell, emphasizing that conflict termination is a process relevant to all social levels, defines the process as "a matter of at least one party in conflict determining to abandon coercive behavior and adopt some form of settlement strategy, through concessions and conciliation."[12] As part of sustainable conflict termination, this process has as its objective the "termination of both parties' conflict behaviour [sic] and the development of a compromise solution involving an abandonment of some goals underlying the original conflict situation."[13] Mitchell contends the process is far from linear and is complicated by myriad factors, including (a) views of relative positions and future prospects, (b) calculations of relevant costs/benefits in light of probable compromise solutions, (c) the dilemma imposed by the entrapment mentality wherein costs are viewed as investments in success, (d) the role of overall or marginal costs/benefits, and (e) doubts regarding the stability of the parties' goal preferences over time.[14] By highlighting these points, Mitchell argues that a process must be actualized to address unresolved issues from a relational perspective—that of the parties in conflict. He argues that the nature of the posthostilities environment necessitates that a conflict termination process address these issues to sustain nonviolent relations. Viewing the process from a military perspective, Rampy provides insight into the practical aspects of termination planning.

Writing to inform military practitioners concerning the relationship between conflict termination and postconflict activities, Rampy contends that "conflict termination is, in large measure, an intellectual process that couples the ends and means at hand with the circumstances of conflict."[15] Without explicitly referencing their works, he connects to both Cimbala's and Mitchell's ideas by noting that the most likely postconflict activities involve "political, economic, socio-psychological and military activities that support conflict termination . . . [including] security measures, intelligence, civil affairs, humanitarian assistance, nation assistance, force redeployment, and other activities."[16] Hence, he recognizes that a process must be in place to address many of the ongoing issues that serve as the basis of the conflict, in conjunction with those that have emerged as a result of the conflict's dynamics.

These three authors have developed the concept of conflict termination as a process, one that regards the broader termination of conflict as an affair encompassing various activities both before and after the actual cessation of violent hostilities. Cimbala insists that the termination of conflict is by all measures intentional and, hence, requires a decision to act. In turn, Mitchell shifts our thinking from the decision point to the factors that influence conflict termination decisions—factors that require an ongoing process to manage unresolved issues. Finally, Rampy highlights the nature of this process by identifying some of the activities that conflict termination processes should include in the posthostilities period. Since conflict termination requires individuals or groups to make a conscious decision—or again, several smaller decisions, some of which may be to abandon the attempt at a noncoercive settlement—to pursue de-escalation toward a less violent coexistence, the theoretical foundation for such a decision-making approach must be explored. To date, the literature on this subject focuses almost exclusively upon rational choice theory as it frames the rational actor model of decision making. Consequently, this perspective's influence requires explanation before analyzing the models themselves.

Rational Actor Approaches

Captured in-depth through the previous chapter, rational choice theory remains one of the most prominent theories of choice. By focusing on the logic of optimal choice, the rational perspective attempts to prescribe the normative ways in which people should make decisions when operating within the guidelines of individual self-interest. Within this paradigm, individuals strive to maximize personal utility; relatedly, organizations strive to maximize profits.[17] It is this self-interested, profit-maximizing perspective that undergirds the rational actor approach.[18]

The utility of termination models rests in their ability to predict the most likely points wherein the cessation of hostility provides an opportunity to initiate the postconflict activities

Rampy identifies as critical components for achieving sustainable conflict termination. Conflict termination models grounded in rational choice theory provide the basis for analyzing the cessation of hostilities phase of the conflict termination process but do not speak to the broader process as outlined in the conflict termination definition (i.e., point and process). This serves as an overarching critique of all rational actor models of conflict termination. Nonetheless, they have the potential, at least theoretically, to predict the point of cease-fire wherein the follow-on phases of the broader conflict termination process can begin and are therefore of great import to both conflict analysts and military strategists.

Classic conflict termination models distinguish the factors most often identified as those that have an influence upon a party's decision to stop fighting. These factors relate directly to quantifiable measures of utility, necessitating utility calculation functions that reflect a cost-benefit ratio regarding gains and losses as well as the costs and benefits of continued struggle.

Wittman: The Zero-Sum, Rational Model

As do most of these theorists, Donald Wittman employs the tenets of the rational actor model to create a mathematically sound model of conflict termination. He assumes that "unless both sides believe that they can be made better off by settlement, the war will continue."[19] Thus, he views the parties in conflict as unitary actors who can accurately and independently measure utility. By extension, this measurement becomes a zero-sum utility factor in that the utilities of both actors embroiled in conflict remain inversely proportional to one another. In this manner, an increase in utility for one party necessitates a comparable decrease for the other, ensuring that unconditional surrender ultimately maximizes the utility for one side (the "victor") while simultaneously minimizing it for the other (the "vanquished").

Using technical equations and utility-maximizing graphs, Wittman claims the factors that hold greatest import for his approach remain the rational actor model's traditionally accepted principles. Specifically, they are (1) the costs of war (namely, military and political—but since the military costs are more visible, he opts to focus on those in terms of logistical resources, manpower, etc.), (2) the probability of winning, (3) the present value of future outcomes, and (4) the joint probability of winning. Treating war and peace as alternative means to national ends, Wittman suggests that it takes two sides to end a war. Through his model, he concludes that "a reduction of hostilities" in terms of the costs associated with continued violence "may reduce the probability of a settlement taking place and thus prolong the war"; consequently, "increasing the probability of winning may not increase the probability of a settlement."[20]

While Wittman admits that information is seldom perfect or complete and that perceptual bias can affect assessments of power and, hence, decisions to discontinue conflict behaviors, he discounts the influence of these factors throughout his analysis. Further, because he focuses upon the unitary actor as decision maker, his work meets his personal goal of "logical clarity" at the expense of reliability and realism.[21] These errors in approach, compounded by his failure to consider the non-quantifiable aspects of psychology and emotion that condition a party's will to fight, erode the predictive value of his utility-based model. This critique moves us toward the works of I. William Zartman, a theorist who relies upon perceptions of utility at the margin while simultaneously assuming stable utility functions.

Zartman: Hurting Stalemate and Imminent Mutual Catastrophe

Zartman's work represents measures of utility at the margin within the rational actor model approach because his focus on a party's motivation to continue the conflict is based upon the ability to harm one or both of the conflicting parties through such continuation (i.e., a *mutually* hurting stalemate).[22] In this way, the cost-benefit aspect of utility maximization dictates that the costs of continuing the conflict far outweigh the benefits that will likely accrue. While Zartman intends his models to be taken in tandem, this text invokes Mitchell's approach and separates them to identify their most salient aspects: the hurting stalemate (HS) and the imminent mutual catastrophe (IMC).[23]

The HS model presupposes that parties in conflict can reach a point wherein an extended period of costly action in the face of little measurable progress compels them to consider other alternatives, that of discontinuing the conflict preeminent among them. As with similar rational actor approaches, this framework assumes that parties have the capacity to identify their costs (of quitting as well as continuing) and that their preference orderings clearly dictate that they should terminate the conflict. It further assumes, without clearly identifying the relevant factors, that parties will exhaust their capacity to continue and will therefore stop fighting, a perspective shared by many analysts.[24] It also assumes that while costs remain high, the perceived probability of (eventually) winning diminishes considerably. On the whole, Zartman's HS approach exhibits flaws similar to those found in Wittman's model: a failure to account for the psychological aspects of conflict and therefore an underestimation of a party's capacity to develop the means to fight when the will remains strong. In this fashion, the will to fight can often eclipse the lack of capacity, forcing people to find alternative tools of violence and, thereby, fulfilling the axiom that "desperate times call for desperate measures." The HS model also suffers from the rational actor model fallacy that rational calculations regarding costs and benefits can be made definitively within highly charged emotional environments. This leads to Zartman's corollary approach, the IMC.

The IMC cannot be detached easily from the HS because parties must presciently foresee an impending disaster that is connected inseparably to their continued participation in the conflict. Zartman envisioned that both parties would be locked in a costly and painful stalemate (HS) with a looming disaster on the horizon (IMC). Simply stated, this perspective assumes that anticipated costs for all parties in conflict increase suddenly and rise sharply. This disaster could manifest in terms of costs or their perceived opportunity for success (i.e., victory) could drastically decline because of continuation. Since this approach remains interlocked with the first, the critique of the HS holds for the IMC as well, with particular emphasis on the parties' inability to collect and process complete, accurate information regarding future events.

Wittman's and Zartman's approaches shaped scholars' thinking regarding conflict termination. Unfortunately, neither their strengths nor their limitations had noticeable influence on developing the US military institutional intellect. The ensuing discussion highlights the ideas of William O. Staudenmaier, Bruce Clarke, Joseph Engelbrecht, and Sam Allotey and others as representatives of US military perspectives of the process.

Staudenmaier: The Strategic Rational Conflict Model

Influenced greatly by the Cold War era's nuclear paradigm, Staudenmaier presents a model with two basic dimensions—one strategic and one rational.[25] Framed in figure 5 as a simple input-throughput-output diagram,[26] he contends his systems model captures conflict termination decision making under the assumption of bounded rationality.[27]

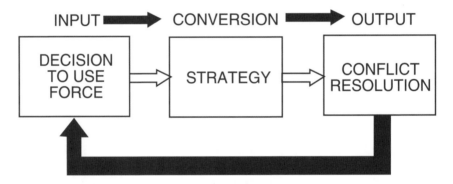

Figure 5. Staudenmaier's Strategic Rational Conflict Model

Returning to the underlying assumptions of rationality, he claims the rational actor model approach remains important based upon its ability to enable decision makers to predict outcomes and, therefore, to manipulate and control strategy.[28] Its assumed predictive value and its reliance upon bounded rationality place this framework within the rational actor model category of conflict termination models.

Staudenmaier advises that this approach is fraught with flaws when viewed in light of the inherent shortcomings of rational actor model assumptions. Decisions to start or stop wars are not taken by unitary actors within the bureaucratic policy arena,[29] perfect information does not exist, and there is no effective means to compare costs and benefits across dissimilar courses of action. This approach simultaneously suffers the error committed by many military thinkers—that of equating conflict termination to final conflict resolution.[30] In spite of these flaws, he maintains his approach is effective for making conflict termination decisions since it provides a means to integrate thoughts regarding the use of force, the selection of a strategy to achieve national objectives, and the decision to "end or continue" the conflict.[31] In the final analysis, Staudenmaier maintains that decisions for conflict resolution result from the comparison of costs (along social, economic, military, and political dimensions) to the value of political objectives.

Clarke: A Rational Model of Incompatible Objectives

Bruce Clarke extends ideas regarding comparing objectives in his discourse on rational conflict termination. Clarke's model (fig. 6) "focuses on a rational-actor model in an attempt to explain the theory involved in conflict termination."[32] He cautions, however, that the process remains embedded within a political context that shapes decisions in significant ways. This said, in his construction of "victory" criteria at the political level, Clarke brings the full focus back to cost-benefit comparisons and utility-maximization functions, stating that victory results when the opponent changes his objectives to coincide or parallel those of his adversary.[33] In this manner, as long as one can continue to prosecute the effort with an advantageous cost-benefit ratio, the conflict will continue. Clarke states the following:

> The primary cause of transition between phases of a dispute . . . is the changing of initial objectives (ends). This change can result from a cost/benefit analysis that indicates that the objective is not worth the price, a change in the external environment, partial or total achievement of the objective, or other situations that reduce or increase how tightly held the objectives are. *This is the key!* (Emphasis in original.) The ability to change objectives of one's opponent is thus the main element that causes transition from one phase to another and thus to successful termination of a conflict.[34]

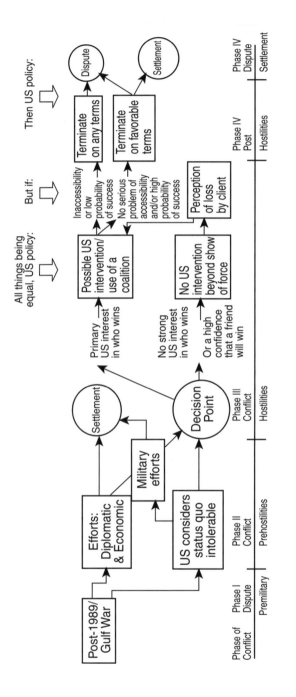

Figure 6. Clarke's Model of US Policy Preferences and Activities toward Conflict

In this manner, Clarke invokes the traditional ideas of the rational actor model and its focus upon measurable, quantifiably comparable utility functions. This approach caused him to create a linear model that begins and ends with a dispute phase, the second stage of which assumes that conflict termination on favorable terms leads to settlement and, by inference, conflict resolution. However, it also only considers the cost-imposing means of making the other side change its calculus. Unfortunately, he would not be the last military thinker to present limited ideas regarding the rational actor model of conflict termination. The most recent military theorist to do so is Joseph Engelbrecht.

Engelbrecht: When a State Stops Fighting

Engelbrecht cites several reasons states stop fighting.[35] Paralleling the rational actor model for the first two theorists, he identifies four theoretical explanations for war termination: (1) winners and losers, (2) cost-benefit ratio, (3) leadership change, and (4) psychological move toward a second-order paradigm. While the first may seem an obvious approach to conflict termination—in that one decides to stop based upon physical incapacity—the second again plays a significant part by enabling the parties to calculate the utility (or futility) of continuing. As with the foregoing approaches, this form of calculation is clearly subject to the critique already offered. His ideas spark interest, however, as he transitions to his third and fourth theoretical perspectives.

A change in leadership—primarily from a hawkish, war-prone leadership, to an authority that is more dovish, or in favor of peace—can create a situation that favors conflict termination, suggesting that factors other than rational calculations have the potential to bring about the cessation of hostilities and act as the genesis of a conflict termination process leading toward final conflict resolution. This transition provides opportunities for new leaders to step away from the policies of those who took the party/nation to war, creating the necessary space for fresh and innovative perspectives toward peaceful coexistence if not complete conflict resolution. This marks the beginning of recognition that the emotive, psychological, and political aspects of conflict play a significant role in initiating courses of action to bring about conflict termination.[36] His fourth factor—the emergence of a second-order change—makes the ultimate break with the rational actor model's ideas toward a more inclusive perspective of the complexity attendant to decision making and its influence on bringing about conflict termination.

Citing the work of Paul Watzlawick, John H. Weakland, and Richard Fisch,[37] Engelbrecht contends leaders may perceive that continued conflictual behaviors threaten principles of superordinate national import. Accordingly, one party perceives the other possesses the capacity to impose a value-threatening change upon the system, one clearly foreshadowing detrimental effects for the internal order. Hence, "at some point the leaders realize the attempted solution (the war itself) becomes the problem . . . [and] they see war termination as a necessary part of a future policy aimed at protecting this value."[38] As an example of this theory in practice, Engelbrecht cites the Japanese emperor's decision to surrender in 1945. He contends the emperor reframed the decision to surrender based upon critical threats to the institution of the emperor and the Japanese national polity: "Future resistance meant that these values were most certainly in jeopardy. The only promise of saving these values lay in giving up all capability to defend them. The emperor made the decision."[39] Engelbrecht's ideas, in concert with others, served as the basis for one of the most comprehensive works on conflict termination to date, that of Sam Allotey and others.

Allotey and Others: Conflict Resolution Framework

Employing the ideas of classic thinkers presented thus far, Allotey and others develop a dynamic, open systems conflict resolution framework that combines the elements of the rational actor model with the less quantifiable elements of psychology and emotion (fig. 7). Based primarily upon Richard Barringer's research,[40] this approach unwittingly combines the ideas of all the foregoing theorists (given that Allotey et al. did not reference the theorists identified as the "classic thinkers") into a *Realpolitik*, power-based model with the potential for other factors to influence the transition between conflict phases.

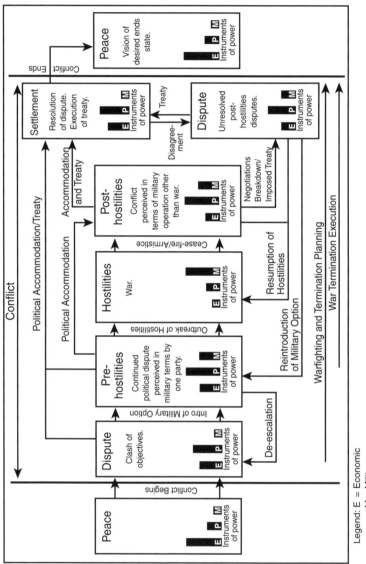

Figure 7. Allotey and Others' Conflict Resolution Framework

Legend: E = Economic
M = Military
P = Political

Unlike its predecessors, this approach acknowledges that war termination does not necessarily equate to conflict termination. These authors assert that terminating conflict entails more than a cease-fire or armistice; it requires the creation of a vision of the desired end state that serves as a bridge toward peace. In fact, they contend that "stopping the fighting is only half the challenge. To prevent the reintroduction of hostilities and achieve a lasting peace, states need to continue working toward resolving conflict. . . . The major difficulties in resolving a dispute lie in the ability to fulfill the conditions for settlement, the psychological implications of war and the nature of the conflict."[41]

While the authors' ideas are correct in this sense, their reliance upon power politics—wherein the victor dictates terms based upon dominant instruments of power—clearly reflects the overwhelming influence of rational actor model tenets. These authors recognize that bureaucratic processes and individual interests frame conflict termination decisions, yet their model fails to account for these factors. Instead, it relies upon conventional utility comparisons across the economic, political, and military instruments of power as the basis for termination decisions. As a heuristic depiction of conflict phasing for power-based conflicts, this model is of some utility; as a viable model of conflict termination—and most certainly to achieve its goal of presenting a framework for conflict resolution as its title implies—it requires the inclusion of nonquantifiable factors—influences recognized by the authors but omitted from the framework's current form.

Of all the approaches outlined thus far, Engelbrecht, and Allotey and others provide the greatest opportunity for factors other than the rational actor model's cost-benefit utility-maximization approach to affect conflict termination policy. Their approaches, however, provide no viable method to account for these influences upon the rational actor model approach and subsequent conflict termination decision-making processes.

Alternatives to Rational Actor Models

In the early 1980s, Mitchell began to move the theoretical foundation of conflict termination away from its classical foundation of rational choice theory and toward exploring the inter-group dynamics that negate a party's ability to employ the rational actor model as a basis for choice. While his original work remains predominately framed by utility functions and cost-benefit analyses, he adds a level of complexity by introducing the idea that *parties in conflict are not unitary actors*. Intraparty cleavages shape their capacity to perform the cost-benefit analyses and utility calculations demanded by the rational actor model.[42] Mitchell's two models, while evolutionary extensions of rational actor models, highlight the inherent dangers of the rational actor approach at opposite ends of the conflict spectrum—escalation and resolution.

The entrapment model (ENT) and the enticing opportunity model (ENO) diverge from the underlying principles of the rational actor model only slightly. Since they present alternative perspectives on termination, beginning with the ENT model, this discussion illuminates their relevance as a bridge toward future research.

Mitchell's ENT represents a paradoxical approach to conflict termination—one that could ultimately result in conflict escalation. Based upon the premise that the cost-benefit analysis is biased because previous costs have been transformed into investments toward future victory, the ENT perspective highlights the fact that parties will continue to struggle when faced with verifiable information dictating the need for termination. Cognitive processes inhibit the parties' abilities to recognize that a distorted sense of impending victory has skewed their perspectives regarding their utility maximizing functions. According to this model, psychological and emotive factors play a role in framing parties' perspectives regarding costs and benefits, as well as investments and probabilities surrounding victory. Mitchell asserts that the ENT model is not irrational since noncalculable factors shape decision makers' perspectives regarding preference orderings and utility functions. It is this idea that gives way to Mitchell's second model, the ENO.

According to Mitchell, the ENO takes a more optimistic view of leaders' capacities to look forward toward positive futures as opposed to becoming entrapped in past or current experiences.[43] Used to create the basis of ripeness (i.e., the conditions wherein parties are more receptive to conflict resolution), this model presumes that parties can learn to embrace positive alternatives while letting go of emotional and psychological commitments to prior sacrifices (in stark contrast to the ENT model). Because the reframing involved with embracing alternatives will most likely include emotive and psychological factors that the rational actor model cannot effectively quantify, this model represents a positive move away from classical conflict termination models. This incremental step is not enough, however. Analysts must capture the complexities of the decision-making process in conjunction with the contextual factors that frame the parties' willingness (including third-party intervenors) to end their violent behavior and begin a conflict termination process.

In *The Structure of International Conflict,* Mitchell contends that decisions regarding conflict termination involve calculations concerning (a) the benefits to be gained by continuing as compared with settling and (b) the costs incurred through continuing as compared with terminating should the conflict end in compromise.[44] He notes, however, that these calculations do not conform to the strictest rules of the rational actor model. Ambiguity of estimates, personal and political factors, and asymmetric evaluations of relative position vis-à-vis the other party shape their determinations.[45] Further, parties in conflict must disaggregate these cost-benefit calculations due to interagency fractionation since "costs and benefits are likely to be unevenly distributed and result in divergent views about the value of continuing or compromising."[46]

Extending this idea, Mitchell and Nicholson contend that "different preference orderings or utility functions *within* parties in conflict can have a major impact in determining when a war will end and when a peace settlement will finally be agreed upon."[47] It is important to note the crucial inference signifying that the shift occurs as a discontinuity within a process regarding conflict termination. Parties in conflict are no longer perceived as unitary actors with the capacity to fulfill the requirements of the rational actor model. Consequently, the rational actor model can no longer serve as the basis for valid conflict termination modeling in cases where groups make termination decisions. Yet, these authors do not discount the value of calculating preference orderings and utility functions; rather, they call for the development of logical processes whereby the preferences of the multiple individuals and factions can be amalgamated into some useful indicator of a party's collective will to engage in a conflict termination process. This type of phenomenon demands additional conflict termination process research.

Summary

The foregoing text presented the dominant models of conflict termination that shape current theory and practice in international relations. For myriad reasons, these approaches fail to capture the dynamic nature of real-world conflict termination decision-making processes. The critiques highlighted herein relate primarily to the invalid assumption of the unitary actor,[48] the foundational tenet of rational choice theory. These rational actor model approaches discount the influence of emotive, psychological, and political factors, all of which must be included as part of the cost-benefit analysis if the models are to have descriptive, explanatory, and predictive value. The rational actor model may incorporate these factors as influences that change the elements in "subjective expected utility" calculations, but empirical evidence of such an approach is absent from contemporary literature.

The most evident move away from the purist application of rational actor model tenets in conflict termination is to be found in Christopher Mitchell's work and in the work of Mitchell and Michael Nicholson. Highlighting the fallacy of the unitary actor approach, Mitchell identifies the need to examine conflict termination decision-making processes within their own context—a dynamic group process that cannot be described by simply applying rational actor model principles.[49] This discussion provides an additional opening for two frameworks that are not based purely upon the rational actor model. Both reflect Mitchell's efforts to present alternative, comprehensive approaches.

Mitchell's work thus recognizes that decision makers charged with taking group decisions regarding conflict termination in no way mirror unitary actors.[50] Rather, the politicized environments within which leaders operate during times of peace, as well as conflict, shape those who make decisions toward termination. With this understanding in the forefront of our minds, Mitchell insists we must "apply some form of Bureaucratic Politics approach to terminating conflict, to abandon restrictive and often misleading assumptions about common goals and single, shared preference orderings within a party in conflict, and to concentrate on intraparty cleavages and their effects on bringing conflicts to an end."[51]

Mitchell's dictum serves as the basis for developing an approach to conflict termination policy development that realistically incorporates intraparty or group dynamics. Developing an understanding of this process must overcome the defects of the rational actor model. It cannot view parties in conflict as unitary actors who rely upon quantifiable utility functions that communicate single preference orderings in the face of incomplete information, dynamic (and sometimes competing) goals, and resource constraints.[52] Conflict termination models must acknowledge that decisions occur within highly politicized environments that are shaped more by negotiation and compromise than by determinations of rational actor outcomes. Consequently, decision makers must reframe approaches to conflict termination policy development, making analyses more inclusive and realistic via the bureaucratic politics model. In light of the endemic limitations of rational choice theory and the rational actor model as a framework for explaining and predicting group decisions, Graham Allison's bureaucratic politics model emerges as the approach best suited to describe, explain, and predict both the characteristics of the interagency process and its likely policy outcomes.

Notes

1. For a compendium of resources related to ending war in general, see Robert Pickus and Robert Woito, *To End War: An Introduction to the Ideas, Organizations and Current Books* (New York: Harper & Row Publishers, 1970).

2. See also Jerel A. Rosati, "The Power of Human Cognition in the Study of World Politics," *International Studies Review* 2, no. 3 (2000).

3. Fred Charles Iklé, *Every War Must End* (New York: Columbia University Press, 1991), 16.

4. See also Lewis A. Coser, "The Termination of Conflict," *Conflict Resolution* 5, no. 4 (1961).

5. See also Michael Handel, "The Study of War Termination," *Journal of Strategic Studies* 1 (1978).

6. For example, USAF doctrine characterizes conflict termination as the set of activities determined to bring about the cessation of hostilities via three mechanisms: (1) the victor imposing its will on the vanquished, (2) mutual negotiated settlement, or (3) settlement brought about by a third party intervenor. As defined within this work, these three conditions may be prerequisites (depending upon the specific context) for conflict termination, but they do not equate to conflict termination as the establishment of a dialogue to explore and resolve the underlying causes and conditions of conflict. For a more in-depth look at the Air Force approach, see also Air Force Doctrine Document (AFDD) 2, *Organization and Employment of Aerospace Power*, 17 February 2000.

7. See also Sam Allotey et al., *Planning and Execution of Conflict Termination* (Maxwell AFB, Ala.: Air Command and Staff College, 1995); see also Ernest F. Estes, *Conflict Termination in Crisis Management* (Maxwell AFB, Ala.: Air Command and Staff College, 1973); see also Leon H. Rios, *Seeking a Final Victory: Creating Conditions for Conflict Resolution* (Carlisle Barracks, Pa.: Army War College, 1993); see also Susan E. Strednansky, *Balancing the Trinity: The Fine Art of Conflict Termination* (Maxwell AFB, Ala.: Air University Press, 1996); and Lt Col Peter W. W. Wijninga (Royal Netherlands Air Force) and Richard Szafranski, *Beyond Utility Targeting toward Axiological Air Operations* (Internet) (Air University Chronicles, 2000 [cited 25 January 2001]), available from http://www.airpower.maxwell.af.mil/airchronicles/apj/apj00/win00/szafranski.

8. See also Sir Basil Henry Liddell Hart, *Strategy* (New York: Praeger, 1954).

9. See also C. R. Mitchell, *The Structure of International Conflict* (New York: St. Martin's Press, 1981).

10. Stephen J. Cimbala, "The Endgame and War," in *Conflict Termination and Military Strategy: Coercion, Persuasion, and War*, eds. S. J. Cimbala and Keith A. Dunn (Boulder: Westview Press, 1987), 2.

11. See also Coser, "The Termination of Conflict"; see also Mitchell, *The Structure of International Conflict;* and see also Barry Schneider, "Terminating Strategic Exchanges: Requirements and Prerequisites," in *Conflict Termination and Military Strategy: Coercion, Persuasion, and War*, ed. S. J. Cimbala and Keith A. Dunn (Boulder: Westview Press, 1987).

12. Mitchell, *The Structure of International Conflict*, 165.

13. Ibid.

14. Ibid., 194.

15. Michael R. Rampy, "Endgame: Conflict Termination and Post–Conflict Activities," *Military Review* 72 (1992): 51.

16. Ibid., 53.

17. See also Paul Koopman and Jeroen Pool, "Organizational Decision Making: Models, Contingencies and Strategies," in *Distributed Decision Making: Cognitive Models for Cooperative Work*, ed. Jens Rasmussen, Berndt Brehmer, and Jacques Leplat (Chichester, England: John Wiley & Sons, 1991); see also Edwin Mansfield, *Applied Microeconomics* (New York: W. W. Norton & Co., 1994); and see also Thomas C. Schelling, *Choice and Consequence* (Cambridge: Harvard University Press, 1984).

18. For a refresher on the assumptions of this approach and its shortcomings as regards the realities of group and individual decision making, see chapter 2.

19. Donald Wittman, "How a War Ends: A Rational Approach," *Journal of Conflict Resolution* 23 (1979): 759.

20. Ibid., 760.

21. Ibid., 745.

22. See also I. William Zartman, *Ripe for Resolution: Conflict and Intervention in Africa* (New York: Oxford University Press, 1989).

23. See also Christopher R. Mitchell, "The Right Moment: Notes on Four Models of 'Ripeness,'" *Paradigms* 9, no. 2 (1995).

24. Jane Holl, former executive director of the Carnegie Commission on Preventing Deadly Conflict, shared this perspective with our research group at the Air Command and Staff College, noting that the party's lack of capacity to carry on the conflict may cause it to terminate its involvement. See Allotey et al., *Planning and Execution of Conflict Termination*, 15; and see also Joseph A. Engelbrecht, Jr., "War Termination: Why Does a State Decide to Stop Fighting?" (PhD diss., Columbia University, 1992).

25. See also William O. Staudenmaier, "Conflict Termination in the Third World: Theory and Practice," in *The Lessons of Recent Wars in the Third World*, ed. Stephanie G. Neuman and Robert E. Harkavy (Lexington, Mass.: D. C. Heath and Co., 1987).

26. Ibid., 17.

27. See also Herbert A. Simon, *Administrative Behavior: A Study of Decision-Making Processes in Administrative Organizations* (New York: Free Press, 1976).

28. Staudenmaier, "Conflict Termination in the Third World," 18.

29. See also Iklé, *Every War Must End*.

30. See also, for example, AFDD 2, *Organization and Employment of Aerospace Power;* and see also Strednansky, *Balancing the Trinity: The Fine Art of Conflict Termination*.

31. Staudenmaier, "Conflict Termination in the Third World," 530.

32. Bruce B. G. Clarke, *Conflict Termination: A Rational Model* (Carlisle Barracks, Pa.: Army War College, 1992), 33.

33. See also Rampy, "Endgame."

34. Clarke, *Conflict Termination*, 8.

35. See also Engelbrecht, "War Termination."

36. See also Allotey et al., *Planning and Execution of Conflict Termination;* and see also Iklé, *Every War Must End.*

37. See also Paul Watzlawick, John H. Weakland, and Richard Fisch, *Change: Principles of Problem Formulation and Problem Resolution* (New York: W. W. Norton & Co., Inc., 1974).

38. Engelbrecht, "War Termination," 36–37.

39. Ibid., 121.

40. See also Richard E. Barringer, with the collaboration of Robert K. Ramers, *War: Patterns of Conflict* (Cambridge, Mass.: The MIT Press, 1972).

41. Allotey et al., *Planning and Execution of Conflict Termination,* 22.

42. See also Leon V. Sigal, *Fighting to a Finish: The Politics of War Termination in the United States and Japan, 1945* (Ithaca & London: Cornell University Press, 1988).

43. See also Mitchell, *The Structure of International Conflict.*

44. See also Paul Lee, *War Termination in a Low-Intensity Conflict* (Carlisle Barracks, Pa.: Army War College, 1988); see also David J. Oberst, *Why Wars End: An Expected Utility War Termination Model* (Carlisle Barracks, Pa.: Army War College, 1992); and see also Sigal, *Fighting to a Finish: The Politics of War Termination in the United States and Japan, 1945.*

45. See also Christopher R. Mitchell, *Cutting Losses: Reflections on Appropriate Timing,* no. 9 ICAR Working Paper (Fairfax, Va.: George Mason University, 1996).

46. Mitchell, *The Structure of International Conflict,* 172.

47. Ibid.

48. Ibid., 185.

49. Christopher R. Mitchell and Michael Nicholson, "Rational Models and the Ending of Wars," *Journal of Conflict Resolution* 27 (1983): 515.

50. See also Graham T. Allison, *Essence of Decision: Explaining the Cuban Missile Crisis* (Boston: Little, Brown and Co., 1971); see also Iklé, *Every War Must End;* see also Mitchell, *The Structure of International Conflict; see also* Mitchell and Nicholson, "Rational Models and the Ending of Wars"; and see also Uriel Rosenthal and Alexander Kousmin, "Crisis and Crisis Management: Toward Comprehensive Government Decision Making," *Journal of Public Administration Research and Theory* 7, no. 2 (1997).

51. Mitchell, *The Structure of International Conflict,* 186.

52. See also Paul Seabury and Angelo Codevilla, *War: Ends and Means* (New York: Basic Books, 1989).

Chapter 4

The National Security Council System

The essence of interagency coordination is the interplay of multiple agencies with individual agendas.

—Joint Pub 3-08, vol. 1
*Interagency Coordination
during Joint Operations*
October 1996

The preceding chapters criticized rational choice theory's inability to capture the true nature of group decision-making processes—those regarding conflict termination in particular. Discussion from this point forward broadens understanding of national security policy making and group choice by establishing the foundation for the remainder of the analysis. Beginning with a discussion of Graham Allison's classical bureaucratic politics model, this chapter identifies the USG actors involved in real-world national security decision-making processes. By highlighting assumptions regarding these actors' shared images and organizational interests,[1] chapter 4 provides the theoretical bridge toward the operationalization of the modern policy-making process. Allison's theory emphasizes the considerations this conceptual framework takes into account.

Allison's Bureaucratic Politics Approach

The overarching perspective that frames the bureaucratic politics model is that "government decisions are made and government actions emerge neither as the calculated choice of a unified group, nor as a formal summary of leaders' preferences . . . [decisions are made within a context of] inordinate uncertainty about what must be done, the necessity that something be done, and the crucial consequences of whatever is done."[2]

This perspective assumes that many actors influence decisions through a dynamic bargaining process shaped by myriad factors. Allison captures the essence of this process as he contrasts it with the following rational choice theory: "In contrast with [the rational actor paradigm], the Governmental (or Bureaucratic) Politics Model sees no unitary actor but rather many actors as players—players who focus not on a single strategic issue but on many diverse intra-national problems as well; players who act in terms of no consistent set of strategic objectives but rather according to various conceptions of national, organizational, and personal goals; players who make government decisions not by a single, rational choice but by the pulling and hauling that is politics."[3] To be an effective player within this arena, Allison contends it is necessary to identify the relevant players who engage in the "pulling and hauling,"[4] determining how that dynamic shapes the larger bureaucratic arena. Thus, decision making is a political process that exhibits three dominant characteristics: (1) "a diversity of goals and values that must be reconciled before a decision can be reached," (2) "the presence of competing clusters of people within the main group who are identified with each of the alternative goals and policies," and (3) "the relative power of these different groups of people included is as relevant to the final decision as the appeal of goals they seek or the cogency and wisdom of their arguments."[5]

The model's major precepts can be repackaged only in limited ways. This work retains the model's original efficacy by presenting the paradigm here as Allison presented it in its original form. Hence, the model's propositions are outlined to distinguish the differences between the rational actor and bureaucratic politics approaches to contribute to conflict termination analyses.

Allison defines the product of the governmental decision process as a "political resultant." He characterizes decision outcomes as *resultants* because they emerge from the decision-making process not as a chosen solution but as the product of "compromise, conflict, and confusion [among] officials with diverse interests and unequal influence."[6] These resultants are *political* because the process that produced the outcome is "best characterized as bargaining along regularized channels among individuals of the government."[7] In this way, an explanation of this model must include an outline of the players, process, and product—Allison's *political resultant*.

In contrast to the rational actor model, the bureaucratic politics model makes conclusive identification of the relevant players considerably more problematic. Rational choice theory presupposes that each individual remains a viable actor in accordance with his or her ability to fulfill the requirements of the model. The bureaucratic politics model invokes a broader, more realistic perspective, designating the players as those "whose interests and actions have an important effect on the government's decisions and actions."[8] According to this view, virtually anyone can become a player in the decision-making process. There are, however, a few parameters that circumscribe influences on the process. The first such parameter is governmental structure.

The structure of the bureaucracy serves to identify the formal and informal players within the governmental decision-making process. The formal players are those who hold positions mandating their participation based upon structural or legal requirements.[9] In this fashion, the president of the United States is compelled to act as a player within the "national security policy game" as a result of structural position (commander in chief and chief executive of the United States) and legally (National Security Act of 1947 and its amendments). Those requirements aside, however, the president naturally would possess the ability to affect governmental decisions through other means and would therefore be considered an informal actor in the absence of formal status. The structure of the position relates directly to the second defining factor—the "stand" actors take within the decision-making process.

Employing the aphorism "Where you stand depends on where you sit," Allison identifies four factors that shape the perceptions and interests that fashion an actor's perspective on policy issues.[10] The analysis presented earlier (the rational choice theory critique that focused upon collective-value dissensus, social interaction and organizational culture, and the pivotal influence of framing) remains particularly salient here. Analysts and decision makers must recognize that actors maintain their respective parochial priorities and perceptions of issues in concert with multilayered and interwoven goals and interests. These generate diverse frames that calculate risk and opportunity differently as they relate to one's "respective" stakes in the game. Further, decision makers experience deadlines that often exacerbate conflicting, competing, and threatening perspectives regarding issues—these promote what Allison calls "faces of issues."[11] Taken in conjunction with the previously identified structural parameters, the development of the actor's stand regarding a particular issue identifies one's position and attitude toward both the decision-making process and its outcome. This "position and attitude" component of the bureaucratic politics model determines an actor's ability to exercise power within the governmental arena.

The dominant characteristic identifying players is their power to influence government decisions and actions. While an extensive body of literature surrounds this concept,[12] Allison maintains that power is "an elusive blend of at least three elements: bargaining advantages, skill and will in using bargaining advantages, and other players' perceptions of the first two ingredients."[13] His schema holds that one's potential sources of power stem from structural position, personal relations, and charisma. In the final analysis, however, he argues that much of an actor's power emanates from his or her ability to demonstrate expertise, control information, gain access to and interact with other players, and affect other players' objectives throughout the game. It is the exercise of this power, based upon the structural position and stand that an actor takes regarding a decision issue, that shapes the bureaucratic politics model's form. Group decision making remains a dynamic negotiating and bargaining process. Within the context of governmental policy making, Allison characterizes the political game's form in terms of action channels, rules of the game, and the environment within which decisions are made.[14]

Social interaction, much like formal negotiation, is not chaotic. Within the decision-making process, social interaction takes the form of "bargaining games [that] are neither random nor haphazard. The individuals whose stands and moves count are the players whose positions hook them on to the action channels. An action channel is a regularized means of taking governmental action on a specific kind of issue."[15] As an example, the War Powers Resolution establishes an action channel regarding the commander in chief's authority to commit troops to combat-prone situations. It prescribes the players (the president and the Congress) and their stands (for the president, flexibility in acting as the commander in chief; for the Congress, limiting presidential authority while providing congressional oversight for the use of force), and is systematized based upon its legal status. Because this action channel is more institutionalized than others, it structures the nature of bargaining and negotiating within the political game by preselecting the major players, determining their points of entry, and distributing the particular advantages and disadvantages of the game across the players.[16] The rules of the game further reinforce these action channels.

Adopting the "rules of the game" metaphor further enhances our understanding of the fundamental nature of this bargaining process.[17] It remains a contest wherein actors compete against one another to reinforce or enhance their overall standing within the government bureaucracy. Noted earlier, actors bargain based upon independent priorities, goals, interests, perceptions, and stands. The parameters that define the acceptable rules of engagement within this bargaining process emerge as the product of constitutional requirements, "statutes, court interpretations, executive orders, conventions, and even culture."[18] These rules have the following three measurable affects on the game: "First, rules establish the positions, the paths by which [individuals] gain access to positions, the power of each position, the action channel. Second, rules constrict the range of governmental decisions and actions that are acceptable. Third, rules sanction moves of some kinds—bargaining, coalitions, persuasion, deceit, bluff, and threat—while making other moves illegal, immoral, ungentlemanly, or inappropriate."[19] Irrespective of their source, however, their combined effect is one of defining the normative ways in which the actors should interrelate with one another within the decision-making arena. In turn, the environment within which the actors function further refines these rules.

The contextual environment of bureaucratic decision making has been characterized as one circumscribed by uncertainty, necessity, and risk. While these represent the macro-level factors, the environment's micro-level aspects complexify group dynamics in ways that invigorate the validity of the earlier rational choice theory critique. Allison argues that the pace, structure, law, and reward of the game interact with uncertainty, necessity, and risk to create a competitive group dynamic that forces "advocates to fight for outcomes . . . players come to fight to 'make government do what is right.'"[20] In this fashion, we see the synthesis of all that has been presented. Individuals as members of groups engage in a negotiation process characterized by competitive bargaining in hopes of developing a decision outcome that best represents their individual priorities, goals, and interests, perhaps in contravention to the context of the crisis under consideration.

Decision makers may select alternatives irrespective of the central issue under consideration due to the nature of a process that produces *political resultants* as outcomes of political bargaining processes. Allison contends that "following Wittgenstein's employment of the concept of a 'game,' national behavior in international affairs can be conceived of as something that emerges from intricate and subtle, simultaneous, overlapping games among players located in positions in a government. The hierarchical arrangement of these players constitutes the government."[21] Accordingly, actors' parochial interests frame political resultants. A fundamental challenge in analyzing the policy-making process is to determine the actors' criteria and preference orderings.

As a facet of the bureaucratic politics model, the criteria and preference orderings for individual and collective decision makers acting within the US bureaucracy prove fluid according to time and context. Closely related to this fluidity, Irving Janis identifies cognitive, affiliative, and egocentric constraints that frame a decision maker's criteria and preference orderings (as well as the remainder of the process).[22] These constraints make rational identification of decision criteria and preference orderings problematic since, according to rational choice theory, the salience of one or more can overshadow an actor's ability to formulate policy outcomes. Therefore, we can conclude that the bureaucratic politics model accounts for these constraints by accepting their influence as part of the political game.

The confluence of the political game's elements entails measurable consequences. Within the context of the universal social order, the policy maker's ability to address the agenda of every individual or group through the bureaucratic process is limited severely. In fact, the policy maker usually finds it impossible to do so. This critique holds for the rational actor model as well since, as Zey contends, people have sets of values that are independent—and sometimes mutually exclusive— of other individuals. Through this comparative approach, then, we must recognize that while the bureaucratic politics model offers a richer description of group decision-making processes, it, too, fails to present a universal remedy for forecasting enigmatic decision-making dilemmas; that is, it proves unable to predict outcomes. Nonetheless, it falls short because decision analysts have not yet perfected our understanding of this approach in ways that distance the model's strengths from its inherent weaknesses.

Effective models describe, explain, and predict complex interactions between and across multiple phenomena. Analysts develop predictive models to envisage future alternatives. They use such models as comprehensible representations of a "number of assumptions from which conclusions—or predictions— are deduced . . . [wherein the] purpose of a model is to make predictions concerning phenomena in the real world, and in many respects the most important test of a model is how well it predicts these phenomena."[23] The bureaucratic politics model does predict two of the following facets of USG decision making quite accurately: (1) the *process* will remain bound by a dynamic political context, and (2) the *outcome* will not reflect a utility or profit-maximizing approach to human choice. While quantitatively grounded analysts would argue that the application proves of limited value due to its inability to predict specific outcomes (the supposed strength of the rational actor approach), its value rests with its ability to describe, explain, and predict the nature of the policy-making process and, therefore, shed light on the shape of the most likely outcome within a real-world context. In spite of its theoretical prowess, the greatest deficiency is that the process itself remains contextually bound—a factor that limits the model's predictive value. Recognition of this deficiency obliges analysts to "shift the emphasis from models which are individualistic and economic to models which are social and contextual."[24]

US Government Decision Making

Individuals consistently prove unable to uphold rational choice theory's tenets because people inherently lack the ability to make utility-maximizing choices in every aspect of their lives. Instead, dynamic goals and preferences, cognitive limitations, resource constraints, and the inability to assign a quantifiable value to each alternative constrain the decision maker's ability to act according to this approach. Fallacies inherent to the unitary actor approach likewise frame the context of group decision making. Limitations that apply to the individual actor hold equally for group decision makers but tend to become magnified in light of ever-present group dynamics. Furthermore, the nature and intensity of the group dynamic that permeates the nonunitary actor generates additional elements that negate the group's ability to engage in utility or profit-maximizing decision processes. Three of these elements have particular relevance: (1) collective value dissensus within the intragroup negotiation, (2) dynamic, interdependent social interaction and organizational culture, and (3) the framing of choice (including the selection of reference points, risk orientation, and preference orderings) as additional constraints impinging on the rational actor model's potential validity. In the end, because people do not always make rational choices, the bureaucratic politics model explains more accurately the nature of decision making within the USG's national security system.

Relying upon Allison's work to establish a baseline, the model's defining characteristics include the players, the process, and the product (the outcome or policy alternatives). Noting that this approach more realistically captures the decision-making process within the government, the framework's strength rests with its ability to effectively describe, explain, and predict the nature of the policy-making process in light of specific contextual factors. Its greatest deficiency, however, remains its inability to predict consistently the specific content of policy decisions (even as process dynamics prove predictable, policy outcomes will vary as one or more of the contextual elements changes). This limitation, however, extends more from its general application than its theoretical foundation. Typically, it is invoked to explain an ex post facto decision. When used to analyze processes and alternatives at the outset of a decision cycle, it rarely acknowledges the unique context of the specific, bounded policy problem.

Using this limitation to guide future research, analysts and theoreticians should reexamine the bureaucratic politics model by grounding it within a specific issue context. As an initial step, this work explores the nature of the conflict termination policy development process in two cases, the Persian Gulf War and the Bosnia conflict. This examination sheds light upon the ways in which interagency conflict—a natural consequence of group decision making according to the bureaucratic politics model—shapes the policy-making process. It illuminates the differences between unitary actor and group decision-making processes, bolstering understanding of the influences these differences have upon conflict theory refinement in light of dissimilar units of analysis (individuals versus groups). Such analysis should enhance decision-making processes in the face of increasing complexity, risk, and uncertainty.

Despite assumptions to the contrary, the USG is not a unitary actor.[25] Christopher Mitchell and Michael Nicholson assert that "different preference orderings or utility functions *within* parties in conflict can have a major impact in determining when a [conflict] will end and when a peace settlement will finally be agreed upon."[26] Discovering that the bulk of the conflict termination research proceeds almost exclusively from the rational actor perspective presents an opportunity for innovative exploration and explanation.[27] While some authors address alternative approaches, a more robust model of conflict termination policy development currently does not exist. Existing research fails to address the effects interagency decision-making conflict has upon conflict termination policy development in terms of conducting comprehensive crisis analysis, framing the desired end state, selecting conflict termination criteria, and developing strategy to achieve conflict termination toward a sustainable peace. To achieve better states of peace[28] through third-party intervention, policy makers must understand the ways in which group decision making influences conflict termination policy development. As demonstrated by Mitchell and Nicholson, intraparty conflict can produce debilitating consequences that adversely affect decisions to end conflict and pursue sustainable peace.[29] An investigation of the policy development processes for the Persian Gulf and Bosnia identifies factors that generate interagency conflict during termination policy development. Such analysis requires definition of the national security policy-making environment.

National Security Policy Making

National security policy making occurs within a highly politicized, bureaucratic context. Accordingly, it assumes that national leaders make national security policy through a process of "decision making by negotiation."[30] Hence, the underlying assumptions of this work parallel Allison's; that is, decision making remains a political process involving differences, negotiation, compromise, and consensus building. To frame this study, specifics regarding the USG policy-making arena are now presented to demonstrate the utility of this approach for similar decision-making contexts. It is important to recognize that this analysis incorporates key policy makers' experiences from various agencies across the USG's interagency process (see app. A for the list of participants and their organizational positions). While this work refers to the "State Department," "Defense Department," and "National Security Council," these organizations are "agencies" within the executive branch's "interagency process." The players in this process—as well as their objectives—may not be as discernable as they appear to be at first glance. It is equally important to acknowledge that the following discussion merely surveys these actors and their positions; it should not be interpreted as the definitive perspective on either. Rather, these brief descriptions orient the reader toward the study's central assumptions. What follows is very much an a priori sketch of the relevant actors. There is utility in addressing the two most obvious participants in the national security policy process—the National Security Council and the Congress—before delving into the specific classifications used to explore the broader interagency process. Figure 3 (refer to p. 9) illustrates the actors involved in the national security policy process.

Primary actors are decision makers involved in the formal decision-making process because of their official government positions. Highlighted earlier, the NSC and the Congress outwardly appear as the two dominant figures guiding the national security process. The NSC is charged with developing a national security policy that, when linked to domestic policy (e.g., economic policy, social programs), will sustain and enhance the nation's security. Yet, the US Constitution grants *only* to the Congress authority to "declare war" and commit troops to known hostile activities abroad.[31] This authority affords the Congress entrée into national security policy formulation on several levels, perhaps most influential being the role the Congress plays in budgetary matters. The Congress controls funding for security policy at all levels (e.g., department budgets, UN contributions, and continuing appropriations bills for troop deployments). Budgetary control, in conjunction with its capacity to hold the commander in chief in check through the War Powers Resolution, ensures that the Congress remains a very active and powerful player in the national security policy-making process.[32] However, as figure 3 clearly illustrates, the NSC and the Congress are not the only players that influence this complex decision process. Because the responsibility for national security policy is split constitutionally between the executive and legislative branches of government, and because others who hold competing perspectives influence both of these branches directly, tensions surrounding the policy process create a dynamic wherein decision making by negotiation becomes the daily reality.

From this viewpoint, the ensuing discussion outlines each of the players identified in figure 3 in terms of their respective roles and potential influence. It is at this point that Morton Halperin and others' study, Bureaucratic politics and foreign policy, pushes Allison's ideas in a more useful direction.[33] By discussing the bureaucratic process in terms of the players' respective shared images and organizational interests, Halperin and others begin to bring into focus the political nature of US government departments, highlighting fissures between players together with disjunctures that hinder process.

Foreshadowing Halperin and others to some extent, Allison observes that the players in the bureaucratic process are identifiable because of the power they brandish in the decision-making arena. To analyze the development of a specific aspect of intervention policy, we must integrate an accurate conception of the individuals, organizations, and contextual factors that influence the development of national security policy beyond the cursory perspective presented above. Alluded to earlier, these four categories of influence are the (1) official actors, (2) quasi-official actors, (3) influential actors, and (4) contextual factors. To conceptualize the research problem more precisely, these participants are examined separately to demonstrate the utility of the analytic approach that undergirds this work. The discussion that follows is an a priori depiction of the national security policy-making process as outlined in figure 3; official actors, quasi-official actors, influential actors, and contextual factors appear as conceptual categorizations for analysis.

Official Actors: The Formal USG Structure

In creating the NSC, the Congress identified the four individuals most responsible for developing national security policy. These four—the president, vice president, and secretaries of state and defense—serve as the official actors. Since 1947, this circle of principals has expanded to include two statutory advisors—the director of Central Intelligence (DCI) and the chairman of the Joint Chiefs of Staff (CJCS). The Defense Department's joint doctrine adeptly captures these actors and their levels of influence (table 1).

The organizational interests and personal convictions these individuals hold shape their respective images regarding intervention. Their individual historical experiences, in conjunction with real-time factors, shape their personal and professional

Table 1
Participation in National Security Council System Activities

		PARTICIPANTS			
		OFFICE OF THE SECRETARY OF DEFENSE	*JOINT STAFF*	*DEPARTMENT OF STATE*	*OTHER EXECUTIVE BRANCH***
	NSC	SECRETARY OF DEFENSE	CHAIRMAN OF THE JOINT CHIEFS OF STAFF	SECRETARY OF STATE	PRESIDENT, VICE PRESIDENT, DIR OF CENTRAL INTELLIGENCE, NATIONAL SECURITY ADVISOR, US REP TO UN, SEC OF TREAS, ASST FOR ECONOMIC POLICY, CHIEF OF STAFF TO THE PRESIDENT, ATTORNEY GENERAL, ET AL.***
N S C S Y S T E M	PRINCIPALS COMMITTEE	SECRETARY OF DEFENSE	CHAIRMAN OF THE JOINT CHIEFS OF STAFF	SECRETARY OF STATE	NATIONAL SECURITY ADVISOR, DCI, US REP TO UN, ASST FOR ECONOMIC POLICY, ET AL.***
	DEPUTIES COMMITTEE	UNDER SECRETARY FOR POLICY OR PRINCIPAL DEPUTY UNDER SECRETARY FOR POLICY	VICE CHAIRMAN OF THE JOINT CHIEFS OF STAFF	UNDER OR ASSISTANT SECRETARY OF STATE FOR POLITICAL AFFAIRS	DEPUTY NATIONAL SECURITY ADVISOR, OTHER DEPUTIES
	INTER-AGENCY WORKING GROUP	ASST OR DEPUTY ASST SECRETARY*	DIRECTOR/VICE DIRECTOR	DEPUTY ASSISTANT SECRETARY OF STATE	APPROPRIATE DEPUTY/UNDER SECRETARIES
	WORKING GROUPS	OFFICE OF THE ASST SECRETARY ACTION OFFICER	JOINT STAFF ACTION OFFICER	DESK OFFICER	US GOVERN-MENT AGENCY ACTION OFFICER

* Office of the Secretary of Defense representatives at interagency working groups may be Assistant Secretaries, Principal Deputy Assistant Secretaries, Deputy Assistant Secretaries, Directors, or Task Force Directors/Members
** A brief listing of other executive branch participants
*** Invited as appropriate

Source: Joint Pub 3-08, *Interagency Coordination during Joint Operations,* vol. I, 1996, II-3.

perspectives. It is to be expected that the historical experiences will differ significantly across these six leading actors, inducing them to render salient select aspects of a particular conflict while downplaying the importance or relevance of others. Consequently, individuals frame crises in different ways, leading them to develop multiple courses of action for dealing with a problem.

While these players may enjoy a few shared images, it is unlikely that those images will remain entirely harmonious over time. Taken in concert with striking organizational interests, these dissimilar shared images impinge upon the group's capacity to develop optimal conflict termination policy options. Irrespective of the number of competing images, the president of the United States remains ultimately responsible for US national security and conflict termination policy.

Few would argue that anyone involved in the policy process has a more difficult path to navigate than does the president of the United States. At the turn of the twenty-first century, America's president serves as both the commander in chief of the world's most powerful military and chief executive officer of the world's remaining superpower. This individual must balance foreign and domestic policy requirements within a very complex, integrated world—one within which these requirements are becoming virtually inseparable. Because these responsibilities and challenges prove multifaceted, the president must craft a domestic policy that sustains international prowess while ensuring that foreign policy does not overextend the capacity of the nation to continue prospering. In today's increasingly interdependent network of monetary and security issues, the opinion that "politics stops at the water's edge" is no longer valid.[34] Indeed, one only needs to observe the effects of international economic market volatility for a short period to realize that the lines separating domestic and foreign affairs are becoming increasingly blurred or, arguably, that they no longer exist in any meaningful sense. It is within this environment that the president must not only develop a coherent vision for foreign and domestic policy but must do so while being influenced by myriad actors whose institutionalized *agency-specific* 'shared images' create cleavages within the interagency process.

As depicted by the downward arrow and apex of the policy triad in figure 3, the president serves as the linchpin of that policy process.

The president must integrate the disparate ideas of the formal policy establishment with those promulgated by actors outside the official circle. In Allison's terms, the "pulling and hauling" of the political environment makes the president's position more uncertain when compared with those held by others in the process. Yet, the president ultimately remains responsible for national security policy formulation and, by extension, conflict termination policy development.

The highest-level decision makers' experiences in World War II identified the need for a more institutionalized process. As a result, the National Security Act of 1947 provided for the National Security Council System (NSCS; i.e., the formalized body of four principals and their requisite staffs) to aid the president with national security decision making. The Department of Defense Joint Publications captures the relationship, noting, "The NSC advises and assists the president in integrating all aspects of national security policy—domestic, foreign, military, intelligence, and economic. Together with supporting interagency working groups, high-level steering groups, executive committees, and task forces, the NSCS provides the foundation for interagency coordination in the development and implementation of national security policy."[35] Recognizing the relationship across the players as a "National Security Council System" focuses attention on the remaining actors' roles when analyzing group decision making.

It is perhaps more difficult to capture the true essence of the vice president's bearing upon policy development than it is to portray any other actor's individual role. After all, the vice president is the only person in government who cannot be removed (except "for cause" through a constitutionally based impeachment process) and who is not responsible to anyone within government. Although elected as the president's running mate, as a point of fact, the vice president does not work for the president. The vice president works for the American people. This perspective does not mean to intimate that the president and vice president embrace mutually exclusive agendas, but it does prompt questions regarding his role in the policy process. Indeed, the vice president tends to share the fundamental images of the president—and, more importantly, their political party—or he would not be the nation's second-ranking executive. Perhaps more to the point, this issue raises questions regarding the vice president's ability to influence the national security policy process in an observably tangible manner. The same characterizations do not apply, however, when discussing the secretaries of state and defense.

In large measure, the hypothesized relationship between the Department of State and the Defense Department served as the genesis for this research. Charged respectively with the responsibilities of preventive diplomacy and national defense, the secretaries of state and defense augment the president and the vice president as statutory players in the national security process. On one hand, the secretary of state is the president's principal foreign policy advisor.[36] On the other, the secretary of defense is the president's principal advisor on national defense.[37] These roles create loyalties to the president, loyalties that sometimes compete with their roles as secretaries of their respective departments. Thus, while a president hopes cabinet-level officers support his or her policy, they may in fact tend to elevate institutional loyalties above presidential desires.[38]

The power of these institutional loyalties creates interagency conflict as the USG attempts to develop both domestic and foreign policy. Allison's aphorism, "Where you stand depends on where you sit,"[39] aptly captures this interagency gap—a gap that causes the USG to develop two opposing halves of an intervention bridge that fail to join in the middle. Three disjunctures stand out as particularly important for conflict termination policy development: philosophical or ideological differences, organizational culture, and operational responsibility.

State Department personnel frame their role in terms of "preventive diplomacy"—diplomats are "on the ground" year-round to fulfill the National Security Strategy's fundamental premise of "engagement."[40] These foreign affairs advisors may tend to be idealistic in their outlook toward the USG's capacity to resolve disputes short of conflict. This perspective prompts them to frame crises quite differently from those in the Defense Department. DOD personnel, because they envision their role in terms of national defense, may tend to be more realpolitik in their perspective on the use of force to resolve conflict.

Moreover, the two departments view differently the role that military forces play in intervention. For the Defense Department, forces intervene to win the war, thus, creating the need to identify allies and adversaries. For the State Department, force becomes the tool of last resort; it must be employed in a minimalist manner to restore conditions in which negotiations can become effective once again. These two views tend to pit the departments against one another in the policy-making process. In the final analysis, the State Department may tend to believe that US diplomacy can have a positive effect on warring parties absent the use of force. Conversely, the Defense Department may believe that some conflicts cannot be resolved without the use of force. Philosophical and ideological perspectives represent only one form of institutional fissure between these two primary entities; organizational culture also emerges as a potential breach.

The State Department's culture differs greatly from that of the Defense Department. While the most obvious difference to an outsider is the structure of the organizations (State resembles a matrix organization with multiple points of overlap; the Defense Department projects a very hierarchically organized quality with little overlap and clearly defined lines of responsibility), in reality the mode of professional interaction and communication flows directly from each organization's structure and its internal leadership. As one example, almost everyone at the State Department is on a first-name basis. Ambassador Robert Gelbard is known as "Bob" to almost everyone within the building. Only at the highest levels are titles used—both in private and in public (e.g., secretary of state). This practice contrasts sharply with that of the Defense Department. There, military titles in the form of ranks and offices circumscribe professional relationships and, more often than not, personal ones as well. Hence, the military adage "salute smartly and carry on" leaves little room for continued public disagreement once a senior official renders judgment; both ranks and positions establish boundaries for interaction and serve as metrics for assigning responsibility and accountability. Conversely, the State Department's apparent lack of an institutional hierarchy makes it appear as if officials are less responsible on the individual level, namely, who is accountable for decisions within the State Department? and how does one know who is responsible? It is this foundational relationship between responsibility and accountability that draws the most definitive cultural distinction between the two departments. Closely related to philosophical or ideological perspectives and organizational cultures, the idea of personal and professional responsibility looms large when evaluating the institutional interests of the respective departments and their secretaries.

While one would hope that both the State Department and the Defense Department would share a parallel vision of responsibility for conflict intervention practices, history reflects that the Defense Department shoulders the majority of the burden in practice. Although the State Department may be committed to being held equally accountable, the scale of intervention operations involving military presence overshadows the State Department's ultimate accountability. When viewed in terms of mission, the State Department may view military presence as an indisputable sign that they have failed—preventive diplomacy faltered, and the military had to be called in to restore some level of civility that diplomacy could not maintain. Hence, to those outside the diplomatic community, the State Department may seem to operate in ways that arrest military participation until the conflict reaches a point wherein the risk for military personnel is heightened as a consequence of delaying military action. Incidentally, this perspective may be shared by the Defense Department, but in the reverse. The diplomats failed, so now we have to go and clean up their mess, but they have put us at risk by delaying our entry (especially when a Noncombatant Evacuation Order [NEO] is required).[41] This form of entry puts lives at stake in large numbers—commanders feel a personal sense of responsibility for decisions that risk the lives of American military personnel. Noting that both the State Department and the Defense Department exercise official voices through their respective secretaries (and with the additional voice of the chairman of the Joint Chiefs of Staff on behalf of the Defense Department), we must realize that the sitting ambassador and regional military person in charge play significant roles in policy development as well. This situation is particularly important if the individual is a presidential protégé and is appointed to that post because of that relationship.

Taken together, these three aspects of the respective departments create an interagency dynamic based upon dissimilar institutionalized shared images. The State Department's internal shared image of idealism, a more flattened organization and a lower degree of operational responsibility, contrasts with the Defense Department's shared image of realism, organizational hierarchy, and a maximum degree of operational responsibility. The chasm between the State Department and the Defense Department does not represent the only fissure across the interagency process—the DCI and the CJCS also have the capacity to frame the four statutory players' understanding of the conflict and the potential courses of action the USG might pursue.

The DCI and the CJCS perform special roles in the national security process. Both serve as statutory advisors to the NSC's four principals. Beyond that parallel, the offices' functional responsibilities begin to diverge. While the DCI serves as a statutory advisor, the intelligence community strives to ensure DCI provides pure intelligence that is devoid of advice. In this capacity, the DCI outlines the context of the crisis for decision makers, providing insight regarding the "what" in relation to a specific conflict—not advice regarding "what to do" about the conflict. It is in this tradition that the DCI strives to provide value-free information—not value-laden advice, as this advisory role might imply. From the DCI's perspective, the community's organizational interests reflect its desire to provide timely and accurate intelligence to all decision makers. The shared image of the intelligence community—remaining value free and providing intelligence but not advice—guides interactions between the DCI and national-level decision makers. Unlike the DCI, however, the CJCS does strive to provide value-laden advice.

The CJCS serves NSC principals while simultaneously serving as the president's top personal advisor on military affairs. Through this role, the chairman of the joint chiefs enjoys direct and unimpeded access to the president and is authorized legally to circumvent the secretary of defense in these communications. While it is unlikely the CJCS would present a position contradictory to the secretary, the CJCS retains latitude to do so if he deems it necessary to preserve national security when military power is employed. Further, because the CJCS typically possesses between 25 and 30 years of military experience before becoming the nation's senior military official, most presidents recognize the value of this warrior's professional training and experience. This statement is not intended to devalue the experience of the State Department officials but to illustrate that the CJCS fulfills a specialized advisory role due to a specific competency. The CJCS's professional and personal values influence his one-on-one advice to the president. An additional factor proves salient in the military's post–Vietnam experience. Military officers desire to retain control of military operations without political interference.

Since the conclusion of the Vietnam War, two shared images of the uniformed military have become public. First, officers band together to avoid the "Tuesday lunch" syndrome; and second, they strive to ensure that ends and means are defined clearly.[42] Such clarity should enable the commander to employ forces efficiently and effectively and with an eye toward extricating them as quickly and safely as possible. In this manner, the CJCS exerts remarkable influence toward policies that produce war termination at the expense of conflict termination and resolution. One can easily see how this advisory role, shaped by the institutional concerns of the military, differs sharply with that of the DCI.

Additional images and interests complexify decision processes beyond the dynamics produced by the NSCS's six statutory players. These actors play an official role but have no statutory mandate for involvement in the process.

Presidential Prerogative Expands the Inner Circle

As illustrated by figure 3, other players inform and influence the national security decision-making process. These additional actors include the Arms Control and Disarmament Agency (ACDA), the US Information Agency (USIA),[43] the intelligence community (all 13 interrelated US government intelligence activities), White House Chief of Staff (CS), the National Security Council Staff, and the assistant to the president for National Security Affairs (APNSA; known informally as the president's national security advisor).

Historically, ADCA plays only a peripheral role in intervention policy processes and, therefore, has virtually no role in conflict termination policy development. Of the agencies involved in the national security process, this entity is the most forward looking in its efforts to halt proliferation and maintain a "stable" armament balance throughout the world (i.e., one that favors US interests). Thus, while ADCA may have a role to play, its functional specificity limits its capacity to provide broad-based advice in situations where the scope of the crisis extends beyond its core expertise. As directed by the Congress, this agency's director "serves as the principal advisor to the President, the National Security Advisor and the secretary of state on arms control, nonproliferation and disarmament issues."[44] Although the agency remains focused on ongoing arms control issues in a strategic sense, its ability to play a powerful role in crises beyond its functional interests remains limited.[45] Consequently, the executive's 1998 USG *Reorganization Plan and Report* states that "ACDA has no formal policy function."[46] While this agency may have performed some limited advisory role in the past, it is apparent that its new parent agency, the State Department, intends to limit its capacity to advise cabinet-level decision makers in the future. This leads to the second "limited partner"—the US Information Agency.

The USIA plays an extremely limited role in interagency intervention policy development and, hence, conflict termination policy development. Given its primary role as that of enhancing public diplomacy, this agency strives to explain US foreign policy to governments abroad while simultaneously engaging foreign publics.[47] USIA has advised principals in only a cursory manner when dealing with complex international contingencies. It provides options for selling US diplomacy abroad, but has exercised only a minor voice in the overall policy process. This is not representative, however, of the influence the next group of quasi-official actors exerts, as they reside within the intelligence community and reflect a clear increase in the capacity of other agencies to influence policy development.

The intelligence community is perhaps one of the most complex within all of Washington. Unlike the State Department or the Defense Department, this community has members positioned within multiple government agencies.[48] For instance, members of the Defense Intelligence Agency (DIA) and State's Bureau of Intelligence and Research (INR) augment Central Intelligence Agency (CIA) intelligence activities.[49] The director of Central Intelligence Interagency Balkan Task Force (DCI/IABTF) provides a particularly relevant example of this type of crossover effort. Through this interagency approach, the task force speaks with one voice when providing the DCI integrated intelligence estimates based upon the views of CIA, the Defense Department, and the State Department experts. This integrative effort is crucial to de-emphasizing parochial agency interests as the members of each individual agency develop working relationships across organizational bounds. However, this type of interagency task force is unique to the Balkans crisis. In other cases, no such structured team exists, and the DCI must assimilate disparate ideas from the various communities.

Given the discussion offered earlier regarding organizational cultures, one can assume that intelligence provided independently by the CIA, DIA, and INR would conform to the institutional images of each respective department. Consequently, the CIA attempts to provide value-free estimates, namely, the DIA, defense-oriented estimates; and INR, diplomacy-oriented estimates. By providing subjective situation estimates that are influenced by institutional positioning, these intelligence agencies frame crises in terms of innate bureaucratic interests instead of the more objective estimate demanded by the rational actor model. While the DCI endeavors to provide value-free estimates directly to the president and the National Security Council, the intelligence community's subcomponents provide estimates to their functional leaders that are framed by their respective institutional environments. The intelligence community collectively provides senior policy makers inputs through multiple points of entry that reflect differing perspectives—the DCI's, the State Department's, the Defense Department's, and others' views as required by the context of the crisis (e.g., the Department of Treasury, National Security Agency, and the Federal Bureau of Investigation). While these three intelligence subcommunities are by far not the only ones that influence intelligence activities, for the purposes of this study, they greatly overshadow all others.

Just as this work is based upon the crucial assumption that the USG is not a unitary actor, the same must be noted for the intelligence community. By identifying the four most influential intelligence actors as the DCI and the dominant executive agencies listed above, we can begin to see that potential cleavages exist within the intelligence community based upon each actor's respective allegiances. Returning to the idea that shared images and organizational interests affect every aspect of an agency's operation, one can begin to distinguish between the divergent patterns of intelligence analysis. These patterns of analysis wield definitive influence on framing the crisis from the bottom up and continually reshape events as they unfold over time. While these actors perform as part of the formal bureaucracy, a distinct cleavage begins to emerge when considering the remaining three quasi-official actors—actors who enjoy a more intimate relationship with the president and usually have extended personal contact with him. These actors are the White House CS and the NSC Staff, led by the national security advisor.

Perhaps more than any other Executive Office of the President (EOP) staff member, the White House CS develops into a member of the president's inner circle in crucial ways. This individual not only keeps the West Wing functioning smoothly but also directs preparation of the president's daily briefing materials. As a result, the CS is usually the next-to-last person (the president being the last) to shape policy before it enters the public, congressional, and interagency arenas. Further, the executive selects this individual not only for his or her professional experience but also because of the personal relationship (namely, demonstrated trust, loyalty, and judgment) he or she shares with the president. The CS gains unique insight into the president's innermost thoughts and feelings, engaging in a give-and-take relationship via regular dialogue. Consequently, the CS becomes one of the president's most regarded advisors and retains the capacity to influence major policy decisions, including foreign affairs initiatives.

It is through this advisory role that the CS serves as an information and access gatekeeper, enabling some to gain access to the president in a timely fashion while impeding or negating others' efforts. This is especially true if the president charges this individual to serve in this capacity. Failure to fulfill this role most assuredly would result in dismissal. This function is vitally important to keeping the president focused on the major issues while subordinating those of lesser import to lower-level decision makers. Linking this idea with Halperin and others' "shared images" elicits a critical question, that is, who decides which issues are critical and which are less critical? Simply stating that the president sets those parameters dismisses the bureaucratic reality of organizational life. The CS has personal ideas regarding what the president needs to know or decide in addition to any guidance proffered directly by the president. The potential power of this advisor cannot be overestimated. The images and interests this person holds most important retain the potential to shape all forms and levels of executive decision making. Nevertheless, an NSC Staff, led by a competent and trusted national security advisor, retains the ability to overshadow the influence of all other actors in the national security policy-making process.

The number of individuals on the NSC Staff has varied over the years, recently averaging between 140 and 160; of these, nearly 100 are involved in the policy functions while the remaining individuals serve as administrative support staff. Of these 100 policy-focused professionals, approximately 70 percent are departmental representatives who are seconded for a short time (usually two years or less) to the NSC Staff; the remaining 30 percent are political appointees selected by the president. Normally, the State Department employees out number the Defense Department representatives by a 3:1 ratio. Together, these two departments contribute roughly 80 percent of the Policy Staff professionals, with other government agencies providing only a handful of organizational representatives.[50] Department representatives rarely occupy the "assistant to the president" and "senior director" positions; political appointees normally serve in these senior advisor and decision-taking positions. NSC staffers play a critical role, however, in that they are the last stop before the president. Charged with coordinating the interagency policy-making process and over-seeing the implementation of presidential decisions, the NSC Staff shapes conflict termination policy in consequential ways.[51] While they dare not risk misconstruing the principals' per-spectives to the president (or anyone else), they can shape of-ficial guidance as long as it does not contradict the position es-poused by NSC principals. More importantly, these principals and their agency members confer with relevant staff members before, during, and after the president makes a decision. It is through such post hoc clarification that the NSC Staff shapes USG policy interpretation and implementation. While the staff works within the mid- and lower-level domains of policy de-velopment, the president's national security advisor remains engaged with the principals who lead each executive branch department.

Much like the senior directors, the assistant to the president for national security affairs is a political appointee who enjoys an extraordinary relationship with the president. Statute does not mandate the APNSA position; rather, "President Eisen-hower created the post to monitor, on his behalf, the operation of the NSC and the various subcommittees."[52] "He is not a statutory member of the NSC or even a 'principal,' except as the President may give him authority in practice."[53] Since the position's inception, presidents consistently have empowered this individual to oversee national security issues and, indeed, have treated this actor as a "principal." Complex factors shape the APNSA's relationship with the president, not the least of which is whether the administration exhibits a predilection for a foreign or domestic policy focus.

In the case of the former, this individual's power and au-thority may overshadow that of the CS. Conversely, when the administration has a predominantly domestic agenda, the APNSA may run a close second to the CS in influence. In ei-ther case, this individual's ability to shape the *policy process* and its *outcome* remains of paramount significance. Given the working relationship the president cultivates with this individual, it is likely that he or she shares the images held most important by the chief executive (e.g., President Richard Nixon and APNSA Henry Kissinger, or President Ronald Reagan and APNSA Colin Powell). In cases where the president projects a predominantly domestic focus, this individual may be empowered to act on behalf of the president where foreign affairs issues are concerned (e.g., President Bill Clinton and APNSAs Anthony Lake and Sandy Berger). Through the exercise of this authority, this individual may personally mitigate a perceived presidential weakness by developing a foreign policy agenda of his or her own when the president envisages little or none. Such a phenomenon presents an opportunity for bureaucratic interests to dominate both intervention and conflict termination policy development as yet another perspective (that of the APNSA connected with his/her shaping of the NSC Staff's) is injected into the policy process.

One can begin to appreciate the complexity of this decision-making apparatus by simply identifying the number of official and quasi-official actors involved in the process—those who have a statutory role as well as those who become influential based upon presidential prerogative or operational precedent. As perplexing as relationships across this inner circle may seem, situating the policy-making process within its more realistic context demands consideration of the influence exerted by those having no official role in interagency policy outcomes.

Influential Actors: Identifying the "Outer" Circle

Figure 3 (refer to p. 9) identifies numerous actors who remain "outside" the official executive branch policy-making circle. These organizations and individuals influence the president as he attempts to function as the nation's chief executive officer, particularly in areas where national security and national interests are not defined clearly. Although figure 3 does not depict all possible influential actors, it does identify those that hold the greatest import for conflict termination policy development. These include international allies and coalition partners; expert advisors; personal confidants, friends, and family; special

110

interest groups; think tanks; the media; the American people; and the US legislature.

Admittedly, this research makes no attempt to examine the interplay between international allies and the USG interagency process. However, failure to acknowledge that friendly, unfriendly, and so-called neutral governments shape the policy process would undermine this work's integrity.[54] Allies and adversaries played particularly important roles in the two crises examined here.

In looking specifically at conflict termination policy, allies help frame the desired end state in a macro sense while simultaneously expanding or limiting courses of action regarding operational strategy. For example, Paul Kecskemeti's analysis of World War II's termination in the form of unconditional surrender aptly points out the Allies' role in shaping the desired end state of total victory.[55] Leaders defined total victory as fighting a war of attrition to the point that peace terms could be "unilaterally imposed rather than negotiated."[56] Through this policy of unconditional surrender, Kecskemeti identifies the Allies' desired end state, conflict termination criteria, and strategy to achieve conflict termination.[57] Collectively, the Allies played a crucial role in developing conflict termination policy. Because it is unlikely that the United States will intervene abroad unilaterally in the future, recognizing the role allies—or ad hoc temporary friendlies—play in shaping intervention policy remains an essential element in understanding how the US interagency process formulates conflict termination policy.

The leverage these allies exert in the US policy process is as multifaceted as the potential combination of allies. As a consequence of today's interdependent web of international relations, it is perhaps more appropriate to speak of rotating "coalition partners" rather than long-term "allies."[58] Crosscutting interests create new opportunities for short-term interdependence[59]—or partnerships President George W. Bush labeled "coalitions of the willing" in the wake of Al Qaeda's "9/11" attack on the World Trade Center—while negating similar opportunities across differing contexts based upon multiple interlocking conflicts.[60] For instance, during the Persian Gulf War, Syria joined forces with the United States to stand against Saddam Hussein's aggression; alternatively, the United States held its long-term ally Israel at arm's length. In both cases, the interests of the coalition partners demanded that the United States temporarily reverse its policy regarding strategic allies and enemies. While this example points to the upper end of the policy spectrum, these decisions shape the capabilities and activities of the force conducting the operational mission.

Coalition partners shape strategy development as policy makers and strategists determine the resources required/available to achieve desired outcomes. This influence takes two forms, namely, active and passive. The active influence of coalition partners is readily observable. Will Great Britain provide forces? If "yes," how many and which capabilities will they bring to bear? If "no," who will make up the resource shortfall? If the country will not provide forces, will it provide subsistence-in-kind in the form of nonmilitary resources or financial support as the Europeans, Japanese, and Germans did during the Persian Gulf War?[61] Again, these forms of participation are easily identifiable and are evaluated as having a direct effect upon the operational mission. Passive forms of participation are not as easy to identify or evaluate.

Passive forms of participation (and nonparticipation) can enjoy levels of influence similar to active forms. The use of pre-positioning and staging locations to amass forces and materiel within the theater of operations increasingly represents a necessary element of US intervention strategy. Relatedly, will an ally or coalition partner authorize overflight for the purpose of bombing a neighboring nonallied country? Take, for example, the case of the 1986 US air strikes on Libya and Spain's refusal to authorize overflight. In this case, *passive nonparticipation* reshaped the US approach to retaliating against Muammar Qadhafi. During the late 1990s, by withholding authorization for flights departing their soil, Saudi Arabia constrained US ability to take offensive action against Iraq in the face of continuing United Nations Special Commission (UNSCOM) violations. Both examples demonstrate that allied relations can limit the USG's options, particularly at the operational level. Allies and coalition partners may agree on the desired end state ("what" needs to be done—the "ends") but may disagree on the strategy to get there ("how" to do it—the "means"). This dichotomous relationship between ends and means resonates with interagency actors who often are divided by the expert advisors.

When evaluating this actor's influence, it becomes difficult to identify structured bases for group inclusion. It quickly becomes apparent that individuals typically become expert advisors as a result of prior government service, exceptional academic record, or their capacity to sell their views to the media and public through radio broadcasts, television appearances, or publications. When an individual shares characteristics of all three, that person will gain entrée into the policy-making process. One example of this phenomenon is Dr. Richard Haass, an expert who has sustained a capacity to advise interagency principals on the Middle East Peace Process. Haass served on President George H. W. Bush's NSC Staff, is a renowned academic and recognized Middle East expert, and oftentimes is invited by prominent media conglomerates to render his opinion on various US foreign policy positions. Added to these credentials, Haass also served as director of a revered Washington think tank, the Brookings Institution. When combined with the three other characteristics, this makes him an individual within Washington's policy elite whose opinion should at the very least be asked for, if not in fact considered at length. These characteristics give Haass and others like him (e.g., Jane Hall Lute and Anthony Lake) influential voices in policy processes. Their influence emerges as a form of authority that proves difficult to link directly to a departmental position on an organizational chart. However, expert advisors are shaped by their past government experience as "in and outers" as well as their personal experiences.[62]

In and outers reappear in important government positions based upon present successes. In other words, "the power to predict has always been the underlying source of the expert's mystique."[63] Those experts whose predictions bear out gain an even greater voice in future decision-making processes, setting off a self-perpetuating cycle wherein accuracy becomes the key to future success (i.e., political appointments). It is through this cycle that expert advisors maintain currency within the political system by maintaining personal and professional relationships with those likely to hold the highest government positions. Accordingly, some expert advisors become personal confidants as well. When dealing with bureaucratic politics, however, that distinction assumes a different meaning.

Closely related to expert advisors are personal confidants, friends, and family.[64] Unlike expert advisors, however, such individuals share no professional competence that guarantees them access. They share a more important characteristic—the principal's unbridled trust and respect in concert with a sustained relationship that extends far beyond professional courtesy. Through the course of this relationship, a principal seeks the individual's opinion on a particular issue that the principal may introduce later in the White House Situation Room or Oval Office. The penetrating characteristic of these advisors is that they lack situational credibility when addressing issues but do share personal relationships that perhaps make them appear more objective or more neutral than official actors involved in the process. The next group of influential actors—special interest groups—proves anything but neutral.

It is a natural phenomenon of democratic government that its heterogeneous population forms characteristic-specific groups to make their individual voices heard. Not only do such groups voice political agendas, but they also contribute financial support to political candidates who advance their positions. An expanding and diversifying US population has spawned many ethnically, racially, socially, economically, and politically based special interest groups. These special interest groups influence the chief executive during the formulation of both domestic and foreign policy. Their power remains bound by their capacity to appeal to a principal's personal or political interests that usually revolve around ideals of justice and equity, preservation of individual rights and liberties, or some other niche. To put these interests and types of advice into perspective, principals often turn to the think tanks.

Recognized for their expertise, sound research, and analytic rigor, these influential institutions play a significant role in shaping a policy maker's understanding of complex issues regarding the position the USG should take in response to a crisis. James Smith contends, "Though personal relationships will always shape the nexus linking knowledge and political decision making, informal ties have been powerfully augmented by formal research and advisory institutions."[65] Analytically rigorous in their own right, these institutions hew to their respective philosophical and political biases.[66]

Whether reflecting conservative or liberal worldviews, think tanks make critical connections between knowledge and power. They begin to develop and refine an awareness of "the politics of knowledge" by creating, organizing, developing, selecting, and disseminating knowledge according to their respective values and interests.[67] Government officials often invite key members of think tanks to participate in policy making. It is not unusual to discover that government agencies may have "implemented the recommendations of Carnegie-supported [or other] groups."[68] The earlier reference to Haass and The Brookings Institution makes clear that Carnegie does not stand alone in terms of access to the policy-making process. Rather, think-tank analysts exert powerful influence over decision makers' views of crises while simultaneously mobilizing public support. It is for this reason that their activities serve as an appropriate bridge to the next set of influential actors, the media.

Just as members of think tanks use their written words to shape the politics of knowledge, so do the media. Unlike the other influential actors identified thus far, the media influences practically everyone's ideas and not just those of the policy elite. In this manner, they play a crucial role in framing crises—much like the roles played by the DCI and the CJCS—but on a much broader scale. Principals remain concerned with the representation and interpretation of their ideas, as evidenced by the fact that each department staffs its own public affairs directorate. Positions promoted by the media can harm or help the president's ability to sell a policy, especially one requiring a commitment of "blood and treasure" on foreign soil.[69] This explicit support (or criticism) of an administration's policies can become a catalyst for action. When reelection prospects appear uncertain, the media's role in shaping policy becomes particularly relevant. Even with the explosion of global information networks, the traditional media remains the primary source for foreign and domestic policy information for the vast majority of Americans. Therefore, the media plays an overwhelmingly influential role in shaping the American public's perspective regarding the activities of government.

Presidents remain concerned about reelection opportunities, endorsement ratings, legacies, and public approval for their actions—especially those actions concerning the stationing of troops abroad. The other principals likewise remain concerned with gaining public approval, or, at the very least, sustaining public ambivalence, for government policies and practices. Relatedly, principals are engaged in protecting the president's public image as it relates to his capacity to ensure that the United States remains a dominant force on the international stage. The lessons of Vietnam, Watergate, and the Iran-Contra Affair caution policy makers that domestic opinion matters and exerts a defining influence on American foreign policy.

The media played a crucial role in shaping American public opinion in each of these events. In Vietnam, Walter Cronkite's description of the Tet Offensive and his implicit statements regarding the government's actions to positively spin wartime losses emerged as one of the earliest efforts of the twentieth-century media to serve as the public's watchdog. Similarly, the Nixon administration's atrocities during the Watergate scandal and the Oliver North conspiracy dealing with the Contras reenergized the media's desire to expose corrupt government. In all three of these cases, the media portrayed a side of government the average citizen could not access.[70] While the literature detailing these three examples proves overwhelming, the relationship between domestic politics and conflict termination in Vietnam highlights the necessity to consider carefully the relationship between domestic politics and foreign affairs.

In her study of war termination in Vietnam, Jane Holl contends that through the analysis of domestic politics one can best understand the policy choices of a nation's leadership during the closing stages of a war.[71] In this manner, domestic considerations definitively shaped US foreign policy and conflict termination decisions. Vietnam is not the first example wherein the media's influence on domestic politics shaped conflict termination policy. Similar domestic considerations emerge in analyses of Japan's decision to surrender to the Allies during World War II.[72] Just as the media serves as the bridge between the American public and Washington's policy elite, domestic opinion serves as the bridge to the final influential actor examined in this work—the Congress.

A pivotal actor in the national security policy-making process as a consequence of budgetary control and the War Powers Resolution, the US Legislature participates in foreign policy development as elected representatives of the American public's interests. Through these representative roles, members of the Congress articulate the people's desires and espouse positions that should parallel their respective constituents' interests. It is this connection between public opinion and congressional authority that exercises the most influence on foreign policy and conflict termination policy development; policy makers perceive that the American public remains concerned with issues of blood and treasure, particularly when a loved one's blood might be spilled on foreign soil. In this vein, the Congress becomes very concerned with exit strategies and bringing the troops home as safely and as quickly as possible. Its focus on this aspect of conflict termination policy reinforces the Congress's official function as legislators.

While their roles as lawmakers and budget authorities provide the Congress entrée into the policy process, albeit through a constitutional back door, this capacity to pass laws restricting the use of force and to withhold funding for military operations provides this body an oversight authority that remains unique across the USG. While the Congress is not a player in the executive branch's interagency process pro forma, it sits at the policy-making table as a formidable shadow negotiator—even in the absence of its physical participation. Every department staff is a legislative liaison office charged with engaging congressional staffers on important policy issues. If a policy cannot be "sold," that policy will eventually fail. In the end, a policy without funding is not a policy but is merely a policy maker's unrealizable desire. This is the most fundamental rule of the game in Washington—the rule everyone understands and the language everyone speaks.

The foregoing discussion merely outlined the roles played by official, quasi-official, and influential actors in shaping foreign and conflict termination policy. But the rules that guide the policy process are not established solely by the actors themselves—they are also bound by the context within which they must operate.

Contextual Factors: Rules Defining the Playing Field

Contextual factors expand or limit a US policy maker's capacity—and willingness—to "color outside the lines" of accepted policy practices. Three factors dominate the foreign policy process: US national interests, the international context, and domestic concerns.

Perhaps the most obvious contextual factor shaping the decision to intervene into a conflict on foreign soil is the answer to the question, What is the national interest? Once again, posing this question requires a cost-benefit analysis. What benefit does the nation gain and at what cost? Are these interests vital, important, or "other"?[73] How does the magnitude of interest influence proposed levels of commitment? Which policy maker ultimately decides whether a crisis impinges upon US national interests? This linkage with national interest shapes the US policy makers' collective ability to convince the media that intervention is required. As a result, national leaders argue that the United States should commit its blood and treasure to achieving positive results for long-term good. While this sounds altruistic on the surface, defining national interests can take many forms short of noble ends.

Executive departments define national interests in terms of their respective shared images and organizational interests.[74] The State Department, for example, may adopt a strong position on the use of force to prevent genocide, defining earlier intervention and humanitarian relief as related to US national interests. In opposition, the Defense Department may push the interagency to frame national interests in more concise terms, asking decision makers to identify clearly the costs of nonintervention and its attendant benefits for comparison with the risks of intervention. From the Defense Department's perspective, the costs in terms of blood and treasure are measured quite easily; yet, the benefits remain ambiguous. Recalling the earlier discussion regarding philosophical/ideological perspectives, organizational cultures, and operational responsibility, these perspectives are recognizable. Taken a step further, these divergent perspectives prompt these two entities to define national interests asymmetrically, creating a fissure that harbors implications for conflict intervention and termination policy development across the highest levels of the policy process. As much as we would like to think that national interests relate primarily to domestic considerations, the international context must be considered when devising foreign policy.

Since the end of World War II, the United States has found it increasingly difficult to isolate itself from activities abroad. In the face of increasingly global economic and security relationships, such isolation is undesirable. For the United States to remain a powerful actor on the international stage, it must enhance its interconnectedness with those nations it endeavors to influence. Activities beyond America's borders continue to influence directly US domestic policy in conjunction with their more obvious relationship to foreign policy. One needs only to examine an underlying reason for the US involvement in the Persian Gulf War—maintaining the free flow of oil for US allies—to find evidence of this relationship. Hussein's potential control of almost 45 percent of the world's oil supply posed devastating effects for the West and its allies in general, for Japan and Germany in particular. After all, these two nations relied heavily upon the Gulf region for their oil supplies and served as the region's principal clients.[75] If Hussein controlled the region's oil supply, Japan and Germany would potentially lose more than any of the other industrialized nations (at least initially—others would likewise feel the effects over time).[76] Underwriting economies is but one form of interdependence; reciprocal security arrangements represent another.

Relations across international actors take on some characteristics of mutually beneficial elements that affect the security of Americans at home. For instance, international organizations such as the Warsaw Pact and the North Atlantic Treaty Organization (NATO) served as deterrent mechanisms. Within the now 19 members of NATO, reciprocal expectations regarding political and military support guided much of US foreign policy throughout the Cold War—and continue to do so today. With the onset of the Balkans crisis in the early 1990s, questions regarding NATO's efficacy prompted a resurgence in US efforts to bolster that organization's capacity to respond to emerging crises. American recognition of this interdependence demands a coherent US foreign policy in the coming years while recognizing that technology and trade will continually transform these types of interdependence. Moreover, national interests and the international context must be evaluated in concert with domestic issues.

Domestic issues and interests play important roles in foreign policy development and decisions regarding conflict termination. While these concerns influence the ways in which policy makers frame US national interests, they also shape the lenses through which national decision makers *see* a crisis. While this discussion can take the form of the classic guns and butter argument, politicians' concerns for domestic issues can reflect a fundamental extension of philosophical and ideological beliefs as much as an outgrowth of economic realities. It is here that we again see the relevance of Allison and Halperin and others. Based upon their respective shared images and interests, individuals and groups make salient sets of priorities that clash with others' desires. Another level of domestic concerns surrounds the policy-making process as well—that of keeping the populace satisfied to ensure an individual politician's (and political party's) future success.

Colloquially speaking, if plagiarism is the sincerest form of flattery, reelection is the most conclusive form of public approval. An individual's desire to continue serving in his or her present political position or higher position parallels how closely one acts upon constituents' desires. In a representative democracy as practiced in the United States, politicians rarely challenge their constituents' most vocal demands, especially if the majority's voice looms loudest. This does not mean that elected officials always vote with their district's simple majority on every issue. It does imply, however, that reelected politicians quickly identify those issues on which they can vote independently and those on which they incur increased political risk when doing so. In this manner, when the public vocally opposes troop deployment to foreign soil or demands the withdrawal of previously deployed forces, elected officials pay attention. These concerns may have little to do with rational choice theory in terms of what is best for the crisis at hand, but may be very rational in light of other contextual factors impinging upon the decision-making process. Such pressures emanate from emotional, political, economic, or social sources, few of which may have any bearing on the crisis into which the USG intervenes. Taken in conjunction with the framing of national interests and the evolving international context, domestic concerns can become a powerful force in developing conflict termination policy for complex international crises.

Clearly, this discussion regarding national interests, international context, and domestic concerns proves inadequate as an overall predictive element for foreign policy development in general, conflict termination policy in specific. However, it begins to frame the types of issues that shape the thinking of those charged with formulating policy and making decisions on behalf of the American populace. This framework provides a mechanism with which to analyze the problems that stem from interagency conflict during conflict termination policy development.

Building Toward New Understanding

Groups make decisions through a multidimensional, dynamically complex, and recursive process, framed by the organizational interests of those who (1) are players in the process, (2) define the rules of the game and its playing field, and (3) make choices based upon competing criteria and asymmetric preference orderings. By capturing the dynamics across the actors within the process, analysts and future decision makers can begin to work within the USG's bureaucratic process to formulate conflict termination policy.

Yet, actors involved in the process of policy making at times *see* crises from the perspectives of their respective organizations and interests, as well as their personal experiences. Cleavages between actors within the interagency process affect US capacity to capitalize synergistically upon all of its re-

121

sources when faced with an international crisis such as the Persian Gulf or Bosnia.

The remainder of this book advances a comprehension of those bureaucratic elements that affect the interagency process's ability to analyze critically the crises it faces, envisage a desired end state, frame and select conflict termination criteria, and formulate a strategy capable of achieving sustainable conflict termination. The next chapter outlines the study's research methodology and conceptual framework.

Notes

1. See also Morton H. Halperin, with the assistance of Priscila Clapp and Arnold Kanter, *Bureaucratic Politics and Foreign Policy* (Washington, D.C.: The Brookings Institution, 1974).

2. Graham T. Allison, "Conceptual Models and the Cuban Missile Crisis," in *International Relations: Contemporary Theory and Practice*, ed. G. A. Lopez and M. S. Stohl (Washington, D.C.: CQ Press, 1989), 124.

3. Graham T. Allison, *Essence of Decision: Explaining the Cuban Missile Crisis* (Boston: Little, Brown and Co., 1971), 144.

4. Halperin, Clapp, and Kanter, *Bureaucratic Politics and Foreign Policy*, 312.

5. Allison, *Essence of Decision*, 157. The quotations within this passage highlight the fact that Allison borrowed these characteristics from Roger Hilsman, *To Move a Nation: The Politics of Foreign Policy in the Administration of John F. Kennedy* (New York: Doubleday, 1967).

6. Allison, *Essence of Decision*, 162.

7. Ibid.

8. Ibid., 164.

9. See also William F. West, "Searching for a Theory of Bureaucratic Structure," *Journal of Public Administration Research and Theory* 7, no. 4 (1997).

10. Ibid; and see also Allison, "Conceptual Models and the Cuban Missile Crisis."

11. Allison, *Essence of Decision*, 178.

12. See also Samuel B. Bacharach and Edward J. Lawler, *Power and Politics in Organizations: The Social Psychology of Conflict, Coalitions, and Bargaining* (San Francisco, Calif.: Jossey-Bass, 1980); see also J. William Breslin and Jeffrey Z. Rubin, eds., *Negotiation Theory and Practice*, 2d ed. (Cambridge, Mass.: The Program on Negotiation at Harvard Law School, 1993); see also Robert Jervis, Richard Ned Lebow, and Janice Gross Stein, *Psychology and Deterrence* (Baltimore, Md.: Johns Hopkins University Press, 1989); see also Paul Koopman and Jeroen Pool, "Organizational Decision Making: Models, Contingencies and Strategies," in *Distributed Decision Making: Cognitive Models for Cooperative Work*, ed. Jens Rasmussen, Berndt Brehmer, and Jacques Leplat (Chichester, England: John Wiley & Sons, 1991); see also Henry

Mintzberg, "The Power Game and the Players," in *Classics in Organization Theory*, ed. J. M. Shafritz and J. S. Ott (Pacific Grove, Calif.: Brooks/Cole Publishing Company, 1987); see also Jeffrey Pfeffer, "Understanding the Role of Power in Decision Making," in *Classics in Organization Theory*, ed. J. M. Shafritz and J. S. Ott (Pacific Grove, Calif.: Brooks/Cole Publishing Co., 1987); and see also I. William Zartman, "Decision Support and Negotiation Research: A Researcher's Perspective," *Theory and Decision* 34 (1993).

13. Allison, *Essence of Decision*, 168.

14. See also Halperin, Clapp, and Kanter, *Bureaucratic Politics and Foreign Policy*.

15. Allison, *Essence of Decision*, 170.

16. Ibid.

17. Ibid. See also, Halperin, Clapp, and Kanter, *Bureaucratic Politics and Foreign Policy*, 104.

18. Allison, *Essence of Decision*, 170.

19. Ibid., 170–71.

20. Ibid., 172.

21. Ibid., 162.

22. Janis lists these constraints as follows: *cognitive*—limited time, multiple tasks, perceived limitations of resources for information search and processing, complexity of issues, ideological commitments, and perceived lack of dependable knowledge; *affiliative*—need to maintain power, status, compensation, and social support, and the need for acceptability of new policy within the organization; and *egocentric* (or self-serving and emotive)—strong personal motive (e.g., greed, desire for fame), arousal of an emotional need (e.g., anger or elation), and emotional stress of decisional conflict. See Irving L. Janis, *Crucial Decisions: Leadership in Policymaking and Crisis Management* (New York: Free Press, 1989), 149.

23. Edwin Mansfield, *Applied Microeconomics* (New York: W. W. Norton & Co., 1994), 16–17.

24. I. E. Morley, J. Webb, and G. M. Stephenson, "Bargaining and Arbitration in the Resolution of Conflict," in *The Social Psychology of Intergroup Conflict*, ed. W. Stroebe et al. (Berlin: Springer-Verlag, 1988), 118.

25. See also Halperin, Clapp, and Kanter, *Bureaucratic Politics and Foreign Policy;* and see also Uriel Rosenthal and Alexander Kousmin, "Crisis and Crisis Management: Toward Comprehensive Government Decision Making," *Journal of Public Administration Research and Theory* 7, no. 2 (1997).

26. Christopher R. Mitchell and Michael Nicholson, "Rational Models and the Ending of Wars," *Journal of Conflict Resolution* 27 (1983): 515.

27. See also Sam Allotey et al., *Planning and Execution of Conflict Termination* (Maxwell AFB, Ala.: Air Command and Staff College, 1995); see also Bruce B. G. Clarke, *Conflict Termination: A Rational Model* (Carlisle Barracks, Pa.: US Army War College, 1992); see also Bruce B. G. Clarke, "Conflict Termination: What Does It Mean to Win?" *Military Review* 72, no. 11 (1992); see also Lewis A. Coser, "The Termination of Conflict," *Conflict Resolution* 5, no. 4 (1961); see also Christopher R. Mitchell, "Ending Conflicts

and Wars: Judgment, Rationality and Entrapment," *International Social Science Journal* 43, no. 1 (1991); and see also Donald Wittman, "How a War Ends: A Rational Approach," *Journal of Conflict Resolution* 23 (1979).

28. See also Sir Basil Henry Liddell Hart, *Strategy* (New York: Praeger, 1954).

29. See also Mitchell and Nicholson, "Rational Models and the Ending of Wars."

30. I. William Zartman, "Negotiation as a Joint Decision-Making Process." *Journal of Conflict Resolution* 21, no. 4 (1977): 619–38.

31. See also Richard G. Stevens, introduction, *The Declaration of Independence and the Constitution of the United States of America* (Washington, D.C.: Government Printing Office [GPO], 1995).

32. It is important to acknowledge here that the status of the War Powers Resolution is debated constantly between the executive and legislative branches. While no president has recognized its authority publicly, every president has complied with its minimal reporting requirements since its inception.

33. See also Halperin, Clapp, and Kanter, *Bureaucratic Politics and Foreign Policy.*

34. This quotation has currency across the USG, so its original source remains a bit obscure. However, Arthur Vandeburg is recognized as espousing this philosophy after World War II, the concept being rooted in Wilson and Lansing's ideas during World War I.

35. Joint Chiefs of Staff (JCS), Joint Pub 3-08, *Interagency Coordination During Joint Operations*, vol. 1, 1996, vi–vii.

36. US Department of State, *Duties of the Secretary of State*, 1997, on-line, Internet, 6 February 1999, available from http://www.state.gov/www/albright/.

37. JCS, Joint Pub 3-08, GL-10.

38. See also Halperin, Clapp, and Kanter, *Bureaucratic Politics and Foreign Policy.*

39. Allison, *Essence of Decision*, 176.

40. See also The White House, *A National Security Strategy for a New Century* (Washington, D.C.: GPO, 1998).

41. Throughout this research, this perspective reflected the Defense Department personnel views on noncombatant evacuation operations (NEO). The Defense Department personnel cited several examples wherein the State Department failed to understand the practical requirements of positioning forces to evacuate US Embassy personnel when crises escalated to a level demanding evacuation. Over time, these types of interactions polarize relations between the departments, creating tension as the State Department wants the evacuation to happen "now" because its people face imminent danger (including the possibility of death), and the Defense Department responds that it needs more time to position the appropriate personnel to evacuate diplomats and their staffs in a safe manner.

42. "Tuesday lunch" syndrome refers to the actions of President Lyndon B. Johnson during the Vietnam War wherein he held Tuesday lunches to designate bombing targets. See also Neil Sheehan, *A Bright and Shining Lie: John Paul Vann and America in Vietnam* (New York: Random House, 1988). Since this experience, military commanders have fought diligently to maintain operational control of the conflict environment while deferring strategic oversight to the political decision makers within the USG. In this manner, the military commander expresses a strong desire for the political decision maker to clearly define "what" they want to accomplish, leaving the "how" of accomplishment in the hands of the professional military expert. For a contemporary perspective, see also H. Norman Schwarzkopf with Peter Petre, *General H. Norman Schwarzkopf: The Autobiography: It Doesn't Take a Hero* (New York: Bantam Books, 1992).

43. It is important to note that effective May 1997, both ACDA and USIA became part of the State Department; integration was completed in 1999. See The White House, *Fact Sheet: Reinventing State, ACDA, USIA, and AID,* 6 February 1999, on-line, Internet, 18 April 1997, available from http:// www.state.gov/www/global/general_foreign_policy.

44. US Department of State, *ACDA: US Arms Control and Disarmament Agency,* 6 February 1999, on-line, Internet, (1997, available from http://www. state.gov/www/publications/statemag/statemag_sep-oct/feature2.html.

45. Ibid.

46. US Department of State, *Reorganization Plan and Report: Submitted by President Clinton to the Congress on December 30, 1998, Pursuant to Section 1601 of the Foreign Affairs Reform and Restructuring Act of 1998, as Contained in Public Law 105-277,* 6 February 1999, on-line, Internet, 30 December 1998, available from http://www.state.gov/www/publications/statemag/statemag_ nov-dec97.featxt2.html.

47. US Department of State, *USIA: On Meeting the Public Diplomacy Challenge,* 6 February 1999, on-line, Internet, 1997, available from http://www. state.gov/www/publications/statemag/statemag_nov-dec97.featxt2.html.

48. For an overview of all 13 USG intelligence activities, access the director of Central Intelligence website via http://www.odci.gov/ic/functions/ html. See Office of the Director of Central Intelligence (ODCI), *US Intelligence Community—Who We Are and What We Do,* 21 September 1998, on-line, Internet, 15 June 1998, available from http://www.odci.gov/ic/functions.html. The National Security Council Staff also staffs an intelligence directorate, but little information is available outlining the specific duties of that "special assistant to the president and senior director." Nor is explicit information available detailing how this individual interacts with the remainder of the intelligence community.

49. In conjunction with creating the NSC and the Department of the Air Force, the National Security Act of 1947 concurrently established the CIA as "an independent agency, responsible to the President through the DCI [Director of Central Intelligence], and accountable to the American people through the intelligence oversight committees of the US Congress." See Office of the

Director of Central Intelligence ODCI, *Central Intelligence Agency,* 21 September 1998, on-line, Internet, 15 June 1998, available from http://www.odci.gov/ic/cia.html.

50. These figures emerged during interviews conducted at the White House from November through December 1998 (exact personnel numbers and ratios were not made available).

51. See also Colin L. Powell, "The NSC System in the Last Two Years of the Reagan Administration," in *The Presidency in Transition,* ed. James P. Pfiffner et al. (New York: Center for the Study of the Presidency, 1989).

52. Ibid., 205.

53. Ibid.

54. See also Vicki J. Rast and Bruce R. Sturk, "Coalitions: The Challenge of Effective Command and Control in Support of the Air Campaign," in *Theater Air Campaign Studies,* ed. Pat Battles (Maxwell AFB, Ala.: Air Command and Staff College, 1995); and see also Robert W. Riscassi, "Principles for Coalition Warfare," *Joint Forces Quarterly* (1993).

55. See also Paul Kecskemeti, *Strategic Surrender: The Politics of Victory and Defeat* (New York: Atheneum, 1964).

56. Ibid., 215.

57. Note, however, that this reflects yet another *cost-benefit analysis* approach wherein the enemy will stop fighting when it can no longer continue the fight (based primarily upon logistical issues in this case since the strategy was one of force attrition). Nevertheless, *Strategic Surrender* is a "must read" for serious students of war and conflict termination.

58. See also Rast and Sturk, "Coalitions: The Challenge of Effective Command and Control in Support of the Air Campaign"; and see also Riscassi, "Principles for Coalition Warfare."

59. See also Lewis Coser, *The Functions of Social Conflict* (New York: Free Press, 1956).

60. See also Louis Kriesberg, *International Conflict Resolution: The US-USSR and Middle East Cases* (New Haven, Conn.: Yale University Press, 1992).

61. See also US House, "Developments in Europe, October 1990" (Washington, D.C.: GPO, 1990).

62. "In and outers" are people, usually political appointees, who serve in one department, return to the private sector, reenter a few years later in another department, then leave government service and the cycle continues. See also Halperin, Clapp, and Kanter, *Bureaucratic Politics and Foreign Policy.*

63. James A. Smith, *The Idea Brokers: Think Tanks and the Rise of the New Policy Elite* (New York: Free Press, 1991), 233.

64. My gratitude goes to Dr. James Lucas at the National War College for identifying this critical omission in my original conceptualization of the policy process.

65. Smith, *The Idea Brokers,* 12.

66. Ibid., 270. For an introduction to many of the most influential think tanks that now influence foreign policy development, see Smith's "Think Tank Directory." Smith surveys 44 of the most prominent think tanks, in-

cluding their origins, finances, staff, programs of research, and their ideological orientations.

67. Ellen Condliffe Lagemann, *The Politics of Knowledge: The Carnegie Corporation, Philanthropy, and Public Policy* (Middletown, Conn.: Wesleyan University Press, 1989), 3–4.

68. Ibid., 10.

69. Blood and treasure refers to the commitment of forces and financial resources to a crisis intervention policy and its ensuing implementation. The American public, policy makers, and media invoke this term when describing the nature of the commitment the United States should make abroad, particularly when "less than vital" interests are at stake (e.g., when describing the nature of US commitments to Kosovo and the Balkans).

70. See also Steven Kull and I. M. Destler, *Misreading the Public: The Myth of a New Isolationism* (Washington, D.C.: Brookings Institution Press, 1999).

71. See also Jayne Ellen Kyrstyn Holl, "From the Streets of Washington to the Roofs of Saigon: Domestic Politics and the Termination of the Vietnam War" (PhD diss., Stanford University, 1989).

72. See also John W. Dower, *Embracing Defeat: Japan in the Wake of World War II* (New York: W. W. Norton & Co./New Press, 1999); see also Joseph A. Engelbrecht Jr., "War Termination: Why Does a State Decide to Stop Fighting? (World War II, Anglo-Boer War, Japan, Great Britain)" (PhD diss., Columbia University, 1992); see also Fred Charles Iklé, *Every War Must End* (New York: Columbia University Press, 1991); and see also Leon V. Sigal, *Fighting to a Finish: The Politics of War Termination in the United States and Japan, 1945* (Ithaca & London: Cornell University Press, 1988).

73. See also The White House, *A National Security Strategy for a New Century* (Washington, D.C.: GPO, 1998).

74. See also Iklé, *Every War Must End.*

75. Joseph Rivas reports that the "US gets 12% of its total oil needs from the Middle East, less Iran (4% from Iraq and Kuwait); comparable figures for Western Europe are 27% and 14% and for Japan, 51% and 14%." The "45 percent figure" emerges from assessments contending Hussein potentially would control outright up to 25 percent of the world's reserves should he gain control of Kuwait and would leverage Saudi Arabia's 20 percent implicitly through sustained coercion. J. P. Rivas, ed., *Petroleum Status of the Western Persian Gulf.* CRS Report to Congress, no. 90–378 SPR (Washington, D.C.: The Library of Congress, 1990), 2. See also Richard E. Rubenstein, *On Taking Sides: Lessons of the Persian Gulf War* (Fairfax, Va.: George Mason University, 1993).

76. Admittedly, this perspective has to be balanced by the reality that the Iraqis would still need a buyer for their oil supply. Should Japan and Germany not purchase Iraqi oil, questions emerge regarding the capacity of Iraq's allies to absorb the surplus. In this manner, the interdependence of this supply-demand relationship would generate detrimental effects for Iraq's economy as well.

Chapter 5

Interagency Fratricide: Bridging the Gap between Theory and Practice

Science would not exist without concepts.

—Anselm Strauss and Juliet Corbin

Interagency conflict termination policy making demands an innovative approach for exploring the ways in which process shapes policy. This chapter explains the techniques employed to conduct this study. What follows, then, is a conceptual bridge that connects the policy-making process with its results. Six core factors are used to measure the indicators of interagency conflict. These core factors are presented in terms of (1) statistically significant correlations, (2) demographic stratification, and (3) emergent theme identification. This approach reveals the crucial factors, their interrelationships, and the implications they hold for conflict termination policy outcomes.[1] Once constructed, the conceptual bridge will bolster understanding of policy process dynamics and generate a more specific comprehension of conflict termination policy development in the Persian Gulf War (1990–91) and the Bosnia crisis (1993–95).

A Basic Conceptual Framework

Anselm Strauss and Juliet Corbin insist concepts are essential because

> by the very act of naming phenomena, we fix continuing attention on them. Once our attention is fixed, we can begin to examine and ask questions about those phenomena (now of course, labeled as concepts). Such questions not only describe what we see, but in the form of *propositions* (hypotheses) suggest how phenomena might possibly be related to one another. Propositions permit deductions, which in turn guide data collection that leads to further induction and provisional testing of propositions. In the end, communication among investigators, including the vital interplay of discussion and argument necessary to enhance the development of science, is made possible by the

specification of concepts and their relationships phrased in terms of propositions (emphasis in original).[2]

Discussion of Allison's bureaucratic politics model, together with identification of the interagency process actors, provided an initial framework for investigating conflict termination policy development. The framework suggested specific propositions regarding expected relationships among strategic actors. These propositions produced six core factors, including the hypothesized relationships depicted in the "Basic Conceptual Framework." Admittedly, an infinite number of factors could influence interagency conflict development during conflict termination policy formulation. The frameworks and models illustrated in figure 8 show relationships between interagency processes and policy outcomes. A refined framework is required to analyze these relationships systematically and thoroughly.

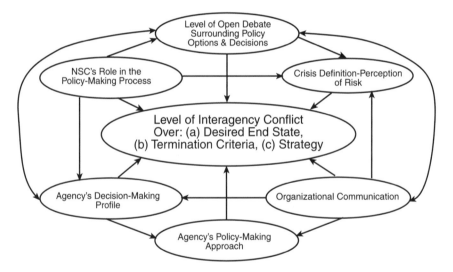

Figure 8. Basic Conceptual Framework

Frameworks and Models

The hierarchical model depicted in figure 9 illustrates measurable relationships between the core factors first outlined in the Basic Conceptual Framework.[3]

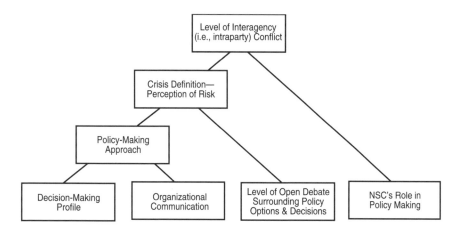

Figure 9. Hierarchical Model: A Framework for Data Collection

The indicators comprising the index labeled *Decision-Making Profile* combine with those constituting *Organizational Communication* to help describe, in conjunction with other core factors, the *Policy-Making Approach* of the agencies under study. *Level of Open Debate,* in conjunction with relevant indicators, helps frame the agency's perspective regarding *Crisis Definition— Perception of Risk.* Once determined, this core factor is explored with regard to the *National Security Council's Role* and relevant indicators to assess *Level of Interagency Conflict.* At first glance, these relationships seem to be, and arguably are, depicted linearly. However, by unpacking the core factors to reveal their component parts—the indicators—it becomes evident that analyzing the core factors and their associated indicators proves anything but linear. Consequently, figure 9 serves as a guide to identify the relationships across the core factors under study so they can be conceptualized, researched, and analyzed.

To accomplish this systematic approach, we must illustrate the core factors identified in figure 9 to outline the proposed interaction between each indicator. Hence, while figure 8 maps the core factors as they most likely interact with one another during the policy-making process, figure 9 provides an operationalizable data framework for statistical analysis. It serves as the basis for the survey questionnaire that supported quantitative survey data collection and analysis.

Assigning Meaning to the Core Factors

In the classic sense, *operationalization* entails creating an "operational definition" that will "concretize the meanings of concepts . . . [laying] out the measuring procedures that provide criteria for the empirical application of concepts."[4] Operational definitions "tell *what to do* and *what to observe* in order to bring the phenomenon defined within the range of the researcher's experience" (emphasis in the original).[5] Taken independently of one another, defining each core factor and its dimensions yielded 44 observation variables that gave rise to 32 survey questions for data collection.[6]

Figure 8 portrays anticipated relationships across the core factors in a realistic yet dynamic fashion. The interaction of these factors is crucial to comprehending the nature of interagency conflict and its influence upon conflict termination policy development. Refer to the models in tandem with their descriptions to ensure complete understanding of the interaction between indicators and across these core factors. Using figure 8 and the *Level of Open Debate Surrounding Policy Options and Decisions* as an example, the ensuing discussion explains how this core factor interrelates with the others.

As conceived, *Level of Open Debate* influences four other core factors: *Crisis Definition—Perception of Risk, Organizational Communication, Agency's Decision-Making Profile*, and *Level of Interagency Conflict*. Simultaneously, three others (*NSC's Role, Agency's Decision-Making Profile*, and *Organizational Communication*) shape *Level of Open Debate*. These relationships appear plausible on the surface. By looking deeper into each of these core factors, however, we can concentrate upon the indicators that comprise each core factor as they relate to the interplay of factors across the framework.

Signed digraph models identify the indicators (also referred to as dimensions) and their hypothesized relationships within each core factor's parameters.[7] These factors represent policy makers' attitudes, perceptions, and beliefs—factors that influence their individual approaches to decision making in conjunction with their collective ability to develop conflict termination policy.

A signed digraph is merely a visual representation of an idea, using a form of cognitive mapping to develop the idea's essential elements.[8] Akin to an engineer's technical schemata or an executive's Pert chart, signed digraphs provide tools for researchers and analysts to envisage ideas and verify their hypotheses. The arrows depicted in these signed digraph models are unidirectional (i.e., one-headed), illustrating initial expectations regarding anticipated relationships between indicators. Although these signed digraphs do not preclude the existence of bi-directionality, they do depict the initial hypotheses investigated for each independent relationship.

Relatedly, the following signed digraphs reflect signs that indicate the presumed direction of the relationship between indicators (+ = congruous or parallel relationship; – = inverse relationship; and, ? = unknown). Each arrow-sign combination depicts hypothesized expectations regarding the patterns of indicators that influence core factors and, ultimately, the level of interagency conflict surrounding policy decisions. Additionally, throughout the signed digraph models, A's refer to *Agency's* and O's to *Other's*. In this manner, *A's* perceptions of *O's* interagency tactics translates to *Agency's* perceptions of *Other's* interagency tactics.

The six core factors serve as the fundamental concepts for analyzing interagency process dynamics, thereby providing one source for data collection—the survey asked policy makers to discuss their experiences in terms of these specific elements. The core factors reveal the crucial relationships these factors hypothesized; their postanalysis depictions reveal the data-generated findings. Bear in mind that the study regards the way(s) people perceive relations between agencies—and that these models capture those perceptions. Having begun the discussion of core factors with the *Level of Open Debate Surrounding Policy Options and Outcomes*, the conceptual unpacking of this signed digraph model illuminates this approach. When this modeling approach and its interpretation are clear, proceed clockwise around figure 8 to examine the five remaining core factors.

Figure 10 addresses the relationship between an agency and its perceptions regarding the attitudes and behaviors others adopt when engaging in crisis policy development. Central to this relational pattern is the level of open debate that takes

133

place between agencies involved in framing policy options and making decisions. The core factors include four of the following aspects of interagency relations that characterize communication patterns:

1. an agency's perceptions of other's conflict orientation—collaborative or competitive,

2. an agency's perceptions of other's level of self-interest—low or high,

3. the nature of departmental relations at the time of initial crisis definition—hostile or collaborative, and

4. the pattern that open debate takes as the crisis progresses over time—increases, remains constant, or decreases.[9]

This study suggests that an agency that views another agency's conflict orientation as "collaborative" will perceive the other agency's self-interest as "low." In this manner, an agency's

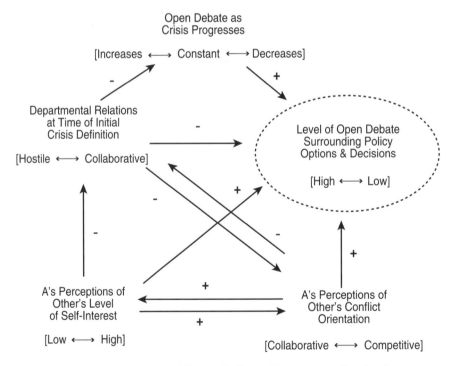

Figure 10. Level of Open Debate (Conceptualization)

134

perception of another agency's conflict orientation should influence directly the level of open debate.

An agency's perception of another agency's conflict orientation should affect the level of open debate indirectly through perceptions of the other's self-interest (see fig. 10, arrow pointing right to left, from conflict orientation to self-interest). In looking at these specific elements, the reverse also seems plausible. The agency's perception of the other's level of self-interest directly affects the level of open debate, yet it also shapes perceptions of conflict orientation as that element relates to the level of open debate (see fig. 10, arrow pointing left to right, from self-interest to conflict orientation).

Open debate in this instance does not necessarily conform to popular ideas concerning candid public debate. Rather, open debate here refers to the levels and types of communication that transpire across the interagency process as these agencies formulate intervention and termination policies. If relations across agencies are hostile at the time of initial crisis definition, we should expect to discover little or no open debate across the agencies. Accordingly, we would expect to find evidence of only limited exchanges across agencies—primarily those that reflect structural (or legal) requirements to communicate with one another. The existence and level of open debate are also likely to influence interdepartmental relations.

This study tests these hypotheses in exploratory fashion to determine which relationships are relevant with regard to the *Level of Open Debate* and the *Level of Interagency Conflict* surrounding crisis analysis. Facets include the desired end state, conflict termination criteria, and a strategy to achieve conflict termination. This approach facilitates testing to identify those elements and relationships that experienced policy makers view as significant in developing interagency conflict. This approach should expose relationships the conceptual framework failed to identify but that prove consequential when analyzing interagency dynamics.

In analyzing these findings, it becomes apparent that *Agency's Perceptions of Other's Conflict Orientation* serves as this core factor's central element (fig. 11). The findings reflecting reciprocal attitudes and behaviors (competition breeds

135

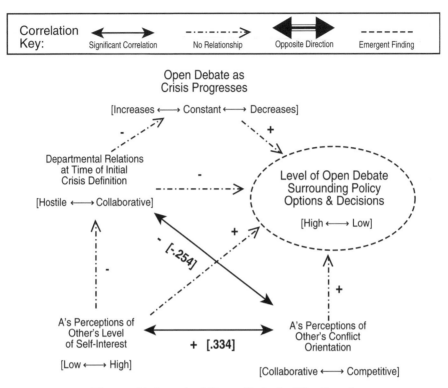

Figure 11. Level of Open Debate (Findings)

hostility; collaboration breeds collaboration) may have seemed obvious. Nevertheless, policy makers' experiences failed to validate the postulated relationship that perceptions of high self-interest promote hostile relationships (expected since actors would be inclined to withhold information to position themselves better vis-à-vis others within the interagency process). Plausible on the surface, the hypothesis failed to consider that a majority of these participants (78 percent) would classify *Other's Self-Interest* as high. In other words, it is clear that perceptions of high self-interest permeate the entire interagency community. Therefore, a high level of self-interest is accepted while developing policy and has little noticeable influence on interagency dynamics. Based upon this approach, the remaining signed digraph models are now depicted in turn, beginning with figure 12, *Crisis Definition—Perception of Risk.*

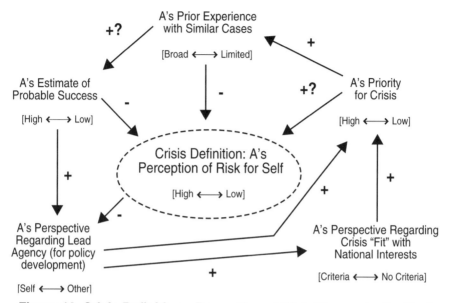

Figure 12. Crisis Definition—Perception of Risk (Conceptualization)

A fundamental assumption of this work is that past experience informs current views. This perspective extends from Tversky and Kahneman's research.[10] Referenced earlier, availability heuristics serve as parameters for interpreting events and for acting upon stimuli that resemble past experience. This core factor (fig. 13) deals exclusively with an agency's perceptions of risk for itself in terms of prior experience with similar cases, the crisis's fit with national interests, and the agency's perspective regarding its responsibility to lead the interagency process during policy development.

"Perception of risk for self" is referenced in bureaucratic values, not in terms of physical risk. Study participants were asked to reflect upon risk in terms of anticipated future engagements—would their actions in the current policy process magnify or detract from their political currency during an impending policy-making process? Would their actions adversely affect job security? The survey instrument, in conjunction with a question that directly addressed perception of risk for self, operationalized these three following indicators: (1) the agency's prior experience with similar cases, (2) the agency's

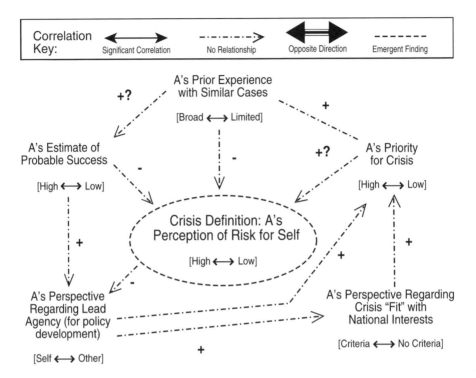

Figure 13. Crisis Definition—Perception of Risk (Findings)

perspective regarding lead agency for policy development, and (3) the agency's perspective regarding the "fit" with national interests. The survey instrument did not address the remaining two indicators—the agency's estimate of probable success and the agency's priority for the crisis. Rather, interviewees explored this issue via the open-ended questions following survey completion as a means to clarify the purpose of the questions and to reinforce response validity and reliability. For the purposes of quantitative analysis, however, the research omitted these two factors.

The fact that data confirmed none of the hypothesized relationships proves curious. It seems obvious, even without the benefit of analysis and a substantial body of literature, that perceptions of risk would shape an agency's policy perspective.[11] Logically, a policy maker's prior experience with similar cases would condition estimates of future probable success and shape perspectives regarding lead agent identification.[12] This element, in conjunction with the agency's perspective regarding the crisis's fit with national interests, should have determined the agency's priority for the crisis and should shape perceptions of risk for that agency. However, the data indicate that no relationships exist among these factors, nor do any exist with regard to the indicator's independent linkage with the core factor itself. For instance, 85.5 percent (59/69) of the study participants related that their agency possessed a broad-based experience with crises such as the Persian Gulf, Somalia, Rwanda, and Bosnia. The original model hypothesized that a "broad" experience base would equate to a "low" perception of risk for self because the agency would benefit from lessons learned, lending confidence and comfort to decision-making processes for similar cases. But the data did not confirm this hypothesis, leading this researcher to rely upon the interview analysis to clarify this lack of relationship.

Analysis to this point indicates that the data clearly supported many constitutive assumptions; yet, this postanalysis signed digraph indicates that data also failed to validate others—and these nonvalidated relationships are of little significance in illuminating sources of interagency conflict.[13] While the foregoing discussions of these two core factors entail a level of complexity in their own right, the anticipated relationships supporting organizational communication take on a life of their own.

One of the most evident influences on interagency relations during crisis policy development is the way in which agencies communicate with one another. Figure 14 begins to address "organizational cultural" issues, but remains limited to those issues that relate to interagency dynamics as affected by cultural issues. Hence, the core factor's dimensions include aspects of culture (department's leadership style, departmental structure, and agency's perceived penalty for failure) that create a pattern of communication framing the interagency tactics an agency employs.

At first glance, the complexity presented through figure 15 has the potential to overwhelm even accomplished statisticians. Yet, examination of the signed digraph model distin-

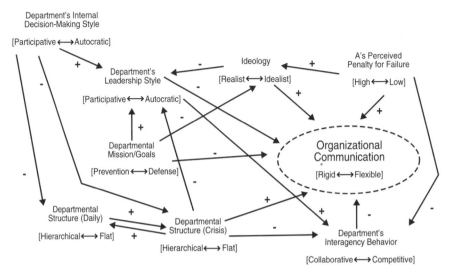

Figure 14. Organizational Communication (Conceptualization)

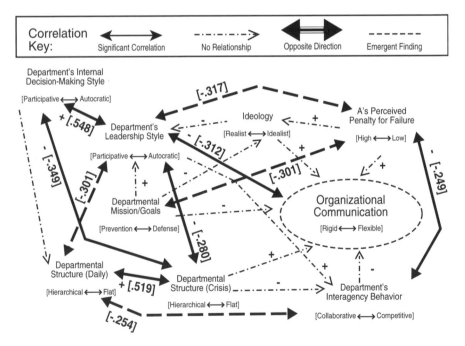

Figure 15. Organizational Communication I (Findings)

guishes the most obvious emergent finding. Diagrammatically, this core factor's point of convergence should be reframed—in terms of Department's leadership style, not organizational communication. The second most valuable indicator within this core factor is Department's internal decision-making style. Given the strong correlation between leadership style and decision-making style, this makes logical sense and is supported by the data. This appreciation of organizational communication enhances our understanding of the fourth factor, agency's policy-making approach.

Implied by its subtitle, this core factor (fig. 16) explores the tactics an agency employs when interacting with others across the interagency process. Although numerous elements influence interagency tactics, the five indicators depicted in the model are proposed as most important. This core factor incorporates the interplay of the agency's ideas of its own policy process, planning focus, and perceptions of accountability, in tandem with its beliefs about its capacity to influence the policy

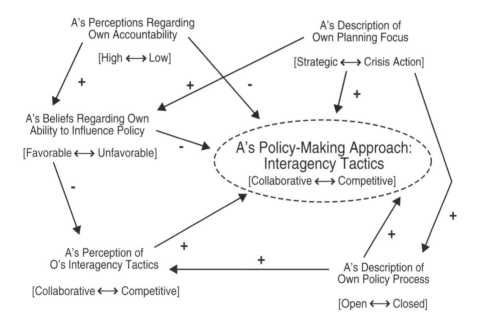

Figure 16. Agency's Policy-Making Approach: Interagency Tactics (Conceptualization)

process as well as its perceptions regarding others' inter-agency tactics (fig. 17).

From a macro perspective, this postanalysis signed digraph model indicates that open policy processes that encourage reciprocal collaboration favorably affect an agency's ability to influence policy. With the analysis of this core factor complete, we can now proceed to the next-to-last factor, agency's decision-making profile: department explores innovative ideas. These dimensions should determine an agency's policy-making approach, signaling whether it tends to interact collaboratively or competitively.

An agency's willingness and capacity to explore innovative ideas at all levels within the bureaucracy signals its receptivity to participative leadership. Much like organizational communica-

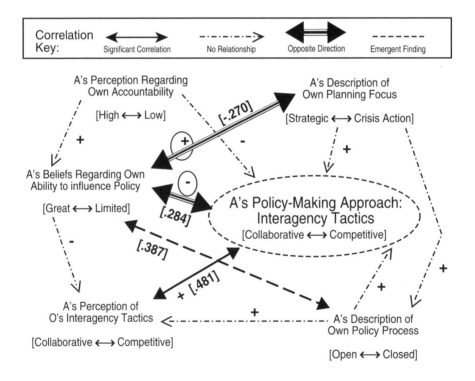

Figure 17. Agency's Policy-Making Approach: Interagency Tactics (Findings)

142

tion (see fig. 14), this core factor (fig. 18) includes elements of organizational culture. For example, educational background appears to influence individuals' skills in analyzing crises in a specific way. A hypothesis that supports this assumption posits that a more technically oriented individual (someone schooled or trained in the hard sciences) will be less likely to propose innovative solutions. He or she will require the types of details that are rarely determinable in social crises and will look for empirically verifiable cause-and-effect relationships when evaluating courses of action.

An individual with a humanities or social science background will be more likely to "see around corners," recognizing that the causes of social conflict are complex and that one conflict is usually interlocked with others in interdependent ways.[14] Hence, a hypothesis for this relationship would speculate that an individual with a humanities or social science educational background will have a great propensity to propose innovative solutions.

As an additional facet of organizational culture, it is important to note that this core factor explores the relationship between individuals' willingness to propose innovative solutions

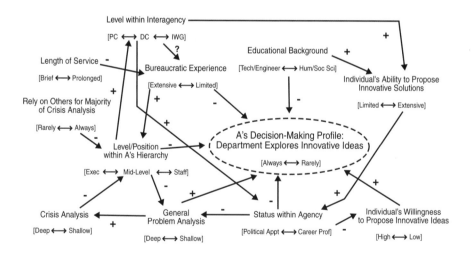

Figure 18. Agency's Decision-Making Profile: Department Explores Innovative Ideas (Conceptualization)

in connection with the department's exploration of those innovative ideas. These factors appear to be correlated directly; that is, a high willingness to propose innovative ideas will lead to the department's exploration of such ideas. These dimensions, however, remain bound by the National Security Council policy-making process.

Figure 19 confirms several critical relationships regarding an agency's decision-making profile. The data failed to support those proposed relationships, however, calling into question the assumptions regarding this core factor's initial operationalization. Merely glancing at the modified signed digraph model provides clues regarding critical elements that share more in common with one's position within the agency than the agency's decision-making profile. Therefore, interpretations of this core factor should focus upon departmental leadership in terms of crisis analysis and innovative solutions. Drawing these tentative conclusions enables us to move forward to NSC's role in the policy-making process.

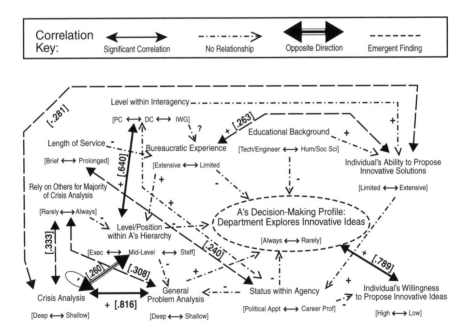

Figure 19. Agency's Decision-Making Profile: Department Explores Innovative Ideas (Findings)

The US National Security Council System represents critical links in the interagency process. The NSC Staff oversees the interagency process as it monitors implementation of presidential decisions as well as those that do not require presidential action. While the preceding five core factors addressed interagency dynamics across all actors, this core factor focuses directly upon the chief actor of the process. Thus, figure 20 represents agencies' perceptions of their ability to influence the NSC and their perceptions of other agencies' abilities to affect policy development. These relationships are expressed and modeled in terms of both formal and informal access and influence.

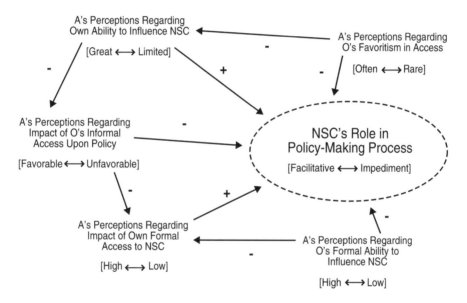

Figure 20. NSC's Role in the Policy-Making Process (Conceptualization)

The postanalysis signed digraph model (fig. 21) depicts no emergent findings among the six indicators. However, the impact of the NSCS, as an agency having the opportunity to control the policy process and shape an individual's ability to influence policy development, cannot be overemphasized. Thus, the NSC's role in the policy-making process demands further exploration.

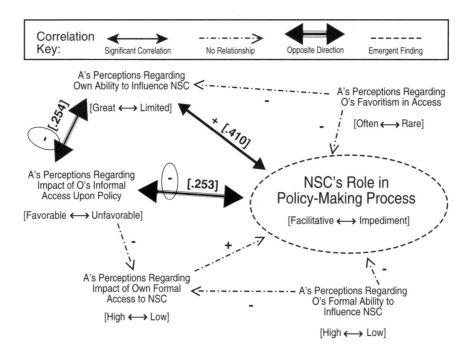

Figure 21. NSC's Role in the Policy-Making Process (Findings)

Indicators, the Hierarchical Model, and Data

The core factors represent the critical components in constructing a new understanding of interagency conflict. In reviewing the signed digraph models, the complexity of the process becomes evident. Many of the indicators identified within specific core factors have the potential to influence others while being influenced by them. However, by treating each digraph's dimensions as indicators of the hierarchical model's core factors, it becomes possible to bring the analysis back to a model-building focus and to a heuristic approach rather than a causal approach. Hence, the original figure 9 appears as figure 22, with the indicators mapped directly onto the core factors to serve as a guide and as a framework for data collection. Ultimately, this framework provides the basis for the officials' estimates of interagency conflict.

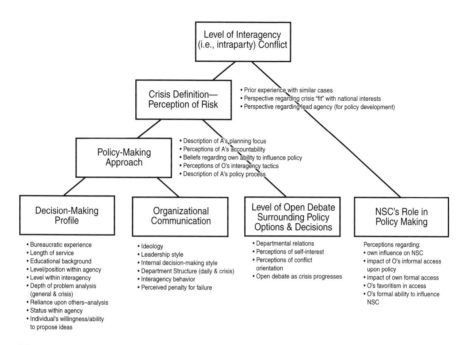

Figure 22. Hierarchical Model: A Framework for Data Collection (with Indicators)

It bears repeating that the interaction of the variables identified herein does not occur in linear fashion. They are presented in a static depiction to operationalize the Basic Conceptual Framework (see fig. 8) guiding this study. As with much of social science research, the real-world interaction of these factors occurs at such a pace and with such extensive interdependence that their isolation proves impossible. Only through such initial conceptualization, however, can we begin to discover the linkages across critical factors. Any patterns that emerge are likely to illuminate further the connection between interagency conflict and the development of conflict termination policy. The central argument is that these six core factors should help theorists and practitioners devise a more comprehensive awareness of interagency conflict and its causes. So, what exactly do these postanalysis signed digraphs begin to tell us about interagency conflict?

Preliminary Conclusions

The foregoing discussion reveals the complexity related to conceptualizing, operationalizing, and analyzing interagency dynamics. A brief summary of the signed digraph model analysis, a discussion regarding the demographic trends identified according to policy-maker stratification, and an introduction of emergent themes that require further exploration through the interview analysis are now warranted.

Core Factor Analysis

Analysis of these six core factors revealed that perceptions remain a critical element in shaping interagency dynamics. To capture these complex findings succinctly, table 2 summarizes the confirmed relationships through the construction of "If . . . , then . . . " propositions. The scaling order equates the first response of the "if" condition with the first response of the "then" condition; the responses enclosed in parentheses for relationships denote correlations. For simplicity, this table summarizes these relationships only once; the reverse relationships remain valid, but the number of statements corresponds with the number of statistically significant correlations. Thus, since figure 10 depicts two significant correlations, table 2 identifies two relationships supported by the questionnaire data.

From a macro perspective, the views of these informed participants tentatively indicate that *communication* and *leadership* play the most crucial roles in shaping interagency dynamics and organizational cultures. The findings suggest that absence of effective communication enables negative stereotypes to affect interagency relations adversely, tending to create or intensify interagency conflict (see fig. 11). Through open communication, decision makers could explain their behaviors and their rationales for high levels of self-interest. Such communication could generate greater understanding across interagency actors and dampen interagency conflict's debilitating effects. Relatedly, leadership appears to play a defining role in developing patterns of organizational communication.

In departments wherein leadership styles facilitate participation, organizational communication patterns tend to be

148

Table 2
Correlational Summary by Core Factor*

Core Factor	IF . . . , THEN . . .
Figure 11 Level of Open Debate	IF agency's perceptions of other's conflict orientation are *competitive (collaborative)*, THEN . . . • departmental relations at time of initial crisis definition are *hostile (collaborative)*. • agency's perceptions of other's level of self-interest are *high (low)*.
Figure 15 Organizational Communication	IF department's leadership style is participative *(autocratic)*, THEN . . . • department's internal decision-making style is *participative (autocratic)*. • departmental structure (daily) is *flat (hierarchical)*. • departmental structure (crisis) is *flat (hierarchical)*. • organizational communication is *flexible (rigid)*. • agency's penalty for failure is low *(high)*. IF departmental structure (crisis) is *hierarchical (flat)*, THEN . . . • departmental structure (daily) is *hierarchical (flat)*. • department's internal decision-making style is *autocratic (participative)*. IF department's interagency behavior is *collaborative (competitive)*, THEN . . . • departmental structure (crisis) is *flat (hierarchical)*. • agency's perceived penalty for failure is *low (high)*. IF agency's perceived penalty for failure is *high (low)*, THEN . . . • departmental mission/goals are oriented toward *defense (prevention)*.
Figure 17 Agency's Policy-Making Approach	IF agency's beliefs regarding own ability to influence policy are *great (limited)*, THEN . . . • agency's description of own planning focus is *crisis action (strategic)*. • agency's policy-making approach: interagency tactics are *collaborative (competitive)*. • agency's description of own policy process is *open (closed)*. IF agency's perception of other's interagency tactics is *collaborative (competitive)*, THEN . . . • agency's policy-making approach: interagency tactics are *collaborative (competitive)*.
Figure 19 Agency's Decision-Making Profile	IF crisis analysis is deep (shallow), THEN . . . • individual's ability to propose innovative solutions is *extensive (limited)*. • rely on others for majority of crisis analysis *rarely (always)*. • level/position within agency's hierarchy is *executive (mid/staff)*. • general problem analysis is *deep (shallow)*. IF general problem analysis is *deep (shallow)*, THEN . . . • rely on others for majority of crisis analysis *rarely (always)*.

Table 2—(Continuation)

Core Factor	IF . . . , THEN . . .
	IF length of service is *brief (prolonged)*, THEN . . . • status within agency is *political appointee (career professional)*. IF level/position within agency's hierarchy is *executive (mid/staff)*, THEN . . . • level within interagency is *Principals Committee [PC] Deputies Committee/Interagency Working Group [DC/IWG]*. IF bureaucratic experience is *extensive (limited)*, THEN . . . • individual's ability to propose innovative solutions is *limited (extensive)*. IF individual's willingness to propose innovative ideas is *high (low)*, THEN . . . • agency's decision-making profile: Department explores innovative ideas *always (rarely)*.
Figure 21 NSC's Role in the Policy-Making Process	IF agency's perceptions regarding own ability to influence NSC are *great (limited)*, THEN . . . • agency's perceptions regarding impact of other's informal access upon policy are *favorable (unfavorable)*. • NSC's role in policy-making process is *facilitative (impediment)*. IF agency's perceptions regarding impact of other's informal access upon policy are *favorable (unfavorable)*, THEN . . . • NSC's role in the policy-making process is *facilitative (impediment)*.

Note: Figure 12, Crisis Definition—Perception of Risk (Conceptualization), reflected no statistically significant relationships and is not included in this summary table.

flexible (see fig. 15). By allowing others to participate in decision making, leaders create an organizational culture wherein individuals perceive that the penalty for failure (for them professionally) is low; these individuals tend to think proactively about crisis prevention. Creating this cooperative organizational culture is associated with collaborative interagency behaviors; when reversed, these conditions prompt interagency competition. As these leadership dimensions shape internal organizational communications, they influence an agency's decision-making approach.

Although not tested stringently through this analysis, the data revealed that when organizational communication is flexible (see fig. 15), crisis analysis tends to be deep (see fig. 19).[15]

Executives characterize their crisis analysis capability as deep and contend that an individual's ability to propose innovative solutions remains extensive (see fig. 19). Policy makers described their general problem analysis as deep and reported that they rarely relied upon others for a majority of their crisis analysis effort. Political appointees' lengths of service tend to be brief, and top-ranking executives serve as members of the interagency principals committee (PC). Likewise, the second- or third-ranking individuals serve as members of the deputies committee (DC), while staff members serve as members of interagency working groups. It appears that when an individual is willing to propose innovative ideas, his or her department explores those innovative ideas. However, it is interesting to note that those with extensive bureaucratic experience are *least able* to propose innovative solutions. This limitation may emanate from a deep appreciation of interagency inertia, or it may be that those having extensive experience perceive that the bureaucracy's structure limits their ability (not willingness) to propose innovative solutions. Specifically, career professionals recognize that political appointees serve in the most influential executive positions and make decisions for their organization throughout the interagency process. In this manner, those with the most extensive experience (career professionals) may feel that they have the least influence on their agency's policy-making approach.

Agency representatives, who characterize their abilities to influence policy as great, described their planning approach as "crisis action oriented" and their policy processes as open (see fig. 17). Such individuals claimed that other's interagency tactics tended to be collaborative and that they responded with reciprocal collaborative behaviors. The characterization of an agency's ability to influence policy as great also held import for perceptions of the NSCS's role in policy making. When an agency member perceived that he or she possessed great influence on the NSCS, the official characterized the influence of other's informal access as favorable. These individuals believed the NSCS should grant access to anyone who—irrespective of governmental or nongovernmental affiliation—may contribute potential solutions for the crisis. When they grant such access, agencies assert that the NSCS facilitates conflict termination policy development. Again, these perspectives indicate that open communication remains one vital element to effective policy making.

Together, these findings indicate that the analysis of interagency dynamics remains complex and that interrelated perceptions, attitudes, and beliefs shape these dynamics. It appears that leadership plays a crucial role in developing cooperative organizational cultures, open communication, and collaborative interagency behaviors. A relationship also appears to exist between these positive dimensions of interagency dynamics and the capacity of individuals to analyze crises deeply and to propose innovative solutions. Finally, the agencies' collective preference for uninhibited NSCS access indicates that decision makers value open communication as the crucial element in effective policy making.

Before outlining the emergent themes that help inform the next phase of analysis, we should consider a few words regarding demographic category findings. These findings are classified according to executive department, one's level within the interagency process, and the case referenced. They illuminate interesting interagency process trends.

Demographic Trends

Differences across the three classifications make apparent that the most pronounced variation exists across the three levels of actors. Recognition of these differences in this impressionistic yet methodical way provides a logical connection with this inquiry's second analytic phase. It creates a link between the analysis performed throughout this chapter and the forthcoming qualitative analysis reported in chapters 6–8.

When assessing differences across departments, the greatest variation existed regarding perceptions of open debate, the use of criteria to prioritize crises, and who conducts a majority of crisis analysis.[16] In the first instance, the White House/NSC and State Department contended that open debate decreased as the crisis progresses, Defense Department asserted that it remained constant, and the CIA felt that open debate increased. This suggests that debate diminished as policy development and implementation became routinized as the crisis proceeds from its initial outbreak to a point wherein decision makers became more focused on departmental operations and less oriented toward strategic policy development. This would also account for the increase in debate by the CIA as its analysts would gather increased amounts of intelligence and convey that information to its functional agencies. Likewise, the Office of the Director of Central Intelligence (ODCI) would take on an expanded information dissemination role within the NSCS. This issue regarding information exchange via open debate requires further exploration through the qualitative analysis. Just as interesting is the dichotomy between State and Defense Departments regarding the use of criteria to prioritize crises.

Although the White House/NSC responses included the range of options from "does" to "does not" as criteria sets, the White House/NSC study participants replied that their use of a criteria set "depends" on other factors (e.g., presidential attention and domestic politics). The Defense Department's responses also covered the range but claimed their department tended to use other criteria (e.g., national interests). The CIA's participants also claimed their agency applied specific criteria. In contrast, the State Department indicated clearly that it did not use criteria to prioritize crises. This difference between the State and Defense Departments highlights one critical area in which organizational cultures differ and may be important for agency views regarding the use of force. It, therefore, demands further exploration through the impending qualitative analysis.

This brings us to the final broad-based difference illuminated through this analysis: views regarding whether the participants conducted a majority of the crisis analysis. The interesting aspect of this finding is that only State Department officials reported they relied on someone else for a majority of the crisis analysis fewer than 25 percent of the time. This raises issues related to interagency communication and information exchange—issues the qualitative analysis should explore.

These three differences regarding open debate, criteria sets, and crisis analysis provide areas for further analysis since they suggest the existence of an organizational cleavage that may frustrate interagency dynamics. Divergence in perception related to informant levels within the interagency process accompanied these departmental differences.

Disparate views exist regarding several dimensions of USG interagency dynamics, including other's level of self-interest, open debate, agency's experience, department's political ideology, organizational communication, department's decision-making style, nature of the policy process, perceptions of other's interagency tactics, and perceptions regarding departmental influence on the NSCS. While specific summaries of each are not presented here, there are intriguing similarities in perspectives between the principals and deputies. There are also apparent major differences between these two levels and the interagency working group.[17] These cleavages generate questions regarding decision makers' perspectives regarding leadership and decision-making styles, the role of prior experience, the nature of organizational communication, and perceptions of other's interagency behaviors. Most importantly, however, these differences across interagency actors raise questions concerning departmental influence on the NSCS. Principals believe their respective departments exercise great influence, and deputies perceive departmental influence as predominantly significant but acknowledge that such influence remains contingent on other factors. In fact, interagency working group members' perspectives regarding influence covered the entire range from great to limited. Together with the issues identified earlier, this difference emphasizes those at the highest level of policy making believe their influence is significant— these are the political appointees who serve as the interagency principals and key deputies. Conversely, those who serve at the lowest level (career bureaucrats, foreign service officers, and military officials) view their influence as mixed, indicating that influence remains contingent upon other factors beyond process structure. This finding demands further exploration, but before proceeding to the qualitative analysis phase, we will examine findings in terms of case specificity that illuminate intriguing patterns.

Although the number of study participants in each category remains too dissimilar to make authoritative comparisons at this juncture, the quantitative data unveiled similarities and differences across indicators within the core factors according to case pairings. Three distinct groupings emerged: the Persian Gulf, the Bosnia crisis, and the interagency experience.

The Persian Gulf and interagency experience groupings shared similar findings in terms of perceptions of departmental interaction, open debate, department's political ideology, planning focus, and the individual's ability to propose innovative solutions; the Bosnia case provided less consistency. After almost 200 hours of interviews, one explanation for this similarity arose from a structural condition. Those involved in the Persian Gulf process at the interagency working group level possessed almost 10 years more experience and were positioned organizationally to develop interagency dynamics in ways that reflect their earlier experiences. These individuals were not positioned to exercise this type of influence during the Bosnia policy process. Hence, officials recreated the organizational dynamics they experienced during that period. Moreover, their subordinates now emulated them, a phenomenon reflected strongly throughout the interviews. This pairing could also be explained through an issue related to timing.

The dimensions of the Bosnia crisis may be dissimilar to the pairing because the interagency developed policy during a new administration's initial weeks when newly appointed decision makers and other actors had yet to establish efficient working relations. This precept may be especially valid for departmental relations and open debate as these dimensions involve communication patterns. Also, the installation of new actors may account for perspectives regarding department's political ideology. Specifically, the Clinton administration may have broken with the Bush administration's realpolitik perspective early in its first term but moved toward a more moderate realist ideology in its second term. In similar fashion, a learning process may have exposed the need to plan for a longer vision during Clinton's second term. Hence, while the administration's planning focus during Bosnia proved one of crisis action response, second-term Clinton administration decision makers (participants with interagency experience from 1996–98) reflected a move toward strategic planning.

155

The idea that the ability to generate innovative solutions is becoming more limited, according to the interagency experience demographic. This may reflect that principals and deputies became more comfortable with making decisions—or perhaps they recognized their role as that of making those decisions. Participants at lower levels within the decision-making process may have perceived this as an action that limited innovation.

These inferences demand further examination regarding the role leadership, decision-making style, and prior experience play in shaping interagency dynamics, as well as the ways in which these individuals define their roles within the interagency process. This last finding may account for the transformation of relations within organizations as depicted by the second classification where interagency experience differs from the Persian Gulf and Bosnia crisis pairing.

The Persian Gulf and Bosnia crisis shared similarities regarding organizational communication, department's internal decision-making style, and agency's perceptions regarding their ability to influence the NSCS. In the first instance, as noted above, an enhanced comfort level with one's responsibilities may create an environment wherein some lower-ranking individuals perceive themselves as less influential. If departmental principals (and deputies) make decisions, this may create the perception that organizational communication is less flexible than in the past. This does not fit with the second finding in this pairing, namely, decision-making style.

The quantitative data reflected that those with interagency experience classified department's decision-making style as participative; yet study participants for the Persian Gulf and Bosnia crisis characterized their departmental decision-making styles as including both participative and autocratic dimensions. Finally, those with Persian Gulf and Bosnia crisis experience perceived their department's influence on the NSCS as great, whereas those within the interagency experience grouping characterized their influence as great but moving toward limited. In the signed digraph analysis presented earlier, those who believe they possess great ability to influence the NSCS characterized the NSC's role in policy making as facilitative. This perspective regarding the NSC's role highlights the final similarity across these cases, illuminating a pairing between the Bosnia crisis and interagency experience.

The Bosnia crisis and interagency experience cases shared similarities across one dimension, namely, NSC's role in the policy-making process. It follows that the gradual shift in a department's ability to influence the NSCS from "great" (Persian Gulf) to "limited" (interagency experience) would mirror perspectives concerning NSCS procedures, from "facilitative" (Persian Gulf) to being an "impediment" to policy making (Bosnia crisis and interagency experience). These findings underscore the necessity of exploring further the influence of leadership, communication, and agency roles on the policy process.

Summarizing findings according to demographic classification proves helpful at this juncture. Table 3 lists the indicators identified as the most divergent according to *Department*, *Level within the Interagency Process*, and *Historical Case*. This visual comparison also illuminates the indicators identified as different for two or more cases (e.g., *Open Debate [Generally]* and *Department's Political Ideology*). Keeping these demographic patterns in mind will facilitate an understanding of the qualitative data analysis.

This analysis provides the basis for analyzing the qualitative data in two ways. First, recognition that the greatest differences exist across the interagency levels (principal, deputy, or interagency working group) provides the basis for organizing the qualitative analysis. Second, the differences related to leadership, agency roles, communication, decision-making styles, use of criteria to prioritize crises, and influence within the policy-making process provide a baseline, in conjunction with table 4, for identifying themes during qualitative data coding. With these points in mind, let us proceed to a brief discussion concerning emergent themes.

Emergent Themes

Given the magnitude of these conclusions, it may prove useful to summarize those findings that should be explored in future research (table 4). Noting that the second phase of investigation relies upon inductive generation of themes from interview data, recording those themes the quantitative data unveiled provides a

Table 3
Summary of Findings: Demographic Stratification

Indicator	Department	Level	Case
Open Debate as Crisis Progresses	X		
Open Debate (Generally)		X	X
Criteria Set	X		
Lead Agent (Self)	X		
Department's Mission	X		
Department's Political Ideology	X	X	X
Majority of Crisis Analysis	X		
Perceptions of Other's Self-Interest		X	
Agency's Experience		X	
Organizational Communication		X	X
Department's Internal Decision-Making Style		X	X
Description of Own Policy Process		X	
Perceptions of Other's Interagency Tactics		X	
Department's Influence on NSC		X	
Planning Focus			X
Individual's Ability to Propose Innovative Solutions			X
NSC's Role in Policy-Making Process			X
Agency's Perceptions Regarding Own Ability to Influence NSC			X
Departmental Relations at Time of Initial Crisis Definition			X

Table 4
Emergent Themes Requiring Further Exploration

Emergent Theme	Issue
Perceptions of Risk	• In what ways does past experience shape conceptions of risk for future engagements? • Does past experience provide a means to evaluate courses of action as a means to diminish risk? • How do perceptions of risk shape ideas regarding penalty for failure as well as organizational communication?
Intervention Criteria	• How do the actors frame national interests? • Who defines whether an issue is related to national interests? • Why do the actors frame criteria sets as metrics for evaluating operational missions vice principles to guide policy development?
Information Exchange across the Interagency	• In what ways does increased perceptions of penalty for failure lead to rigid communication? • In what ways does participative decision making make communication more flexible? • Why do those with open policy processes believe they have a great influence on policy development? • What role does the protection of bureaucratic equities play in information exchange?
Leadership and Interagency Dynamics	• What role do leaders play in creating perceptions of risk for both their organizations and its members? • What do leaders within hierarchically structured organizations "do" that makes their people feel as if they have a high degree of participation in decision making? • Why do executives, who have the least bureaucratic experience, believe they conduct deep analyses vis-à-vis the specialists (i.e., the staff members)?
Perceptions of Other's Interagency Tactics	• How salient are notions of reciprocity? Do the actors recognize reciprocal behaviors in the midst of crisis policy making? • Do actors see others (or self) as taking active measures to protect their equities during policy making?
Roles and Missions	• What role does the NSC Staff play in shaping the overall interagency dynamic?

logical starting point. The analysis generated 14 unanticipated relationships; these are grouped into six emergent themes. Discussed later within the context of the qualitative analysis, table 4 provides a snapshot of issues the quantitative analysis raised but left unresolved. These issues do not present an entirely new research problem. Quite the opposite, in fact—grounded theory methodology generates additional questions for exploration through the remainder of the research. This book does not deal with these issues in the form of research questions per se; nonetheless, they provide additional themes to stimulate the upcoming qualitative data analysis.

Complementary Analyses

This chapter constructed the bridge between the academic theory of group choice and the researchable practice of real-world interagency decision making. Employing a twofold strategy of complementary quantitative and qualitative analyses brings into focus interagency conflict's effects on conflict termination policy development. Quantitative (survey) data tested the original assumptions and hypotheses depicted through the six core factors. In related fashion, the impending qualitative (interview) data analysis provides contextual richness for the correlation coefficients identified as significant within each core factor. Hence, they simultaneously address the specifics of the ability of the interagency process to develop conflict termination policy for the cases under investigation.

The remainder of the book builds upon the interim conclusions presented here by analyzing the interviews conducted with select government officials (see app. A). Using an inductive coding process to examine qualitative data (creating the picture from the bottom up rather than overlaying a prestructured design from the top down), interview analysis revealed 26 interrelated factors.[18] This chapter highlighted concerns related to six of these themes (risk, criteria, information exchange, leadership, interagency tactics, roles and missions; see table 4) as issues in need of further exploration through the qualitative analysis. These themes are classified as ideas dealing with the ways in which (1) dynamic themes related to policy making shape the interagency process dynamics and policy outcomes, (2) contextual parameters serve as boundaries for the policy process, and (3) crosscutting effects influence both dynamic themes and contextual parameters. Together with the survey results, these themes bring into sharp relief the nature of the interagency processes employed during the Persian Gulf War and Bosnia crisis. On the surface, a great deal of interplay occurs between these two categories throughout the policy-making process. In-depth analysis revealed that the policy makers' experiences confirm overarching (macro) and supporting (micro) themes based upon interrelationships among the original 26 factors.

In light of the complexity of this approach, there is utility in modeling these themes to portray their cumulative interrelated influence. As illustrated in figure 23, this model depicts the interaction between those factors—*Contextual Parameters, Dynamic Themes*, and *Crosscutting Effects*—that mold the interagency process during conflict termination policy development.[19]

The ensuing three chapters deal specifically with one overarching (macro) theme, explaining in detail the confluence of its supporting (micro) themes. Chapter 6 begins to explain this alternative approach by visualizing the relationships between

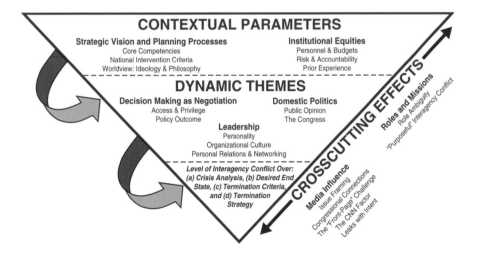

Figure 23. Interagency Conflict: Contextual Parameters, Dynamic Themes, and Crosscutting Effects

the *Dynamic Themes* and *Contextual Parameters*, in concert with the *Crosscutting Effects*. As figure 23 indicates, the *Dynamic Themes* directly influence the level of interagency conflict during termination policy development. They are therefore discussed as the first category of emergent themes (refer to fig. 23's middle area). These themes concern the ways in which interagency dynamics influence interagency conflict in terms of *Leadership*, *Decision Making as Negotiation*, and *Domestic Politics*. Figure 23 also illustrates that *Strategic Vision and Planning Processes* and *Institutional Equities* influence the *Dynamic Themes* relationships that are examined through chapter 7. Finally, chapter 8 unveils the *Crosscutting Effects* of *Roles and Missions* and *Media Influence*, discussing the ways in which these emergent themes influence both *Dynamic Themes* and *Contextual Parameters*. In the end, this influence serves as another factor in generating interagency conflict over termination policy development.

Notes

1. For the complete discourse regarding the statistical analyses involved in this study, see Vicki J. Rast, "Interagency Conflict and United States Intervention Policy: Toward a Bureaucratic Model of Conflict Termination" (PhD diss., George Mason University, 1999), 197–410. The reporting of these findings is simplified here to ensure their meaning does not get lost in the numbers.

2. Anselm L. Strauss and Juliet M. Corbin, *Basics of Qualitative Research: Grounded Theory Procedures and Techniques* (Newbury Park, Calif.: Sage Publications, 1990), 62; and see also H. Blumer, *Symbolic Interaction* (Englewood Cliffs, N.J.: Prentice-Hall, 1969).

3. The construct and impetus for this approach came from Prof. Daniel Druckman. See also Daniel Druckman and Justin Green, *Political Stability in the Philippines: Framework and Analysis*, ed. Karen A. Feste, vol. 22, *Monograph Series in World Affairs* (Taiwan, ROC: University of Denver [Colorado Seminary], 1986).

4. See also Chava Frankfort-Nachmias and David Nachmias, *Research Methods in the Social Sciences*, 4th ed. (New York: St. Martin's Press, 1992).

5. Ibid.

6. Special appreciation goes to two colleagues—Susan Allen Nan and Ilana Shapiro. They independently piloted the interview schedule, providing advice and ideas toward creating a more feasible interview technique, the one ultimately employed throughout this work. Additionally my gratitude extends to the Delphi panel participants. The panel consisted of three of the

four dissertation committee members and three student colleagues, two of whom participated in the pilot while the third refined this research throughout its conceptual development. I would like to again thank Susan Allen Nan, Ilana Shapiro, and John Windmueller for their participation in this panel. For further information regarding the Delphi technique, see also Colin Robson, *Real World Research: A Resource for Social Scientists and Practitioner-Researchers* (Oxford, United Kingdom: Blackwell, 1993).

7. Developed within graph theory and applied across multiple fields, the signed digraph model is an excellent tool for brainstorming relations across several factors as they influence a concept under study. I am grateful to Prof. Christopher Mitchell for introducing this technique to me during coursework at the Institute for Conflict Analysis and Resolution, George Mason University, Fairfax, Virginia. For rigorous presentations of signed digraph theory, see Russell W. Belk, "It's the Thought That Counts: A Signed Digraph Analysis of Gift-Giving," *Journal of Consumer Research* 3, no. 3 (1976): 155–62; see also Gary Chartrand, Linda Lesniak, and Mehdi Behzad, *Graphs & Digraphs* (Monterey, Calif.: Wadsworth & Brooks/Cole Advanced Books & Software, 1986); Patrick Doreian and Andrej Mrvar, "A Partitioning Approach to Structural Balance," *Social Networks* 18, no. 2 (1996): 149–68; and see also Hian Poh Yap, *Some Topics in Graph Theory* (Cambridge & New York: Cambridge University Press, 1986).

8. For an extensive explanation of signed digraphs, see Russell W. Belk, "It's the Thought That Counts," 155–62; see also Chartrand, Lesniak, and Behzad, *Graphs & Digraphs*; Doreian and Mrvar, "A Partitioning Approach to Structural Balance," 149–68; and see also Yap, *Some Topics in Graph Theory*.

9. In the tradition of grounded theory, I originally did not identify the pattern of debate over time as one of the dimensions relating to this core factor. Rather, this element emerged from conversations with professionals who noted that the change in the pattern over the cycle of the conflict is perhaps more telling than the level of open debate at the beginning of the crisis. Thus, this element emerged as a concept requiring further exploration, and I added to it the survey instrument after developing the original conceptual framework. Again, I would like to point out that this is one of the crucial strengths of conducting research on social conflict through this methodology: It demands that the researcher employ a recursive process to incorporate emerging concepts as the analyst "gets smarter" regarding the problem being explored.

10. Amos Tversky and Daniel Kahneman, "Judgment under Uncertainty: Heuristics and Biases," *Science* 185, no. 4157 (1974): 1124–31.

11. See, for example, Kenneth J. Arrow, "Risk Perception in Psychology and Economics," *Economic Inquiry* 20 (1982): 1–9; see also C. F. Camerer, "Individual Decision Making," in *The Handbook of Experimental Economics*, ed. J. H. Kagel and A. E. Roth (Princeton, N.J.: Princeton University Press, 1995); Steven R. Elliott and Michael McKee, "Collective Risk Decisions in the Presence of Many Risks," *KYKLOS* 48, no. 4 (1995): 541–45; Vincent Follert, "Risk Analysis: Its Application to Argumentation and Decision-Making,"

Journal of the American Forensic Association 18, no. 2 (1981): 99–108; Irving L. Janis and Leon Mann, "Coping with Decisional Conflict," *American Scientist* 64, no. 6 (1976): 657–67; Robert Jervis, "Political Implications of Loss Aversion. Special Issue: Prospect Theory and Political Psychology," *Political Psychology* 13 (1992): 187–204; Daniel Kahneman, "Judgment and Decision Making: A Personal View," *Psychological Science* 2, no. 3 (1991): 142–45; see also Daniel Kahneman, Paul Slovic, and Amos Tversky, eds., *Judgment under Uncertainty: Heuristics and Biases* (Cambridge: Cambridge University Press, 1982); T. Kameda and J. H. Davis, "The Function of the Reference Point in Individual and Group Risk Decision Making," *Organizational Behavior and Human Decision Processes* 46 (1990): 55–76; Jack S. Levy, "Prospect Theory and International Relations: Theoretical Applications and Analytical Problems. Special Issue: Prospect Theory and Political Psychology," *Political Psychology* 13, no. 2 (1992): 283–310; Jack S. Levy, "Prospect Theory, Rational Choice, and International Relations," *International Studies Quarterly* 41, no. 1 (1997): 87–112; P. Slovic and S. Lichtenstein, "Preference Reversals: A Broader Perspective," *American Economic Review* 73 (1983): 596–605; Amos Tversky and Daniel Kahneman, "Loss Aversion in Riskless Choice: A Reference Dependent Model," *Quarterly Journal of Economics* 41 (1991): 1039–61; Amos Tversky and Daniel Kahneman, "Rational Choice and the Framing of Decisions," *Journal of Business* 59, no. 4, 2 (1986): S251–S78; Amos Tversky and Peter Wakker, "Risk Attitudes and Decision Weights," *Econometrica* 63, no. 6 (1995): 1255–80; Thomas S. Ulen, "The Theory of Rational Choice, Its Shortcomings, and the Implications for Public Policy Decision Making," *Knowledge: Creation, Diffusion, Utilization* 12, no. 2 (1990): 170–98; and see also Mary Zey, "Criticisms of Rational Choice Models," in *Decision Making: Alternatives to Rational Choice Models*, ed. Mary Zey (Newbury Park, Calif.: Sage Publications, 1992).

12. Quantitative data regarding this indicator—*Agency's Estimate of Probable Success*—were not collected. Future research should analyze this dimension (see fig. 12).

13. Note that these relationships are not "invalid" statistically because the "null hypothesis" was not tested. However, correlation coefficients did not prove statistically significant based upon participant responses included in this government employee purposive sampling frame (i.e., the 135 participants listed in app. A).

14. See also Louis Kriesberg, *International Conflict Resolution: The US-USSR and Middle East Cases* (New Haven, Conn.: Yale University Press, 1992).

15. A two-tailed test of correlation is significant at the 0.05 level (–.262, n=68).

16. Although other differences exist, these three present the most interesting findings. Hence, this discussion is limited to these three interdepartmental cleavages.

17. For an in-depth discussion, see Rast, "Interagency Conflict and United States Intervention Policy," chap. 8.

18. It is important to note that I stratified the 135 participants according to agency and *then* identified 75 individuals for data coding and analysis. This approach both ensured a representative sample from each agency and protected the data from any bias that I may have held toward a particular individual, either positive or negative.

19. My deepest appreciation goes to Tracy Ann Breneman-Penas and Larissa Fast for their help in developing this innovative framework.

PART II

Analysis and Findings

Chapter 6

Dynamic Themes:
Leadership, Negotiation,
and Domestic Politics

Data analysis across all three levels of the interagency process led to the discovery of the following three process-related themes: (1) the role of leadership, (2) decision making by means of a negotiation process, and (3) the ways in which domestic politics influence policy outcomes. Policy makers referred most often to the theme of *leadership*, an overarching (macro) theme comprised of three supporting (micro) themes. Reportedly, the most significant element in terms of shaping policy outcomes, leadership is discussed first since it emerged as the dominant theme affecting interagency dynamics within the policy-making process.

Leadership

The most universally consistent comments regarding effective development of conflict termination policy revolved around leadership, particularly the president's ability to lead his principals and the nation.[1] Recall that quantitative analysis revealed 10 significant statistical correlations across indicators in the signed digraph model (fig. 24), indicating that the core factor should be reframed in terms of department's leadership style rather than organizational communication. Hence, it is reassuring that the qualitative analysis likewise indicated that leadership remains a crucial factor in shaping interagency dynamics. In fact, almost half of those interviewed cited a relationship between leadership and policy development.[2]

Several noted that the system does not fail to produce sound policy, but rather, leaders fail the system.[3] These officials contended that airing strong opposing views is healthy for the process, as it dampens the groupthink phenomenon. However, they likewise noted that leaders must "harness the friction that may become debilitating" to control the institutional process.[4]

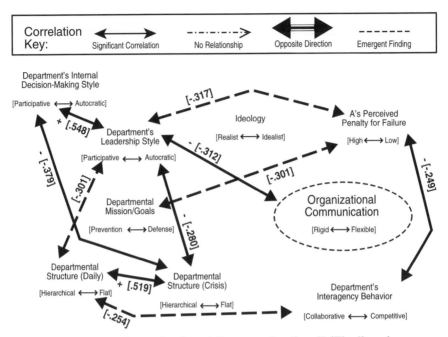

Figure 24. Organizational Communication II (Findings)

One high-level State Department official asserted "it is usually the fault of leadership, not the process, that impedes policy from energizing."[5] From the highest levels, leaders must present coherent policy visions. Decisiveness generates teamwork, provides a cohesive perspective to all government agencies regarding the president's policy choices, and communicates effectively with the public to mobilize domestic support for security policy initiatives. One principal noted, "More than anything else, the lack of a coherent policy at the highest level is the problem [in generating interagency conflict]. From the very top, there must be articulated a vision and a policy. In their absence, these fiefdoms will always push their agendas (e.g., human rights, energy)."[6]

The essence of this perspective permeated nearly every conversation I had with these experienced policy makers. More than any other issue, interagency participants agreed that a leader who effectively communicates a clear policy vision remains *the determining factor* in generating collaborative interagency dynamics and ensuring policy successes. The words of a National

Security Council principal echoed this sentiment, "When the system has to push the president, it does not work—the president must lead the NSC."[7] Clearly visible leadership, then, can move the bureaucracy in a focused direction. The absence of such a leader allows interagency conflict to fragment the policy process as personalities overwhelm the policy-making structure. Consequently, although not explored via the quantitative analysis, a majority of the participants identified *personality* as an element that proved central to the development and character of interagency dynamics. The salience of personality's relationship to leadership triggered its classification as leadership's first supporting (micro) theme.

Personality

Study participants followed their comments concerning leadership with ideas regarding the role personality plays in developing interagency dynamics. Again, while thoughts surrounding these two themes proved diverse, these professionals agreed that the policy-making system is *personality-driven, especially at the upper levels.* Accordingly, the system's success extends from the president's personality; hence, its direct linkage to leadership. One Defense Department official noted, "Every president stamps his identity in some way on the administration. How policy is formed is largely reflective of the character of the president. If [the president is] disengaged . . . the opportunities for power centers to form is [*sic*] there. If they have an ideological bent, it comes through."[8] Once the president establishes the tone for interagency relations, the department principals' personalities define each agency's internal and external operational boundaries.

Separating "leadership qualities" from "personality characteristics" is a difficult task, one beyond the scope of this book. The important factor for this analysis is that *interagency officials perceive that the two remain linked.* Thus, in the same vein as leadership, personalities shape the nature of the interagency process and are, therefore, at least partially responsible for the substantive outcome of the policy process. This perspective materialized as markedly salient for those in the White House and National Security Council Staff where four out of five people referenced personality as a factor in shaping

171

interagency dynamics, compared with only half of the State Department, Defense Department, and CIA officials. Together, these officials insist the president's and principals' (namely, the vice president and secretaries of state and defense) personalities shape the institutional process in distinct ways. Crucial issues related to this personality dynamic encompassed the "strength of the principal" and the "ego factor."

Repeatedly, and across all agencies, the "strength of the principal" emerged as an element dominating interagency dynamics and subsequent policy development. Multifaceted elements, decision-making style, and ego appeared as the most consistently referenced characteristics related to perceptions of a principal's strength within the interagency environment. Decision-making style becomes a factor in the perceived strength of a principal as subordinates observe interactions with others both inside the agency and across the government. When interagency actors identify a particular principal as a strong player at the highest level, subordinates at the deputies and interagency working group levels feel empowered to push their positions at their respective levels. Such behaviors increase interagency conflict as people become more entrenched in their own positions, communicating that they remain unwilling to "listen" to alternatives. Because "procedures are personality driven," people enter the policy-making process at lower levels with the attitude that "if I've got the influence, then I'm going to overrule you, particularly if my principal is stronger than yours." Individuals from both State and Defense Departments described this phenomenon, noting that the strength of the secretaries of state and defense accounted for much of the interagency dynamic and process output. In fact, references to William Perry serving as the "de facto secretary of state" proved widespread, as did comments regarding the nature of the relationships between Henry Kissinger and William Rogers, Caspar Weinberger and George Schultz, and Madeleine Albright and William Cohen. In each pairing, study participants claimed that personality tended to drive the policy-making process. According to a National Security Council member, the strength of these personalities becomes especially important during periods of transition where "patterns are established based either upon personalities or the entropy of the bureaucratic organization of the people who try to keep the train running."[9] An element related to this perception regarding a principal's strength is his or her ego.

As with most personality dimensions, the nature of one's ego (i.e., one's desire to enhance personal power and prestige) can engender both positive and negative implications for interagency dynamics. On the positive side, an actor's desire to satiate his or her ego may impel an individual to act. However, acting before conducting comprehensive analyses can be (and usually is) detrimental to policy development and its implementation. More often than not, this seems to be the effect of personal ego impinging on the policy process. One informant asserted, "So much of the interagency process is done so that 'I' will be successful—not so much that we'll achieve broader goals. . . . It's not only the big names, but it's the little names . . . and their efficiency reports. I see policy as being driven by personal career goals—a lot of their inclination is driven by that."[10]

Others supported this view, relating the nature of ego to competitive behaviors by noting that "institutions are not competitive, personalities are." The effects of these competitive personalities most often manifest in interagency meetings wherein actors vie for the president's or APNSA's (i.e., the president's national security adviser) ear. Study participants referred often to this phenomenon. One senior government official remarked that he never realized the prominence of this "macho ego" factor until he experienced it throughout the interagency process. It has been his observation that even in meetings on national policy, egos play an important role as people "role-play" for the president's attention saying, "I'm tougher Mr. President, watch me. . . . I need to be heard."[11] This competition closes interagency communication channels and stymies innovative thinking as egos overwhelm reason during crisis analysis, thereby biasing the shape of proposed courses of action (COA) during planning. The negative effects of this dynamic become acute during crises. One high-ranking State Department official noted, "The interagency process is truncated during crises—influence depends on the personality and power of the secretary and a couple of other people at the senior levels."[12]

This truncation holds implications for emergent conflict termination policy in terms of crisis analysis and option generation. Moreover, findings presented in chapter 5 raised the issue that internal departmental leadership should be explored in terms of its relationship to crisis analysis and innovative solution generation. Indeed, this qualitative finding reinforces this proposition. Given the salience of personality, it is worthwhile to report the ways in which these individuals framed the connection between leaders' personalities and the development of organizational culture.

Organizational Culture

Seven of 10 study participants identified organizational culture as a crucial element in the development of interagency dynamics. Policy officials disclosed that perceptions of their own agency and their perceptions of others served as a significant factor in their inability to understand one another, a factor explored further in the forthcoming discussion of "core competencies." Recall that the signed digraph model labeled *Organizational Communication* (refer to fig. 24) tested relations between many dimensions of organizational culture, including ideology, leadership and decision-making styles, penalty for failure, organizational structure, interagency behavior, and patterns of organizational communication, concluding these elements of organizational culture should be explored in terms of the role leadership plays in developing each indicator.[13] Organizational culture affects interagency dynamics in the following three pronounced ways: (1) establishes the organizational climate, including decision-making styles, (2) shapes communication patterns, and (3) influences innovative thinking. Together, these three factors inform perceptions of one's own agency as well as others.

A leader's personality shapes an organization's climate because "the personality of leadership drives the agenda for the organization."[14] This agenda included identifying and prioritizing issues as well as setting parameters for the nature of relationships within one's own agency and the agency's interrelationships with others. Concerning issues, the cliché "my boss's priorities are my priorities" is particularly fitting within government agencies wherein promoting "institutionally shared images" becomes an important metric for determining an individual's career success. The connection here is that an interagency actor often will seize upon his or her principal's priorities regarding the importance of particular issues *even when* this individual knows that his or her interagency counterpart does not share that perspective and is unlikely to yield. For example, it is customary for interagency actors to come into conflict regarding the use of military force to assist in nation building or humanitarian relief operations. Because an individual must represent the principal's views as if they were his or her own, differences on substantive issues create interpersonal conflict, the subsequent tension is then transformed into interagency conflict on a broader scale. This type of polarized dynamic relates to another major component of shared images—the beliefs one agency holds about other government agencies.

While diverse views exist regarding the organizational cultures of all agencies across government, the most pronounced differences permeate relations between the Departments of State and Defense. Officials consistently described "State's view of Defense" and "Defense's view of State," yet *not one* of these study participants shared a perspective contrary to the shared image he or she described. In this manner, State reportedly believes Defense "has all the toys" (i.e., resources) but does not want to "use" them. Similarly, Defense sees State's primary aim (and the NSC Staff's to a lesser degree) as putting troops in harm's way for issues that are not within the country's "vital national interests." Shared across all three levels of the interagency process, these perceptions create an interagency climate wherein decision makers—*especially at the lower levels*—recognize only confirming evidence of these stereotypes while failing to acknowledge disconfirming information (i.e., they are acting to minimize their individual "cognitive dissonance"). Over time, these stereotypes bolster self-perpetuating cycles of interagency conflict within the interagency process. Officials respond with reciprocal behaviors, increasing tension across the policy-making process while simultaneously proving unable to distinguish behaviors designed to decrease interagency conflict intensity. This propagates each agency's skewed ideas regarding others taking active measures to protect their respective institutional equities (i.e., as any asset that adds value to or is the defining characteristic of an agency, one that becomes a substantive input into the policy process) during crisis policy making.[15] Although not the only factor in establishing decision-making style, these perceptions play significant roles in framing decision-making dynamics as these polarized perspectives help to generate "bureaucratic turf battles" at all levels of the interagency process.

Most pronounced at the interagency working group (IWG) level, turf battles occur because individuals prove unwilling to challenge publicly their principal's stated positions. Absent a clearly articulated presidential position that is echoed by the principals, stereotypical beliefs about one's own agency and others create situations wherein standard operating procedures and dogmatic application of institutional perspectives negate officials' abilities to secure consensual decisions at lower levels. An additional difference in organizational culture related to decision-making styles exacerbates the following phenomenon: Individuals within the State Department tend to behave as consensus builders; conversely, Defense Department officials tend to behave as decision takers.

Policy makers repeatedly described this difference between consensus builders and decision takers, insisting that such a difference in decision-making style can paralyze the policy process. One National Security Council official stated his experience underscores the idea that "decision making by consensus is used by departments to avoid taking decisions [and] accountability."[16] In speaking on the Bosnia policy process, another high-ranking official noted, "Bosnia has a consensus-driven system starting from the top. This makes it easy to be obstructionist and encourages hedgehog behaviors. A consensus approach tends to drive people toward the bureaucratic behaviors . . . it encourages turf battles."[17]

This continual drive for consensus manifests itself in tangible ways as Defense officials attend interagency meetings to "take decisions" on issues. After numerous interactions, Defense Department representatives within a consensus-oriented administration become increasingly frustrated as they "spend an entire meeting watching people dance with each other" when the Defense representative wants an explicit decision, observing, "When they start dancing again, that creates conflict."[18] An overwhelming emphasis on generating consensus around a policy creates interagency conflict as those who must develop the strategy's tangible facets to implement the policy feel Washington officials waste crucial time creating a sense of buy-in at the expense of determining operational and tactical details. While the effects of an overemphasis on a consensus-oriented policy process can generate interagency conflict, the same can be said of an autocratic decision-taking style.

The influence of personality again comes to the fore as decisions made in spite of bureaucratic turf battles or a zealous drive for consensus usually result from pre-existing personal relationships among individual members of the interagency process. Some of these decisions are taken through a governmental ad hoc body known as the "Kitchen Cabinet," a group mobilized when the president (or principals within their own agencies) surrounds himself with a few trusted advisors. The president (or principal) selects these advisors based upon interpersonal chemistry—their personalities and established personal relationships. During times of crisis policy development, "increased pressure leads to the increased likelihood to circumvent the ordinary decision-making machine and use the 'Kitchen Cabinet.'" A State Department official noted that this tendency for a principal to sit down with a limited group of hand-picked people from his or her own bureaucracy creates conflict. This approach disenfranchises people from both policy development and its subsequent implementation while perpetuating the conditions for continued conflict during future interagency engagements.[19] The preceding quantitative analysis that indicated departments with less participative leaders correlated with higher perceptions of penalty for failure that, in turn, related to competitive interagency behaviors (see fig. 24) reinforces this finding. The patterns of communication principals establish for their organizations further inflame these conditions.

Leadership plays a crucial role in developing the parameters for communication, a critical component in establishing the "rules of the game" for interagency conduct.[20] The interviews revealed three additional elements related to communication patterns not captured in the original signed digraph model. These three components regard (1) the structure of communication patterns, (2) information exchange, and (3) the nature of the interagency debate. An argument can be made that the first necessarily influences the other two; therefore, let us begin this discussion with the structure of communication patterns.

Communication Patterns

Perceptions regarding the structure of communication patterns within agencies remained mixed. Several portrayed information exchange as "linear and closed"; others characterized it as "recursive and open." Officials from both departments of State and Defense observed that patterns tend to change over the life cycle of a crisis, becoming more structured over time as formalized, issue-specific chains of command (within both departments) are clarified. Overall, however, the study participants agreed that communications across the government remain too compartmentalized. This compartmentalization results from the absence of interoperability (i.e., the ability of different agencies to work together seamlessly, based on either human or technological incompatibilities) or dilemmas exacerbated by dissimilar organizational cultures.[21]

In the first instance, interoperability challenges emanate from physical and technological disjunctures. With the exception of the Secure Video Teleconferencing System (SVTC), no method exists for multiple decision makers to exchange and discuss sensitive or classified information, save a face-to-face meeting within one room. Obviously, the logistical demands inherent to this approach become debilitating over time as the number of meetings expands to consume the decision-maker's calendar.[22] This said, no governmentwide interconnected classified computer system (or unclassified for that matter) exists, nor has there ever been one to this point. Complicating information exchange is the reality that many government officials do not want to record their views because such records are subject to public release via the Freedom of Information Act (FOIA). Records create an accountability issue, and, according to one high-level official, most interagency actors do not want to be held to that standard. An intangible interoperability issue compounds this challenge as diverse organizational cultures operate using different languages—these vocabularies and their meanings are not always congruent across interagency domains.

Highlighted in the discussion regarding perceptions across departments, the State Department's and NSC Staff's organizational cultures strive to sustain an interagency environment that enables these agencies to "keep all of their options open." Consequently, these agencies avoid specificity when framing their proposals. In the words of a high-ranking Defense Department official, "this is an anathema" to military officials. At the same time, State Department officials tire of the Defense Department's unyielding demand for clarity and precision, particularly regarding definition of the desired end state. Defense's expectations are reinforced through joint doctrine and training—State Department possesses no such doctrinal structures. Consequently, State Department officials interpret such demands as an excuse for Defense to "do nothing." These types of cleavages encourage departments to "hand off" the problem to others as they adopt a more passive approach to policy formulation and information exchange. Hence, State Department's and the NSC Staff's *implicit* demand for ambiguity and flexibility clashes with Defense's *explicit* drive for clarity and precision. Taken together, the data supported the quantitative finding that when *Departmental Relations at Time of Initial Crisis Definition* are perceived as "hostile," *Agency's Perceptions of Other's Conflict Orientation* tended to be "competitive." In other words, if the departments interrelate within an environment characterized by an inability to discuss a particular crisis due to organizational cleavages, then they will behave competitively toward one another *from the outset*. In related fashion, these perceived competitive behaviors are associated normally with "high" *Perceptions of Other's Level of Self-Interest*. These differences go well beyond mere words. They often induce detrimental effects for interagency dynamics, especially when related to information exchange. The lack of effective information exchange can produce serious consequences for interagency dynamics and the policy outcome of that process.

Policy officials universally agree on the one issue that "information is power." While most asserted that people did not withhold information in times of crises or the development of "high policy" (i.e., national security or national defense), a few respondents cited instances wherein individuals controlled information flow to manipulate policy outcomes. Officials use information to shape the policy process and to provide their respective principals a competitive advantage within the interagency arena as they attempted to protect their respective bureaucratic equities. Controlling information exchange is only one issue related to communication patterns; the nature of the exchange presents another dilemma.

Two factors shape the nature of interagency exchange: the number of actors within the process and the actors' most salient objectives during the communication process. In the first instance, several study participants noted, "as the importance of the issue increases, the importance of avoiding leaks increases—the more important the issue, the more likely the experts will be excluded." While there may be no deliberate plan to exclude experts, their detachment results from decision makers' efforts to "know who knows." Policy makers endeavor to avoid information leaks due to the information's sensitivity.[23] Habitually, then, expertise is traded to maintain secrecy—a practice that again foreshadows grave implications for crisis analysis and option generation. Discussed earlier, the Kitchen Cabinet's negative consequences reemerge as important in shaping information exchange. Further, the actors themselves possess personal objectives for their participation in information exchange sessions. While some hope to enhance their (and other's) understanding of the issue, when parochial interests intrude, actors create interagency conflict by not listening to others involved in the process. One individual involved at the IWG level captured this problem succinctly: "There's very little discussion among people—they come to the table with a set of views that are 'deployed' but not discussed. There is relatively little give-and-take and no debate. Debate goes on within an agency . . . but bureaucracies come together with separate bottles—each has its own container and [it] is not shared around."[24]

A principal reinforced this observation by saying that a lack of communication *at all levels* generates interagency conflict. He went further to say that conflict is exacerbated by the "perceived proprietary interest" in a genuine policy that makes a group of policy makers believe that "one agency considers that it has either the primary or sole responsibility for carrying out a given piece [yet] others feel they should have a role—this creates tension; or, one agency or small group's feeling that a particular party is competent and information is dispensed on a "need to know basis." For example, I was trying to work my way into [the CIA] and was told 'we can't release anything to you, but the DCI is communicating with the secretary of state directly'—it did not happen."[25] These elements related to information exchange help mold the third aspect of communication, the nature of the interagency debate surrounding crises. The level and nature of the interagency debate depends upon the issues, the personalities involved in the exchange, and timing in terms of the impending crisis's nature. Additionally, debate tends to be more open at the higher levels and less so at the lower levels. Invoking an almost universally understood metaphor, one NSC principal asserted that the interagency's IWG-level process should indeed resemble a "food fight" as these people are charged to protect their agency's respective equities. This official maintained that only decision makers at the deputies' committee and principals' committee levels are authorized to "negotiate away" such equities. Further, another official asserted, "high open debate [exists] horizontally at the highest levels, but not necessarily vertically."[26]

An NSC Staff member aptly described the generic nature of interagency crisis debate:

> What tends to happen is that when the crisis erupts, you've got to sort out what's going on. Inherently, there's a lot of debate on what the crisis is, what's important to us, [and] how it will evolve. There's a sphere of debate on the nature of the crisis and then debate on what's going on resumes at a lower level. Immediately, after you sort out "what's the situation?" [and] then decide how to respond, there's a high level [of debate regarding] interests, level of response, [and] options for responding. Then, in course of discussion, you merge toward consensus. The situation peaks, then you determine what the response should be.[27]

While this perspective logically describes issue-related factors, it does not account for the other two conditions governing the debate—personalities and timing—conditions that can promote or stifle debate.

Debate surrounding policy options tends to *increase* under four circumstances: (1) when no consensus on crisis definition or policy options has been achieved, (2) when individuals are unhappy with the initial decisions, (3) when principled differences of opinion exist regarding capabilities, and (4) when crisis parameters evolve or change abruptly. With the exception of the third element, the study participants offered little in the way of a constructive rationale for debate to increase based upon principled differences. Instead, their experiences substantiated ideas regarding strong personalities and the need for individuals to satisfy their egos (discussed earlier). Personalities, then, can increase the debate within the interagency forum. Combined with interpersonal relations, personality factors seem to decrease debate.

Debate tends to *decrease* under four conditions: (1) when time pressures demand immediate action, (2) when things are going well and there is agreement across the interagency, (3) when key decisions have already been made, and (4) when the principal takes a position and makes that position public. One can recognize the dampening affect that the first three conditions would have on open debate because of the environment within which policy decisions are made. The rationale for this last condition relates directly to the earlier discussion of personalities, personal relationships, and shared images in terms of the risk associated with putting forth a perspective contrary to the principal's stated position.

Together, these three elements—the structure of communication patterns, information exchange, and the nature of the interagency debate—serve as indicators of an organization's internal culture. These elements help us understand a particular communication pattern's influence on an individual's willingness to promote innovative thinking.

Bear in mind that the quantitative analysis produced no significant relationship between an individual's ability to propose innovative solutions and individual's willingness to propose innovative ideas.[28] It is important to bring this relationship into focus as the evidence sheds new light on this disjuncture. While officials conveyed they felt able to propose innovative solutions for crises, they maintained that other factors limited their agency's exploration of these ideas. The most salient inhibitor seemed to be the "inertia of the bureaucratic process" that is tied to *prior experience*. Put succinctly, if an agency's prior experience with a situation has prompted it to develop contingency plans to deal with future occurrences or even a "folk memory" of what worked and did not work the "last time," then opportunities to think innovatively about new situations diminish. This is known across government as the "plan in the can" phenomenon. Defense Department officials stated there is a genuine recognition of openness to ideas but also acknowledged that senior members of the Joint Staff act as filters based upon their personal experiences and desires, often dismissing ideas more junior officials would classify as innovative. From the perspective of a Defense Department IWG-level interagency participant, "The department isn't really interested in innovation or creative ways . . . this is a result of our organizational culture."[29] This ability to recall prior experience is linked to two additional conditions that impinge on innovative thinking—the pressure of other business and the desire to pronounce options consistent with an agency's respective shared images.

It is common for government officials (those at the levels interviewed for this study) to work an average of 14 to 16 hours a day, five to six days every week. These "noncrisis" time demands prove astonishing. During periods of acute crisis, the workday elongates significantly. Within this time-constrained environment, it becomes extremely difficult to reach consensus on issues toward achieving "closure." A Defense Department official characterized this by saying, "Up to a certain point you can discuss anything, but on the big issues you can only throw the bomb in the organization once or do it all the time and no one listens. People are not morally afraid; there just is a certain imperative. . . . People can talk out-of-the-box, but not get out-of-the-box."[30]

The daily pressures of doing business coupled with the desire to remain active in the policy process limit willingness to propose solutions that move beyond the agency's (or interagency's) shared prior experience. This prior experience shapes the images of an organization's current sense of purpose and produces constraints on conceptualizing new approaches to deal with complex crises. A senior State Department official characterized this by saying, "For everyone who wishes to walk through the gates of the future, the path is blocked by 10,000 guardians of the past."[31] Finally, it is important to recognize that these study participants perceived that organizational culture and training biases affected their ability to think innovatively during conflict termination policy development.

This discussion addressed the organizational culture issue previously in terms of one's desire to be seen as a team player by continuing to share (and promote) the images of the principal and his or her organization. Consequently, officials believe this factor stifles creativity at the lower levels and influences the nature of communications between deputies and principals. One State Department official characterized the dynamic this way: "As the stakes get higher, as people have committed their resources, energy, and prestige, etc., receptivity to out-of-the-box thinking declines and the willingness of intermediate supervisors to up-channel is limited. The internal debate gets limited too."[32]

Similarly, a Defense Department official noted, "Proposing innovative solutions makes it harder to get consensus. The thought process is, 'If it's outside, there's a hidden agenda . . . what's he trying to slip by me?' That's the psychology of the interagency."[33] In the experience of one State Department official, an environment wherein some principals believe performance "should be judged on how well we made the case and carried out what you intended to do"[34] reinforces this perspective. Because of the dilemma created by shared images, individuals are not willing to promote options to higher levels that have the potential to be seen as "flaky" even though they believe such options warrant further exploration. A State Department official claimed this dynamic limits receptivity to out-of-the-box thinking.

In the final analysis, State Department officials agreed with outsiders who characterized their agency as a "process oriented" organization, one whose organizational culture conflicts with the Defense Department's self-reported "results oriented" perspective. Comments within the State Department (and NSC) reflected a relatively greater receptivity to innovative thinking. Conversely, those from the Defense Department (and CIA) highlighted the "what has worked in the past" mentality, an attitude reinforced by training and one that limits both willingness and ability to think innovatively during periods of intense crisis policy making. A senior Defense Department official conveyed an interesting perspective, asserting that military members at the operational level (i.e., theater level) are not trained to think through all the steps beyond war fighting because this is not "their role." Rather, this individual stressed that the State Department and the NSC should be considering the postconflict environment and that the "key is for all the principals to have the perspective across the board and to understand the whole issue."[35] This official, however, offered no insight regarding the ways in which the State Department and the NSC would communicate postwar objectives to the operational level commander to enable the commander to execute operational courses of action toward achieving—or, at least, establishing the conditions to achieve—those postwar objectives. More importantly, this mentality again reflects the sequential thinking that governs intervention strategy: the Defense Department, somewhat in isolation from other executive agencies, strives to achieve its military objectives and then *hands off* the situation to the State Department and the NSC.

The foregoing discussion highlighted the ways in which divergent organizational cultures affect decision-making styles, communication, debate, information exchange, and innovative thinking.[36] Reinforced by self-perpetuated stereotypes, this organizational cleavage remains pronounced between the Departments of State and Defense. In the face of such disjunctures, *policy is made in spite of the system* designed to produce policy outcomes. As a rule, this policy output results from pre-established personal relationships and networks. Therefore, "personal relations and networking" are discussed here together as the final micro theme relating leadership to the interagency dynamics that shape the substance of policy outcomes.

Personal Relations and Networking

Chemistry between personalities enables policy makers to engage in personal relationships that significantly affect inter-agency dynamics. While the preceding discussion of *personalities* primarily reflected the adverse consequences individual personalities bring into being, those personal relationships people develop both *within* and *across* agency boundaries influence interagency dynamics in constructive ways.[37] Positive and respectful interpersonal relations shape collaborative inter-agency behaviors. At the same time, however, a few officials emphasized that principals could (and do) sideline individuals in terms of "playing the game" if they are not trusted or if the principal prefers one individual to another based upon a pre-existing personal relationship. The evidence also revealed a tendency to push issues up the policy-making chain if individuals do not like one another at lower levels. These behaviors emerged as the few negative effects personal relationships can have on interagency dynamics. For the most part, experienced inter-agency officials insisted personal relations shape interagency dynamics in positive, effective ways.

More than a third of those interviewed lauded the benefits of personal relationships, noting that "relations between principals make development of foreign policy doable."[38] In fact, these officials universally agreed that personal relationships develop *the* positive interagency dynamic that makes the system work. One policy maker characterized the utility of interpersonal relations in this manner: "If the personal relationship goes away, the lines of communication are cut off . . . the system breaks down. If it's not there, integration occurs only because people want it to—if they don't like it, they close it down."[39] Although the drawbacks of Kitchen Cabinet approaches have been presented, it is important to acknowledge that many study participants viewed this approach as also producing useful results.

The efficacy of the Kitchen Cabinet approach to policy making becomes evident as the president and principals surround themselves with small groups of advisers with whom they feel personally connected. One senior Defense Department official remarked, "Relationships determine who gets included in these things."[40] A State Department official echoed this sentiment, stating "if people are known by decision makers and considered important, they will be in the loop whether the normal hierarchy and communication patterns would include them or not."[41] A DC-level participant contended these individuals operate first "from a personal relationship platform to each other," relationships forged in *prior experience*—not through the current interagency exchange.[42] The general perspective, as characterized by one Defense official, is that "you don't develop relationships in a crisis."[43]

Perhaps the most important aspect of personal relationships and networking is the recognition that breakthroughs in policy development emerge from pre-existing personal relationships that enable policy makers to set aside their competing institutional interests and interact with one another on a private level. As one convincing example, an NSC official pointed out that during the last two years of the Reagan administration, the "haircut group" developed policy for relations with China. A group of close friends across government who were both interested and knowledgeable regarding China policy met during periods blocked on their calendars as "haircut." It is intriguing that these policy makers felt they needed to "work around" the formal policy process. This alternative practice grew from pre-existing personal relations these individuals shared. The practice exemplifies that personal relationships and networking play a crucial role in policy development, even going so far as to serve as a substitute for an officially structured, USG-sanctioned process.

The patterns described above illustrate the powerful influence personal relationships and networking have in creating a positive interagency dynamic designed to overcome those competitive interagency behaviors that hamper policy making. In this vein, the influence of pre-existing personal relationships cannot be overemphasized and must be considered in any analysis regarding the national security policy-making process.

The foregoing discussion illustrated that leadership remains the most influential element in the policy-making process, one that affects interagency dynamics at all levels (i.e., IWG, DC, and PC). Not only is a clearly articulated top-down vision required, but leaders must also remain cognizant of the ways in which their actions as principals (and "bosses") create, exacer-

187

bate, or diminish interagency conflict. As leaders interact with actors across the interagency process, their personalities shape organizational cultures—including perceptions of risk for the individual if he or she deviates from the agency's shared images or the principal's stated policy position. Further, these leaders rely upon personal relationships and networking to develop national security policy. The case analyses concerning the Persian Gulf and Bosnia (forthcoming chap. 9) bolster this idea.

With an understanding of the study participants' perspectives concerning the role leadership plays in shaping interagency dynamics, let us move on to the second macro theme associated with process' influence on substance, that of "decision making as a process of negotiation." According to the policy makers interviewed for this study, personal relationships also play a crucial role in developing this interagency negotiating process.

Decision Making as Negotiation

Decision making by negotiation shapes policy choices within a bureaucratic environment.[44] Two micro themes emerged regarding the relationship between decision making and negotiation: The first relates to the interagency process in terms of access and privilege and results from pre-existing personal relationships; the second concerns the nature of the policy outcome.

Access and Privilege

Figure 21 (refer to p. 146) reminds us that the evidence failed to support a statistically significant relationship between the indicator relating *Agency's Perceptions Regarding Other's Favoritism in Access* and the core factor characterizing perceptions of the *NSC's Role in Policy-making Process.*

Privileged access to officials within the NSC System is an accepted practice, with departments of State and Defense spokespersons most often being the privileged actors. Many study participants noted that such access is necessary to ensure the policy-making process is as inclusive as possible in light of operational security concerns (e.g., troop protection or intelligence source protection). In fact, of the 21 participants who discussed privileged access, only two (one each from State and Defense) felt such informal contact with the NSC could pose detrimental consequences for policy making, as it provided an opportunity for one agency to shape the NSC's perspective before any other. Government officials perceived that this privileged access favorably influenced policy development. One high-level official captured his perspective by saying, "Because it's from those informal contacts that you're most likely to get innovative ideas and out-of-the-box thinking—[people are] less likely to be competitive in a crisis if [they] know each other."[45] Another informant described this privileged access as having favorable effects on policy development because "what the NSC does is receive and transmit information. They condition the activities of the interagency."[46] It is important to note, however, that these study participants distinguished access from influence.

Access does not equate necessarily to an ability to shape the perspective of the NSC.[47] Repeatedly, officials noted that while privileged access allows many individuals the opportunity to shape policy, personal relationships provide some individuals with greater capacity to influence policy. One high-ranking State Department official described it in this manner: "I think they all have access but that's separate from influence. Some are privileged in their influence depending on the APNSA."[48] An NSC principal echoed this perspective, noting that personality and relational dimensions permit access as well, and saying, "Because these folks [NSC Staff members] come from different departments, [they] have informal contacts."[49] The influence of personality and personal relationships again comes to the fore in terms of enabling select individuals to access and to influence the policy-making process.

Since some are able to influence the substance of policy because of their entrée into the process, another facet of networking emerges as personalities and personal relationships—not organizational structures—create opportunities to influence policy outcomes. The recognition and acceptance of this idea is what leads those with an open policy process to believe they influence policy development in fundamental ways (i.e., have great influence). After all, irrespective of the policy process's nature (i.e., open or closed), personal relationships, not the nature of the process itself, serve as prerequisites affecting one's ability to influence both the policy process and policy outcomes. The findings enhance the quantitative findings presented in figure 25. These personal relationships lead directly to a discussion of the second micro theme concerning negotiation, the policy outcome.

Policy Outcome

In analyzing interviews regarding the policy outcome resulting from the interagency negotiating process, an unambiguous theme emerged: The interagency process is a negotiating process wherein decision makers compromise to reach consensus regarding a middle-ground option. This decision-making process takes longer, delays actions, and dilutes policy outcomes, often producing a "least common denominator" course of action. Added to this, each interagency actor enters the negotiation with clearly defined boundaries—boundaries the individual is not authorized (and perhaps remains unwilling) to cross. One principal characterized the process in this manner:

> You get a much more muddled set of choices via negotiation that may contain inherent contradictions. It's a bit like [the] Congress and the War Powers Act—it tries to staple two houses of [the] Congress together. The problem with negotiated positions equates to a significant risk of the camel as a product of committee: You may not want a camel with two humps, may not want any humps at all. You may produce a policy position that is less clear-cut, has inherent contradictions—like stepping on the accelerator and brake at the same time. It may be unsuited to the problem [as] other agendas are pursued with less focus on the problem at hand. While negotiation generates increased unity on the US side, it may come at the price of a policy position that is not well targeted, and one with extra baggage.[50]

This passage summarizes the essence of decision making by means of negotiation. It also highlights another theme regarding this decision-making process by claiming that negotiation increases unity on the US side. While study participants acknowledged that this negotiation process has a tendency to produce incrementally derived suboptimal outcomes, they simultaneously asserted that decision making through negotiation is required if the government hopes to achieve buy-in regarding policy implementation. One principal declared that "officials make consistently suboptimal decisions that get us where we want to go—we bend, but do not fracture."[51] These officials unanimously contend that this approach does not conform to the tenets of rational choice theory and its rational actor model of decision making.

A State Department official remarked that policy making is "all about negotiation—that's the way policy is made."[52] The individual went on to say that "rational actor models assume an understanding of what's 'actually' in the national interest. If using it descriptively, it's a tautology. It presumes one can tell what's in the national interest—12 others outside the government have other versions not in the national interest. I do not think anybody knew or has a way to figure out what's in the national interest. There is a presumption of a "clear" thing in the national interest. So the negotiation and the accident of who the players are—a government without a CIA or Air Force—you get different outcomes."[53]

This individual's experience reflects two important critiques of the rational actor model decision-making approach described in chapter 2. First, the informant notes that there is no clear, unified understanding of national interests. The most basic assumption of rational choice theory asserts that an individual knows one's goals and that these goals remain static over time or for some period.[54] Recall that this assumption's validity proves ineffectual when applied to the group choice setting wherein diverse individual cognitive maps encode mismatched values and goals. Divergent cognitive maps create intragroup conflict surrounding problem definition. Here, an experienced interagency actor pronounced that this dilemma characterizes the interagency process in terms of attempts to clarify national interests (i.e., problem definition in this sense). A DC-level actor corroborated this perspective, indicating that the unitary actor model does not fit reality because the government is not a unitary actor with a single goal or policy vision: "Cost-benefit analysis assumes unity of action . . . policy is not made this way."[55] Hence, this individual confirmed that the interplay of certain actors influences the interagency's negotiating process. The individual illuminates a second critical feature of the policy process by intimating that "accident" may dictate who the players are in any given interagency process.

Through an agency representative's inclusion—or indeed, his or her exclusion—the national security policy process generates different policy outcomes.[56] Recognition of this interagency dynamic moves the USG policy-making process further away from a rational actor model. The assumptions of rational choice theory dictate that the most appropriate individuals be included in every interagency exchange. Instead, as many have indicated, the identification of actors is based somewhat on personal relationships and personality characteristics. In the final analysis, a DC-level representative aptly described the overall negotiation process and its influence on policy development: "The bureaucracy affects the decision—it's not entirely a rational actor [process]—time is a compressing factor. People do try to make rational decisions as they analyze as best they can. There are conflicting points of view [and people] go for the middle ground. It comes back to leadership."[57] This individual brought the macro theme of negotiation back to the starting point for this analysis—leadership. Interagency actors perceive leadership as the most significant element in creating an interagency dynamic capable of negotiating policy to meet the interagency's most demanding criterion—actionability, as evaluated through the lens of interagency buy-in during implementation.

As a metric, actionability must likewise account for another factor—domestic politics' influence on both interagency dynamics and policy outcomes. The nature of this negotiation is tempered through the prism of domestic politics, namely, efforts to shape public opinion and the roles of the Congress.

Domestic Politics

Domestic politics play a crucial role in shaping the ways in which agencies interact while boasting significant impact on policy outcomes.[58] Two streams capture the nature of this influence: (1) the influence of public opinion and (2) the influence of the Congress on interagency decision makers. In the first instance, policy makers across the government share a heightened sensitivity to the public's desire to avoid "another Vietnam" or "Somalia" debacle and to prevent American casualties at all costs. These desires relate directly to prior experience. When looking at the two historical cases explored through this research and the data provided by these officials, bear in mind that the Vietnam experience overshadowed contemporary thinking at the highest levels of government as well as across the vast majority of America's adult populace (the "baby-boomer" generation in particular). One CIA official remarked, "This is a country wherein the public and the politicians are unwilling to accept casualties. So that when they see people being killed, they want to engineer, to borrow Kissinger's term, a solution. The problems can only be ameliorated—they look for an empirical solution."[59]

This perspective is not lost on interagency decision makers, themselves products of this national culture. Officials across government concurred that the use of force remains a function of politics and is something that can be decided only when sustainable domestically. From this perspective, domestic politics influences interagency dynamics as policy makers use the media to shape public opinion while remaining attentive to their constituents' desires as measured through public opinion polls. Another conduit to convey public opinion to the executive branch is through the Congress.

The earlier depiction of the policy process in motion asserted that the Congress plays a multifaceted role in national security policy development. Fittingly, two vital elements emerged concerning the ability of the Congress to influence interagency dynamics: partisan politics and the power of the purse. (Obviously, budgetary control generates implications for policy outcomes. The ensuing chapter discusses congressional influence from that substantive perspective.)

With regard to partisan politics, officials across all three levels disclosed that decision makers within the NSC System, State Department, and Defense Department pay close attention to congressional views, especially when the potential exists for military engagement. This is not so much in terms of the War Powers Resolution as hypothesized earlier but more to gain advantage within the executive's interagency process to regulate policy outcomes. An NSC principal declared, "We take [the] Congress into consideration on everything we do."[60] Reported in a November 1989 Defense Department *White Paper*, the daily activities of the Pentagon vis-à-vis congressional reporting put this relationship into perspective:

> The frequency and range of interchanges between DOD and the Congress is truly remarkable. The July 1989 Defense Management Report cited 2,500 telephonic and 450 written inquiries from [the] Congress to DOD *every working day*. Congressional reports and audits require the equivalent of 900 full time employees on a continuing basis. Largely in addition to those efforts, there are over 500 people in the Pentagon whose only job is to deal with the Congress or respond to routine Congressional requests. In turn, there are over 1,500 Congressional staffers who deal nearly exclusively in defense issues.[61]

The rationale for including this supporting material is to highlight again that relationships persist across the three primary interagency actors (i.e., the NSC System, State, and Defense) and the Congress. These relationships provide actors opportunities to shape congressional opinion regarding policy development. Further, these actors recognize that these relationships exist and use "off line" communications to leverage the interagency process in their favor. In effect, the Congress becomes a "shadow negotiator" within the executive's interagency process. This condition manifests itself in two distinct ways. As one example, officials indicated that part of President William Clinton's 1993 unwillingness to put forth a position contrary to that of Gen Colin Powell (CJCS) with regard to the use of the military in Bosnia emanated from the White House's appreciation of Powell's enduring relationship with the Congress. The Clinton administration recognized that the Congress would support Powell's viewpoint to not introduce troops into Bosnia (1993–95). Many officials indicated that the CJCS used his advantage within the interagency process to avert US ground troop participation. Albeit for opposite reasons, a different CJCS clashed with the Clinton administration a few years later regarding the use of ground troops for the Kosovo crisis (1999).

Gen Hugh Shelton (CJCS) purportedly informed President Clinton that the use of airpower—in the absence of ground troops—would exacerbate the ongoing Kosovo conflict, the refugee situation in particular.[62] Although connections between the CJCS (in terms of both the office and the person) and the Congress remain ambiguous, this situation provides another probable example of the military-congressional relationship. Despite calls from within the Congress to use ground troops, the Clinton administration stayed the course with airpower alone. The effects of the second form of influence, that of partisan politics, prove far less subtle.

Analysis revealed the political nature of the national security policy-making process. One CIA informant described this aptly by saying, "interagency conflict is becoming more intense than ever before. Partisan politics, combined with the tendency for the Legislature to assert itself, has killed the imperial presidency and reasserted its role in foreign policy matters."[63] While most data of this kind reflected the nature of interagency dynamics for the Bosnia policy development process, they likewise demonstrated that the Persian Gulf policy process was not immune to this influence, as "most Democrats did not want to support military action."[64] Even with United Nations resolutions supporting the use of force to expel Hussein from Kuwait, the US Congress nevertheless voted on the use of military force practically on the eve of war.[65] Many perceived this as a congressional attempt to reassert itself within the executive-dominated foreign policy arena.

Although advantage as a shadow negotiator and partisan politics represent merely two examples of congressional influence on interagency dynamics, this type of tactical advantage engenders strategic implications for the policy-making process. The Congress plays a related role through its authority to control the nation's fiscal affairs. Thus, while the public influences congressional perspectives and is made aware of their representative's perspective via the media-promoted rhetoric that surrounds crisis decision making, the implications attendant to congressional budget authority cannot be overstated.

The Congress retains pronounced influence on the policy process through its ability to shape policy outcomes. Legislative liaisons in all executive departments work diligently to lobby the Congress to gain and sustain support for policy initiatives (if possible, before making these initiatives public). This influence relates directly to the substantive outcome of the policy process, but again plays a role in shaping interagency dynamics. Specifically, Defense Department officials observed that in the absence of a continuing resolution or appropriations bill to support troop deployment, the Defense Department recognizes that it will have to absorb the costs of foreign intervention. This creates interagency conflict by perpetuating the stereotypes regarding the use of force for intervention activities that do not relate clearly to US national interests—national interests the president has failed to define and communicate effectively. This perspective relates back to leadership: Actors within all agencies perceive one of the president's (and his administration's) primary responsibilities as defining and articulating the national interests that frame his presidency as a means to establish the nation's guiding vision. Defense Department officials characterized this as State Department "having their hand in our pocket." From a Defense Department perspective, these monies are required to prepare the force for the next major theater contingency. Therefore, using them to fund State Department initiatives that the Defense Department opposes ensures, in their minds, that the United States cannot sustain a military force capable of "fighting and winning the nation's wars."[66] It is in this manner that congressional action—or the threat of inaction, in this case—plays a major role in sustaining negative stereotypes across agencies while exacerbating interagency conflict.

From this brief analysis, it is clear that domestic politics—in terms of public opinion and the influence of the Congress (as a government actor outside the formal interagency process)—plays a crucial role in shaping both interagency dynamics and policy outcomes. In conjunction with leadership and decision making as negotiation (and their supporting micro themes), domestic politics serves as a compelling factor in shaping interagency actor attitudes and behaviors. It is critical to note, however, that while these three macro themes emerged as those exerting the greatest influence on interagency dynamics, the data also revealed two crosscutting effects that impinge upon both dynamic themes and contextual parameters. These crosscutting effects are framed as (1) roles and missions and (2) media influence. These elements mold both the ways through which interagency dynamics affect the substantive policy outcome and the ways in which contextual parameters influence interagency dynamics, and ultimately, policy outcomes.

Interpretation of Findings

The findings related to dynamic themes (i.e., decision making as negotiation, domestic politics, and leadership as seen in fig. 23) indicate that Allison's bureaucratic politics model characterizes the interagency policy-making process in terms of the ways in which the process identifies the players and the players frame the process dynamic. The most salient factors shaping the process itself materialize in the form of the leadership provided by the president and the principals, in tandem with the individual decision makers' personalities and the nature of the personal relationships they share with others. In this manner, the finding conforms to Allison's propositions regarding the player identification, their perspectives or "stands" on the issues (as framed by organizational cultures and shared images), and the influence they exercise within the policy process in terms of shaping interagency dynamics and policy outcomes. Personalities, personal relationships, and organizational culture play an associated role in developing the process dynamics Allison anticipated.

Individuals actively control information exchange, manipulating the interagency negotiation process to achieve policy outcomes that undeniably emerge as "political resultants" in Allison's classic sense. Bureaucratic infighting occurs at lower levels of the interagency process but tends not to be as prominent at the principals or deputies levels unless the issue under consideration threatens the core values or equities of the department or institution (e.g., readiness, budgets, or the strength of diplomacy). Further, once a principal makes public his or her institution's position, the parameters are set—crisis definition and option generation are then bound by that principal's perspective. This pronouncement can create interagency conflict across the IWG as actors become increasingly resistant to "negotiating away" their respective principal's stated perspective—even if the nature of the crisis compels such reconsideration. Organizational cultures dictate that reversals can come only through the statements and actions of the principals themselves. This is not to allege that intradepartmental debate ends. Rather, it suggests that public interagency debate will (potentially) divert its focus from the problem under consideration as the actors become increasingly loyal to their principals in cases wherein the debate is framed as a bureaucratic fight, one whose "primary" purpose is to protect and preserve one's particular equities.

Government officials agree that the policy-making process should be, and indeed is, an exercise in decision making by negotiation. Only through such a process can the USG generate and sustain the required buy-in toward a broader consensus, one that is clearly not a "rational actor" approach in terms of subjective expected utility. This consensus approach then becomes the critical component in implementation. When decision makers fail to generate adequate buy-in through the interagency process, departments act in fulfilling policy mandates but operate only at the margins by exercising their inherent bureaucratic powers during the stated policy's interpretation and implementation.[67]

Having determined that these findings conform to the first two elements of Allison's bureaucratic model, analysis of those themes wherein the contextual parameters of the process shape interagency dynamics by framing the dynamic themes discloses another layer of complexity regarding process. Through the analysis of the findings presented here and those that emerge via the two upcoming chapters, we should be able to determine whether Allison's third and final modeling precept fits the interagency process. We will do this by discovering the ways in which these dynamic themes and contextual parameters influence policy alternatives, simultaneously explaining the ways in which the contextual parameters that circumscribe the policy process shape interagency dynamics.

Notes

1. The literature on leadership is perhaps one of the largest bodies of scholarship in existence, both from an analytical perspective and from a personal memoir standpoint. See also an overview of leadership as it relates to decision making and foreign policy as is provided by Chester Barnard, *The Functions of*

the Executive (Cambridge, Mass.: Harvard University Press, 1938); see also Lee Roy Beach et al., "Image Theory: Decision Framing and Decision Liberation," in *Decision-Making and Leadership,* ed. Frank Heller (Cambridge, Mass.: Cambridge University Press, 1992); see also Boutros Boutros-Ghali et al., *Essays on Leadership: Perspectives on Prevention* (New York: Carnegie Corp. of New York, 1998); see also George Bush, "American Leadership and the Prevention of Deadly Conflict," in *Essays on Leadership;* see also Jimmy Carter, "Searching for Peace," in *Essays On Leadership;* see also Howard Cooper Deshong III, "Resolution and Disillusion: Bureaucratic Politics and the Reagan Administration's Counterterrorism Policy, 1982–1986" (PhD diss., Tufts University, 1996); see also Arne Garborg, "Garborg's Heart'n Home Collection: Leadership" (Bloomington, Minn.: Garborg's, Inc., 1993); see also Mikhail Gorbachev, "On Nonviolent Leadership," in *Essays On Leadership;* Jayne Ellen Kyrstyn Holl, "From the Streets of Washington to the Roofs of Saigon: Domestic Politics and the Termination of the Vietnam War" (PhD diss., Stanford University, 1989); see also Irving L. Janis, *Crucial Decisions: Leadership in Policymaking and Crisis Management* (New York: Free Press, 1989); see also John Thomas Preston, "The President and His Inner Circle: Leadership Style and the Advisory Process in Foreign Policy-Making" (PhD diss., Ohio State University, 1996); see also Edgar H. Schein, *Organizational Culture and Leadership* (San Francisco: Jossey-Bass Publishers, 1992); see also Desmond Tutu, "Leadership," in *Essays On Leadership;* and see also Victor H. Vroom and P. W. Yetton, *Leadership and Decision Making* (Pittsburgh, Pa.: University of Pittsburgh Press, 1973).

2. This qualitative analysis is not laden with numbers and statistical references; rather, where most illuminating, this discussion uses phrases such as "a majority" or "almost half" to clarify the frequencies of particular themes. Note that these percentages, where included, refer to the percentage of those whose interviews were selected for inclusion in this qualitative analysis. Unless otherwise noted, these figures relate to the qualitative coding sampling. Hence, a reference to "50 percent of those at the NSC" equates to "6 out of 12," not 10 out of 19. Finally, this research does not attempt to transform this grounded theory categorical analysis into a quantitative presentation of these thematic findings.

3. See also Leslie H. Gelb and Richard K. Betts, *The Irony of Vietnam: The System Worked* (Washington, D.C.: The Brookings Institution, 1979) for an historical example that reflects this position.

4. All quoted items in this chapter and subsequent chapters come directly from the interview transcripts that support this research. Where possible, this research frames quotations in terms of the individual's level within the interagency process, departmental affiliation, and the case with which he or she is associated.

5. State Department official, US Deparment of State, Washington, D.C.

6. Ibid.

7. National Security Interagency Policy-making official, Executive Office of the President, Washington, D.C.

8. Defense Department official, US Department of Defense, Washington, D.C.

9. National Security Interagency Policy-making official.

10. Ibid.

11. For another account of this phenomenon, see also Leon V. Sigal, *Disarming Strangers: Nuclear Diplomacy with North Korea* (Princeton, N.J.: Princeton University Press, 1998). The account captures the most recent diplomatic crisis between the United States and Korea regarding nuclear arms.

12. State Department official.

13. For additional facets related to organizational culture, see Nimet Beriker and Daniel Druckman, "Simulating the Lausanne Peace Negotiations, 1922–1923: Power Asymmetries in Bargaining," *Simulation and Gaming* 27, no. 2 (1996): 162–83; Jennifer A. Chatman and Sigal G. Barsade, "Personality, Organizational Culture, and Cooperation: Evidence from a Business Simulation," *Administrative Science Quarterly* 40 (1995): 423–43; Michael I. Harrison and Bruce Phillips, "Strategic Decision Making: An Integrative Explanation," *Research in the Sociology of Organizations* 9 (1991): 319–58; see also J. Steven Ott, ed., *Classic Readings in Organizational Behavior* (Pacific Grove, Calif.: Brooks/Cole Publishing Co., 1989); Andrew M. Pettigrew, "On Studying Organizational Cultures," *Administrative Science Quarterly* 24, no. 4 (1979): 570–81; see also Edgar H. Schein, "Defining Organizational Culture," in *Classics of Organization Theory*, ed. J. M. Shafritz and J. S. Ott (Pacific Grove, Calif.: Brooks/Cole Publishing Co., 1987); see also Edgar H. Schein, "Group and Intergroup Relationships," in *Classic Readings in Organizational Behavior*, ed. J. S. Ott (Pacific Grove, Calif.: Brooks/Cole Publishing Co., 1989); and see also Amarjit S. Sethi, *Developing Excellence through Imaginative Organizational Culture: A Strategic Systems Approach* (Ontario, Canada: University of Ottawa, 1994).

14. National Security Interagency Policy-making official.

15. An *institutional equity* is defined as any asset that adds value to or is the defining characteristic of an agency, one that becomes a substantive input into the policy process. This theme is discussed in detail in chapter 7 as an emergent macro theme.

16. National Security Interagency Policy-making official.

17. Ibid.

18. Defense Department official.

19. This condition is visible at many levels across the interagency process but is particularly acute in terms of the "headquarters field" relationship. Several study participants with experience outside Washington noted that an attitude persists wherein those in the field believe Washington's policy makers are too disconnected from the contextual realities of crises on the ground to make adequate decisions. This said, there is at times a "Washington can do whatever it wants" attitude toward following the directions of the USG. Halperin et al. discussed this situation as well—the findings here reinforce its continued existence. See also Morton H. Halperin, with the assis-

tance of Priscila Clapp and Arnold Kanter, *Bureaucratic Politics and Foreign Policy* (Washington, D.C.: The Brookings Institution, 1974).

20. See also Graham T. Allison, *Essence of Decision: Explaining the Cuban Missile Crisis* (Boston: Little, Brown and Co., 1971); and see also Halperin with the assistance of Clapp, and Kanter, *Bureaucratic Politics and Foreign Policy.* Recall also that this research contains survey findings indicating that relations across departments correlate with *Agency's Perceptions of Other's Conflict Orientation*, which, in turn, correlate with *Agency's Perceptions of Other's Level of Self-Interest* (see fig. 11).

21. For example, during the Persian Gulf War, the military's failure to achieve full interoperability resulted from dissimilar communication equipment that would not allow different services to talk with one another during the execution of the mission.

22. This generates another organizational dilemma. If the principal or deputy is involved constantly in meetings, how is he or she supposed to "run" an agency and deal with other pressing matters? Hence, this approach becomes a "nonstarter" from the perspective of the decision maker.

23. For a more in-depth examination of this issue, see also James D. Thompson, "Organizations in Action," in *Classics of Organization Theory,* and see also James D. Thompson, *Organizations in Action: Social Science Bases of Administrative Theory* (New York: McGraw-Hill, 1967).

24. Intelligence Community official, Washington, D.C.

25. National Security Interagency Policy-making official.

26. Ibid.

27. Ibid.

28. For an additional perspective on innovative thinking, see Johan Kaufmann, "The Middle East Peace Process: A New Case of Conference Diplomacy," *Peace and Change* 18, no. 3 (1993): 290–306; Jacques Paul Klein, telephone conversation with author, 20 November 1998; and Eleanor Farrar McGowan, "Rational Fantasies," *Policy Sciences* 7, no. 4 (1976): 439–54.

29. Defense Department official. The Defense Department's perspectives on innovative thinking remained mixed. This perspective imparts only one view. It is highlighted here to demonstrate that this individual made a direct connection between innovative thinking and organizational culture. An outside reader clarified this perspective, noting that there is another level of analysis involved. Contingency plans are devices to expedite decisions within the Defense Department. There is a time issue inherent in this—they feel that others need to demonstrate that the conditions do not fit the contingency plan. From this official's perspective, it is not a matter of being resistant to innovation; rather, it is a matter of all the prework and analysis that generated the contingency plan—work that the Defense Department is hesitant to discard unless other agencies provide a better alternative.

30. Ibid. This dichotomy addresses one of the aspects this research attempted to investigate, namely, the tendency for people to think something happens one way in theory, but behaviors and attitudes actualize in a different manner in practice. Hence, the ability for people to think outside the box but

not "get" outside that box provides evidence that this theory-practice fissure exists.

31. Ambassador Jacques Paul Klein provided this insight; permission to attribute granted by Ambassador Klein, telephone interview with author, 20 November 1998.

32. State Department official.

33. Defense Department official.

34. State Department official.

35. Defense Department official.

36. An ever-expanding literature continues to enhance our understanding of communication, debate, and information exchange. See, for example, Gary Bornstein, Danny Mingelgrin, and Christel Rutte, "The Effects of Within-group Communication on Group Decision and Individual Choice in the Assurance and Chicken Team Games," *Journal of Conflict Resolution* 40, no. 3 (1996): 486–501; Gary Bornstein et al., "Within- and Between-group Communication in Intergroup Competition for Public Goods," *Journal of Experimental Social Psychology* 25 (1989): 422–36; Angela M. Bowey, "Approaches to Organization Theory," *Social Science Information/Information sur les Sciences Sociales* 11, no. 6 (1972): 109–28; Nathan Caplan, "Social Research and National Policy: What Gets Used, by Whom, for What Purposes, and with What Effects?" *International Social Science Journal* 28, no. 1 (1976): 187–94; see also John S. Carroll and John W. Payne, "An Information Processing Approach to Two-Party Negotiations," in *Research on Negotiation in Organizations*, ed. Max H. Bazerman, Roy J. Lewicki, and Blair H. Sheppard, *Handbook of Negotiation Research* (Greenwich & London: JAI Press, Inc., 1991); Steven R. Corman, "A Model of Perceived Communication in Collective Networks," *Human Communication Research* 16, no. 4 (1990): 582–602; Chester A. Insko et al., "The Role of Communication in Interindividual-Intergroup Discontinuity," *Journal of Conflict Resolution* 37, no. 1 (1993): 108–38; see also Paul Koopman and Jeroen Pool, "Organizational Decision Making: Models, Contingencies and Strategies," in *Distributed Decision Making: Cognitive Models for Cooperative Work*, ed. Jens Rasmussen, Berndt Brehmer, and Jacques Leplat (Chichester, England: John Wiley & Sons, 1991); James R. Larson Jr., Pennie G. Foster-Fishman, and Christopher B. Keys, "Discussion of Shared and Unshared Information in Decision-Making Groups," *Journal of Personality and Social Psychology* 67, no. 3 (1994): 446– 61; Todd J. Maurer and Robert G. Lord, "An Exploration of Cognitive Demands in Group Interaction as a Moderator of Information Processing Variables in Perceptions of Leadership," *Journal of Applied Social Psychology* 21, no. 10 (1991): 821–39; see also M. Minsky, *Semantic Information Processing* (Cambridge, Mass.: MIT Press, 1968); Charles Pavitt, "Another View of Group Polarizing: The 'Reasons for' One-Sided Oral Argumentation," *Communication Research* 21, no. 5 (1994): 625–42; Alan Ned Sabrosky, James Clay Thompson, and Karen A. McPherson, "Organized Anarchies: Military Bureaucracy in the 1980s," *Journal of Applied Behavioral Science* 18, no. 2 (1982): 137–53; Pierre Thomas, "Interagency FBI-CIA Tensions Defy Decades of Ef-

202

forts to Resolve Them," *The Washington Post*, 3 May 1994, A4; Earl A. Thompson and Roger L. Faith, "Social Interaction under Truly Perfect Information," *Journal of Mathematical Sociology* 7, no. 2 (1980): 181–97; see also Richard E. Walton and John M. Dutton, "The Management of Interdepartmental Conflict: A Model and Review," in *Classic Readings in Organizational Behavior*, ed. J. S. Ott (Pacific Grove, Calif.: Brooks/Cole Publishing Co., 1989); and John Zaller, "Information, Values, and Opinions," *American Political Science Review* 85 (1991): 1215–38.

37. The academic and popular literatures describe personal relationships and networking in myriad ways. See, for example, Carroll and Payne, "An Information Processing Approach to Two-Party Negotiations"; Corman, "A Model of Perceived Communication in Collective Networks"; Patrick Doreian and Andrej Mrvar, "A Partitioning Approach to Structural Balance," *Social Networks* 18, no. 2 (1996): 149–68; see also Peter M. Haas, "Introduction: Epistemic Communities and International Policy Coordination," *International Organization* 46 (1992); Joseph J. Molnar, "Comparative Organizational Properties and Interorganizational Interdependence," *Sociology and Social Research* 63, no. 1 (1978): 24–48; see also Ian E. Morley, "Intra-Organizational Bargaining," in *Employment Relations: The Psychology of Influence and Control at Work*, ed. Jean F. Hartley and Geoffrey M. Stephenson (Oxford, England: Blackwell, 1992); see also Sabrosky, Thompson, and McPherson, "Organized Anarchies: Military Bureaucracy in the 1980s"; and James D. Westphal and Edward J. Zajac, "Defections from the Inner Circle: Social Exchange, Reciprocity, and the Diffusion of Board Independence in U.S. Corporations," *Administrative Science Quarterly* 42, no. 1 (1997): 161–83.

38. Intelligence Community official.

39. Ibid.

40. Defense Department official.

41. State Department official.

42. Ibid.

43. Defense Department official.

44. It is important to reiterate here that this study is not a study of negotiation; rather, it examines the interagency process by determining whether the decision-making process is a negotiation. For a review of the literature related to decision making *and* negotiation, see Samuel B. Bacharach and Edward J. Lawler, "Power Dependence and Power Paradoxes in Bargaining," *Negotiation Journal* 2 (1986): 167–74; see also Carroll and Payne, "An Information Processing Approach to Two-Party Negotiations"; William A. Donohue et al., "Crisis Bargaining in Intense Conflict Situations," *International Journal of Group Tensions* 21, no. 2 (1991): 133–53; Ole Elgstrom, "National Culture and International Negotiations," *Cooperation and Conflict* 29, no. 3 (1994): 289–301; see also Hrach Gregorian, *Congressional-Executive Relations and Foreign Policymaking in the Post–Vietnam Period: Case Studies of Congressional Influence* (Waltham, Mass.: Brandeis University, Department of Politics, 1980); Roderick M. Kramer, Pamela Pommerenke, and Elizabeth Newton, "The Social Context of Negotiation: Effects of Social Identity and Interpersonal Accountability on Ne-

gotiator Decision Making," *Journal of Conflict Resolution* 37, no. 4 (1993): 633–54; Jack S. Levy, "Prospect Theory, Rational Choice, and International Relations," *International Studies Quarterly* 41, no. 1 (1997): 87–112; see also Michael Nicholson, "Negotiation, Agreement and Conflict Resolution: The Role of Rational Approaches and Their Criticism," in *New Directions in Conflict Theory: Conflict Resolution and Conflict Transformation*, ed. Raimo Vayrynen (Newbury Park, Calif.: Sage Publications, Inc., 1991); J. P. Perry Robinson, "The Negotiations on Chemical-Warfare Arms Control," *Arms Control* 1, no. 1 (1980): 30–52; see also Alvin E. Roth, "An Economic Approach to the Study of Bargaining," in *Research on Negotiation in Organizations*, ed. Max H. Bazerman, Roy J. Lewicki, and Blair H. Sheppard, *Handbook of Negotiation Research* (Greenwich & London: JAI Press, Inc., 1991); Leigh Thompson, Erika Peterson, and Susan E. Brodt, "Team Negotiation: An Examination of Integrative and Distributive Bargaining," *Journal of Personality and Social Psychology* 70, no. 1 (1996): 66–78; see also Raimo Vayrynen, ed., *New Directions in Conflict Theory: Conflict Resolution and Conflict Transformation* (Newbury Park, Calif.: Sage Publications, Inc., 1991); and I. William Zartman, "Negotiation as a Joint Decision-Making Process," *Journal of Conflict Resolution* 21, no. 4 (1977): 619–38.

45. National Security Interagency Policy-making official.

46. Ibid.

47. For various views on the relationship between access and privilege in organizational decision making and foreign policy, see also Larry W. Boone, "An Assessment of Organizational Decision-Making for Simple and Complex Problems" (PhD diss., University of Pittsburgh, 1987); see also Deshong, "Resolution and Disillusion: Bureaucratic Politics and the Reagan Administration's Counterterrorism Policy, 1982–1986"; see also Hanna Yousif Freij, "Perceptions and Behavior in U.S. Foreign Relations Towards the Republic of Iraq" (PhD diss., University of Pittsburgh, 1992); see also Hyun Kim, "Rationality, Bureaucratic Politics, and Cognitive Processes in Foreign Policy Decision-Making: An Analysis of the United States Policy Decisions Towards Japan, 1948–1954" (PhD diss., City University of New York, 1996); see also Agnes Gerges Korbani, "Presidential Working-System Style, Cognition, and Foreign Policy: A Comparative Study of U.S. Decisions to Intervene Militarily in Lebanon in 1958 and 1982" (PhD diss., Northwestern University, 1989); see also Paul Andrew Kowert, "Between Reason and Passion: A Systems Theory of Foreign Policy Learning" (PhD diss., Cornell University, 1992); see also James David Meernik, "Presidential Decision-Making and the Political Use of Military Force" (PhD diss., Michigan State University, 1992); see also Cynthia Biddle Orbovich, "Cognitive Style and Foreign Policy Decisionmaking: An Examination of Eisenhower's National Security Organization" (PhD diss., The Ohio State University, 1986); see also Philip John Powlick, "The American Foreign Policy Process and the Public" (PhD diss., University of Pittsburgh, 1990); and see also Qingshan Tan, "U.S.-China Policy: A Function of Strategy or Process?" (PhD diss., Emory University, 1989).

48. State Department official.

49. National Security Council official.

50. Interagency official, Executive Office of the President.

51. Ibid.

52. State Department official.

53. Ibid.

54. See also Geoffrey Brennan, "What Might Rationality Fail to Do?," in *Decision Making: Alternatives to Rational Choice Models*, ed. Mary Zey (Newbury Park, Calif.: Sage Publications, Inc., 1992).

55. Interagency official.

56. Take, for example, the revelation that the military chiefs of staff remained "out of the loop" when President William Clinton decided to retaliate against Osama Bin Laden in both Afghanistan and the Sudan. Their inclusion in this process may well have led to a different course of action. See also Seymour Hersh, *The New Yorker*, 12 October 1998.

57. Interagency official.

58. Domestic politics, especially public opinion, play a significant role in the development of policy. See, for example, Christopher Dandeker, "Public Opinion, the Media, and the Gulf War," *Armed Forces and Society* 22, no. 2 (1995): 297–302; William P. Eveland Jr., Douglas M. McLeod, and Nancy Signorielli, "Actual and Perceived U.S. Public Opinion: The Spiral of Silence During the Persian Gulf War," *International Journal of Public Opinion Research* 7, no. 2 (1995): 91–109; James D. Fearon, "Domestic Political Audiences and the Escalation of International Disputes," *The American Political Science Review* 88, no. 3 (1994): 577–92; see also Douglas Charles Foyle, "The Influence of Public Opinion on American Foreign Policy Decision-Making: Context, Beliefs, and Process" (PhD diss., Duke University, 1996); see also Nathalie Julia Frensley, "Domestic Politics and International Conflict Termination: The Dynamic Group Theory of Conflict Processes with Northern Ireland as a Test Case" (PhD diss., University of Texas at Austin, 1996); see also Martha Liebler Gibson, "Weapons of Influence: The Legislative Veto, American Foreign Policy and the Irony of Reform" (PhD diss., University of Colorado at Boulder, 1991); see also Holl, "From the Streets of Washington to the Roofs of Saigon"; Shanto Iyengar and Adam Simon, "News Coverage of the Gulf Crisis and Public Opinion: A Study of Agenda-Setting, Priming, and Framing," *Communication Research* 20, no. 3 (1993): 365–83; Sut Jhally, Justin Lewis, and Michael Morgan, "The Gulf War: A Study of the Media, Public Opinion and Public Knowledge," *Propaganda Review* 8 (fall 1991): 14–15, 50–52; see also Andrew W. Katz, "Public Opinion, Congress, President Nixon, and the Termination of the Vietnam War" (PhD diss., The Johns Hopkins University, 1987); Jon A. Krosnick and Laura A. Brannon, "The Media and the Foundations of Presidential Support: George Bush and the Persian Gulf Conflict," *Journal of Social Issues* 49, no. 4 (1993): 167–82; see also Steven Kull and I. M. Destler, *Misreading the Public: The Myth of a New Isolationism* (Washington, D.C.: The Brookings Institution Press, 1999); Bradley Lian and John R. Oneal, "Presidents, the Use of Military Force, and Public Opinion," *Journal of Conflict Resolution* 37, no. 2 (1993): 277–300; Suzanne L. Parker, "Toward an Understanding of 'Rally' Effects: Public Opinion in the Persian Gulf War," *Public Opinion Quarterly* 59, no. 4 (1995): 526–46;

Philip J. Powlick, "The Attitudinal Bases for Responsiveness to Public Opinion among American Foreign Policy Officials," *Journal of Conflict Resolution* 35, no. 4 (1991): 611–41; Robert D. Putnam, "Diplomacy and Domestic Politics: The Logic of Two-Level Games," *International Organization* 42, no. 3 (1988): 427–60; see also Robert Rothstein, "Domestic Politics and Peacemaking: Reconciling Incompatible Imperatives," *The Annals of The American Academy of Political and Social Science* 392 (1970); see also Bruce Russett and Thomas W. Graham, "Public Opinion and National Security Policy: Relationships and Impacts," in *Handbook of War Studies*, ed. Manus I. Midlarsky (Boston: Unwin Hyman, 1989); see also John Spanier and Eric M. Uslaner, *How American Foreign Policy Is Made* (New York & Washington, D.C.: Praeger Publishers, 1974); Norman C. Thomas, "The Presidency and Policy Studies," *Policy Studies Journal* 9, no. 7 (1981): 1072–82; and see also John Zaller, *The Nature and Origins of Mass Opinion* (New York: Cambridge University Press, 1993).

59. Interagency official.

60. National Security Interagency Policy-making official.

61. See also the Special Assistant to the Secretary and Deputy Secretary of Defense, Department of Defense (DOD), *White Paper—Department of Defense and Congress* (Washington, D.C.: U.S. Department of Defense, 1989).

62. Michael Hirsh and John Barry, "How We Stumbled into War," *Newsweek*, 12 April 1999, 38–40.

63. Intelligence Community official.

64. Ibid.

65. George Bush, *Statement on the United Nations Security Council Resolution Authorizing the Use of Force against Iraq* (The George Bush Presidential Library, 1990), on-line, Internet, 3 April 1999, available from http://www.csdl. tamu.edu/bushlibrary/library/research/research.html.

66. One principal made an interesting and innovative observation regarding military funding. He said, "If you follow Powell's dictum, we would have lost the support and would not be enjoying the budgets we have today. To maintain a strong military we had to keep the military relevant for today's problems to prepare for tomorrow's problems. This is why we needed to play role in Haiti, Bosnia, Somalia, etc., while at the same time building a military to handle Korea, China, etc."

67. Officials referenced numerous examples of such policy decisions throughout the interview process. During the 1983 Lebanon crisis, for example, the Defense Department stationed a US Marine Corps unit off shore for quick evacuation purposes in lieu of positioning US Army troops on the ground. While the positioning of the Marines met policy requirements, the Defense Department selected the Marine component with the foreknowledge that it was *not* the most appropriate or prepared military unit for the mission. More recently, during the evacuation mission in Somalia that simultaneously attempted to capture warlord Mohammed Farah Aidid, Defense employed Black Hawk helicopters in place of the more appropriate AC-130H gunships. As a 17-hour firefight ensued during the rescue attempt on 3 October 1993, "elite units of the US Army's Rangers and Delta Force were ambushed by Somali men, women

and children armed with automatic weapons and rocket-propelled grenades." See Frontline, *Ambush in Mogadishu*, PBS, 1999, on-line, Internet, 27 March 2002, available from http://www.pbs.org/wgbh/pages/frontline/shows/am bush/etc/synopsis.html. Because of this effort to protect bureaucratic equities—the US Army's "go it alone attitude" in this case—18 Americans died and 84 others were wounded.

Chapter 7

Contextual Parameters: Environmental Factors Channel Interagency Dynamics

Decision makers frame policy options within a politically constrained environment. Domestic and international political contextual parameters determine the nature of the interagency process "playing field" while simultaneously selecting the "players." When making decisions regarding crisis intervention and conflict termination policy, attitudes and behaviors surrounding strategic vision and planning processes and institutional equities hold sway over interagency actors' approaches to the policy process. Based upon their capacity to mold the interagency dynamic, strategic vision and planning processes, tend to shape the policy process in crucial ways as they clarify institutional equities; consequently, this theme frames our understanding of the ways in which contextual parameters influence interagency dynamics.

Strategic Vision and Planning Processes

It follows logically that strategic vision and planning processes would function as a critical component of contextual parameters as its complementary dynamic theme is leadership (i.e., leadership emerged as the most salient theme that shapes interagency dynamics as identified in chap. 6). The substantive extension of leadership manifests itself in those issues surrounding the nature of the strategic vision and planning processes that guide the interagency process toward policy outcomes.[1] Three interdependent issues related to strategic vision and planning processes emerged: (1) political vision, (2) shared images, and (3) a tactical focus. Supporting subthemes relate to core competencies, national interests and intervention criteria, and worldview influence (in terms of ideology and philosophy).

209

Acknowledging the potential crosscutting effects of this theme, strategic vision channels process dynamics—and hence, policy outcomes—through its ability to either enhance cohesion or further fragment the interagency process from the outset of crisis analysis. Policy makers who participated in the study (especially those below the principals level) felt that a clearly articulated strategic vision diminishes interagency conflict by providing all agencies a goal around which to coalesce.[2] Alternatively, the absence of strategic vision creates (or exacerbates) interagency conflict that adversely affects policy outcomes. In characterizing the post–Cold War era, one State Department official remarked, "There's no strategic vision—none similar to NSC-68 which carried us to the end of the Cold War. That strategy and doctrine carried us for 45 years."[3] DOD officials consistently echoed this perspective, one remarking, "We are fast approaching the point 'where the inbox rules' and knee-jerk reactions [prevail] with no larger vision for how this fits into the strategic vision [and] without even thinking how this fits into the larger picture. Again, personality and credibility often override the process. Political vision is lacking, therefore, so is the political will."[4]

This lack of strategic vision, coupled with the inability to mobilize political will, creates an environment wherein disparate perspectives concerning *Roles and Missions* reinforce dissimilar crisis analyses while seemingly supporting divergent views regarding potential US policy options. This dilemma stems from fragmented images (i.e., they are not "shared images") that dominate crisis analysis, option generation, and course of action development.

Introduced earlier through the reference to NSC-68's Cold War–era efficacy, post–Cold War interagency actors do not share a common image regarding the nature of threats to national security and, therefore, the USG's most appropriate responses. Although post–Cold War national security and military strategies of "engagement/enlargement" have attempted to provide such a vision through their associated "shape, respond, prepare now" approaches, executive agencies have not yet embedded evenly the vision (and its requirements) throughout their organizational cultures.[5] A senior State Department official characterized this problem by saying, "One of the things that drives the current period is the lack of shared images on the nature of threats and the use of force. The assumption in the argument is that people want to employ [Defense Department] resources, but the military does not."[6] The absence of shared images enables personalities to dominate the process, generating a policy outcome and COA that remain disconnected from a broader strategic vision. The result of philosophical differences, this defect allows the Congress and the media to engage in the substantive aspects of policy development. A State Department principal asserted, "Quite often, those of us in government, the civilians, take each crisis as it comes with very little reference to a policy document. If a serious action, it will work its way up to the PC and president if necessary. It brings with it things that are not necessarily . . . part of a policy document—the Hill and what the media is saying about it."[7]

Another State Department official corroborated the following idea regarding the role of policy (or lack thereof) in guiding interagency decision making: "The interagency process is cumbersome; [it] necessarily works well at [the] working level [IWG] when people understand clear policy lines and you're tracking. When making new policy it can be very time consuming. Within the standard IWG, DC, PC process, when there are contentious issues, there's not enough discipline and agencies in this [Clinton's] administration frustratingly reopen decisions and take each . . . to the Hill—that's Washington. If you have a core team with a mandate, then it works."[8] The absence of an overarching strategic vision—one coalescing around shared images reinforced by a mutual understanding of roles and missions—adversely affects intervention planning for complex crises as decision makers focus on short-term or immediate tactical, rather than longer-term strategic issues. In so doing, analysts and decision makers alike tend to focus on select nodes of a problem (i.e., honing in on individual trees) as a substitute for a systems approach that explores the entire problem within its own dynamic context (i.e., analyzing the trees within their broader organic context of the forest). Such an oversight holds grave implications for conflict termination policy development.

One of the most pronounced cleavages across the inter-agency process regards the actors' perspectives regarding planning. The interagency process embodies no comprehensive planning mechanism to integrate the various agencies' incongruent visions (when such visions exist). Unfortunately, the Clinton administration's Presidential Decision Directive (PDD) 56 has not abridged interagency fissures. This is due partly to the way in which it is administered (final plans are held tightly by the NSC Staff) and partly because a PDD cannot "fix" an organizational cultural problem within the executive branch. Thus, the absence of leadership and dissimilar organizational cultures are responsible, in part, for producing this dynamic. According to one NSC Staff member, the NSC Staff tries to engage in forecasting and strategic planning, but they remain mired in the "crisis of the day." Relatedly, although the State Department operates an office entitled "Strategic Planning" (SP), it too is consumed by "the crisis *du jour*." One State Department official characterized SP's problem in this manner, "There are so many crises—State has an interest in almost all of them. If you are SP, Strategic Planning, you are marginalized. Yes, [strategic planning] is a good idea, but it is never effectively used in that way. No one at State has come up with a way to integrate effective strategic planning into daily operations."[9] "DOS/SP gets into much of day-to-day stuff more than the long-term vision, it's not a J-5 [J-5 is the Joint Staff's strategic planning component and is part of the chairman's staff within the Defense Department]. The successful SPs don't do long-term stuff—they put out fires (i.e., crises) for the secretary. SP is marginalized if focused on the long term."[10] Hence, within the State Department no imperative exists to perform long-term strategic planning. This omission conflicts with the Defense Department's approach whose strategic planning office actually conducts strategic planning.[11] A Defense Department deputy captured the essence of this cultural divide by stating "[You] have State who doesn't understand backwards planning coming into contact with DOD who does that kind of planning. Now [you] have an institutional battle—the breakthrough comes in terms of personality. If you get good personality matches, you get good policy: Personality matches make this happen. This 'Let's go and do something' approach is prevalent in other agencies."[12]

Inherent in this approach, according to one experienced policy maker, is the unwillingness of interagency actors to "ask the tough questions" (e.g., How long will this take? . . . Ten years, no way [we're not doing that]—eight months, maybe).[13] Additionally, an NSC official contended, "Going through the process to develop options/strategies is very useful for [the president]. The military does not understand that interagency planning at the policy level is a process that creates choices, not a plan . . . a plan is worthless, but planning is everything."[14] In the words of another official, this disconnect regarding agency planning approaches and their resultant plans ensures that even "if there is a vision, there's no strategy to achieve it."[15]

The net effect of this chasm is that the policy process is driven more toward the development of tactical options as a substitute for the strategic vision necessary to guide national security policy and crisis response activities. Each agency agreed that the policy process is reactive and tactically focused, promoting across all agencies an ad hoc response to the crisis *du jour*. The research methodology employed by this study cannot confirm conclusively whether this tactical focus *causes* this reactive planning and response cycle (nor can it conclusively support the reverse relationship). However, it is interesting to reflect upon one State Department official's perspective—a perspective that links strategic vision directly to planning and crisis action response—"There is not too much of a distinction between strategic and crisis action planning. If you started at the beginning of the administration and get a vision, you use the crisis to advance the interests you have already identified. In that sense, crisis management is the fire you are waiting for."[16]

Two factors related to strategic vision promote interagency actors' collective inability to capitalize on, or prepare for, the crisis of the moment. First, while no fault of their own, because the lower-level actors have not internalized a strategic vision to guide their activities, they lack insight regarding the specific crisis as it relates to US national interests, national security, and the broader geopolitical context. This assumes, of course, that leaders have defined and articulated US national interests (an issue

213

discussed later in this section). This myopic focus retards the earliest stages of crisis analysis wherein decisions are made that frame the conflict's underlying causes and conditions and, by extension, potential responses. This problem continues to hamper policy development as lower-level actors clarify issues for successive interagency levels (i.e., DC and PC).

Second, time and resource constraints accompanying crisis analysis magnify these problems. Contrary to the rational actor model's tenets, agencies possess neither unlimited time nor unbounded resources (e.g., number of people to work the crisis or capacity to access "pure" intelligence). Such limitations greatly compress analysis and response cycles for each crisis while negating the decision maker's ability to respond in terms of a broader strategic vision (again, assuming one has been developed and articulated).

Reflecting on the theory framing this analysis, it is crucial to acknowledge that issues related to strategic vision and planning processes shape initial inputs and anchoring points by injecting disparate information into the interagency's policy process during policy development's initial stages—these issues continue to reinforce initial inputs and anchoring points well into the production of policy outcomes. Consequently, disparate inputs regarding political vision and shared images reflexively propel the planning process toward a tactical-level focus, moving away from the strategic vision required to guide the overarching planning and response processes. The effect of this tactical perspective and its ensuing response process manifests visibly in the interagency's policy outcomes; because the views of the desired end state are politicized at the government's highest levels, people remain unwilling to ask (and, indeed, answer) tough questions concerning crisis analysis and response. An NSC principal adeptly characterized the problem as one related to organizational culture by stating, "[The pol-mil planning process] has [an] advanced planning process—different from the military's deliberate planning. The [object of the] deliberate planning process is to provide a plan—the product of the advanced planning process is to create options, the policy maker wants choices. Below the policy maker, the strategizer level of DOD wants objectives."[17]

This cleavage reveals one of the interagency's most disturbing disjunctures, a fissure that ultimately prevents decision makers from developing effective conflict termination policy. Interagency actors remain unable to translate policy-maker choices into measurable objectives that can be operationalized in terms of (1) a viable strategy and (2) the identification of conflict termination criteria to guide that strategy toward the desired end state. Issues surrounding core competencies, national interests and intervention criteria, and agency worldviews (including ideological and philosophical perspectives) serve as substantive inputs for framing strategic vision, thereby shaping planning processes. Taking each in turn, the ensuing discussion explains their importance and provides evidence for those relationships.

Perceptions of Core Competencies

Arguably, this research could have analyzed issues related to core competencies in terms of the clarity of roles and missions discussion presented in the next chapter. While a direct relationship exists as an agency's core competencies (i.e., the activities for which an agency trains and equips as its functional roles)[18] distinguish its ability to perform certain roles while negating others, the connection between core competencies and strategic vision is of particular import. Specifically, the lack of a substantive comprehension of each agency's core competencies (i.e., the expertise each brings to bear as a product of one's roles and missions) creates and exacerbates interagency conflict, ultimately giving rise to suboptimal policy outcomes. Misunderstandings regarding core competencies generate iterative cycles that fragment policy makers' perspectives regarding the national interests that form strategic vision's foundation.

An acute misunderstanding of core competencies exists across interagency decision makers. This confusion emanates from the lack of connectivity across agencies and leads to "finger pointing" (i.e., one manifestation of interagency conflict) and increased media activity. One Defense Department official characterized the problem by insisting that "interagency conflict results from a lack of understanding of each agencies'/departments' (intra- and inter-) capabilities and a lack of connectivity between your short-range crisis reaction types and your long-range visionaries.

215

That's a corollary to 'you've got to have strategic vision'—and we don't have it."[19]

The agencies' respective organizational cultures—particularly those of the NSC, State, and Defense—intensify this lack of understanding, prompting nonuniformed decision makers to view the use of force as a surgical instrument within the conduct of diplomatic operations. An NSC principal described this tendency the following way:

> Through most of the Cold War, virtually everyone had some understanding of the military. That is now the exception rather than the rule. We have been saved from an even worse disaster by Goldwater-Nichols giving the Chairman (CJCS) a clearly political role, which the CJCS did not have prior to Goldwater-Nichols. It is a serious problem because fundamentally, unless you have been in the military, things always [get] screwed up. It never goes as planned. To many of the high officials now, the military is this sort of flawless medical instrument—"a nice clean little war."[20]

This lack of understanding goes beyond perceptions of a "nice clean little war" in that the NSC and State Department fail to understand force employment's logistical requirements. A State Department principal remarked that part of the problem begins with his agency and the NSC Staff: "One of the limitations in this building and at NSC [is that] there is an over-emphasis on the theory of the practice of politics and diplomacy, but not enough on the hands-on experience of multiaircraft tasking packages. There isn't enough attention paid to how we maintain the force— that is the specialist argument we started out with."[21]

This official's ideas identify another issue related to perceptions of core competencies, the perpetual debate regarding whether a decision maker must be a technical specialist or a managerial generalist. A structural conundrum exists across organizational cultures within the interagency and their grasp of core competencies. The interagency process is designed to bridge gaps in decision makers' understandings of core competencies. Yet, precisely because *nonuniformed* personnel are educated, trained, and rewarded by an organizational culture that emphasizes nonmilitary means to manage and resolve crises while *uniformed* personnel are educated, trained, and rewarded (especially at the operational level) according to an organizational culture that focuses almost exclusively on the use of force to control the crisis environment, the USG employs very few individuals who understand or have internalized the asymmetric images held by both cultures. In essence, then, the decision makers remain isolated from one another as they develop, employ, and refine their respective core competencies, impelling them to analyze crises in terms of their "mutually exclusive" experiences. As a result, few officials understand the linkages and disjunctures between the strategy of diplomacy and the operational art of war.

Leaders' failures to integrate fully these dichotomous cultures expand this chasm across all levels of the interagency process. Misperceptions of core competencies shape substantive inputs to the policy process as perspectives on what you think you *can do* (i.e., substantive inputs) shape ideas regarding what you *should do* (i.e., policy outcomes). This perspective stifles innovative thinking regarding roles and missions, forcing the visionary and planning processes "into the weeds" (i.e., tactical level). Individual agencies further distort this "can-should" relationship as they frame national interests and intervention criteria in isolation from other executive agencies.

Framing National Interests and Intervention Criteria

A very interesting relationship between national interests and intervention criteria exists in terms of the relationship between interests and values.[22] The analysis revealed that decision makers framed *interests* by evaluating potential alternative futures; conversely, decision makers framed *values* more broadly in terms of past commitments or current/future humanitarian issues. Hence, perspectives on interests and values differ concerning foreign policy,[23] illuminating a distinct cleavage across officials representing different agencies. Interests tend to relate to diplomatic, economic, and military prowess (e.g., maintaining oil flow from the Persian Gulf to the United States and its allies). Alternatively, values concern social aspirations (e.g., preventing or mitigating humanitarian disasters abroad or maintaining a positive return on a prior investment). This dichotomy extends from the dissimilar images that shape asymmetric visions of the US role in the world, reflecting perspectives that fail to distin-

217

guish among "supreme, vital, strategic, and tactical interests."[24] This muddled, multifaceted conception of national interests enables prior experiences, perceptions of risk, and individual personalities to dominate debate regarding intervention criteria.

Perceptions regarding the use of criteria to prioritize a crisis remained mixed. In fact, a majority of the officials queried via survey contended their agency did apply formal criteria; the remaining reported their agencies had no formal criteria, but instead relied upon informal criteria. Perspectives regarding criteria usage split almost evenly across the three levels of the interagency process.[25] Interview data reinforced this finding, concurrently revealing that recollections of prior experience— especially in terms of risk—helped decision makers array formal intervention criteria. Alternatively, perceptions related to domestic politics, media spin, and presidential desires tended to frame informal criteria.

The Defense Department tended to cite formal criteria more often than the other agencies. These officials invoked interpretations of the Weinberger Doctrine that remained bound by their professional experience. One Defense Department principal noted that "criteria for involvement were those in the Weinberger Doctrine—this was the benchmark and nobody else had such a thing. . . . We tried to apply the Weinberger Doctrine with these criteria in mind: (1) vital national interests, (2) clear political objectives, and (3) [a] reasonable strategy for achieving goals, and (4) have all other means been exhausted prior to the introduction of forces. Finally, . . . Weinberger always asked if it was sustainable with the American people."[26]

This official continued by asserting that the State Department has consistently rejected these criteria—principles the Defense Department has guarded vigorously since their introduction in the 1980s. One Defense Department principal characterized this as an educational process for both the military and other government agencies. Referencing Secretary of Defense William Perry's speeches regarding "criteria for intervention," this official contended, "There's an increased awareness on the part of the military in terms of understanding (a) why military force is used and (b) what we hope to achieve with military force."[27] This tendency to apply the Weinberger Doctrine leads military professionals to assess the risks of conducting the mission in terms of costs (i.e., blood and treasure) and feasibility (i.e., probability for success or failure). The war fighter's prior experience, in both training and combat, influences these assessments regarding costs and feasibility. As an example, one official noted that the "Weinberger criteria [were] discussed formally and informally on the Joint Staff. There's a story that became a tone-setter early on [in the Bosnia policy development] . . . someone brought General Powell a map and he remarked, 'Looks like Dien Bien Phu.'"[28] Risks are evaluated likewise in terms of "vital national interests," clarity of political objectives, and the use of force as a last resort (i.e., all other means have been applied and, by definition, have failed). Although an abridged version of the evaluative process that characterizes the Defense Department assessment process, the crucial aspect of this finding is that members across the agency share this viewpoint concerning the process for framing intervention criteria. The same cannot be said for the NSC, State Department, and CIA, agencies that delineate intervention criteria according to their respective institutional viewpoints. Perhaps the crucial difference with regard to these agencies' ordering of intervention criteria is that State Department and the NSC Staff reverse the priority given to criteria vis-à-vis DOD's ranking of identical criteria.

It is appropriate, based upon these findings, to conclude that these agencies do not discount the importance of those criteria DOD regards as preeminent. However, they emphasized that the informal criteria of "domestic politics" and "presidential attention" tend to eclipse other criteria in the policy-making process. Domestic politics play a seminal role in terms of both public opinion and special interest group activity because of its capacity to energize partisan politics. Relatedly, the media's ability to focus attention on issues that, for the president, could be politically sensitive ensures that both the NSC (and NSC Staff) and State Department increase their efforts to resolve those problems. Consequently, the media perspective influences intervention criteria and goals, particularly those related to humanitarian values; the case analyses in chapter 9 make this precept more apparent. The president's attention further refines NSC and State Department perspectives as issues the executive becomes personally involved with take on a higher priority, effectively overshadowing any other criteria.[29] A State Department principal remarked that his agency measures policy and, by extension intervention criteria, in terms of whether it (1) has been "articulated," (2) is "sustainable," and (3) is "the best use of resources."[30] Another State Department D.C.-level official noted that even when national interests are considered as criteria, they are defined very broadly as economic issues (i.e., dealing with business) or concerns for the safety of citizens abroad. In fact, one State Department official claimed, "We do not [use criteria]. It's systemic—State tends to treat everything as an equal priority. In the end, we do try to look at things in accordance with national security interests, but it happens after the fact."[31]

An NSC principal contextualized the use of criteria across the interagency process, noting that "criteria happen least in a crisis." Instead, the critical factors become the "level of interest at stake, political sensitivity, [and] how fast events are moving."[32] The absence of a clearly articulated national security policy that builds upon identifiable national interests interpreted similarly across the interagency process ensures that these agencies independently frame intervention criteria according to their respective departmental interests, not US national interests as a whole. Chapter 6 illuminated the ways in which interagency dynamics shape policy outcomes; here again, the role of personality and the influence of personal relationships emerge as critical components of the policy process. In the final analysis, the absence of mutually accepted principles to frame and evaluate intervention criteria enhances the potential for the strength of personality to exert a defining influence on both intervention criteria development and decisions regarding force employment.

Clearly articulated national interests provide the substantive goal around which the interagency process can envisage, develop, and implement policy. Ambiguity creates interagency conflict during the process of policy making as disagreements over national interests harden the agencies' perspectives regarding role expectations toward developing policy and the missions they will perform to fulfill that policy mandate. This tension generates ambiguity of purpose and manifests itself in the resultant policy outcomes. These policy outcomes evaluate issues in terms of past commitments, not future prospects. In this way, the problems intrinsic to psychological entrapment affect policy outcomes.[33] Such an approach mirrors Mitchell's "entrapment model" while discounting the possibilities of alternative futures as presented in his "enticing opportunity model."[34] One principal's argument supporting intervention into Bosnia echoed this rationale, "We spent 40 years building Europe to this level,"[35] inferring that *because* the United States has "so much invested" in Bosnia's past, it could not afford to remain uninvolved in its future. Perspectives regarding past investments and alternative futures reflect the decision makers' ideologies and philosophies, thereby providing an appropriate segue into the final supporting theme regarding strategic vision and planning processes—that connecting worldviews to ideologies and philosophies.

Worldviews: Ideologies and Philosophies

Worldview is not a new concept among philosophers, cultural historians, and social scientists, yet it is only beginning to gain currency across all disciplines.[36] The description offered by Oscar Nudler contextualizes this concept's significance by highlighting the effects of conflicting worldviews, "Both 'world' and 'frame' refer then to a set of assumptions or principles which enable us to structure situations and, by the same token, make them real for us. . . . Worlds (are) rooted in fundamental need (for meaning). . . . Now we can see why conflicts between worlds may be so hard to handle: they may imply alternative, competing ways of meeting the need for meaning and, therefore, they may be perceived as putting in danger our way, a way on which all the rest of what we are depends."[37]

From this perspective, worldview takes on greater significance when agencies within the policy-making process engage "in conflict" as they strive to meet their respective needs for meaning (part of which is captured by their self-described roles and missions). A DOD principal captured this implication concisely, "Friction is always present: Fundamental differences of opinion over vital interests—this generates a certain amount of friction. I don't think it's necessarily unhealthy. You get friction between departments. The State Department differs from the way the

Defense Department views the world—their relative view affects the definition of the situation."[38] Worldviews, then, shape the definition of the situation for agency decision makers in the following two crucial ways: (1) according to the decision makers' ideological perspectives regarding the use of force and (2) in terms of their philosophy for the employment of military forces.

Ideology plays an important role in the development of worldview as it shapes the ways in which agencies perceive the geopolitical environment and their roles within it. In this context, ideology refers to one's perspective regarding the use of force to bring about desired results. Analyzing this concept from a peace research perspective, Michael Banks contends, "The sharpest distinction [between the realist and idealist] is to be found in their respective attitudes toward the use of force as a means of conflict management. Conservatives [realists] accept it and seek to refine it, direct it rationally, and minimize it. Liberals [idealists] try to escape from it, seeking refuge in law, international organizations, and a great variety of piecemeal modifications."[39] Although Banks draws a sharp distinction between the two main ideological approaches regarding the use of force, this theoretical dichotomy is not so pronounced in practice. Analysis by department, level within interagency, and case indicated that with the exception of the State Department, interagency actors characterize their agencies as predominantly *realist* where foreign and national security affairs are concerned. The interviews supported this finding as well, but they also highlighted additional issues that further demonstrate the ways in which ideology becomes a substantive input to the policy-making process. Actors across the interagency process agree that the USG is comprised predominantly of realists. However, another theme emerged consistently across the interviews—one concerning morality and values.

Policy making also includes an *idealistic* element that manifests itself in the formation of "moral" policy. One State Department deputy noted, "There is a moral and religious component to our policy that has nothing to do with strategy."[40] A State Department principal maintained it is too difficult to generalize regarding ideological perspectives because such alignments are issue specific. This official categorized *realism* as regarding those

222

issues related to diplomatic relations and the regular conduct of diplomacy; *idealism*, in his view, included issues related to human rights, democracy, and, to some degree, the environment. Another State Department official further delineated the organizational culture of that agency by claiming the geographic bureaus (e.g., Bureau of European and Canadian Affairs) tend to be more *realistic* in their outlook since they focus on interest-related issues, while the functional bureaus (e.g., Bureau of Democracy, Human Rights, and Labor) tend to remain more *idealistic* as they focus on value-related issues. In contrast to the State Department's mixed ideology, the NSC Staff and Defense Department characterized their ideological perspective as overwhelmingly *realist* in nature. This ideological cleavage between agencies generates interagency conflict as it perpetuates those destructive stereotypes discussed previously within this work. A Defense Department principal characterized the problem in this manner, "Within the senior levels at the State Department and the NSC Staff, there's a left-wing bent toward value-laden policies rather than interest-laden policies. They push to get US forces involved in pursuit of liberal values . . . that's a left-wing bent."[41] Actors within the policy process further politicize these stereotypes as they ascribe political party affiliations to interest- and value-laden perspectives.

One State Department official expressed this through a political party stereotype, "Republicans see people as nation-state actors—Democrats tend to look at issues."[42] From this perspective, stereotypes classifying Republicans as *realists* who pursue interest-related issues clash with those characterizing Democrats as *idealists* who pursue value-laden issues. These types of classifications shape interagency dynamics in terms of *process* (namely, exacerbating and amplifying preexisting cleavages between organizational cultures and mobilizing agents in terms of domestic politics) and *policy outcomes* in terms of the substantive inputs introduced into that process. The philosophies these agencies employ as a reflection of their respective ideological perspectives make this relationship evident.

Philosophy plays a crucial role by providing a system of principles that guide each agency's views concerning the use of force. An NSC principal emphasized that "philosophies provide the overall parameters for interagency conduct."[43] Competing philosophies regarding the use of force assert enormous influence if the principals do not share a sense of teamwork. Products of polarized ideology, dissimilar philosophies fragment definitions of national interests, intervention criteria, and, hence, strategic vision. Together, these fissures decrease trust across agencies and further perpetuate harmful stereotypes. These factors interact to produce divergent views on the appropriate use of force in times of crisis, creating a dynamic wherein the Defense Department perceives that the State Department sees military force as a tool to be manipulated. As evidence, an NSC principal remarked, "It is ironic that State is eager to use force when it hits a snag in diplomacy."[44] A Defense Department principal likewise asserted, "The problem we are having is that other agencies commit our force—it has now become the punitive arm to slap people around."[45] A Defense Department deputy presented another corroborative viewpoint, "The State Department [people] . . . most of what I've heard there is they like to use military force on the edges—things like no-fly zones, shaping diplomatic purposes, humanitarian operations, stability operations, shows of force—more in a preventive mode to discourage aggression and encourage stability."[46]

Consequently, the Defense Department *perceives* that the State Department's (and NSC's) *first inclination* is to use force. A State Department official similarly reflected this perspective, claiming that "State Department people can be pretty strongheaded on the requirement to use force, but they do not always understand implications of the use of force. The State Department wants to use force first—DOD is always the biggest hindrance to the use of force."[47]

These asymmetric philosophies regarding the use of force reflect the State Department's "sense of urgency to do something" and, conversely, the Defense Department's "caution signal." Projecting perspectives at opposite ends of the force employment continuum, this dynamic produces a polarized relationship that further expands the gap between diplomats and war fighters. It is demonstrated in like manner by the State Department's desire for ambiguity and the Defense Department's drive for specificity (a topic discussed in the ensuing chapter as a factor related to clarity of *Roles and Missions*).

Ultimately, ideological and philosophical differences create a prism through which dissimilar worldviews envisage asymmetric definitions of national interests and intervention criteria, thereby producing fragmented, nonparallel strategic visions among interagency actors. Occurring within the context of a nonintegrated planning system, these disparate visions generate dissimilar perspectives regarding core competencies, national interests, and intervention criteria, resulting in asymmetric commitment levels regarding the strategy to achieve the stated policy outcome. These substantive inputs to the policy process hold sway over interagency dynamics and, in turn, the resulting policy outcome. The final overarching theme, however, may hold the greatest import for bureaucratic policy making wherein substance regulates process as attitudes toward *institutional equities* circumscribe interagency process dynamics.

Protection of Institutional Equities

An institutional equity is any asset that adds value to, or is the defining characteristic of, an agency. From this perspective, Allison's maxim asserting that "where you stand depends on where you sit" aptly captures the process that distinguishes an agency's respective institutional equities. Government officials repeatedly invoked his words to characterize the nature of their institutional equities, reflecting Allison's ideas unequivocally through descriptions of bureaucratic stakes they strive to protect. Resources (e.g., budgets, personnel, and equipment) and functions (i.e., the respective agencies' roles and missions) emerged as the most tangible assets departments view as equities. Even so, intangible factors continuously refine agencies' views regarding their respective equities. These intangible factors include "perceptions of risk and accountability" and, referenced earlier, "prior experience." Beginning with the tangible factors of personnel and budgets, the ensuing discussion demonstrates the ways in which these three factors shape departmental viewpoints regarding their (and others') respective equities. Efforts to protect and bolster these equities shape substantive inputs to the policy process.

Personnel and Budgets

The resources and functions each agency controls serve as defining elements of each agency's identity. These elements take their most visible forms in terms of the personnel, budgets, assets, and responsibilities departments regard as their own. As will be made clear through the *Clarity of Roles and Missions* discussion in the next chapter, perceptions of confusion and overlap exist regarding these responsibilities when agencies take part in the interagency process. Despite this ambiguity within the interagency, boundaries remain unmistakable when one's own institutional equities are at stake. Further, in the cases where agencies lack large budgets and operate with limited numbers of people, the ability to function—optimally—becomes the most protected institutional equity. Beginning with NSC, let us work through each of the major actors.

The NSC Staff is constrained by its size (i.e., approximately 150–180 people). One of its primary goals is to protect the long-term legacy of the presidency. Indeed, many officials associated with the Bosnia crisis (1993–95) and those with ongoing interagency roles (1996–98) characterized the goal as a fundamental responsibility, one that compels the NSC Staff to react to media reports and to respond to congressional pressures. Concurrently, as "coordinator" of the executive's interagency process and the last stop for policy review before sending an issue to the president, this agency "wants to achieve compromise above all else." Thus, while maintaining relations with the media and the Congress that enhance the president's legacy remains a priority, its most protected equity—*its defining characteristic*—is its capacity to build consensus across the interagency process. Although this equity is projected inward toward the intergovernmental relations of US agencies, it has played a supporting role in developing both State's and Defense's institutional equities.

At the most basic level, interview data indicated that the State Department defined its *central equities* as (1) the strength of its diplomacy, (2) its uninterrupted worldwide presence, and (3) its

226

identification as the USG's foreign policy leader. A State Department deputy captured their essence, "The closer you get to an institution's core interests, the more competitive a department gets. The State Department's core interests tend to be process-oriented and institutional. The reputation of the Foreign Service, the role of the ambassador, the conduct of American foreign policy through . . . traditional diplomacy . . . [maintaining] a non-isolationist perspective in the world."[48] Clearly, functional responsibilities dominate the State Department's views regarding its equities. The State Department's capacity to perform its mission often reveals the nexus wherein political and military equities clash. This nexus illuminates the resource-related equities that appear as the Defense Department's visible assets.

Of all the agencies, the Defense Department controls the preponderance of resource equities—equities that comprise the military's very soul, troops and budgets.[49] Perspectives surrounding these two factors remain linked to the Defense Department's organizational culture and its conceptions of leadership. The first, issues related to troops, manifests as an institutional bias in the following two interrelated ways: (1) the number of people the agency commands coupled with (2) the command responsibility that agency extends to its people. The military recognizes that it has the largest personnel tally, making it an easy target for the "lowest common denominator" phenomenon highlighted earlier. Interagency decision makers recognize that the Defense Department personnel *are* the lowest common denominator because no other agency possesses the capacity to organize, mobilize, and lead people as effectively as the Defense Department. Recognition of this status on the part of the Defense Department officials makes them even more cautious when contemplating the use of forces since they, more than any other decision makers across the interagency process, grasp fully the gravity of putting troops in harm's way.[50] The commander-subordinate loyalty relationship that exists within the military's organizational culture molds this perspective.[51]

Mission lethality and the potential for loss of life (both US troops and others) demand that the Defense Department officials protect this equity as fervently as possible. Efforts to protect this equity do, however, create interagency conflict and further perpetuate negative stereotypes. For example, an NSC principal asserted that the "JCS will not recommend to the chairman anything that derogates force protection."[52] Because of this hesitance, contended one State Department official, the American political and bureaucratic context is "obsessed by force protection. This leaves the force less capable of filling other missions."[53] Troop protection is not the only equity the Defense Department officials strive to protect. Budgets (and, by extension physical assets) are regarded highly as well, the protection of which augments the Defense Department's reservation to volunteer for those "other missions" the foregoing State Department official referenced.

The size of the Defense Department's budget is important in its own right; of greater significance is its size when compared to that of the State Department. According to one Defense Department principal, the asymmetry of the budgets between the departments of Defense and State generates problems for interagency relations:

> State has taken a much higher hit than Defense in resources. [The] Congress does not want to give them the resources, and State is forced to close embassies. When you consider how much we rely upon diplomats, and we give them nothing to do the job—they [i.e., the Congressional Foreign Affairs Committee] deal with funds based upon political whims. Albright talks about the $270 billion [Defense budget]—they have $18 billion—they cannot run foreign policy on that money. I do not blame her [Secretary of State Albright]—the answer is to give them more.[54]

While these figures are based upon late 1990s funding levels, the overwhelming fiscal disparity between these agencies did not occur overnight and is readily apparent. The State Department is forced to sustain its diplomatic operation with roughly 7 percent of the total Defense Department budget. Arguably, the need to develop, procure, and maintain billion-dollar weapons systems, supporting equipment, and personnel requires a much larger operating and maintenance budget for DOD. However, the Defense Department recognizes, based upon its prior experience, that ongoing State-initiated contingencies involving the use of forces will deplete vital monies intended for readiness and training, thereby, adversely affecting the military's ability to fight and win the nation's wars—the ultimate purpose for its existence.[55] Discussed previously, the following dynamic produces interagency conflict: "The perception [within] this building [i.e., Defense Department] is that the State Department runs around with their hand in our pocket. The State Department's view is that if the Defense Department has all the toys, why won't you use them."[56] Gen Colin Powell captured one such conversation in his memoirs when then-UN Ambassador Madeleine Albright asked him, "What's the point of having this superb military that you're always talking about if we can't use it?"[57] From the beginning of an interagency process regarding possible crisis intervention, the Defense Department's efforts to protect troops and budgets serve as substantive inputs to the policy process, thereby generating interagency conflict with those who do not hold these institutional equities salient. While the NSC and Departments of State and Defense remain the primary actors in the interagency process, the Intelligence Community—the CIA in particular—likewise plays a significant role as the protection of its functional equities links directly to the substantive inputs around which the interagency dynamic is formed.

Introduction of the "Intelligence Community" (see chap. 4) identified this actor's primary goal as that of presenting timely, objective estimates of the situation. However, comprised of 13 distinct but interrelated intelligence activities, the different actors within the Intelligence Community share this image regarding objective estimates, but not necessarily a sense of ownership regarding the estimates it collectively produces. One CIA official noted that competition becomes a factor if certain intelligence agencies "don't have all the knowledge and won't defer to those 'in the know.' "[58] In this manner, equities across the Intelligence Community reflect their institutional affiliations (e.g., State's "Bureau of Intelligence and Research" and the military's "Defense Intelligence Agency").

Notions regarding these respective equities must be placed within the overall interagency context.[59] According to one IWG-level informant, this tendency to "protect our own rice bowls" creates interagency competition and defines the boundaries of both agency interaction and resource commitment, each of which directly influences policy outcomes. One NSC principal noted that the principals exacerbate this problem through their inattentiveness to the details of crisis intervention, "I would find budgeting/mechanical issues of concern—it's rare to see these come up at PC/DC levels—PCs just say, 'Do it.' "[60] This conduct pushes equity-based discussions back down to the lower levels— levels wherein decision makers are rewarded for competitively protecting their respective equities. Perceptions regarding risk and accountability further refine perspectives regarding institutional equities.

Risk and Accountability

Agencies frame risk and accountability very differently across the interagency process.[61] DOD identifies troops as its central equity, one to protect and avoid risking at all costs. On the other hand, the State Department frames risk to its equity of diplomatic viability in terms of sustaining worldwide diplomatic presence. These equities clash when the Defense Department must employ its troops to evacuate the State Department personnel when crises erupt. It is not the evacuation that creates the clash of equities; rather, it is the *perceived delay* by the State Department, according to the Defense Department perspective, that increases the risk to military personnel. As argued earlier, this emanates from the absence of a universal comprehension of each other's core competencies, but the resulting conflict exposes yet another organizational culture dimension that holds significant import for equity protection. In essence, diplomats and war fighters act upon asymmetric conceptions of time.

Diplomats regard their mission as one of extended duration— they are there "for the long haul." Conversely, war fighters view their role as one of "getting in, accomplishing the mission, and getting out." Thus, the risk to Defense Department's equities increases exponentially as the troops remain engaged. This reality serves as the impetus for Defense Department's petition for clearly defined objectives and end states. For diplomats, while intensity may vary at specific moments, risk remains relatively constant over time as they are "on the ground" before troop deployment and remain there long after troops return to their home bases. This creates interagency conflict as, in the view of one

State Department official, equity is also framed in terms of an agency's "place in control of an issue, [its] political currency."[62] A State Department principal noted that during the Lebanon example cited previously (chap. 6), the Defense Department remained unwilling to entertain State Department views regarding the positioning of the Marines offshore, "That has been traditionally regarded by our armed forces as encroachment."[63] Hence, a clear connection exists with the roles and functions discussion and the *Clarity of Roles and Missions* debate examined in chapter 8. The other side of the risk issue related to equity protection is the notion of accountability.

Accountability remains a multidimensional concept, but two elements hold great importance for equity framing—accountability in terms of "commission" and "omission." In the first instance, agencies exhibit risk-averse behaviors regarding accountability as they tenaciously avoid committing decisions to paper, thereby preventing them from becoming part of an official government record.[64] Not only does recording or publishing decisions lead to heightened risks of leaks (again, for the political opposition this serves as fuel for their antiadministration policy rhetoric), but they also increase the decision maker's accountability if the policy fails. For example, a DOD principal recounted the US experience in Panama with regard to objectives, "The Bush administration went into Panama with four objectives—three were attained within 48 hours. Yet, we could not get Noriega, the fourth objective. I think this was prime in the White House and the Pentagon—we found him and it did become a victory. By making Noriega an objective, we were more vulnerable to failure."[65]

In this manner, government officials desire not to hand their political opposition the noose with which to hang them publicly (i.e., here, the potentially damaging effects of domestic politics dominate policy-making conduct). The absence of such a record, albeit public or private, diminishes continuity across the interagency process as individual actors emerge from meetings with incongruent, perhaps contradictory, perspectives regarding what the policy *is* and what it *means*. The need to avoid unnecessary risks while simultaneously bolstering institutional equities further complicates perceptions of policy making. The interactive effects of accountability continue to permeate the process as the need to avoid unnecessary risks and protect institutional equities mandates active participation in the interagency process to avoid "accountability via omission."

Agencies fear being pulled into situations that adversely affect the institutional equities described earlier, while simultaneously increasing risk and accountability for their departments. Such fears require agency representatives to become involved in the policy process as early as possible to avoid the phenomenon of *accountability via omission*. Specifically, a widespread concern exists that the interagency will make ineffective and inappropriate decisions if one's own agency is not involved early in the decision-making process. Bush captures the essence of this concern when reflecting upon his presidency, "Brent [Scowcroft] and Jim [Baker] did get moderately crosswise, but very rarely. Jim worried that he might be excluded from a decision that affected his department. As a former chief of staff, he knew how a strong-willed presidential advisor, if backed by a president, can easily isolate a cabinet member."[66] Reports in the aftermath of the Sudan bombing effort of 20 August 1998—implying that the White House truncated (or, indeed, bypassed) the interagency process in its haste to act—further validate this concern. Given the discussion of troops as DOD's primary equity and a recognized lack of understanding regarding core competencies across the interagency process, this anxiety remains particularly acute for the military. An NSC principal recognized this anxiety, observing, "It is ironic that State is eager to use force when it hits a snag in diplomacy. The military [is reluctant] to get involved. In a sense, they are holding the bag . . . will have their budget eaten up."[67] Decision makers' prior experiences further reinforce these fears of accountability via omission.

Prior Experience

With the exception of diplomats and national leaders who have served in a long-term career capacity, few share images arising from a "collective prior experience" to the same degree as do uniformed professionals. For those individuals, prior experience is ingrained as part of one's professional heritage—institutionally and personally. Only the military promotes a professional military education system that regularly (and repetitively at different levels) educates its members on leadership, historical conflicts, and the art and science of war fighting. This recurring educational process institutionally emphasizes lessons learned from past conflicts as it generates an assumption that future conflicts will be similar to those prior experiences. Decision makers then interpret these lessons in light of current personal experiences and those shared by the senior officials they strive to emulate. When personal experiences remain limited to comparable organizational cultures with little or no opportunity for sustained cross-fertilization, the emphasis of lessons learned generates a tendency to perpetuate stereotypes. One State Department official noted that stereotypes do come to the fore within the interagency process, "Everybody to a certain extent meets their stereotype. For example, CIA analysis is always pessimistic. DOD always thinks the State Department is trying to take resources and commit troops. The State Department always thinks DOD is unwilling to employ forces."[68]

These stereotypes, based upon prior experience, shape perspectives regarding risk and accountability to one's institutional equities, especially personnel and budgets. The agencies' perspectives regarding their own and others' equities frame inputs to the interagency process by determining the salience of goals and establishing the level of commitment these agencies dedicate to policy implementation. Agencies' respective internal evaluative processes, according to one State Department official, compel them to conduct a "cost-benefit analysis from [the vantage point of] their interests, not the national interest."[69] Consequently, interagency actors protect their respective equities at lower levels because of process design—the principals' stands further constrain subordinate level actors' abilities to compromise. Within this environment, senior leaders do not provide midcourse corrections for this behavior because, in the words of one State Department principal, "The president and senior officials do not begin to understand how the problems bubble up. They don't understand that people protect their turf."[70] According to an NSC official, the effect on the day-to-day policy-making approach is that these turf battles "keep splitting the differences until the policy is neutered."[71]

Yet, if decision makers employ this negotiating process fully, interagency discussions regarding equities provide the feasibility check for building consensus around a policy and its ensuing implementation. It is in this tradition that the interagency process attempts to produce integrative outcomes through negotiation. Only through such integrative outcomes can respective agencies commit fully to policy execution. Referenced earlier in chapter 6, the unintended consequences of such a lack of commitment are clear when analyzing Lebanon and Somalia, two cases wherein the shortsighted protection of bureaucratic equities brought about disastrous results. It is in this manner that perspectives concerning institutional equities play a commanding role in shaping the substantive inputs that guide the policy process.

This discussion of strategic vision and planning processes and institutional equities demonstrates the ways in which interagency participants characterize the influence of the contextual parameters that shape interagency dynamics. Before proceeding to a discussion of the crosscutting effects of the two remaining emergent themes—roles and missions and media influence—let us briefly recapture the essence of these relationships to highlight the ways in which substantive inputs shape interagency dynamics.

Interpretation of Findings

The analysis presented within this chapter elucidated the ways in which contextual parameters framing the policy process shaped *interagency dynamics* (see fig. 23, p. 161). These contextual parameters shape criteria selections and preference orderings, thereby illustrating the third tenet of Allison's bureaucratic politics model, whereby negotiated policy outcomes emerge as *political resultants* rather than the utility maximizing calculation extending from rational choice theory's criteria-based cost-benefit analysis. One stimulus inspiring these political resultants arises from the distorting effects surrounding misconceptions of substantive inputs to the policy process in terms of the contextual parameters discussed here. As such, these themes regarding substance-process relationships (i.e., the ways in which context shapes interagency dynamics) emerged to complement the process-substance themes (i.e., interagency dynamics influence on shaping outcomes) presented in the previous chapter. This substance-process relationship manifests in two interrelated ways—through the strategic vision and planning processes that filter and control inputs into the process and the institutional equities that serve as the framework for those inputs.

Factors within strategic vision and planning processes shape the agencies' perspectives regarding the crisis the interagency process strives to address. Dissimilar political visions fragment policy process inputs while simultaneously exacerbating interagency conflict. The absence of clearly articulated goals around which the agencies can coalesce stems from disparate shared images regarding the nature of the crisis itself, in conjunction with the ambiguity surrounding the respective roles each agency should play in policy formulation and implementation. This ambiguity emanates from divergent perspectives regarding the utility of planning—perspectives that, in the absence of strategic vision and shared images, force the planning process toward a nodal, tactical-level focus as a substitute for a systems-based, strategic perspective. A governmentwide misunderstanding of agency-specific core competencies further reinforces this tendency to focus on tactical-level issues.

Precisely because agencies fail to understand the nature of another's expertise that flow from roles and missions, the flawed expectations each agency holds for its partners in the policy-making process creates interagency conflict. This discord appears particularly salient with regard to the expectations the State Department has of the Defense Department (and vice versa). Intensified by contrasting organizational cultures, each agency's respective definition of national interests and intervention criteria further amplify mutual misunderstanding.

The analysis demonstrates that decision makers frame national interests differently—a variation made evident through perspectives regarding *interests* and *values*[72] and their influence on shaping intervention criteria. Those who evaluate alternative futures tend to frame intervention criteria in more formal language that focuses on interests in terms of diplomatic, economic, and military supremacy, noting that formalized intervention criteria (e.g., the Weinberger or Powell doctrines) shape perspectives regarding the use of the military for crisis intervention. Alternatively, those who make connections with past investments or the need to prevent humanitarian crises abroad frame intervention criteria in terms of values. These values shape intervention criteria differently, tending to rely upon informal intervention criteria (e.g., presidential attention) to shape perspectives on the use of the military for crisis intervention. These perspectives arise from the worldviews each agency embraces—worldviews shaped by their respective ideologies and philosophies regarding the use of force (i.e., war fighting) and forces (i.e., noncombatant roles and missions).

Worldviews retain particular import for the ways in which agencies define a crisis. Ideology plays a major role in shaping perspectives on the use of force for crisis management. Although the realist worldview dominates the interagency process, the existence of a moral component in the framing of US policy creates an arena for competing interest- and value-laden definitions of national interests and intervention criteria to clash. Where the use of force is concerned, the interaction of these dichotomous interest- and value-laden perspectives creates interagency conflict. This conflict is evident in the philosophies regarding the use of force wherein *realists* generally contend that force should be used to promote interests whereas *idealists* generally argue that force should be used to secure values. The perpetuation of stereotypes and the influence of partisan politics tend to enlarge this ideological-philosophical chasm, creating an interagency dynamic in which perceptions of dissimilar worldviews exacerbate interagency conflict. It is crucial to acknowledge that interagency conflict is not always dysfunctional. Interagency conflict that clarifies roles and missions, core competencies, risk, feasibility, and related issues can be instrumental to effective policy development. However, the interagency conflict addressed here tends to shut down communication channels so that the decision makers *cannot* achieve clarity regarding those types of issues. These polarized perceptions materialize via the institutional equities these agencies strive to protect.

Paralleling Allison's perspective, this work demonstrates that parochial interests frame political resultants (see chap. 4). The findings presented here support that precept, albeit from a more positive, less parochial, perspective. Through discussions of the agencies' respective institutional equities, the interagency process conducts a systematized feasibility check while educating decision makers regarding the respective core competencies each agency brings to bear during crises. Each agency's need to protect (and advance) its respective equities is reflected through a competitive interagency dynamic that ensues regarding "personnel and budgets" and "risk and accountability," as framed by the decision makers' prior experiences.

Shaped by the need to protect institutional equities within a bureaucratic environment wherein decisions are made via negotiation, these multiple, dissimilar, and sometimes competing strategic visions and planning processes generate divergent criteria selections and preference orderings regarding the use of force (or forces in noncombatant roles) to manage crises. These criteria and preference orderings become the substantive inputs for the decision maker's understanding of unambiguous termination policy.

In the end, a dangerous cleavage exists between interagency decision makers regarding the development of termination policy. This cleavage remains most pronounced between decision makers in State and Defense Departments. A Defense Department official provided a fitting transition into this discussion of conflict termination policy, "A military person understands conflict termination and exit strategy. DOS understands trip wires—they understand things differently. In the military, we are warfighters [*sic*]—[that is how we] are brought up. . . . Their [DOS] mindset [*sic*] is different—they are more concerned about the individual person, we're concerned about the mission. Their mission is diplomacy, our mission is to respond when diplomacy fails. They're supposed to complement one another."[73]

Toward refining our understanding of this fissure, the ensuing chapter discusses the final category of emergent themes—those having crosscutting effects on both dynamic themes and contextual parameters. To bring these ideas together, chapter 9 draws conclusions based upon this analysis, integrating the quantitative and qualitative findings through the examination of policy development for the Persian Gulf War and the Bosnia crisis.

Notes

1. For literature related to strategic vision and planning, see also Sam Allotey et al., *Planning and Execution of Conflict Termination* (Maxwell AFB, Ala.: Air Command and Staff College, 1995); Stephen J. Andriole, "Decision Process Models and the Needs of Policy-Makers: Thoughts on the Foreign Policy Interface," *Policy Sciences* 11, no. 1 (1979): 19–37; Karen A. Bantel, "Comprehensiveness of Strategic Planning: The Importance of Heterogeneity of a Top Team," *Psychological Reports* 73, no. 1 (1993): 35–49; see also John T. Fishel, *Liberation, Occupation, and Rescue: War Termination and Desert Storm* (Carlisle Barracks, Pa.: Strategic Studies Institute, US Army War College, 1994); Vincent Follert, "Risk Analysis: Its Application to Argumentation and Decision-Making," *Journal of the American Forensic Association* 18, no. 2 (1981): 99–108; see also Richard O. Mason, *Challenging Strategic Planning Assumptions: Theory, Cases, and Techniques* (New York: Wiley, 1981); Eleanor Farrar McGowan, "Rational Fantasies," *Policy Sciences* 7, no. 4 (1976): 439–54; Paul Charles Nutt, "Some Guides for the Selection of a Decision-Making Strategy," *Technological Forecasting and Social Change* 19, no. 2 (1981): 133–45; see also Robert L. Rothstein, *Planning, Prediction, and Policymaking in Foreign Affairs: Theory and Practice* (Boston: Little, Brown, and Co., 1972); Norman C. Thomas, "The Presidency and Policy Studies," *Policy Studies Journal* 9, no. 7 (1981): 1072–82; Mark van de Vall, "Utilization and Methodology of Applied Social Research: Four Complementary Models," *Journal of Applied Behavioral Science* 11, no. 1 (1975): 14–38; see also Raimo Vayrynen, ed., *New Directions in Conflict Theory: Conflict Resolution and Conflict Transformation* (Newbury Park, Calif.: Sage Publications, Inc., 1991); and Larry A. Weaver and Robert D. Pollock, "Campaign Planning for the 21st Century: An Effect-Based Approach to the Planning Process," in *War Theory*, ed. M. Kwolek and G. Story (Maxwell AFB, Ala.: Air Command and Staff College, 1995), 13–20.

2. Gordon Allport provides a theoretical basis for this intergroup behavior with regard to racial prejudice in his classic, *The Nature of Prejudice*. It is interesting to note that his "contact hypothesis" holds here as well, as diverse groups coalesce around goals to achieve a greater outcome—one they could not achieve independently. Through this "integration," dissimilar groups achieve true conflict resolution. See Gordon W. Allport, *The Nature of Prejudice* (New York: Anchor Books, 1958), 320.

3. State Department official, US Department of State, Washington, D.C.

4. For an outstanding abridged analysis of NSC-68 and its legacy, see also S. Nelson Drew, ed., *NSC-68: Forging the Strategy of Containment, with Analyses by Paul H. Nitze* (Washington, D.C.: Institute for National Strategic Studies, 1996).

5. See also, for instance, The White House, *A National Security Strategy of Engagement and Enlargement* (Washington, D.C.: Government Printing Office [GPO], 1994); and see also The White House, *National Security Strategy of the United States* (Washington, D.C.: GPO, 1991).

6. State Department official.

7. Ibid.

8. Ibid.

9. Ibid.

10. National Security Interagency Policy-making official, Executive Office of the President, Washington, D.C.

11. Note that the CIA also has a quasi-strategic planning function in terms of its "early warning" intelligence activities. However, their focus is on collecting information and interpreting it for decision makers to use in developing options. In this manner, they are not responsible for developing "strategic plans" in the same vein as the NSC and Departments of State and Defense.

12. Defense official, US Department of Defense, Washington, D.C.

13. Interagency official, Executive Office of the President, Washington, D.C.

14. National Security Interagency Policy-making official.

15. Ibid.

16. State Department official.

17. National Security Interagency Policy-making official.

18. Core competencies for the State Department include diplomacy and negotiation and for the Defense Department, war fighting and military operations other than war (MOOTW), including peacekeeping.

19. Defense Department official.

20. National Security Interagency Policy-making official.

21. State Department official.

22. For a broader discussion of national interest framing and its relationship to policy development, see also Allotey, *Planning and Execution of Conflict Termination;* see also Andriole, "Decision Process Models and the Needs of Policy-Makers: Thoughts on the Foreign Policy Interface"; see also L. Benjamin Ederington and Michael J. Mazarr, eds., *Turning Point: The Gulf War and US Military Strategy* (Boulder: Westview Press, 1994); Paul A. Gigot, "A Great American Screw-Up. The US and Iraq, 1980–1990," *The National Interest*, no. 22 (1991): 3–10; see also Hyun Kim, "Rationality, Bureaucratic Politics, and Cognitive Processes in Foreign Policy Decision-Making: An Analysis of the United States Policy Decisions Towards Japan, 1948–1954" (PhD diss., City University of New York, 1996); Zeev Maoz, "Framing the National Interest: The Manipulation of Foreign Policy Decisions in Group Settings," *World Politics* 43, no. 1 (1990): 77–100; see also W. A. Reese, *The Principle of the Objective and Promoting National Interests: Desert Shield/Storm—A Case Study* (Washington, D.C: Industrial College of the Armed Forces, 1993); and Albert R. Tims and M. Mark Miller, "Determinants of Attitudes toward Foreign Countries," *International Journal of Intercultural Relations* 10, no. 4 (1986): 471–84. Similarly, for an expanded perspective on intervention, see Lorraine

M. Belliveau and John F. Stolte, "The Structure of Third Party Intervention," *Journal of Social Psychology* 103, no. 2 (1977): 243–50; Elizabeth Heger Boyle and Edward J. Lawler, "Resolving Conflict through Explicit Bargaining," *Social Forces* 69, no. 4 (1991): 1183–204; Peter J. Carnevale and Patricia A. Keenan, "The Resolution of Conflict: Negotiation and Third Party Intervention," in *Employment Relations: The Psychology of Influence and Control at Work*, ed. Jean F. Hartley and Geoffrey M. Stephenson (Oxford and Cambridge: Blackwell, 1992), 225–45; William A. Donohue et al., "Crisis Bargaining in Intense Conflict Situations," *International Journal of Group Tensions* 21, no. 2 (1991): 133–53; see also Jay Morgan Parker, "Understanding Intervention: The Utility of Decision-Making Theory" (PhD diss., Columbia University, 1991); Gregory A. Raymond, "Democracies, Disputes, and Third-Party Intermediaries," *Journal of Conflict Resolution* 38, no. 1 (1994): 24–42; see also James D. D. Smith, *Stopping Wars: Defining the Obstacles to Cease-Fire* (Boulder, Colo.: Westview Press, 1995); Earl A. Thompson and Roger L. Faith, "Social Interaction under Truly Perfect Information," *Journal of Mathematical Sociology* 7, no. 2 (1980), 181–97; Oran R. Young, "Intermediaries and Interventionists: Third Parties in the Middle East Crisis," *International Journal* 23 (1967), 52–73; Oran R. Young, "Intermediaries: Additional Thoughts on Third Parties," *Conflict Resolution* 16, no. 1 (1972): 51–65; and see also I. William Zartman, *Ripe for Resolution: Conflict and Intervention in Africa* (New York: Oxford University Press, 1989).

23. It is important to note that framing interests and values in terms of *domestic policy* would also include enhancing the political currency of the presidency, the Congress, and the political parties, each according to their respective "strategic interests."

24. See also Charles. W. Freeman Jr., *The Diplomat's Dictionary*, revised ed. (Washington, D.C.: United States Institute of Peace, 1997).

25. The ratios across the three levels in terms of "does/does not" use criteria were principals level, 11/14; deputies level, 19/14; and interagency working group, 5/6.

26. Defense Department official.

27. Ibid.

28. Ibid.

29. See also Daniel Druckman and Benjamin J. Broome, "Value Differences and Conflict Resolution: Familiarity or Liking?" *Journal of Conflict Resolution* 35, no. 4 (1991): 571–93.

30. State Department official.

31. Ibid.

32. National Security Interagency Policy-making official.

33. Tatsuya Kameda and Shinkichi Sugimori, "Psychological Entrapment in Group Decision Making: An Assigned Decision Rule and a Groupthink Phenomenon," *Journal of Personality and Social Psychology* 65, no. 2 (1993): 282–92; C. R. Mitchell, "Classifying Conflicts: Asymmetry and Resolution," *Annals of the American Academy of Political and Social Science* 518 (November 1991): 23–38; Jeffrey Z. Rubin et al., "Factors Affecting Entry into

Psychological Traps," *Journal of Conflict Resolution* 24, no. 3 (1980): 405–26; and see also Jeffrey Z. Rubin, Dean G. Pruitt, and Sung Hee Kim, *Social Conflict: Escalation, Stalemate, and Settlement*, 2d ed. (New York: McGraw-Hill, Inc., 1994).

34. See also Christopher R. Mitchell, *Cutting Losses: Reflections on Appropriate Timing, ICAR Working Paper #9* (Fairfax, Va.: George Mason University, 1995).

35. Ibid.

36. For a broader explanation of worldview theory, see also Jayne Seminare Docherty, "When the Parties Bring Their Gods to the Table: Learning Lessons from Waco" (PhD diss., George Mason University, 1998); Amitai Etzioni, "The Crisis of Modernity: Deviation or Demise?," *Journal of Human Relations* 21, no. 4 (1973): 370–93; see also Hanna Yousif Freij, "Perceptions and Behavior in US Foreign Relations Towards the Republic of Iraq" (PhD diss., University of Pittsburgh, 1992); Arnold A. Lazarus, "Theory, Subjectivity and Bias: Can There Be a Future?," *Psychotherapy* 30, no. 4 (1993): 674–77; see also Dario Moreno, "Ideology and United States Central American Policy under Carter and Reagan" (Ph.D., University of Southern California, 1987); Oscar Nudler, "On Conflicts and Metaphors: Toward an Extended Rationality," in *Conflict: Human Needs Theory*, ed. J. Burton (New York: St. Martin's Press, 1990), 178–87; see also Byeong Chul Park, "Generational Problems and Their Effect on Foreign Policy" (New York: Department of Sociology, Syracuse University, 1991); W. James Potter, "Examining Cultivation from a Psychological Perspective: Component Subprocesses," *Communication Research* 18, no. 1 (1991): 77–102; and see also Dennis J. D. Sandole and H. van der Merwe, *Conflict Resolution Theory and Practice: Integration and Application* (Manchester & New York: Manchester University Press, 1993).

37. Nudler, "On Conflicts and Metaphors," 178.

38. Defense Department official.

39. Michael Banks, "Four Conceptions of Peace," in *Conflict Management and Problem Solving: Interpersonal to International Applications*, ed. Dennis J. D. Sandole and Ingrid Sandole-Staroste (New York: New York University Press, 1987), 262.

40. State Department official.

41. Defense Department official.

42. State Department official.

43. National Security Interagency Policy-making official.

44. Ibid.

45. Defense Department official.

46. Ibid.

47. State Department official.

48. Ibid.

49. The reference to troops here is understandable. The reference to budgets is not meant to derogate the military's image; this theme of budget

protection emerged repeatedly as one Defense Department officials regarded as critical to its survival.

50. It is critical to note this author's distinction between the "use of force" and the "use of forces." The "use of force" relates directly to the employment of military technologies in a war-fighting capacity to bring about the desired result. Alternatively, the "use of forces" conveys a message that the NSC utilizes military personnel in some other capacity, one that does not involve (necessarily) the employment of forces for a combat mission. It is important to note that the distinction is not intended to communicate that an ego factor shapes the first. On the contrary, it is the commander-subordinate loyalty relationship discussed here that creates caution on the part of commanders to put troops in harm's way, irrespective of the mission.

51. See also Benjamin O. Davis Jr., *American: An Autobiography* (Washington, D.C.: Smithsonian Institution Press, 1991).

52. National Security Interagency Policy-making official.

53. State Department official.

54. Defense Department official. Numerous government officials called attention to the "games" the Congress plays regarding funding. Another individual noted that the Congress responds to funding contingencies in three primary ways. First, if they support the operation and feel the Defense Department has the funding to cover it, the Congress does nothing. Alternatively, if they support the operation and feel the Defense Department lacks sufficient funding, the Congress passes a supplemental appropriations bill to fund the contingency without taking additional monies from the Defense Department. Finally, if they do not support the operation, they deny funding for the particular activity undertaking the operation, effectively diminishing its capacity to fulfill the policy mandate. The Congress, however, would hold that these actions fulfill its constitutional prerogative—indeed its mandate—to check the executive branch and monitor foreign policy by controlling funding.

55. Recall the earlier discussions of national interests and strategic vision that highlighted these "State initiated" purposes tend to fall outside the national interests from the Defense Department's perspective since they tend to reflect value-laden policies, not interest-laden judgments.

56. State Department official.

57. Colin L. Powell and Joseph E. Persico, *My American Journey* (New York: Random House, 1995), 576.

58. Intelligence Community official, Washington, D.C.

59. It is important to acknowledge that other institutional equities exist as well. For example, the Department of Justice is playing more of a role as they focus on "dotting the i's and crossing the t's." This can lead to delays and constrained rules of engagement (e.g., more narrowly interpret the Geneva and Hague Conventions). Additionally, the Office of Management and Budget (OMB) is taking on a larger role much earlier in the policy development process by asking, "Who is going to pay?" for these contingencies.

60. National Security Interagency Policy-making official.

61. The literature on risk and risk avoidance remains one of the most diverse, spanning multiple fields (from psychology to economics). See, for example, Kenneth J. Arrow, "Risk Perception in Psychology and Economics," *Economic Inquiry* 20 (1982): 1–9; C. F. Camerer, "Individual Decision Making," in *The Handbook of Experimental Economics*, ed. J. H. Kagel and A. E. Roth (Princeton, N.J: Princeton University Press, 1995), 587–703; Steven R. Elliott and Michael McKee, "Collective Risk Decisions in the Presence of Many Risks," *KYKLOS* 48, no. 4 (1995): 541–45; see also Follert, "Risk Analysis: Its Application to Argumentation and Decision-Making"; D. M. Grether and C. R. Plott, "Economic Theory of Choice and the Preference Reversal Phenomenon," *American Economic Review* 69 (1979): 623–38; see also US House, "Risk/Benefit Analysis in the Legislative Process" (Washington, D.C.: GPO, 1979); see also Irving L. Janis and Leon Mann, *Decision Making: A Psychological Analysis of Conflict, Choice, and Commitment* (New York: Free Press, 1977); Robert Jervis, "Political Implications of Loss Aversion, Special Issue: Prospect Theory and Political Psychology," *Political Psychology* 13 (1992): 187–204; see also Daniel Kahneman, Paul Slovic, and Amos Tversky, eds., *Judgment under Uncertainty: Heuristics and Biases* (Cambridge: Cambridge University Press, 1982); Daniel Kahneman and Amos Tversky, "Prospect Theory: An Analysis of Decision under Risk," *Econometrica* 47 (1979): 263–91; Jack S. Levy, "Prospect Theory and International Relations: Theoretical Applications and Analytical Problems, Special Issue: Prospect Theory and Political Psychology," *Political Psychology* 13, no. 2 (1992): 283–310; Jack S. Levy, "Prospect Theory, Rational Choice, and International Relations," *International Studies Quarterly* 41, no. 1 (1997): 87–112; Paul Slovik, "The Construction of Preference," *The American Psychologist* 50, no. 5 (1995): 364–71; Amos Tversky and Daniel Kahneman, "Loss Aversion in Riskless Choice: A Reference Dependent Model," *Quarterly Journal of Economics* 41 (1991): 1039–61; Amos Tversky and Daniel Kahneman, "Rational Choice and the Framing of Decisions," *Journal of Business* 59, no. 4 (1986): S251–S78; Amos Tversky, Paul Slovic, and Daniel Kahneman, "The Causes of Preference Reversal," *American Economic Review* 80 (1990): 204–17; and Amos Tversky and Peter Wakker, "Risk Attitudes and Decision Weights," *Econometrica* 63, no. 6 (1995): 1255–80. While the accountability literature is not as diverse, an overview is provided by John S. Carroll and John W. Payne, "An Information Processing Approach to Two-Party Negotiations," in *Research on Negotiation in Organizations*, ed. Max H. Bazerman, Roy J. Lewicki, and Blair H. Sheppard, *Handbook of Negotiation Research* (Greenwich & London: JAI Press, Inc., 1991), 3–34; see also Hrach Gregorian, *Congressional-Executive Relations and Foreign Policymaking in the Post–Vietnam Period: Case Studies of Congressional Influence* (Waltham, Mass.: Brandeis University, Department of Politics, 1980); Roderick M. Kramer, Pamela Pommerenke, and Elizabeth Newton, "The Social Context of Negotiation: Effects of Social Identity and Interpersonal Accountability on Negotiator Decision Making," *Journal of Conflict Resolution* 37, no. 4 (1993): 633–54; and

Michael G. O'Loughlin, "What Is Bureaucratic Accountability and How Can We Measure It?" *Administration and Society* 22, no. 3 (1990): 275–302.

62. State Department official.

63. Ibid.

64. This fact became a reality for this research as well. I quickly realized that these actors did not record decisions or their analytical processes on paper (save a limited number of highly classified documents that could not be included in this work). Consequently, I had to modify the research methodology by deleting the archival content analysis I originally planned to conduct. As one example, a State Department official communicated that their Strategic Planning office had written a couple of papers on conflict termination for the Persian Gulf War. When I asked if I could review them, this official replied, "I don't know where they are—we don't keep records of such things."

65. Defense Department official.

66. George Bush, "American Leadership and the Prevention of Deadly Conflict," in *Essays on Leadership: Perspectives on Prevention* (New York: Carnegie Corp. of New York, 1998), 36.

67. National Security Interagency Policy-making official.

68. State Department official.

69. Ibid.

70. Ibid.

71. National Security Interagency Policy-making official.

72. For a more general theory of the interplay between values and interests in negotiation, see Dan Druckman and K. Zechmeister, "Conflict of Interest and Value Dissensus: Propositions in the Sociology of Conflict," *Human Relations* 26 (1973): 449–66; Daniel Druckman, "Situational Levers of Position Change: Further Explorations," *Annals of the American Academy of Political and Social Science* 542 (November 1995): 61–80.

73. Defense Department official.

Chapter 8

Crosscutting Effects: Roles and Missions and Media Influence

The themes analyzed through the two previous chapters (dynamic themes and contextual parameters) share a crosscutting ability to influence policy outcomes as well as interagency dynamics. While this research framed them in terms of their influence on the latter and not the former, there can be no mistake that a tendency exists for the informants' ideas regarding roles and missions and media influence to affect both dynamic themes and contextual parameters. It is appropriate, then, to analyze these two crosscutting effects as the bridge between interagency dynamics and policy outcomes. Shown earlier as the elements outside the inverted triangle in figure 23 (p. 161), crosscutting effects exercise considerable influence on interagency conflict during the development of termination policy.

Clarity of Roles and Missions

Returning to the postanalysis signed digraph depicting crisis definition (see fig. 13, p. 138), recall that the quantitative analysis of questionnaire data revealed no significant relationship between *Agency's Perspective Regarding Lead Agency (for policy development)* and any other indicator within the signed digraph model. Little confusion regarding roles and missions is present at the highest levels of policy development. Without providing specifics, one principal remarked, "Senior management knows what it has the lead for and what it does not. The White House is the top level—the chief executive. Some on the National Security Council staff assumed authority they do not have."[1] Government officials identified the president, the NSC (and NSC Staff), and State Department as the three actors most responsible for developing termination policy.[2] This finding supports the original conceptualization of the policy process (depicted in fig. 3, p. 9), which shows the four statutory actors that constitute the NSC as being most responsible for developing national security policy. However, within this complex network of relationships, the president must establish and articulate unambiguously the nation's policy vision. Included in this role is the responsibility to establish the vision for the desired end state.

One informant noted that "the end state and goals [are] defined by the secretary of defense and the president. Nevertheless, the secretary of state has significant, if not overriding, influence on the identification of the end state. Usually, the Assistant to the President for National Security Affairs (APNSA) has the greatest influence over the president—whether it is formal or informal is hard to tell. The agency with the greatest informal influence on the NSC is State . . . [because] the NSC does not have a game plan."[3]

A high-ranking State Department official reinforced this perspective, asserting that it is the State Department's "job to create a vision for the desired end state."[4] These diverse perspectives regarding the NCA's role and the State Department's influence provide evidence for continuing conflict among agencies over roles and responsibilities concerning end-state definition. There are, however, traditionally accepted notions regarding agency roles.

The NSC Staff remains responsible for policy coordination and implementation oversight. The State Department plays an essential role in this process since it is responsible for formulating the nation's foreign policy and maintaining diplomatic relations abroad. In turn, the Defense Department is responsible for winning the nation's wars[5] and for advising civilian policy makers regarding the use of military force. Finally, the Intelligence Community (namely, CIA, DIA, INR, NRO [National Reconnaissance Office]) is responsible for providing intelligence to support policy makers and war fighters. On the surface, these roles seem well defined and mutually exclusive. This is true only in theory, however; policy making includes other dimensions that generate interagency conflict—dimensions that blur the otherwise clearly defined roles and missions outlined above. Moreover, the seemingly clear distinctions conceal overlaps in the process.

Role Ambiguity

According to an IWG-level participant, these roles and missions have sufficient overlap to create confusion and generate tension across the interagency environment, "I don't think we have a coherent interagency process—we have few examples of coherent interagency vision or strategic planning. The problem is that we have different responsibilities, missions, and capabilities within these agencies. The problem is there is some overlap and often there are not [sic] clear lines of responsibility."[6] Overlap in an environment where responsibilities are not clearly defined leads to the second source of interagency conflict regarding roles and missions—that of resisting a role to protect one's respective equities.

Role resistance seems to resonate compellingly within the Department of Defense. Along with other interagency actors, the Defense Department noted a hesitance on the part of the military to get involved in missions not defined explicitly as their traditional war-fighting role. Again, the idea of shared images applies as Defense Department personnel adhere to a stringently circumscribed perspective on the military's role and the missions it should perform. According to an NSC source, "You have an inherent tension in civil-military conflicts between the need for a logistics capability on the ground and the fact that a lot of these tasks are more civil-oriented. When the US government needs to move, plan, etc., there's one organization that does this stuff—the military. But the Pentagon does not believe it is its job to do civil affairs stuff—building wells, transportation, etc., but other, responsible agencies cannot do it right away."[7]

A sentiment echoed by the State Department, the Defense Department agrees it has been less than proactive about embracing these "nontraditional" missions. A Defense Department official noted that the Department's cultural bias plays into this as well, "We forget that we work for civilians and if the NCA have established new perspectives for the nation, then we need to accept that."[8] In essence, Samuel Huntington's ideas regarding continuing tension in civil-military relationships retains as much, perhaps more, import for contemporary interagency relations as they did throughout the post–World War II era.[9] The role the NSC Staff plays in the policy process exacerbates these cultural differences and tends to generate interagency conflict across the three major actors within the policy process.

As described in chapter 4, the NSC Staff serves as the president's policy coordinator and implementation supervisor.[10] However, officials with 1990s experience indicated that the NSC Staff assumed a role beyond coordinating while abdicating responsibility for implementation oversight. A State Department deputy captured the essence of this transition, "Paradoxically, the NSC [Staff] now dominates the process. Because it is now dominant, it deals with all the issues, but only episodically. It exacerbates the problem by not paying attention except to the 'crisis of the day.' That decreases pressure for State and Defense to work together, so they continue to do their own things. The NSC [Staff] does not do a good job of forcing people to work together."[11]

A Defense Department official asserted that the NSC Staff has now transformed itself into a position wherein the "NSC's desire to be the State Department, OSD [Office of the Secretary of Defense], etc., . . . their desire to be the 'prime mover' rather than the 'prime shaper' has created confusion about who's in charge."[12] An NSC official echoed this perspective, "For the NSC and State there is friction over leadership in foreign policy issues—it can become institutional or personality driven."[13] This dilemma is especially critical for implementation where a lack of policy oversight enables bureaucratic equities to resurface. The official continued, "There's no consistent management at the top so implementation is not smooth and the bureaucratic differences reassert themselves in implementation. I've seen that happen fairly often because it's very hard to have consistent policy management. It's harder than policy making. The NSC has to be the policy manager, not just the broker of the policy decision."[14]

A principal focused this issue by saying, "Statute specified the roles of the CINC, et cetera, but that's not the only thing that specifies how we deal with these roles. The judgment and capabilities of the people who occupy these posts—sometimes people don't know their roles."[15] This role ambiguity creates an interagency dynamic that paralyzes the policy process as actors become polarized with regard to each other and shift their focus from the crisis at hand to their immediate crisis in the White House Situation Room. Interagency negotiations take place in other venues as well. This example makes the point that the actors lose focus on the needs of those whom they are supposed to serve (i.e., those in the field), only to focus on their respective bureaucratic needs vis-à-vis others engaged in the policy process. In addition to these role-identification dilemmas connected to departmental missions, a parallel roles and missions issue enables substantive aspects of policy formulation to shape interagency dynamics. Highlighted in the previous chapter's analysis of interagency dynamics, the perception that the interagency process intends the IWG-level exchange to be a "food fight by design" presents a particular challenge for conflict termination policy development.

"Purposeful" Interagency Conflict

A higher level of interagency conflict exists at the IWG-level when compared with the deputies and principals levels (refer to chap. 6). One principal affirmed this finding, saying, "First, it is designed that way for [a] useful purpose: Each agency is assigned certain responsibilities and authorities—the process is designed to look after those. Second, the process has an underpinning of good sense in that it forces the bureaucracy to seek compromise rather than having a 'first among equals.' It forces people to stay within their boundaries rather than directing them . . . compromise rather than dictate."[16]

In similar fashion, a deputy noted, "junior people draw the initial battle lines, but not the outcome."[17] This perspective has become so ingrained, according to this deputy, that the standard joke from the NSC Staff and the State Department with regard to the Defense Department's position on troop employment is "Whatever the action is—the standard answer is 20,000 troops (one Division) and $2 billion."[18] Senior decision makers expect lower-level actors to protect their respective agency's bureaucratic equities throughout the interagency policy-making process. When lower-level actors feel limited in their ability to protect institutional equities, they push the issue up to the next level for decision. In this manner, a principal submitted that "most action officers feel their duty is not to decide, but to clarify."[19]

The ensuing struggle to protect institutional equities generates interagency conflict, especially at the lower levels. These blinders negate actors' abilities to analyze the entire crisis spectrum for fear of "negotiating away" their respective equities. Through institutional entrenchment and rigidity, interagency decision makers create a self-perpetuating dynamic of interagency conflict. The conflict's continuation or escalation impairs the USG's capacity—in terms of both "will" and "skill"—to explore all of its potential options for dealing with complex contingencies. An NSC official claimed this problem goes beyond the "you can't see the forest for the trees" metaphor, "The more you see, you realize you don't see other stuff. It's not just the forest or the trees, there's a mountain, an ocean, and a planet."[20] During complex crises, the problem then becomes one of agencies focusing myopically on their individual trees (their respective equities) at the expense of the forest (the interests of the parties in conflict), the mountain (US national interests), the ocean (regional interests), and the planet (global interests).

The foregoing discussion reveals ways in which experienced policy makers think about issues concerning *Roles and Missions*. Clearly, these issues relate to both process and substance. First, the absence of mutual understanding regarding roles creates interagency conflict surrounding responsibilities, accountability, and missions. That dynamic unfavorably shapes policy outcomes as agencies fail to clarify roles and missions during policy formulation—a problem that carries over into policy implementation. This condition intensifies greatly when actors within the interagency process (1) abrogate the leadership role others perceive they should fulfill, (2) try to assume the roles of others, or (3) attempt to compel others to perform roles and missions they perceive to be the responsibility of another organization. Secondly, the perceived need to protect institutional equities when entering the policy-making process generates (or exacerbates) interagency conflict. In this way, the substantive inputs to policy making in terms of resource protection adversely affect interagency dynamics. This discussion highlights that this cross-cutting theme can hold grave consequences for the ability of the interagency process to develop conflict termination policy in terms of effective crisis analysis, the vision for the desired end state, conflict termination criteria, and the strategy to achieve conflict termination. The media plays a similar crosscutting role.

Media Influence

Perhaps more than any other theme that emerged from the interviews, the ways in which the media influences both the process and substance of the USG policy machine remain difficult to isolate and cannot be categorized neatly into the process-substance and substance-process categories undergirding this framework. Therefore, arguments apply to both of these categories based upon the data provided by the informants. The two relationships are separated artificially here for the purpose of analysis; bear in mind, however, that the data revealed substantial crosscutting effects with each issue outlined below. The role the media plays in developing the interagency dynamic—while concurrently shaping the substantive input to the policy process—remains extremely complex and somewhat intangible. In other words, it is difficult to trace empirically or precisely the influence the media has on interagency dynamics, substantive inputs to the policy process, and resulting policy outcomes. One State Department principal captured the essence of this difficulty, noting, "I do not know at the end of the day how much press/media concerns drive foreign policy. But I know that it does to some extent— you can feel, see, and sense it."[21] The data indicated unquestionably, however, that the media is seen as playing a role in shaping both relationships. One of the most critical roles played by this influential actor in terms of the substance-process relationship is reflected in the media's ability to advance substantive inputs that move the policy process in a particular direction. The media plays a crucial role in shaping the substance-process relationship in terms of framing the issue, providing a feedback loop to the Congress (and the public), and developing a "move it off the front page" phenomenon.

Issue Framing

Interagency actors perceive that the media plays a fundamental role in framing issues for both the decision maker and the public. According to one Defense Department principal, the media shapes people's views of the world when they get up in the morning, it is "the drama of the iron curtain crumbling—watching history unfold every morning in the headlines. It creates a preoccupation." This individual continued, "The media helps frame the question . . . reminds you that it's important and everyone is hoping for an improved professional response. Once something is hot, there's an increased preoccupation with media perceptions."[22]

Another Defense Department principal identified Washington as a "one issue town," claiming that "everyone reads the *Early Bird* and they are all influenced by that."[23] Yet another official, this one from the State Department, insisted that one of the most influential questions is how the issue gets cast into the public domain, "*Who* writes the *Foreign Affairs* article?" Although unable to authenticate this figure beyond mere anecdotal evidence, two State Department officials independently reported that the State Department's intelligence function provides *almost 50 percent* of the USG's intelligence collection capability. The difference between the State Department and the remainder of the Intelligence Community is that they take advantage of open sources, a method the other intelligence activities do not employ to the same degree. According to these informants, media reports are one component of this open-source approach. Others remarked that decision makers within the Congress get much of their information from the media, perhaps on a far broader scale when compared with internal government intelligence sources.

Congressional Connections

The media reports the perspectives of Washington notables (e.g., Richard Haass and Susan Woodward) while reflecting the views of respected think tanks as well. Once the views of these personalities gain currency with the media and the public, they provide the Congress a baseline for calling expert witnesses during congressional hearings.[24] These witnesses' views help shape the Congress's approach to national security policy, the funding of troop deployments in particular. Highlighted earlier, managing executive-legislative relations is of the utmost import for interagency decision makers. This communication network between the media and the Congress relates to another aspect of this actor's influence upon domestic politics in terms of the substance-process relationship—media reporting generates a "move it off the front page" phenomenon within the interagency process.

"Front Page" Challenge

The data showed that a perception exists wherein "if it is in the newspaper, it is real." A State Department official went so far as to say that "if I had to choose between a brilliant cable or inside story by a 23-year old in the *Washington Post*—if you wanted to enforce the policy, choose the *Washington Post*."[25] While this perspective relates to the issue of the media driving policy, it also reveals the sense of urgency policy makers share for moving issues off the front pages of the nation's most respected, most widely read newspapers. Another State Department official claimed the media does not drive policy but admitted that decision makers consider the media as a factor in every action, "The media is certainly one of the factors you take into account every time. You ask, How is the media going to play it? What sort of criticism will we get . . . how [do we] handle the criticism?"[26] It does not drive, but is a factor!

Decision makers and politicians do not trivialize the magnitude of this substantive factor and its effect on the policy process. One Defense Department principal made the connection between the media, domestic politics, and the Congress by arguing, "The press and public opinion and politics are the ultimate drivers even in international crises because the senior people—the president, vice president, and cabinet-level members—are politicians so they have got to focus on the realistic political room they have got. If they do not know, they will take a poll and run with it. . . . The principals say, 'What can I sell?'"[27]

Consequently, the media shapes the policy-making forum through its attempts to define issues, manage relationships with the Congress, and mold public opinion (indeed, domestic politics in general) regarding the nature of the crisis and the most appropriate US policy response.[28] With an understanding of the media's capacity to shape substantive inputs, it is logical to proceed to the ways in which these substantive inputs influence interagency dynamics and resulting policy outcomes. This process-substance relationship is captured through concerns surrounding the "CNN factor," the potential for press guidance to drive policy, the use of leaks, and the capacity for "the necessity to manage the media" to deplete the interagency process of critical intellectual, emotional, and psychological capital.

CNN Factor

Decision makers across the interagency process remain concerned with the effects of the "CNN factor."[29] Simply put, actors within the White House/NSC Staff and State Department remain cognizant of the media's ability to shape public and world opinion; consequently, decision makers remain attuned to the media's activities.[30] While this issue relates to the substance-process aspects of policy making, process-substance conditions emerge in terms of the potential for press guidance to drive policy. One tangible measure of this process-substance relationship manifests itself in time and numbers of people agencies employ to develop press guidance. Although unable to make reliable comparisons across agencies, it is important to recognize that the State Department's Office of Press Relations utilizes 10 people who spend an average of 200 hours per five-day work week *before 1200* (i.e., noon) developing press-related guidance for the "1230" press briefing. Activities *after* the 1230 press briefing vary, but my observations over a four-month period revealed that much of these people's day(s) is consumed by efforts to respond to media inquiries generated at this 1230 briefing. A State Department principal provided another perspective regarding the media's influence, "Here, within State, [and] at NSC and OSD, the most senior policy formulators spend a lot of time planning for public affairs. Jamie Rubin [assistant secretary of state for Public Affairs and State Department spokesman] is Albright's closest policy advisor—Steinberg and Berger [deputy

APNSA and APNSA, respectively] spend a lot of time talking with Rubin about public affairs."[31]

An NSC official echoed that point of view by saying, "You can issue a very important policy pronouncement, but if it gets no attention, it doesn't really matter—press guidance does become policy."[32] Another State Department principal scoffed that "press guidance is called long-range planning."[33] A Defense Department official remarked, "If you're always in a crisis and always worried about CNN and the *Washington Post*, you're never able to get out of that dilemma."[34] The media's capacity to garner policy-making attention to the degree that it does affect interagency relations adversely and inhibits interagency exchange. By way of example, a State Department official reported that the NSC Staff's standard practice had been to brief the media's perspective on an issue before engaging in an interagency discussion of the matter. Following that practice, "during the first Carlucci-led NSC meeting, the person got up to brief the media's reporting first. He said, 'No, that comes at the end of the meeting, not the beginning.'"[35] Unlike his predecessor, Carlucci would not let the media drive the interagency process and the policies it produced. Another way in which media relations affect interagency dynamics is through "intentional leaks."

Leaks with Intent

Leaks emanate from two sources—protestors and champions—but for one purpose—to shape the decision-making process in terms of both interagency dynamics and substantive policy outcomes. The previous chapter confirmed that actors across the government agree that the interagency process makes decisions via negotiation as it strives to generate consensus-based policy outcomes. This consensus approach then becomes the indispensable component during implementation. However, increasingly the USG experiences leaks to the media by anonymous actors (i.e., protestors) who disagree with a policy. An NSC principal supported this proposition by stating, "Look at the press—those who have been stymied go to the press to attack those who stymied them."[36] One high-ranking Defense Department official noted that leaks reflect organizational culture and leadership as well, "If the people do not like the policy, they will leak it. [Secretary of Defense] Perry had no leaks—he respected their views and the people respected him. It all starts with the leadership qualities of the [people] at the top."[37]

An NSC deputy claimed the process occurs in this fashion, "What happens is, if people do not agree they call 'Mike' at the *New York Times*—'Mike, can you believe what they are trying to get me to do?'"[38] In these instances, the source of the leak is an interagency official who disagrees with the policy and, therefore, invokes the media to shape public and, perhaps, congressional perspectives of the crisis and the nature of the USG's most appropriate response. Such actors *intend* to fragment the policy process and create interagency conflict in hopes of gaining greater support for their position, a position that remains contradictory to espoused USG policy (and hence, outside the interagency's shared images). A Defense Department principal remarked that the media shapes interagency dynamics further because "friction between personalities is driven by the press—it's easier to talk 'win-lose' than about the issues."[39] This dynamic instigates additional adverse consequences as attention given to managing this aspect of the interagency dynamic depletes the process of vital intellectual and emotional capital. Such depletion "zaps the psychological energy of everyone,"[40] in the words of one Defense Department principal, intimating that this prevents innovative thinking as well. In this manner, decision makers purposefully use leaks to shape interagency dynamics and, therefore, the substantive outcome(s) of the process. The second source likewise intends to use leaks to shape the interagency process, but for a different purpose.

Halperin and others contend that most leaks emanate from the White House.[41] The officials' experiences captured in this study support Halperin's supposition, noting that most leaks are in fact "official leaks with intent." These "leaks with intent" occur for the following three reasons: First, to shape proactively the image of the crisis and the USG's corresponding policy; second, to signal or communicate with allies and adversaries; and, third, to test public reaction to policy options (i.e., floating a "trial balloon"). A State Department principal noted the reason for the first is very simple, observing, "If there are leaks not provided as the official guidance, I do not know about them. Official leaks are 'leaks with intent.' The purpose of giving someone an exclusive [is to] help *you* shape *their* story—they're not going to have an opportunity to do a lot of checking around. . . . There is a re-emphasis on dealing with key media before the story is written— a move to make ourselves more available to media officials."[42]

While this practice shapes Washington's interagency dynamic, its purpose is to likewise signal allies and adversaries regarding the USG's intentions. During the Persian Gulf War, for example, decision makers used the press extensively. One NSC principal declared, "CNN was very instrumental—used to signal Hussein, the Iraqis, and the allies—we were very open about that."[43] A State Department deputy echoed this perspective, noting "press guidance elements of policy are central as they shape US and in-ternational views. There has to be a very direct connection be-tween press guidance and policy."[44] From this perspective, the data demonstrated that those who agree with the policy position use leaks to shape the public's understanding of the crisis and the nature of the US response while communicating US resolve to people both at home and abroad.

Collectively, analysis indicates unambiguously that the media does play an important role in shaping both the substance-process and process-substance relationships that mold the emergent themes. The substance-process relationships ap-peared through those issues wherein the media frames the is-sues, provides feedback to the Congress, and develops the "move it off the front page" phenomenon. The process-substance rela-tionships emerged from those issues related to interagency dynamics in terms of the level of attention given to press guid-ance, the CNN factor, the "use of leaks," and the media's ability to exacerbate friction between decision makers while depleting the interagency process of crucial intellectual and psychological energy. Referring again to the *Interagency Conflict* model (see fig. 23), we can begin to see the ways in which these themes inter-relate as they build upon one another and exacerbate the "Level of Interagency Conflict over (a) crisis analysis, (b) desired end state, (c) termination criteria, and (d) strategy."

Interim Summary

Informants disclosed that ambiguity surrounding roles and missions and the impact of media influence shape not merely the substance of policy but also the process of policy making. Together, these emergent themes affect the development of interagency dynamics and the substantive inputs into the policy process. When placed along side the dynamic themes and contextual parameters, these crosscutting effects tend to amplify interagency conflict over the development of termination policy. The case analyses that follow (chap. 9) demonstrate the ways in which these dynamic themes, contextual parameters, and crosscutting effects shaped termination policy development for the Persian Gulf War and Bosnia crisis.

Notes

1. National Security Interagency Policy-making official, Executive Office of the President, Washington, D.C.

2. NSC Staff and State Department officials conveyed an expectation that taking the "lead" for policy development is indeed the *independent role* of each agency, but not necessarily *their collective* responsibility.

3. Intelligence Community official, Washington, D.C.

4. State Department official, US Department of State, Washington, D.C.

5. Since the end of the Cold War, this narrow definition of Defense Department responsibilities has become a source of conflict within the interagency process. DOD has used this (or at least the Joint Chiefs of Staff have) to avoid extensive participation in complex contingency scenarios.

6. Intelligence Community official.

7. As a point of clarification, joint and service doctrines provide for DOD participation and leadership in such actions. However, this NSC official identified Defense Department's reticence to become involved in roles distinct from war fighting.

8. Defense Department official, US Department of Defense, Washington, D.C.

9. See also Samuel P. Huntington, *The Soldier and the State: The Theory and Politics of Civil-Military Relations* (Cambridge: The Belknap Press of Harvard University Press, 1957).

10. Colin L. Powell, "The NSC System in the Last Two Years of the Reagan Administration," in *The Presidency in Transition*, ed. James P. Pfiffner et al. (New York: Center for the Study of the Presidency, 1989), 204–18.

11. State Department official.

12. Defense Department official.

13. National Security Interagency Policy-making official.

14. Ibid.

15. The use of *CINC* does not refer to the president of the United States as "commander in chief" of the Armed Forces. Rather, "the acronym 'CINC' refers to the commander of a unified or specified command." See Armed Forces Staff College (AFSC), AFSC Pub 1, *The Joint Staff Officer's Guide*, 1993), I-4. Note that Secretary of Defense Donald Rumsfeld changed DOD's lexicon in 2002 to identify one "commander in chief"—the POTUS. For consistency throughout this work, the heretofore-accepted doctrinal term *CINC* is used to place the ideas within their original context.

16. Interagency official, Executive Office of the President, Washington, D.C.

17. Ibid.

18. Ibid.

19. Ibid.

20. National Security Interagency Policy-making official.

21. State Department official.

22. Defense Department official.

23. The *Early Bird* is a publication prepared by the American Forces Information Service (AFIS/OASD-PA). Circulated daily (and now available on the Internet), it seeks "to bring to the attention of key personnel news items of interest in their official capacities. It is not intended to substitute for newspapers and periodicals as a means of keeping informed about the meaning and impact of news developments." See AFIS/OASD-PA, *Early Bird* (Washington, D.C.: Current News Service, The Pentagon, 1998), 1. This publication (which averages 28 pages) is a compilation of foreign-policy relevant articles from the major news organizations around the world (e.g., *New York Times, Washington Post, Washington Times, International Herald Tribune*, and *London Sunday Times*). Defense Department official.

24. While I did not perform a statistical analysis to support this supposition, Dr. Susan Woodward is a participant in this research not because of her publishing record on the Balkans crisis (which is noteworthy on its own merit) but as a result of the number of times the Congress called her to testify regarding US policy in the Balkans. I drew a connection between media reports citing her views and the congressional hearings in which she participated. This same connection can be made, and, I believe, statistically supported, between Dr. Richard Haass' currency in the media and his ability to act as an unofficial advisor to the president on Middle East issues. While certainly not the only reason for Haass' continuing influence, such media exposure does translate into policy influence on some level. This, however, is the subject of a different analysis and is offered here as an observation and justification for Woodward's selection as a participant in this study.

25. State Department official. "Cables" are the USG's (especially the president's and State Department's) primary means of communicating official policy within the USG and abroad.

26. State Department official.

27. Defense Department official.

28. A rich literature discusses the media's influence in molding public opinion and policy development. For insight into these phenomena and the media's influence on the two cases addressed later in this work, see Thomas D. Beamish, Harvey Molotch, and Richard Flacks, "Who Supports the Troops? Vietnam, the Gulf War, and the Making of Collective Memory," *Social Problems* 42, no. 3 (1995): 344–60; Johan Carlisle et al., "Symposium—Special Gulf War Forum," *Propaganda Review*, no. 7 (1990): 5–34; Noam Chomsky, "Twentieth Century American Propaganda," *Propaganda Review* 8 (Fall 1991): 8–11, 37–44; see also T. L. Coleman, *News Media: Should They Play a Role in Crisis Management* (Carlisle Barracks, Pa.: US Army War College, 1989); Christopher Dandeker, "Public Opinion, the Media, and the Gulf War," *Armed Forces and Society* 22, no. 2 (1995): 297–302; W. Phillips Davison, "News Media and International Negotiation," *Public Opinion Quarterly* 38, no. 2 (1974): 174–91; Michael Dobbs, "U.S. Starts Process of Army Aid; Some Allies Resist Bosnian Project," *The Washington Post*, 21 December 1995, A35; Matthew C. Ehrlich, "Taken by Storm: The Media, Public Opinion, and US Foreign Policy in the Gulf War," *Journalism and Mass Communication Quarterly* 72, no. 1 (1995): 251–52; William P. Eveland Jr., Douglas M. McLeod, and Nancy Signorielli, "Actual and Perceived U.S. Public Opinion: The Spiral of Silence During the Persian Gulf War," *International Journal of Public Opinion Research* 7, no. 2 (1995): 91–109; Douglas C. Foyle, "Public Opinion and Foreign Policy: Elite Beliefs as a Mediating Variable," *International Studies Quarterly* 41 (1997): 141–69; Dina Goren, "The News and Foreign Policy: An Examination of the Impact of the News Media on the Making of Foreign Policy," *Research in Social Movements, Conflicts and Change* 3 (1980): 119–41; see also Hrach Gregorian, *Congressional-Executive Relations and Foreign Policymaking in the Post–Vietnam Period: Case Studies of Congressional Influence* (Waltham, Mass.: Brandeis University, Department of Politics, 1980); see also Shanto Iyengar, *Is Anyone Responsible? How Television Frames Political Issues* (Chicago: University of Chicago Press, 1991); Shanto Iyengar and Adam Simon, "News Coverage of the Gulf Crisis and Public Opinion: A Study of Agenda-Setting, Priming, and Framing," *Communication Research* 20, no. 3 (1993): 365–83; Sut Jhally, Justin Lewis, and Michael Morgan, "The Gulf War: A Study of the Media, Public Opinion and Public Knowledge," *Propaganda Review* 8 (fall 1991): 1415, 50–52; see also D. V. Johnson, *Impact of the Media on National Security Policy Decision Making* (Carlisle Barracks, Pa.: US Army War College, Strategic Studies Institute, 1994); Elihu Katz et al., "Symposium: Journalism in Crisis and Change," *Journal of Communication* 42, no. 3 (1992): 5–107; Jon A. Krosnick and Laura A. Brannon, "The Media and the Foundations of Presidential Support: George Bush and the Persian Gulf Conflict," *Journal of Social Issues* 49, no. 4 (1993): 167–82; Ven Hwei Lo, "Media Use, Involvement, and Knowledge of the Gulf War," *Journalism Quarterly* 71, no. 1 (1994): 43–54; see also Frank Spurgeon Morrow Jr., "The U.S. Power Structure and the Mass Media" (PhD diss., The University of Texas at Austin, 1984); see also Office of the United States Secretary of Defense (OSD), *Conduct of the Persian Gulf War, Final Re-*

port to Congress Pursuant to Title V of the Persian Gulf Conflict Supplemental Authorization and Personnel Benefits Act of 1991 (Public Law 102-25) (Washington, D.C.: GPO, 1992); Zhongdang Pan and Gerald M. Kosicki, "Voters' Reasoning Processes and Media Influences During the Persian Gulf War," *Political Behavior* 16, no. 1 (1994): 117–56; Suzanne L. Parker, "Toward an Understanding of 'Rally' Effects: Public Opinion in the Persian Gulf War," *Public Opinion Quarterly* 59, no. 4 (1995): 526–46; see also Philip John Powlick, "The American Foreign Policy Process and the Public" (PhD diss., University of Pittsburgh, 1990); Edward W. Said and Barbara Harlow, "The Intellectuals and the War," *Middle East Report* 21, no. 4 (1991): 15–20; Jack G. Shaheen et al., "Media Coverage of the Middle East: Perception and Foreign Policy," *Annals of the American Academy of Political and Social Science* 482 (November 1985): 160–73; Robert Stallaerts, "Forging War. The Media in Serbia, Croatia and Bosnia-Hercegovina," *Tijdschrift voor Sociale Wetenschappen* 40, no. 1 (1995): 102; Albert R. Tims and M. Mark Miller, "Determinants of Attitudes toward Foreign Countries," *International Journal of Intercultural Relations* 10, no. 4 (1986): 471–84; James Toth, "Demonizing Saddam Hussein: Manipulating Racism as a Prelude to War," *New Political Science* 21–22 (spring–summer 1992): 5–39; Patrick Wilcken, "The Intellectuals, the Media and the Gulf War," *Critique of Anthropology* 15, no. 1 (1995): 37–69; John Zaller, "Information, Values, and Opinions," *American Political Science Review* 85 (1991): 1215–38; and see also John Zaller, *The Nature and Origins of Mass Opinion* (New York: Cambridge University Press, 1993).

29. With the proliferation of newscasts and cable talk shows (e.g., *Meet the Press* and *Face the Nation*), this study in no means intends to imply that CNN, Inc., is the "only" influential media conglomerate. It is used here euphemistically to capture the broader media element. For an interesting viewpoint on this issue, see also Marc D. Felman, *The Military/Media Clash and the New Principle of War: Media Spin* (Maxwell AFB, Ala.: Air University Press, 1993); and see also US Army Headquarters, Department of the Army, "Information Operations and Battlefield Simulation/Digitization," *Military Review* 75, no. 6 (1995).

30. It is interesting to note that the comments related to press guidance influencing policy emanated primarily from the NSC Staff and the State Department—the Defense Department informants made no mention of this connection. By department, the ratio of overall references to the media was White House/NSC, 50 percent; State Department, 50 percent; Defense Department, 23.3 percent; and, CIA, 66.7 percent.

31. State Department official.

32. National Security Interagency Policy-making official.

33. State Department official.

34. Defense Department official.

35. State Department official.

36. National Security Interagency Policy-making official.

37. Defense Department official.

38. National Security Interagency Policy-making official.

39. Defense Department official.

40. Ibid.

41. See also Morton H. Halperin, with the assistance of Priscilla Clapp and Arnold Kanter, *Bureaucratic Politics and Foreign Policy* (Washington, D.C.: The Brookings Institution, 1974).

42. State Department official.

43. National Security Interagency Policy-making official.

44. State Department official.

PART III

Conflict Termination Policy Development

Chapter 9

Developing the
Endgame—Termination Policy
for the Persian Gulf and Bosnia

It is more than coincidental that popular discourse refers to the vision of the desired end state as the "endgame."[1] Such terminology intimates an underlying perspective regarding the bureaucratic political process and is, therefore, an implicit extension of the "game" metaphor used to describe Allison's bureaucratic politics model of decision making. Dissimilar approaches to leadership, decision making as negotiation, domestic politics, strategic vision and planning processes, and institutional equities determine the "face of the issue" each agency perceives as most important, while shaping analytical perspectives to minimize the distressing effects of cognitive dissonance (chap. 2). The findings provided evidence regarding the influence of this face-of-the-issue component on policy development, suggesting that termination policy must be thought of in terms of the following four themes that emerged from both cases: the development of crisis analysis, end-state vision, termination criteria, and termination strategy. To contextualize these findings within real-world interagency processes, this chapter traces interagency conflict's effects on the policy processes of the Persian Gulf War and the Bosnia crisis along the lines of these four themes.[2] Crisis analysis emerged as the most critical aspect of Termination Policy development because it frames the remaining three policy components—the desired end state, termination criteria, and strategy; consequently, it serves as the anchoring point for the remainder of this discussion.

Crisis Analysis

Crisis analysis provides the foundational perspective around which policy makers frame the three remaining termination policy components. Leadership directly affects crisis analysis. The absence of strategic vision coupled with the lack of an integrated planning process empowers decision makers to develop perspectives on crises that remain bound by disparate worldviews. Dissimilar conceptions of roles and missions (i.e., theirs and others) and the need to protect institutional equities further restrict these perspectives.

In the first instance, the absence of a strategic vision enables decision makers to frame crises differently because of dissimilar organizational cultures and competing institutional equities. A product of asymmetric worldviews, dissimilar shared images regarding ideology and philosophical perspectives concerning the use of force prompt agencies to ascribe different meanings to crises. The State Department tends to view crises as part of the continually evolving global landscape. Accordingly, State adopts a process-oriented analytic approach to analysis. Defense, on the other hand, tends to view crises as situations with identifiable beginning and ending points. Defense's views are therefore substance-oriented with an accompanying tendency to fractionate crises into distinct phases wherein milestones must be chronologically (or serially) achieved before proceeding to the next phase; that is, it is a linear process with clear turning points.[3] Magnified within an interagency process that lacks an integrated planning mechanism, these differences permit department-specific worldviews to dominate crisis analysis as the absence of structure generates considerable latitude for interpretation.

Decision makers generally fail to recognize the extent to which subconsciously constructed worldviews affect conflict dynamics and their respective analytical processes. Accordingly, the USG endeavors to superimpose its perspective onto others when dealing with both interest- and value-laden issues. Such an ethnocentric approach lacks cultural appreciation and impels US leaders to promote "good guy/bad guy" stereotypes regarding adversaries.[4] Demonization of the enemy negates decision makers' ability to look at the conflict *in toto* for fear of becoming an apologist for those whose practices contributed to the actual crisis, yet whom the USG feels compelled to support.[5] It likewise creates an environment wherein concerns about face-saving prevent leaders from engaging in a more collaborative approach.[6] Hence, the conclusion that a groupthink phenomenon develops during crisis analysis, one made evident by decision makers' unwillingness to examine more rigorously the underlying causes and conditions of conflict.[7] One State deputy characterized this unwillingness by saying, "Part of the process is that no agency [or] person wants to express a view that gets them put *outside* the system. In terms of 'bad guys/good guys' . . . if you raise those issues, you find yourself outside the shared images."[8] This fear of being outside the shared images of one's agency further distorts national interest definition and the framing of intervention criteria.

The most critical aspect concerning the presence or absence of shared images for crisis analysis materializes in the answer to the question When does a conflict start? The response to this inquiry rests in part with the perceptions decision makers attach to their roles during crisis intervention. Their roles are defined partially by institutional equities. A State deputy contended "different departments have different views on what a crisis is—that's related to self-interest. In part, the interagency conflict is over the definition of the crisis—which is directly tied to their self-interests."[9] Examination of roles and missions ambiguities alongside defense of institutional equities clarifies their relationship with crisis analysis.

In addition to the effects of role ambiguity highlighted earlier, this problem manifests itself further in the absence of an integrated analytical mechanism. Because no one agency controls or "owns" an entire crisis response effort, the lack of cross-fertilization results in interagency misconceptions of core competencies. One National Security Council principal asserted, "To try to figure out [how] to make a . . . complex civil emergency operation work is a [heck] of a puzzle . . . no one understands the whole puzzle and everyone comes at it from a different perspective."[10]

This insulated effort curtails crisis analysis as mutually exclusive analyses lack a "systems approach" that capitalizes upon the core competencies each agency brings to bear upon the problem. Because no interagency mechanism exists to conduct long-term forecasting, agencies independently engage in crisis analysis *after* eruption (e.g., humanitarian crises). One State principal noted, "So much depends on individuals that it isn't the process at fault—it's the failure to utilize the process in decision making, a failure to look in advance at what are likely to be future challenges. All too often we wait for a crisis to erupt before developing a policy. You never know how it might erupt."[11] Lower-level analysts and decision makers push independent postfacto perspectives upward to the highest levels whereby the principals attempt to synthesize fragmented images of the "puzzle." This approach complicates planning and crisis response unnecessarily because principals remain reluctant to get involved with the details of the planning process (e.g., identifying contingency operation funding sources). Such inaction pushes the fundamental progenitors of interagency conflict back down the interagency hierarchy where decision makers dogmatically protect their respective equities.

Discussed in greater detail throughout the earlier analysis, perceptions regarding the need to protect institutional equities play a central role in developing "competitive" interagency tactics when perceptions of self-interest are "high" (see fig. 11, p. 136). Additionally, the quantitative analysis revealed that when an *Agency's Perceived Penalty for Failure* ranked high, that *Department's Interagency Behavior* tended to be "competitive" (see fig. 15, p. 140). The interagency's lower-level members remain tied to their respective agencies and perceive that their failure to protect institutional equities equates to professional failure. The desire to avoid this failure (and its penalty; see fig. 15) generates competitive interagency tactics. Further, divergent conceptions of time (compounded by a general lack of time due to the pace of interagency activities) exacerbate this perceived need to protect institutional equities, prompting agencies to frame national interests and intervention criteria independent of others' inputs and, therefore, differently from one another.

Contending views regarding interest- versus value-laden national interests and intervention criteria intensify interagency conflict as agencies promote discordant assessments regarding the definition of conflict and the utility of armed intervention. Such analysis results in a tendency to exaggerate or overestimate operational requirements as a means to protect institutional equities and delay action. Relatedly, the NSC Staff's operating procedures intensify these differences when it responds to congressional pressure or media influence *rather* than taking action based upon principled guidance from the White House. Together, these factors—dissimilar worldviews, asymmetric conceptions of roles and missions, and the need to protect institutional equities—create a narrow analytical approach that compels decision makers to focus on tactical rather than strategic issues. This approach emerged as the most crucial flaw related to crisis analysis since the nature of this analysis—occurring in the initial stages of the policy debate—shapes termination policy's remaining elements.

Ultimately, because decision makers focus on tactical-level issues, their approaches to crisis analysis tend to analyze the nodes of the system, failing to recognize the value of the relationships across nodes that make the system one entity.[12] Alternatively, some tend to be incapable of recognizing that a systemic phenomenon is at work yet perceive that tactical actions serve the national interest. Either way, such tactical focus restricts the interagency's ability to evaluate the underlying causes and conditions of the crisis, thereby negating its ability to develop a policy that can achieve long-term conflict termination as a step toward sustainable conflict resolution. Data supported these findings for both cases examined here, illustrating as well how two distinct presidential decision-making styles can both lead the interagency toward the same tactically focused conclusion.

Case Examples/Crisis Analysis

The Persian Gulf and Bosnia crises transpired during two different presidential administrations that exercised different decision-making styles. The Bush presidency was a decision-taking administration; the Clinton presidency, a consensus-building administration.[13] Despite these differences in style, both administrations focused on select critical nodes of the conflict system rather than on the system as a whole. The decision-making style distinction is relevant for the remainder of this analysis since it relates to the leader's development of strategic vision and the widely held assumption that leaders who provide strategic vision are able to fulfill policy mandates because an integrated planning process supports implementation of that strategic vision. However, the analysis generated the conclusion that neither administration promoted an effective interagency dynamic and each, therefore, retarded integrated planning.

The Persian Gulf War

In this case, the "Gang of Eight," or, as Bush and Brent Scowcroft labeled it, the "core group," developed policy and made all decisions in a practical sense.[14] These eight principals shared a common worldview—one wherein the *realist* paradigm dominated their philosophies regarding the use of force. Inherent in this *realist* approach proved the notion that the territorial boundaries of sovereign nations should remain inviolable. Aggression against such borders, irrespective of the provocative acts of one or more parties, "will not stand"[15] and must be rebuked by "all necessary means."[16] The maintenance of international borders remained a high priority for this administration, one that the president successfully communicated to the American public as a vital national interest, in part by demonizing Saddam Hussein.[17] In consultation with his core group, the president acted decisively, but perhaps too commandingly as his leadership and decision-making styles prevented the interagency process from undertaking a thorough analysis of the crisis and debating the issues.

The president's decisive leadership enhanced implementation at the operational and tactical levels, but the absence of integrated interagency planning truncated the crisis analysis process. Regional and issue-specific experts were excluded, producing a policy outcome framed by four "strategic objectives"[18] that could, *at best*, merely return the conflict to a status quo antebellum because these objectives failed to address the underlying causes and conditions of conflict. Consequently, the crisis analysis process did not consider the broader conflict spectrum, including the Kuwaiti's provocative actions against Iraq that Hussein purportedly interpreted as an economic act of war.[19] Such oversight ensured any acceptable termination of the immediate crisis would be, at best, one-sided. The shared images of these top advisors and the president prevented them from acknowledging other issues in the conflict because their *realist* worldview demanded an immediate response to Hussein's aggressive "unprovoked invasion" of Kuwait.[20] One State Department principal characterized the issue of crisis analysis as it related to termination policy development in the following manner:

> Once the shooting started it was too late to get meaningful input from expert levels of the bureaucracy into nontechnical decisions being made at the highest level, such as conflict termination. I think that the president would have been well-advised to seek agency views on conflict termination involving various battlefield scenarios. Without being in any way bound by those views reflecting greater expertise than what could be available among the handful of top advisors, this would have given the president the benefit of ideas that might have aided him in forming his own decisions. . . . In fact, on some key decisions involving termination, I suspect that the only people involved in discussing the matter were the president, Scowcroft, Cheney, and Powell. . . . At various times during the period from the Iraqi invasion of Kuwait until the cessation of hostilities and the cease-fire talks at Safwan, efforts by the Bureaus of Near East Affairs (NEA) and Political Military Affairs (PMA) to interject ideas about the "endgame" or conflict termination, or even guidelines for General Schwarzkopf at the Safwan cease-fire talks, were rebuffed.[21]

In the end, decisive leadership developed a strategic vision for prosecuting the war but not for sustaining peace. Because the "core group" prevented the interagency process from defining, describing, and framing the crisis through the eyes of substantive experts, the decision makers failed to develop and evaluate options that could address strategic, rather than tactical, issues. It is clear that incongruent conceptions of roles and missions further debilitated the interagency's integrated development of policy for this crisis. When Hussein made clear that he was willing to wage war with the United States (and the international coalition), the core group overwhelmingly emphasized the military course of action, thereby diminishing its ability to integrate diplomatic, economic, and military options into a cohesive approach. In this manner these leaders, propelled by shared images regarding the use of force,[22] constrained crisis analysis and option generation.[23] The core group managed the initial analytical effort for the Bosnia crisis (1990–93) much in the same manner as it had for the Persian Gulf, an approach that experienced little modification with a change in executive administrations.

The Bosnia Crisis

While the Bush administration remained embroiled in the Iraq crisis, the Balkans began to implode. The analytical

271

process used to frame action in the Gulf produced a "policy of abstinence" vis-à-vis the Bosnia crisis. The words of a Bush administration NSC principal captured the following analytical process:

> We applied the process we had to Bosnia, the same as Iraq, but came to a different conclusion than the Clinton administration. Starting with US national interests, other than humanitarian, we found interests to be marginal unless it spread to Kosovo and Macedonia. We looked at the conflict in Bosnia and whether the application of US/NATO force was an appropriate way to try to deal with the conflict. We determined it could not be done at a cost which the American people would be willing to pay and at a cost commensurate with the benefits. And, could we get our forces back out? We could not ensure the last two questions in the affirmative, so we did not go in.[24]

Whereas the Bush administration concluded that intervention into a sovereign nation was not in the best interests of the United States, the Clinton administration reached a quite different conclusion . . . though not immediately.[25] The factors discussed above (i.e., absence of strategic vision, lack of an integrated planning process, disparate worldviews, differing conceptions of roles and missions, and competing institutional equities) similarly influenced the analytical process the Clinton administration employed as it took office in 1993. As a result of interagency conflict and executive indifference, these factors delayed intervention until 1995.

According to one NSC principal, Scowcroft's and Lawrence Eagleburger's experiences with the former Yugoslavia overshadowed the interagency's analysis of the crisis.[26] As a result of their influence, agencies continued to frame the crisis in Bosnia as a "case of a relatively artificial country breaking apart and we had little interest outside humanitarian." Secretary of State Baker characterized the situation by saying the United States "didn't have a dog in this fight."[27] Although the leadership physically changed in January 1993, this adjustment largely affected the political appointees, not the career bureaucrats and military officials who continued to share the Scowcroft–Eagleburger image of "Bosnia imploding." Relatedly, worldview gaps between State and Defense enlarged as General Powell held steadfastly to the previous administration's analysis whilst his incoming peers across government increasingly urged the United States to take action in light of intensified media pressure. Clinton's executive mandate exacerbated this cleavage, since he had campaigned (and won) based upon a domestic platform that refocused political attention onto internal issues at the expense of foreign affairs.

In this sense, the Clinton administration's strategic vision proved myopic as it turned a blind eye on the events in the former Yugoslavia to honor its campaign commitment to the domestic agenda. Ambassador Richard Holbrooke criticizes the Clinton administration for this ambivalent approach and apparent trade-off, noting that the president's preeminent foreign policy campaign issue (1992) was Bosnia.[28] However, the administration failed to act until the galvanizing events involving genocide in mid-1995.[29] The Bosnia crisis worsened in the absence of strategic vision,[30] an absence that in Holbrooke's eyes perpetuated the "deep division within the new team."[31] The absence of an integrated planning approach amplified this void.

At the beginning of the executive transition, decision makers faced an added challenge that shaped interagency planning. The new principals (and those replaced two and three layers down within each agency) engaged in competitive behaviors in an effort to "get the president's ear."[32] These behaviors further impaired the planning process as these principals' actions unconsciously closed communication channels in an effort to control their respective bureaucracies. In the absence of preexisting personal relationships, communication and planning became isolated further. This isolation intensified Defense's perceptions that State wanted to embroil the military in another Vietnam- or Somalia-like "quagmire."[33] Here again, the need to protect institutional equities magnified the disparate worldviews and philosophies regarding the use of force,[34] ensuring gridlock within the administration until the media reported the atrocities that "remind[ed] the world that international conventions and moral law were being violated and demand[ed] that the major powers take decisive military action."[35] These media reports further reinforced disparate agency worldviews as the State Department identified the Serbs as the aggressors while Defense took a more balanced view by insisting that all parties in conflict shouldered some level of responsibility. This fissure became especially influential in the creation of different end-state visions.

Exacerbated by a change in leadership in 1993, the analytical process that framed the crisis in Bosnia shared the same basic deficiencies as that of the Persian Gulf. However, the problem with leadership in this instance was not that it commanded *too strong* a role, but rather, that it failed to establish the tone for the administration and allowed interagency decision makers to drift according to their respective subcurrents for over two years.

As the process drifted, tension across the interagency actors intensified, leading to the development of a flawed intervention process. In effect, the Dayton Peace Accords produced *interagency* termination policy in name only—the military and civilian components of that intervention remained separated, again demonstrating that the absence of an integrated planning process encourages agencies to develop courses of action based upon disparate worldviews and the protection of their institutional equities. The following question has been a long-term problem: Are the senior State Department executives or Defense Department flag officers in charge?[36] The protection of equities and inflexibility regarding roles and missions—on the part of all agencies—led to the development of two mutually exclusive, serially connected courses of action (i.e., the military Implementation Force [IFOR] and the civilian implementation missions). In the final analysis, these problems ensured the approach used by the interagency decision makers to analyze the conflict focused on the independent nodes of the Bosnia crisis, not the "Balkans" as a system so that affecting one component could leverage another to move the system toward a comprehensive desired end state. However, this supposition presumes that the administration had, in fact, articulated such a desired end state, a topic explored in a later section of this chapter.

Summary:
Crisis Analysis

These approaches to crisis analysis revealed two recurring defects—one related to information exchange; the other related to strategic vision. First, decision makers continually excluded expert participation (i.e., people with culturally or crisis-specific knowledge) in both the crisis analysis and the decision-making processes. While the latter proves somewhat understandable, mistakes pertaining to the former ensure decision makers initially frame crises with limited information, prompting them to make decisions based upon potentially flawed assumptions and incongruous worldviews. Yet, the problem goes beyond excluding expert knowledge. *Asymmetric* knowledge of conditions on the ground reinforces a groupthink dynamic because information is not shared across or within agencies (with the experts). One Defense principal characterized the problem by saying, "There are immense amounts of ignorance being shared because information is not shared. You go to the PC or the DC meetings— the Deputy Secretary/Undersecretary—these folks do not have all the information in their heads because they are the top folks. It is terrible how ignorant the process is because it is top-down in these committees/groups and they do not have time to get, or to know, all the facts and the right people are not there with the information."[37]

This lack of information inhibits the principals' and deputies' capacities to develop policy as decision makers *decontextualize crises* to fit their understanding in light of their prior experience (i.e., Tversky and Kahneman's availability heuristic dominates). Perceptions of interagency relations that perpetuate negative stereotypes further magnify these skewed perspectives. These stereotypes produce competitive dynamics that reinforce misconceptions of roles and missions and drive the policy process toward the lowest common denominator—the use of force framed by tactical perspectives.

Tactical perspectives impel analysts and decision makers to focus on a conflict system's critical nodes while hampering the development and articulation of the necessary strategic vision required to promote a clearly defined desired end state. In this manner, decision makers truncate required "backwards planning" processes from the very beginning. The lack of integration across the interagency process generates an analytical approach based upon flawed assumptions and narrow perspectives regarding opportunities upon which the intervenors could capitalize. These missed opportunities manifest themselves by generating limited visions for the desired end state.

Desired End State

The foregoing dimensions of crisis analysis cannot be viewed in isolation from the process wherein decision makers construct their vision for the desired end state.[38] The factors highlighted above, along with their limitations, carry over into the development of this vision as perspectives concerning the nature of the crisis influence views regarding the "post-intervention destination." Bertram Spector captures the essence of this relationship as follows:

> The way a dispute is framed can constrain the options for resolution. If the parties view the conflict in nationalist, ethnic, or ideological terms, escalation of the dispute and recourse to violence may be inevitable. Definitions that delimit the meaning of the conflict to simplistic stereotypes, that villainize the adversary, that place total blame on the other party, and that emotionalize the conflict often promote early impasse and give way to conflicts that appear impervious to negotiation or mediation. The principals become inflexible. Bosnia, Somalia, and Rwanda are some recent examples of such conflicts.[39]

The development of this vision occurs through a political process of decision making as negotiation, one that remains intensely political at the highest levels—one that is channeled by anticipated roles, personalities, and institutional equities. According to one high-ranking government official,

> The problem is that the definition of the end state is a political process. You cannot, almost by definition, define it without going through the messiness of the political process. . . . Defining the [desired] end state . . . cannot be done absent what you have to do to get there. Agencies will always measure against what has to be done to get there. When you layer upon that personal factors—egos, power—it is difficult. People tentatively have a stake in this sort of situation. Then there are the distractions, the lack of consistent attention, [and] so many other things going on.[40]

Layered upon this political process is the tactical-vision problem, an issue exacerbated by dissimilar organizational cultures and a lack of integrated planning. A Defense principal acknowledged the tendency of his department to think tactically concerning the end state: "In our discussions in the 'Tank,' we did not give a lot of attention to clearly defining conflict [termination] in the context in which you're looking at it. Someone would say 'What are we trying to do?' but I can't remember us talking a lot about 'If he takes this action, then. . . .' Our discussions were almost more tactical than strategic in this sense."[41]

It is important to recall that agencies across the USG do not feel Defense should establish the end-state vision since it is not the lead agent for policy development. To perform its missions, however, Defense planning and doctrine rely upon clearly articulated end states from which to develop operational campaign plans. Yet, because the interagency process fails to debate the issues, compare analytical approaches, and integrate planning mechanisms, the perception generally held within Defense is that *no other agency* is developing this vision, and it must address these issues to protect its institutional equities. If the NSC Staff and State Department *are* developing this vision, the findings surrounding these two crises indicated that they are not communicating that vision through the interagency process. One Defense principal offered that his department's "ability to influence [end-state vision] is not good—within the department, there's a fair capability to create conflict termination and exit strategies. Defense has a high strategy development capability, but the department's ability to influence [end-state vision] is not good. You rarely see the State Department or NSC Staff working the desired end state. In other words, 'What's the end state you want to occur?' and work backwards from there—that rarely occurs in State or NSC."[42]

Experiences throughout these two crises indicated that for both the NSC Staff and State Department the definition of an end state does not hold the same significance as it does for Defense, thus highlighting a significant cultural fissure. One NSC principal noted, "End state is a military planner's term of art. Every time we have a discussion within the interagency that rests on nomenclature that one segment has grown up with, we have problems. End state was a key one. [We] avoid words like control, strategy—we had to methodically strip out the nomenclature and substance. . . . Avoiding proprietary nomenclature can be really important to hammering-out an end state or a tentative strategy."[43]

This difference in significance is magnified by decision makers' prior experiences—experiences that prompt Defense officials and others who served during the Vietnam War to push the interagency toward a clear definition of the desired end state. A Defense principal captured the essence of this perception, "The most important question is absolutely the end state. I point to Vietnam and ask (1) 'What is the political end state you expect to see?' (2) 'What does the military situation have to do to [achieve] number one?' and, (3) 'Can we do it?' In Vietnam, we never thought through the political end state—can you do it? If we tried to do the same thing in Somalia, we would still be there. The development of the end state is bottom-up instead of top-down."[44]

The answers to these three questions are not apparent immediately if one hopes to achieve systemic change because of armed intervention. They require intense debate by individuals who can collectively see the entire "puzzle" through their institutional perspectives, but who can simultaneously put aside their institutional equities when developing policy. However, failing to address these questions can lead to applying force with unanticipated negative effects, thereby worsening the conflict between adversaries.[45] The lethality of force demands that the interagency process and its decision makers address these issues *before* force employment. Defining the end state cannot be generated via a "bottom-up" approach wherein tactical realities dictate strategic vision "in the moment." Yet, the absence of such a top-down vision intensifies Defense's need to define an exit strategy as a critical component of intervention strategy.[46] Defining exit strategy *first*, especially in terms of a timeline, again promotes a lowest common-denominator solution wherein the USG employs forces with no clear vision for their role in achieving a satisfactory termination according to clearly defined criteria, termination policy's third major component.

Case Examples: Desired End State

Similar to the discussion of crisis analysis, the issues concerning end-state vision materialized differently in these two cases. Senior-level decision makers framed no strategic end state for the Persian Gulf War beyond a return to the status quo antebellum.[47]

The Persian Gulf War

One Defense deputy noted, "In the Persian Gulf War, our intention was to repulse the Iraqi invasion of Kuwait . . . talking about getting at a modern-day Hitler."[48] One CIA official shared this perspective by asserting, "I don't think they had an end state. Originally, [it was a] cease-fire, end of conflict. The problem is the immediate end state for the war was fairly clear, but [there was] no clear policy after that. Keeping Saddam Hussein in his box was not an end state—sanctions are not a policy, they're a policy tool."[49] A Defense principal likewise reflected this perception, "I do not think we had political objectives. . . . The political objectives were to kick Iraq out of Kuwait—that was it. There was no consideration for conflict termination—'Where do you want to be politically in 20 years?' 'What are the strategic decisions for this part of a world?' None of that was considered!"[50]

Evidence for these views emerged at the time of the cease-fire. Because agencies responded independently to the crisis in terms of their respective core competencies, decision makers created a phased approach toward achieving a desired end state, one framed only in terms of the four limited political objectives identified overtly as US policy objectives.[51] However, the leaders introduced no integrated political, economic, and social/psychological objectives until *after the cease-fire* when the military recognized it would have to assist in the post-conflict humanitarian effort (including maintaining combat air patrols [CAP] to prevent Iraqi aircraft, save helicopters, from flying in the northern and southern no-fly zones). Deployed military units initially provided support for humanitarian aid and civil affairs functions. It is significant that the military was not prepared, either psychologically or materially, to do so; thus, a crucial omission in planning emerged because the planning process failed to link war fighting with diplomacy.

In effect, the decision makers in this case developed a limited strategic vision through a process that ensured the military would "hand the situation back" to the ambassador and country team once a cease-fire occurred. This handoff resulted from the absence of an integrated interagency planning mechanism that could debate the issues and compare various analyses of the crisis. Such a process could have anticipated these needs from the outset of the conflict, especially since public rhetoric and the military's psychological operations (PSYOP) attempted to assure the Iraqi populace that the US-led coalition waged war against Hussein as their rogue leader, not against them as individual citizens. The logic of this approach manifested itself in the identification and selection of military targeting objectives,[52] yet there was no recursive linkage to the political objectives to create a comprehensive approach for the long-term reintegration of Iraq into the global community.

The Bosnia Crisis

In August 1995, the nature of the humanitarian crisis in Bosnia brought together two disparate worldviews related to armed intervention. Those mobilized by value-laden concerns accentuated media reports of the massacres in Srebrenica and market-place bombing in Sarajevo. At the same time, those mobilized by interest-laden concerns stressed the adverse effects of NATO's damaged credibility.[53] Prior to this point, however, the president did not create an image (i.e., a definition of task, a purpose, or an end-state vision) around which the public or policy could coalesce. The ongoing congressional power struggle vis-à-vis the executive branch further complicated the development of an end-state vision as the CJCS did not want to use troops on the ground; the Pentagon had congressional support—and knew it.[54] In conjunction with this dynamic, the disparate views around this question of end state held by State and Defense paralyzed the policy process. A CIA official noted that "the humanitarian factor also applied to Bosnia. During the deliberations, State was in the forefront of those who thought we should bomb—the Pentagon was very reluctant. DOD's main concerns were (a) what are we going to bomb and (b) once you start, what's the end state?"[55]

The agencies framed their answers to the second question in terms of their worldviews and the assumptions their ideologies made salient. Although a long passage, the words of one Defense official capture the nature of this fissure, bringing into stark relief the contrasting views held by State and Defense:

> State assumed Milosevic would go away. We saw him as the linchpin—State thought student protests would be effective and also thought we'd take on a broader role with war criminals and we'd remove Milosevic and Mladic. We left them in place. Our vision of the end state was to come up with the right lines on the map and balance the power through the "Train and Equip" plan written here without much input from the State Department. It was trotted out and State saw it and said, "Holy cow, we thought you were going to put the Bosniacs in power and pull Milosevic out." They (State) did all the negotiation with Bosnia and we did all the negotiation with the other side. We ended up with State seeing Milosevic as a threat—their vision was so different from ours and they didn't see it. We had a balance of power whereas State thought we'd come to the aid of those abused. We now have a situation where you have two entities instead of one. We were dealing with Milosevic—he's got the guns. So we balanced the power out and State assumed there would be an imbalance of power they could come in and negotiate. I think Holbrooke's view was to end the fighting—we do a lot of those simplistic things. Holbrooke's view was "How do I stop this war?" The State Department was more Pollyannaish—[their] focus was on future trade, etc. State takes a very simplistic view—"Everyone will see the situation through our lenses. Because the US is there, everyone will work cooperatively with one another." I don't think State recognized that they are political entities, not ethnic entities. Holbrooke was a realist—[he] balanced the power. State's view was Bosnia would be part of "engagement and enlargement" and then we'll move out.[56]

For Bosnia, this cleavage ensured that once decision makers decided to introduce forces into the conflict, they did so with no clear vision of any desired end state; rather, they fell victim to the "do something" syndrome. The absence of such vision prompted decision makers to agree on an "end date"—in place of an end state—as an effort to "sell" troop deployment domestically, to both the public and the Congress. A State Department deputy contended, "People say they're trying to create a desired end state, but we can't do it—the actors have to. We are good at short-term stopping the fighting. The biggest difficulty is to make political decisions to act. The media and Congress—Congress tends to be 'quick in and out.' The media is looking for failure . . . good news is not reportable."[57]

An NSC principal claimed the interagency did not establish a desired end state for Bosnia but did frame termination criteria in the form of "benchmarks." This official claimed, "We do not talk about end states, we talk about 'benchmarks.' We came up with 8 or 10 benchmarks for Bosnia. For example, when the militaries of the three have a structural transparency such as the 'cross-observation' exercises that took place before the [Berlin] Wall came down. If you satisfy most of the criteria for most of the benchmarks, you do not need a military force on the ground. We fleshed this out with a 'cheat sheet' from the guys at State to run with the details."[58]

The implied end state here reflects operational, indeed tactical, thinking, "You do not need a military force on the ground."[59] This recollection also demonstrates that the planning process remained isolated as the NSC worked with only one agency—the State Department—to develop the plan. Concurrently, the Defense Department developed a different end-state vision that remained isolated from the interagency process, one that it later "sold" to US civilian decision makers *after* it had been adopted by the North Atlantic Council (NAC). With reference to the IFOR mission, the military plan directing this effort noted that the terms of the Peace Agreement would play a large role in defining the political end state. Further, it highlighted the diplomatic-military fissure by stating that NATO's mission was not linked directly to the end state. It did, however, outline four possible conditions that, when achieved, could be deemed an end state in Bosnia-Herzegovina. These conditions included the following:

1. parties' adherence to the military requirements of the Peace Agreement, especially the absence of violations or unauthorized military activities;

2. parties' demonstration of a commitment to continued negotiations to resolve differences;

3. creation of civil structures to assume responsibility and monitor compliance with the Peace Agreement; and

4. establishment of conditions for ongoing nation-building activities.

This proposed vision attempted to establish the "destination" for the intervention but one that remained tactically focused due to the absence of an integrated planning mechanism.

Summary: Desired End State

These two cases illustrate that the dearth of innovative thinking surrounding the development of a vision for the desired end state is the product of a nonintegrated planning mechanism that attempts to synthesize separate crisis analyses only at the highest levels of decision making. Structural cleavages create interagency conflict that further stymies useful interagency debate. Because the process remains focused on tactical-level issues, one of the primary concerns becomes the development of an exit strategy irrespective of the underlying conditions on the ground between the parties in conflict. Therefore, termination criteria, when developed, may or may not be connected with a vision for the desired end state.

Termination Criteria

Perhaps more than any other emergent theme, developing conflict termination criteria reflected the decision maker's reliance upon the same cost-benefit mentality that undergirds rational choice theory. When considering armed intervention agency worldviews, institutional equities and domestic politics shape definitions of national interest, intervention criteria, and, ultimately, termination criteria. One Defense principal noted, "Our entry is not usually declared with a clear view of how we're going to get out. In the Gulf War, I don't think people had a clear sense of exit strategy; Bosnia is hands-off, [and] in Somalia we went in with a set of laudable objectives. Outside of 'feel good criteria,' we didn't look at all the possible outcomes and regional developments."[60]

It is this perception that the termination criteria tend to reflect feel-good criteria as a product of dissimilar worldviews, defense of institutional equities, and responses to domestic politics that drives the development of termination criteria to their most basic and tactically focused level, eventually pushing for force withdrawal irrespective of changes in the basic conflict.[61] When the previous chapter discussed relationships across these factors, the findings indicated that domestic politics and media influence play a particularly important role in framing these termination criteria.

Power struggles between the Congress and the executive branch inject irreconcilable images into the process of developing termination criteria. On the one hand, the Congress wants to exercise its constitutional prerogatives concerning the use of US force abroad (e.g., via the War Powers Resolution or, more generally, the domestic political process). On the other, the Congress must reflect the desires of the populace it represents, a factor expressed usually through pressure to bring the troops home as quickly as possible. In conjunction with the former, the Congress pushes the president, as commander in chief, to express termination criteria in terms of ending US participation—criteria that do not relate necessarily to ending the conflict itself. A deputy-level State Department official characterized this congressional pressure by stating, "[The] Congress starts by saying 'stop the slaughter and get it off the front pages,' but then they say 'stop spending money and bring the troops home. ' We are in for six months . . . and then Congress says bring the troops home. Congress pushes to get in, then blows a whistle to get out much more quickly."[62] The media reports this congressional pressure in partisan ways, thereby exacerbating interagency conflict regarding the best form of intervention and the definition of termination criteria.[63] Relatedly, in their effort to frame the issues, the media tends to promote the idea that the United States must act as part of its moral obligation as the world's sole remaining superpower.

Media images push the limits of policy development by stressing the "should do something" part of policy well before critical analysis is performed to determine what intervention—armed or otherwise—"can" do. Policy makers did not indicate that the media should refrain from performing this role, as it helps frame critical issues. Rather, officials argued that this added pressure demands the principals lead the interagency process in vetting all possible courses of action, their most likely results, and their relationships to termination criteria development.[64] In this sense, the capacity of the media to influence policy exacerbates congressional pressures to define termination criteria largely in terms of exit strategies.

Together, these factors frame termination criteria in terms of measurable milestones, but ones that take the parties to the *point of a cease-fire* but not beyond. This focus upon the cease-fire as the preeminent termination criterion perpetuates a cleavage in the interagency process and intensifies conflict between disparate worldviews. This interagency dispute promotes a fissure between the political and military objectives that "establish the nature of the conflict."[65] In essence, Defense defines its role as bringing about the cease-fire through the application of overwhelming force. Once achieved, the salience of institutional equities and roles and missions debates comes to the fore as Defense perceives its role as one of war fighting, not nation building. Defense views these postconflict civil affairs activities as State Department responsibilities.[66] This further reflects the military's "get in, do it, get out" mentality, a perspective that remains tied to strategy and "courses of action." Findings regarding the development of termination criteria in these two cases present interesting conclusions.

Case Examples: Termination Criteria

Policy makers—both diplomats and war fighters—proved unable to translate effectively the stated political objectives into clear, concise, and adequately measurable termination criteria. This inability is demonstrated throughout these two cases.

The Persian Gulf War. It is clear that the Bush administration developed termination criteria (i.e., the four strategic objectives for US involvement that became the UN objectives for the Gulf War) in pursuit of a limited end state—reestablish the status quo antebellum. This policy contained the added objective of maintaining regional stability by impairing Hussein's ability to act aggressively but not damaging his military strength to the degree that it could no longer act as a counterbalance to Iran.[67] These five criteria focused on establishing the conditions to produce a cease-fire, yet not terminating the Iraq-Kuwait/Iraq-Coalition conflict in any tangible sense, as they failed to address the underlying conflict issues or create innovative solutions to transform the parties' goals beyond those issues. In this sense, these five termination criteria became the end state, one that could be fulfilled only through a strategy of conflict containment—an approach that similarly characterized the Bosnia crisis.

The Bosnia Crisis. The absence of an articulated end-state vision makes the identification of conflict termination criteria problematic since agencies cannot be assured that their actions will help them arrive at their desired destination if that destination has not been determined, agreed upon, or communicated. The foregoing reference to the IFOR plan did intimate, however, that one possible end state could be achieved by securing the four elements it proposed.[68] Outside that proposal, however, no clearly articulated interagency termination criteria existed. The absence of such criteria led one Defense deputy to remark, "The interagency's primary interest in Bosnia was to contain it from spreading—[that's] the reason we went to Macedonia."[69]

The insertion of forces and IFOR did bring about a cease-fire and prevent international spillover, but the conflict expanded as it migrated to other venues (e.g., the Kosovo-Yugoslav crisis). An NSC principal adeptly captured this perspective, "We go too far if we think conflict termination [i.e., cease-fire] is the end state—we're still there. We got the shooting to stop in October 1995, [but] we have expended enormous resources and energy. We must leave in place the mechanisms to prevent further flare-ups."[70] Developing mechanisms to prevent further flare-ups must be included in any strategy that employs specific courses of action to achieve clear termination criteria as a step toward achieving a desired end state. As such, termination strategy development is the final component of conflict termination policy; it is discussed as the final topic of this chapter.

Summary: Termination Criteria

In both cases, decision makers failed to acknowledge the relationship between termination criteria and the political objectives that shape the vision of the desired end state. Because of this disjuncture, termination criteria took the form of goals that emerged from a decision-making process in which the experts were excluded and those with the least situation-specific knowledge made decisions based upon incomplete assessments and limited crisis analysis.[71] The product of a tactical-level perspective, termination criteria provided benchmarks for activities that produced temporary cease-fires but failed to address underlying conflict issues.[72] Therefore, these actions failed to induce systemic, lasting change. The data from the cases illuminated an interrelated pattern. Crisis analyses frame desired end states that, in turn, lead to the identification of termination criteria. In turn, these criteria influence conflict termination strategy development, the substance of the final emergent theme. The words of a Defense principal integrate the findings presented thus far by establishing a relationship between interagency conflict and the development of termination criteria:

> Interdepartmental conflict makes it harder to agree on what conflict termination criteria are because what often a negotiation process signals is that they did not agree on policy outcomes. You get selection of "mushy" criteria that each side interprets prospectively in their own way—no one wants to push the discussion and get a tentative handshake. You'll not really be pressed by events—we see this in Bosnia . . . we don't have any idea whatsoever as to what the end state looks like. The main criterion is to get through the next decision period. Now there is an expectation that this could not go on forever, but we have not agreed on what we're going to do—the problem is not going to go away.[73]

Hence, the ideas reflected herein provide an appropriate transition into the final emergent theme that addresses how the USG is going to do what it intends to do—that of termination strategy and, ultimately, course of action development.

Termination Strategy

The most extensive interagency fissure emerged when considering the relationship between the three themes discussed above and the development of termination strategy to achieve the desired result. Deciding *how* to achieve your end state in terms of definitive courses of action is the point at which the three previously discussed themes converge. Decision makers often agree that something should be done on the macro level but developing consensus regarding the form that action will take proves far more difficult. Interagency conflict emanates from dissimilar organizational cultures and mutually exclusive planning processes that empower skewed perceptions of institutional equities and roles and missions to polarize decision makers as they develop intervention and termination strategy. Domestic political influence amplifies these difficulties by further constraining strategic options. Beginning with organizational culture, this discussion reviews each of these factors to demonstrate their influence on termination strategy development.[74]

Dissimilar organizational cultures influence termination strategy development by shaping the nature of interagency communications. Disparate organizational cultures arrest innovative thinking and perpetuate stereotypes that exacerbate misunderstanding, thereby truncating debate regarding COA development. Friction between nonuniformed conceptions regarding civilian control of the military and the war fighter's perspective regarding civilian control hampers interagency communication as military officials want civilian leaders to establish the strategic vision for intervention (i.e., the desired end state and termination criteria) but leave the development of operational strategy in the hands of the war fighter.[75] For many within the military, Gen George S. Patton Jr.'s maxim appropriately reflects this relationship, "Never tell people how to do things. Tell them what to do and they will surprise you with their ingenuity."[76] For some, this perspective captures the essence of the military's view of civilian control of the military, a view that is not shared universally by decision makers and one that amplifies planning fissures as misaligned conceptions of roles and missions prompt agencies to exclude others from the development of strategy. Further, when leaders do not demand that interagency actors collaborate when developing courses of action, this planning fissure expands much in the same manner as that caused by the independent crisis analysis processes discussed previously. As a result, the interagency process fails to produce an integrated, sustainable approach for termination strategy.

As each agency develops its own approach, the interagency process fails to employ synergistically all of its instruments of power (i.e., diplomatic, economic, informational, psychological, sociological, and military) in the creation of termination strategy. These independent approaches rely instead upon the phased or serial development of strategy that artificially separates diplomatic and military courses of action. Hence, a "virtual handoff" occurs once the president decides to employ the military (i.e., the diplomat passes responsibility for the crisis to the war fighter).[77] The net result is that decision makers collectively fail to capitalize on potential opportunities because their perceived need to protect institutional equities (both functional and resource-based) closes these windows. For example, war fighting is seen as Defense's role, not State's. Similarly, the conduct of diplomacy dictates that military officials do not negotiate on behalf of the USG. Consequently, the absence of an integrated interagency planning mechanism produces strategies aimed at creating temporary cease-fires but not sustainable conflict termination. No bridge spans these mutually exclusive conceptions of roles and missions. Domestic political concerns amplify the importance of developing a strategy to achieve a cease-fire while inhibiting the development of courses of action that move toward sustainable conflict termination.

Domestic perceptions of the "American way of war" play a significant role in perpetuating the termination strategy gap. The United States purportedly remains unwilling to accept American casualties, relies upon overwhelming force to coerce its adversaries quickly and decisively (the Powell Corollary to the Weinberger Doctrine), and impels respected national leaders to demonize the enemy's leader(s) as a means to mobilize public support.[78] In the first instance, perceived unwillingness to accept casualties compels the interagency process to develop an *exit strategy* as its first order of business.[79] This exit strategy presupposes the existence of an end date. In this manner, decision makers develop strategy with a focus, first and foremost, on getting out—not with a vision toward creating the conditions that will bring about sustainable conflict termination. In order to get out, this strategy must stop the fighting decisively through the application of overwhelming force.

Using overwhelming force creates difficulties for developing termination strategy since force application rarely resolves conflict. Overwhelming force has the potential to end conflict by creating a "conflict pause," but because force alone cannot resolve conflict, that pause may prove to be a mere hiatus. In the words of one Defense principal, "[T]he rule there is that if conflicts are to be resolved and an enduring agreement produced, then all the factions to the agreement must believe that what results is better than not having an agreement. They must somehow believe they benefit more from the agreement than fighting, or it will come up again. Clearly, those conditions did not exist in the Bosnia Peace Agreement or Kosovo either. You can't get conflict resolution—you can get a cessation of hostilities through the threat of force, but you can't get conflict resolution."[80] Obviously, a cost-benefit calculus gives rise to this perspective. However, what is important here is the recognition that force by itself cannot bring about conflict resolution, which, by definition, implies permanent termination. Perhaps it is this growing recognition that generates the third theme related to termination strategy—that of demonizing the enemy.

The practice of demonizing the enemy to mobilize popular domestic support for military action abroad enjoys a long history.[81] The nature of this demonization is changing, however, as increasingly governments purportedly take military actions against rogue leaders, not their oppressed civilian populaces.[82] Portraying a myopic view of the enemy channels public perspective, both domestic and international, making it easier to "sell" military intervention to both constituencies. It is important to note that this demonization process can be captured in a sound bite or a "bumper sticker," thereby perpetuating negative images of the adversarial leader, not the innocent people who strive to survive under his (or her) "tyrannical rule." Yet, this demonization process limits the decision maker's ability to develop an effective strategy as the need to use power and coercion against a "demonized other" comes to dominate views framing all potential courses of action. The salience of this power projection need drives strategy toward a constant state of escalation and results in the application of overwhelming force. However, overwhelming force cannot bring about sustainable termination short of extermination.[83] An NSC principal contended the demonization of Saddam Hussein during the Persian Gulf War as one of the United States's "greatest mistakes." A Defense principal echoed this perspective, "From a public relations perspective, you create a situation where you can no longer deal with the enemy in a rational fashion—like Castro—you can only deal with him through third parties. The only exception to this was Nixon to China. I believe that one of the only near-term ways out of the Iraq situation is to help redefine Saddam Hussein—don't make him a hero, but change the perception."[84]

The emphasis here on limiting one's ability to "deal with the enemy in a rational fashion" implies that such actions restrict COA development and create public expectations that negate the decision maker's ability to refine policies. Such boundaries further constrain the strategist's capacity to consider all possible options when framing COAs toward conflict termination. A brief examination of these factors' manifestation in the two cases begins to integrate the findings. Noting that the three previous sections addressed several of these themes (e.g., dissimilar organizational cultures, institutional equities, and roles and missions) and because their effects influence strategy development, this application focuses specifically upon the connection between strategy and mutually exclusive planning processes as this linkage serves as the bridge between the desired destination and the vehicle used to get there.

Case Examples: Termination Strategy

The development of the plan connecting desired ends with available means remains perhaps the most perplexing aspect of policy formulation. The Persian Gulf and Bosnia cases demonstrate the nature of this challenge.

The Persian Gulf War. The air operations planners understood that neither President Bush nor the American public would accept large numbers of casualties.[85] This recognition generated an implicit end-state vision, one that struggled to ensure the Iraqi people would not harbor hatred for the United States as a result of a massive aerial bombing campaign that killed civilians and irreparably damaged their way of life. This condition prompted the development of an integrated air plan that judiciously selected targets with that implicit condition in mind. However, the Defense Department developed this strategy directly with the NSC Staff and the president, obtaining little input from State. In the perceptions of one State deputy, this strategy—coupled with the public relations effort to drive a

291

wedge between the populace and the leader while demonizing Hussein—enabled Bush to pronounce the coalition would "go in, liberate Kuwait, and that was it."[86] He emphasized that everyone knew "George Bush would make the decision."[87] This rhetoric constrained innovative thinking and the development of other options. One NSC principal noted the following:

> We looked at [conflict termination] before the bombing started. We did not have unanimity however. Before the bombing started, before congressional approval, it was a debate about whether or not there should be a conflict. In this case, State and JCS would have preferred a resolution short of conflict—Iraq be induced to withdraw without military action. [Cheney and Scowcroft] (and the president, although he kept quiet) thought that such an outcome would have been a disaster for the US. We had gotten ourselves into a position where there had to be a conflict. If Iraq had withdrawn too quickly, he still had 100,000 troops on the border and we would have lost strategically and long-term.[88]

Getting themselves "into a position where there had to be a conflict," President Bush and his National Security Advisor (Scowcroft) turned to Cheney and Powell to develop the strategy to eject Hussein from Kuwait.[89] This dilemma was created in part when the president dispatched senate delegations to tell Hussein that the United States believed Iraq now had "a central role to play in the Middle East." Hussein began to interpret these overtures as carte blanche approval to take action to rebalance the region's power relations based upon Kuwaiti-imposed economic disparity.[90] Ambassador April Glaspie's 25 July meeting did little to dissuade Hussein from pursing a military strategy toward that goal. In fact, William Reese indicates that Glaspie told Hussein, "We have no opinion on the Arab to Arab conflicts like your border disagreement with Kuwait."[91] Reese postulates that Glaspie's statement, taken in conjunction with the United States's apparent apathy toward Iraq's convergence of 100,000 troops on the Kuwaiti border in the 11 days prior to 25 July, led Hussein to believe he had free reign to exact as much punishment as he deemed necessary from Kuwait. The development of this strategy flowed primarily between these four decision makers and the military planners (including the war-fighting commander) to the virtual exclusion of career diplomats. Crisis analysis occurred absent the presence of regional and cultural experts—the same non-military experts were excluded from strategy development.[92] Because the administration did not define clearly the type of postwar peace it sought in terms of an end state, the four political objectives served as de facto termination criteria.[93] Yet, translating these objectives from the political arena to the operational war-fighting environment illuminated the disconnect between diplomacy and warfare as the cease-fire ensued.

The policy-makers' failure to bridge this gap created the subsequent impression *once the war was over* that the termination strategy (and indeed, the war itself) left the situation in the Gulf unfinished. The most visible aspect of this "unfinished business" concerned the extent to which the administration demonized Hussein, yet "allowed" him to remain in power. While other examples exist, this emerged as the most poignant reminder that "the decisions on ending the war also highlighted the failure to keep political and military objectives in synch."[94] One possible reason for this disconnect was the handoff that occurred through the phased approach of the war fighter's presence becoming dominant when diplomacy "failed" and then diminishing upon cease-fire. Although the term *exit strategy* was not commonplace in 1991, DOD commanders felt they had fulfilled their role, and it was time to "pass" the posthostilities effort to nonmilitary agencies. These agencies had not been involved with combat planning and proved ill prepared for the impending challenges. The development and implementation of this termination strategy, then, remained in the hands of a few individuals (i.e., the core group), the same individuals who prosecuted the war effort but remained intellectually ill equipped for the posthostilities "peace" that followed. Consequently, this case illustrates how serial strategy development artificially separated diplomatic and war-fighting COAs. Evidence for this rests with the fact that for more than a decade after the cease-fire, the United States and a dwindling number of its coalition partners remain embroiled in an oscillating pattern of air strikes to "put Hussein back in his box" as he oversteps the 1991 boundaries demarcated by the United States and the United Nations. The United States remains similarly engaged in the Balkans more than seven years after the signing of the Dayton Peace Accords.

The Bosnia Crisis. Identifying termination strategy for the Bosnia crisis as it relates to a desired end state proves difficult as it remains unclear whether a precise end state was envisaged when the decision makers initially formulated policy between 1993 and 1995 (i.e., the Dayton Peace Accords). Relatedly, the absence of a clear end state ensured termination criteria would remain ambiguous. This ambiguity affected termination strategy development as the Implementation Force (and later, Stabilization Force [SFOR]) seemed to be "muddling through." One component of that strategy did emerge clearly, however, as policy makers established a timeline that drove strategy. Discussed earlier, this timeline produced an exit strategy that remained tied to a 12-month exit date. The evidence shows that Defense insisted on establishing an exit strategy because it felt the Clinton administration failed to articulate an end state that would ensure it could eventually bring the troops home. One Defense principal noted that "DOD was forced to go to this because in the interagency there was not much discussion on exit strategy. This forced a little bit of discipline into it."[95] An NSC principal offered an additional rationale for the end date, "After Dayton, people thought there had to be a deadline. I don't think people were lying, but they were not being intellectually rigorous. But it was in the campaign period, so the administration avoided having public debates—that reluctance to 'front-burner' Bosnia impeded a rational policy process. [In] the consensus-driven system you get rational work, but it's much harder and [you] have to deal with dysfunctional behaviors—it takes greater effort."[96]

The reference to domestic politics (namely, the administration's "reluctance to 'front-burner' Bosnia") is important here since it remained apparent that senior decision makers recognized beforehand that one year would prove insufficient. At the same time, however, they suspected they could not gain public and congressional support for anything longer.[97] An NSC principal insisted, "The real end state we are after will only be achieved 5, 10, 20 years after the military presence that is there to support the political/civilian implementation process. Until this civilian implementation can carry on by more conventional means (i.e., without the presence of three NATO divisions on the ground), we'll use a whole combination of traditional, nonmilitary means not to have NATO troops on the ground. We're talking about a transitional presence—how do you know when the job is done?"[98]

For reasons previously discussed, the military developed a termination strategy to induce a cease-fire that would create the environment for civilian agencies (governmental and nongovernmental) to improve the humanitarian situation. Defense's organizational culture and conceptions of roles and missions curtailed the military's willingness to consider other missions (e.g., pursuit of war criminals) that may have expedited civilian implementation of the Dayton Peace Accords. The Clinton administration's lack of leadership and absence of strategic vision provided no alternatives for strategy development, leaving the military to, in the words of one government official, "craft an end state for itself."[99] Again, this gap between the diplomatic and military missions became visible, as did the chasm between a strategy to induce a cease-fire and one to create the conditions for a sustainable peace.

Summary: Termination Strategy

In both cases national decision makers agreed US intervention was required to stop the bloodshed and protect US national interests, yet securing agreement regarding the nature of those interventions remained problematical. Dissimilar organizational cultures promoted nonintegrated planning processes that enabled agencies to frame strategies for conflict termination independently and, ultimately, in ways that protected their respective institutional equities as defined by department-specific roles and missions. Concerns regarding domestic politics restricted strategy development as decision makers used public opinion and the Congress to leverage others' views on the use of force. In the end, this generated a strategy that sought to bring about what should be termed war termination in the form of a cease-fire, but that failed to move beyond that point in time to the development of conflict termination policy as the bridge toward sustainable peace. Applying overwhelming force to attain cease-fire became the de facto policy goal and its subsequent measure of merit.

Synergistic Effects

The effects of interagency conflict on conflict termination policy development can be captured through a brief synopsis. Once reiterated, the final discussion interprets the effects of these findings.

1. Dissimilar organizational images regarding the appropriate use of force create different meaning for/of a crisis and stimulate interagency conflict that hampers termination policy development by stifling interagency communication.

2. Decision makers fail to recognize ways in which their respective worldviews (i.e., political ideologies and philosophies regarding the use of force) shape their conscious (and subconscious) analytical processes, prompting leaders to demonize the enemy as they artificially dichotomize the nature of the crisis into "good guy/bad guy" frames.

3. Decision makers frame the crisis in terms of their roles in crisis intervention; roles defined by institutional equities. Role ambiguity and the absence of an integrated planning mechanism amplify the need to protect respective institutional equities.

4. The absence of strategic vision and the lack of an integrated planning approach impel decision makers to focus on parts of the system (i.e., nodes) while ignoring the system as a whole. This approach expands the gap between diplomats and war fighters as they each fail to understand the other's core competencies and, as such, fail to maximize the effects of their integration.

5. Because decision makers focus on tactical-level issues, analytical processes examine isolated nodes of the system (i.e., independent parts of the broader conflict system), thereby restricting the interagency's ability to evaluate the underlying causes and conditions of conflict and

negating its ability to develop policy toward a sustainable solution.

6. Leaders who establish organizational cultures that limit innovative thinking and create perceptions that the inability to protect equities equates to professional failure (for which, the penalty is high) exacerbate the tendency to protect institutional equities. This generates conflict at the interagency working group level.

7. The NSC Staff's operating procedures intensify interagency conflict when it responds to media or congressional pressures rather than acting upon principled guidance from the White House.

8. The development of end-state vision is a political process of "decision making by negotiation" and is channeled by anticipated roles, personalities, and institutional equities.

9. Agencies across the USG evaluate the importance of a desired end-state vision differently, generating a "lowest common-denominator" policy and leading to the development of "exit strategies" as a means to ensure force withdrawal irrespective of the longer-term implications of armed intervention.

10. Domestic politics and the media play a crucial role in framing termination criteria. Public opinion demands a "bloodless war"; the Congress manipulates funding to control foreign policy; and, the media appeals to the emotional side of everyone, compelling the government to "do something" before adequate analysis is conducted.

11. Together, these factors exacerbate interagency conflict and frame termination criteria in terms related to the cessation of hostilities, measurable milestones, and exit strategies but not to the conditions required for sustainable conflict termination as defined throughout this work.

12. In the absence of an articulated strategic vision, disparate organizational cultures and prior experience shape termination strategy via their capacity to arrest innovative

thinking, stifle interagency communication, and truncate analytical debate.

13. Agencies develop independent analyses, end-state visions, criteria, and strategies for conflict termination—senior leaders attempt to synthesize these perspectives, yet these decision makers usually possess little, if any, expertise with the contextual specifics of the crisis.

Together, these findings ensure that interagency conflict—working at all levels of the process but in a very pronounced fashion at the initial levels, that is, the interagency working group level—negates the USG's capacity to develop termination policy with a focus on the following:

1. thorough crisis analysis,

2. an unambiguous desired end state,

3. termination criteria that move the parties in conflict toward a long-term solution as they act as indicators of progression or regression, and

4. development of an agreed-upon and realistic strategy to achieve such a solution.

The agencies' preoccupation with their respective equities creates a dynamic wherein agencies develop strategies that commit their respective resources *only at the margins* of intervention in practical terms. This institutional conservatism impedes the USG's ability to analyze the crisis critically and thoroughly so that COAs can be developed appropriately based upon the specific conflict's context—thereby producing integrated strategies that could potentially transform the underlying sources of conflict and move the parties toward sustainable conflict termination in the postintervention environment. Rather, salience accompanies those bureaucratic factors that remain most pronounced within the interagency process—each respective agency's institutional equities, both functional and resource-based.

In practice, conflict termination policy centers on simply bringing an end to open hostilities—as has been illustrated by the cases addressed herein—but little concerted effort is applied toward developing a policy approach addressing the broader issues of the conflict itself. The Realpolitik paradigm acts as a constraint on this entire process since the USG seems most concerned with reestablishing territorial boundaries and "legitimate" governments while ignoring the conditions that precipitated conflict. As of 2003, this omission remains pronounced in US dealings with both Iraq and the former Yugoslavia.

Developing conflict termination policy for complex contingencies is the process that ideally should merge diplomacy and war fighting. Yet, while the nature of the gap between diplomats and war fighters ensures the interagency process develops policy to bring about war termination in the form of a cease-fire, it fails to achieve conflict termination in the form of a sustainable peace. Because policy emerges through a process of "decision making by negotiation," defects in leadership, voids in strategic vision, dissimilar organizational cultures, disparate worldviews, the perceived need to protect institutional equities, and the absence of integrated interagency planning mechanisms to conduct ongoing crisis analysis and option generation magnify this gap. Efforts to demonize the enemy further constrain innovative thinking and thwart strategy development. Relatedly, the immediate need to save face or to enhance future credibility leads to conflict escalation and the application of overwhelming force for limited objectives, the achievement of which can "at best" return the crisis to the status quo antebellum rather than establish the conditions for a better state of peace. In assessing the Bosnia crisis, a State Department principal captured the nature of this gap by saying, "It may be politically impossible to do the right things."[100]

Ultimately, faulty analyses of the crisis result from intense interagency conflict that generates an inability to create an agreed upon (and achievable) vision of a desired end state. This, in turn, promotes an inability to agree upon or establish clear criteria for terminating the conflict. By extension, promulgation of ambiguous termination criteria impedes the development of an effective strategy for termination, save for bringing about an end to the fighting through the application of overwhelming military force.

Notes

1. At the time of this initial research, NATO began bombing Yugoslavia to "degrade" the Serbs' capacity to continue their ethnic cleansing campaign against the ethnic Albanians in Kosovo. The media continually referred to the desired end state of this bombing activity by asking USG officials, "What is the endgame?"—a concept adapted from the game of chess. See also, for example, M. A. Sutherland and H. M. Lommer, *1234 Modern End-Game Studies with Appendix Containing 24 Additional Studies* (New York: Dover Publications, 1968). Yet, the international relations literature cites this concept of endgame as well. See, for example, Stephen J. Cimbala, "The Endgame and War," in *Conflict Termination and Military Strategy: Coercion, Persuasion, and War*, ed. S. J. Cimbala, *Studies in International Security Affairs and Military Strategy* (Boulder: Westview Press, 1987), 1–12; see also Stephen J. Cimbala, *U.S. Military Strategy and the Cold War Endgame* (Ilford, Essex, England: F. Cass, 1995); see also Robin Cohen, *Endgame in South Africa?: The Changing Structures and Ideology of Apartheid* (Trenton, N.J.: Africa World Press, 1988); see also Stuart Croft, ed., *The Conventional Armed Forces in Europe Treaty: The Cold War Endgame* (Brookfield, Vt.: Dartmouth Publishing Co., 1994); see also Charles M. Hubbard, *The Burden of Confederate Diplomacy* (Knoxville: University of Tennessee Press, 1998); Michael R Rampy, "Endgame: Conflict Termination and Post–Conflict Activities," *Military Review* 72 (1992): 42–54; see also David Rohde, *Endgame: The Betrayal and Fall of Srebrenica, Europe's Worst Massacre since World War II* (New York: Farrar, Straus and Giroux, 1997); and see also Strobe Talbott, *Endgame: The inside Story of Salt II* (New York: Harper & Row, 1979).

2. By design, this work does not provide the historical contexts for these two cases. For a list of background, historical, and analytical references on these two cases, see also Append ix, F, "Case-Specific Literature: The Persian Gulf and Bosnia" in Vicki J. Rast, Interagency Conflict and U.S. Intervention: Toward a Bureaucratic Model of Conflict Termination" (PhD diss., George Mason University, 1999).

3. Daniel Druckman, "Social Psychology and International Negotiations: Processes and Influences," in *Advances in Applied Social Psychology*, ed. Robert F. Kidd and Michael J. Saks (Hillsdale, N.J.: Lawrence Erlbaum Associates, Publishers, 1983), 51–81; see also Daniel Druckman and Justin Green, *Political Stability in the Philippines: Framework and Analysis*, ed. Karen A. Feste, vol. 22, *Monograph Series in World Affairs* (Taiwan, Republic of China: University of Denver [Colorado Seminary], 1986); and Daniel Druckman, Jo L. Husbands, and Karin Johnston, "Turning Points in the INF Negotiations," *Negotiation Journal* (1991): 55–67. In the current military planning jargon, the terms *phases, branches,* and *sequels* describe the possible outcomes of operational and tactical plans.

4. This process is not uniquely American but occurs across all cultures. The inference here, however, is the particular effect it has on US policy making.

5. This practice holds import for *termination strategy* development as well, the implications of which are discussed further in an upcoming section.

6. See also Jeffrey Z. Rubin, Dean G. Pruitt, and Sung Hee Kim, *Social Conflict: Escalation, Stalemate, and Settlement*, 2d ed. (New York: McGraw-Hill, Inc., 1994).

7. The literature on groupthink has expanded in recent years. For an overview of this phenomenon and its relationship to group dynamics and conflict resolution, see J. Brockner, "The Escalation of Commitment to a Failing Course of Action: Toward Theoretical Progress," *Academy of Management Review* 17 (1992): 39–61; see also Maryann Kathleen Cusimano, "Committing the Troops: New Perspectives on United States Military Deployments" (PhD diss., Johns Hopkins University, 1993); Randy Y. Hirokawa and Dierdre D. Johnston, "Toward a General Theory of Group Decision Making: Development of an Integrated Model," *Small Group Behavior* 20, no. 4 (1989): 500–523; see also Irving L. Janis, *Crucial Decisions: Leadership in Policymaking and Crisis Management* (New York: Free Press, 1989); Irving L. Janis, "Groupthink: The Desperate Drive for Consensus at Any Cost," in *Classic Readings in Organizational Behavior*, ed. J. Steven Ott (Pacific Grove, Calif.: Brooks/Cole Publishing Co. 1989), 223–32; Tatsuya Kameda and Shinkichi Sugimori, "Psychological Entrapment in Group Decision Making: An Assigned Decision Rule and a Groupthink Phenomenon," *Journal of Personality and Social Psychology* 65, no. 2 (1993): 282–92; Walli F. Leff, "Groupthink," *Omni* 3 (1981): 26–27; Clark McCauley, "The Nature of Social Influence in Groupthink: Compliance and Internalization," *Journal of Personality and Social Psychology* 57, no. 2 (1989): 250– 60; see also Robert K. Merton, "Bureaucratic Structure and Personality," in *Classic Readings in Organizational Behavior*, ed. J. S. Ott (Pacific Grove, Calif.: Brooks/Cole Publishing Co., 1989); and Christopher P. Neck and Charles C. Manz, "From Groupthink to Teamthink: Toward the Creation of Constructive Thought Patterns in Self-Managing Work Teams," *Human Relations* 47, no. 8 (1994): 929–52.

8. Although beyond the scope of this research in an empirical sense, this crisis analysis process is complicated further within a multinational environment wherein each actor shares part but not all of the images that frame the crisis, as well as only portions of the goals that shape the multinational response. As an example, a State principal noted that in Bosnia the "Europeans looked at separate divisions and the Americans wanted to produce a multiethnic society." State Department official, U.S. Department of State, Washington, D.C.

9. Ibid.

10. National Security Interagency Policy-making official, Executive Office of the President, Washington, D.C.

11. State Department official.

12. A *node* is one critical component of a system. Acting against this critical component will affect the system, but it may not change the nature of the system on the strategic level. To bring about systemic change, the system must be affected beyond the independent nodes, or the nodes must be affected in an integrated fashion to bring about the desired result. For example, the crisis in the Balkans is comprised of several nodes that synergistically form a system. Geographically, Bosnia, Macedonia, Montenegro, Kosovo, Albania, Serbia, and

so forth, represent independent nodes. Together, these nodes form the Balkan system. Nodes can take many forms—political, economic, military, social, and so on. Affecting a particular node in isolation from the others cannot, in most instances, bring about systemic change. Hence, in the Balkans generally, and with regard to the 1999 Kosovo crisis in particular, focusing upon President Slobodan Milosevic's actions in isolation from the activities of the Kosovar Liberation Army and other actors most likely will fall short of affecting sustainable systemic change.

13. This work recognizes that the Bosnia crisis did not manifest itself in 1993 when President Clinton took office. However, since this research analyzes the effects of interagency conflict on conflict termination policy development, beginning this analysis with the Bush administration is of little utility since the data indicated that the interagency process became energized surrounding this crisis only *after* Clinton took office.

14. This "core group" included Dan Quayle (vice president), James Baker (secretary of state), Richard Cheney (secretary of defense), Brent Scowcroft (APNSA), Lawrence Eagleburger (deputy secretary of state), Robert Gates (deputy APNSA and, later, director of the Central Intelligence Agency), and John Sununu (White House chief of staff). Most officials generally identify Colin Powell (chairman of the Joint Chiefs of Staff) as the "eighth" member of the "Gang of Eight." See also George Bush and Brent Scowcroft, *A World Transformed* (New York: Alfred A. Knopf, 1998).

15. See also Gordon S. Brown, *Coalition, Coercion, & Compromise: Diplomacy of the Gulf Crisis, 1990–91* (Washington, D.C.: The Institute for the Study of Diplomacy, Georgetown University, 1997); and see also Bush and Scowcroft, *A World Transformed.*

16. George Bush, *Statement on the United Nations Security Council Resolution Authorizing the Use of Force against Iraq, The George Bush Presidential Library,* 1990, available on-line, Internet, 3 April 1999, http://www.csdl.tamu.edu/bushlibrary/library/research/research.html.

17. During the period 1990–1991, President Bush made at least 51 public references to the "Gulf War" and 175 to "Saddam" and "war." By doing so, the president kept the issue in the forefront of the American consciousness and created a sense of connection with the public. Likewise, Bush made 11 public references linking Saddam Hussein to Hitler during this period. See *The George Bush Presidential Library* at http://www.csdl.tamu.edu/bushlibrary/library/research/research.html. For a discussion of demonization and its effects in this case, see Edward W. Said and Barbara Harlow, "The Intellectuals and the War," *Middle East Report* 21, no. 4 (171) (1991): 15–20; and James Toth, "Demonizing Saddam Hussein: Manipulating Racism as a Prelude to War," *New Political Science* 21–22 (spring–summer 1992): 5–39.

18. "Strategic objectives" is offset here since it can be argued that the four objectives were *primarily* regional in nature, thereby equating to operational objectives, not strategic objectives. For the Persian Gulf War, the four stated US national policy objectives were (1) "Immediate, complete, and unconditional withdrawal of all Iraqi forces from Kuwait"; (2) "Restoration of Kuwait's legiti-

mate government"; (3) "Security and stability of Saudi Arabia and the Persian Gulf"; and (4) "Safety and protection of the lives of American citizens abroad." See also Office of the United States Secretary of Defense, *Conduct of the Persian Gulf War, Final Report to Congress Pursuant to Title V of the Persian Gulf Conflict Supplemental Authorization and Personnel Benefits Act of 1991 (Public Law 102-25)* (Washington, D.C.: Government Printing Office (GPO), 1992).

19. See also Pierre Salinger and Eric Laurent, *Secret Dossier: The Hidden Agenda Behind the Gulf War* (New York: Penguin Books, 1991).

20. A majority of the congressional documents of the period characterizes the Iraqi invasion of Kuwait in this manner. The Congress took its lead, perhaps, from the president's State of the Union Address, 29 January 1991, where he labeled Iraq's action as an unprovoked invasion. See George Bush, *Address before a Joint Session of the Congress on the State of the Union*, 29 January 1991, on-line, Internet, 1 December 1998 available from http://www.csdl.tamu.edu/bushlib/papers/1991/91012902.html.

21. State Department official.

22. Many outside this research have argued that the military's institutional equity of demonstrating its combat effectiveness compelled the Defense Department to promote going to war with Iraq. See also, for example, Michael R. Gordon and Bernard E. Trainor, *The Generals' War: The Inside Story of the Conflict in the Gulf* (Boston: Little, Brown and Co., 1995). Throughout the research, however, study participants across government reported that General Powell (and Secretary Baker) remained hesitant to use force, arguing instead that economic sanctions needed more time. Powell's objection is noted in Bush and Scowcroft's memoirs, *A World Transformed*, as well as his own, see also Colin L. Powell with Joseph E. Persico, *My American Journey* (New York: Random House, 1995).

23. See also Vicki J. Rast, "The Iraq–Kuwait Crisis: Structural Deprivation Leads to Revolution," in *Intervention Design in Conflict Analysis and Resolution: Theory, Practice, and Research*, ed. L. A. Fast and V. J. Rast et al. (Fairfax, Va.: Institute for Conflict Analysis and Resolution, George Mason University, 1998).

24. National Security Interagency Policy-making official.

25. For a published account reflecting the perspectives of Bush, Cheney, and Powell, see also Susan L. Woodward, *Balkan Tragedy: Chaos and Dissolution after the Cold War* (Washington, D.C.: The Brookings Institution, 1995); and see also Warren Christopher, *In the Stream of History: Shaping Foreign Policy for a New Era* (Stanford, Calif.: Stanford University Press, 1998).

26. National Security Interagency Policy-making official. This principal said, "They were tainted with their experiences in Yugoslavia in the late '50s and early '60s. Their view was Bosnia would light up like a Christmas tree (the 1991 to 1992 situation). They feared spillover and misread the situation—it would not spillover into Europe but would be contained. Powell was irrelevant to that—the political forces were reluctant because Eagleburger and Scowcroft (State and White House) had their heels dug in." David Gompert, a senior NSC member during the Bush administration, characterized the Bush administra-

tion as being "divided and stumped" in its approach to Bosnia. See also David C. Gompert, "The United States and Yugoslavia's Wars," in *The World and Yugoslavia's Wars*, ed. Richard H. Ullman (New York: Council on Foreign Relations, 1996). However, the data analyzed here indicate that Scowcroft's and Eagleburger's perspectives ensured a status quo policy approach.

27. See also James A. Baker III, *The Politics of Diplomacy: Revolution, War, and Peace, 1989–1992* (New York: G. P. Putnam's Sons, 1995); and see also Warren Christopher, *In the Stream of History: Shaping Foreign Policy for a New Era*. See also Warren Zimmerman, *Origins of a Catastrophe* (New York: Times Books, 1996).

28. See also Richard C. Holbrooke, *To End a War* (New York: Random House, 1998).

29. Ibid.

30. For illustrative purposes, one perspective regarding a "strategic vision" for the Bosnia crisis might take the form of ending the conflict while establishing the mechanisms to resolve interparty conflict for the short-, mid-, and long-term eras. This approach would include developing confidence-building measures in terms of the security/military, political, economic, and social environments. See James Macintosh, "Confidence-Building Measures—a Conceptual Exploration," in *Confidence Building Measures and International Security*, ed. R. B. Byers et al. (New York: Institute for East-West Security Studies, 1986), 9–29. This strategic vision is far different from the ideas surrounding "preventing spillover" and "containment," perspectives that drove US policy in the Balkans. This broader geopolitical approach would require decision makers to analyze the crisis through a systems approach that identified those political, economic, security, military, and social factors requiring transformation toward resolving the conflict. This approach could envisage bringing Bosnia back into the international community as a continuing partner for economic prosperity and continued peace in Europe. This vision would necessitate the development of a larger framework for a sustainable peace and would then lend itself to an operational end-state vision to achieve the broader strategic vision. Note, however, that such an envisaging process requires decision makers (and analysts) to focus their vision through the real-world constraints that affect one's ability to intervene in these crises. As such, this example is offered here merely to clarify the meaning of strategic vision and remains overly simplistic in its development.

31. See also Holbrooke, *To End a War*.

32. Ibid. Holbrooke notes that nothing generates more heat in the government than the question of who is chosen to participate in important meetings.

33. Susan Woodward maintains that analyses regarding the unwillingness to use force (until 1995) reserve the harshest criticism for UN generals on the ground and defense establishments for obstructing military engagement for fear of losing soldiers' lives. Author is quoted. She asserts that this reluctance provided a cover for major disagreements between the major powers about objectives in the Balkan peninsula and the absence of a policy toward the conflict. This was made clear when military airpower defended safe areas. Such

use was largely motivated by Bosnian Serb defiance. See also Woodward, *Balkan Tragedy: Chaos and Dissolution after the Cold War*. Mark Bowen captures the implications of the "Somalia syndrome" in *Black Hawk Down: A Story of Modern War* (New York: Atlantic Monthly Press, 1999), a best-selling book transformed into a major motion picture.

34. For a discussion regarding the theory of interplay between interests and values where intensified conflict of interest serves to polarize the parties on ideologies or values, see Daniel Druckman and Justin Green, "Playing Two Games: Internal Negotiations in the Philippines," in *Elusive Peace: Negotiating an End to Civil Wars*, ed. I. William Zartman (Washington, D.C.: The Brookings Institution, 1995), 299–331.

35. See also Woodward, *Balkan Tragedy*.

36. For a discussion of this phenomenon, see also Richard D. Challener, *Admirals, Generals, and American Foreign Policy, 1898–1914* (Princeton: Princeton University Press, 1973).

37. Defense Department official, US Department of Defense, Washington, D.C.

38. Recall from chapter 1, this work defines the *end state* by extending the US military's joint doctrine definition to include social factors. Specifically, Joint Pub 3-07, *Joint Doctrine for Military Operations Other Than War*, defines the *end state* as "What the National Command Authorities want the situation to be when operations conclude—both military operations, as well as those where the military is in support of other instruments of national power." Note that this work expands the definition to include the political, economic, military, *and social/psychological* conditions that exist in the posthostilities period. Decision makers and planners must make each explicit to ensure they consider these factors throughout the policy-development process. For a review of this concept of end state, see also Frederic E. Abt, *The Operational End State: Cornerstone of the Operational Level of War* (Fort Leavenworth, Kans.: US Army Command and General Staff College, 1988); see also Sam Allotey et al., *Planning and Execution of Conflict Termination* (Maxwell AFB, Ala.: Air Command and Staff College, 1995); James H. Anderson, "End State Pitfalls: A Strategic Perspective," *Military Review* 77, no. 5 (1997): 93–95; see also Andrew Bair, "Which End-Game in Bosnia?" *Strategic Forum*, no. 16 (1995); see also Khaled Bin Sultan, *Desert Warrior: A Personal View of the Gulf War by the Joint Forces Commander* (New York: HarperCollins Publishers, 1995); see also US Congress, "Postwar Economic Recovery in the Persian Gulf" (Washington, D.C.: GPO, 1991); see also US House, "Options for Dealing with Iraq" (Washington, D.C.: GPO, 1992); see also US House, "Post–War Policy Issues in the Persian Gulf" (Washington, D.C.: GPO, 1991); see also US House, "U.N. Role in the Persian Gulf and Iraqi Compliance with U.N. Resolutions" (Washington, D.C.: GPO, 1991); see also US House, "U.N. Role in the Persian Gulf and Iraqi Compliance with U.N. Resolutions" (Washington, D.C.: GPO, 1992); see also JCS, Joint Pub 3-07, *Joint Task Force Commander's Handbook for Peace Operations*, 1995; D. M. Last, "The Challenge of Interagency Cooperation in International Peace

Operations: A Conference Report," *Peacekeeping & International Relations* 24, no. 1 (1995): 5; see also H. Norman Schwarz-kopf with Peter Petre, *General H. Norman Schwarzkopf: The Autobiography: It Doesn't Take a Hero* (New York: Bantam Books, 1992); and see also US Senate, "Middle East" (Washington, D.C.: GPO, 1991).

39. Bertram I. Spector, "Creativity Heuristics for Impasse Resolution: Reframing Intractable Negotiations," *The Annals of the American Academy of Political and Social Science* 542 (1995): 81–99.

40. Interagency official, Executive Office of the President, Washington, D.C.

41. Defense Department official.

42. Ibid.

43. National Security Interagency Policy-making official.

44. Defense Department official.

45. For example, as the NATO air campaign against Yugoslavia entered its 10th day, the media continued to report that the air strikes exacerbated the refugee situation as "about 164,000 ethnic Albanians have been expelled from Kosovo by government forces" and were fleeing into the neighboring countries of Albania, Macedonia, and Montenegro UNHCR (United Nations High Commissioner for Refugees). See "Refugee Crisis," *The Washington Post*, 2 April 1999, A22. Included in answering the three questions posed above (as part of recursive crisis analysis) *should be* the anticipation of the effects of aerial bombardment. Clearly, decision makers failed to anticipate the magnitude of this undesired effect as this refugee migration destabilized the entire region.

46. See also Michael D. Gilpin, *Exit Strategy: The New Dimension in Operational Planning* (Carlisle Barracks, Pa.: US Army War College, 1997).

47. For illustrative purposes, as an extension of a broader strategic vision, one "potential" end-state vision for the Iraqi–Kuwaiti crisis might have included the reintegration of Iraq into the regional power base, beyond a mere counterbalance to Iran. See, for example, Zbigniew Brzezinski and Brent Scowcroft, *Differentiated Containment: U.S. Policy toward Iran and Iraq* (Council on Foreign Relations, 1997, on-line, Internet, 26 March 1999), available from http://www.foreignrelations.org/studies/transcripts/contain.html. Such political integration would have necessitated the resolution of long-standing differences between Iraq and Kuwait (e.g., territorial boundaries and ownership of the Rumaila oil fields). This political issue extends to the economic vision as well, noting that the reintegration of Iraq into the world economy would serve as one method to dampen the tension between Iraq and Kuwait. Relatedly, OPEC and the international community could open additional markets for the Iraqis as an avenue to help them recover their financial losses sustained as a result of the Iran-Iraq War. These political and economic "carrots" could be used to entice Iraq to halt its military expansion. In turn, as a good faith gesture, Iraq could be convinced to shift the funds spent on military expansion to domestic social programs, rebuilding the infrastructure of the country and bolstering public support for the Hussein regime. Admittedly, this end-state vision may seem implausible given

the events of the last 20 years—both before the Gulf War and in its aftermath—in terms of Hussein's treatment of his populace. However, the important aspect of developing this vision is identifying the conditions of conflict through a system's approach to crisis analysis. This approach would provide the specifics for the strategic vision; and, therefore, the end-state vision that addresses the political, economic, military, and social conditions required to establish a sustainable peace. This approach differs greatly from the "containment" vision used to frame the four "strategic" objectives proffered during the Gulf War; objectives that focused on Hussein as a node within the system, rather than the overall system itself.

48. Defense Department official.

49. Intelligence Community official, Washington, D.C.

50. Defense Department official.

51. Again, the four objectives were (1) "Immediate, complete, and unconditional withdrawal of all Iraqi forces from Kuwait"; (2) "Restoration of Kuwait's legitimate government"; (3) "Security and stability of Saudi Arabia and the Persian Gulf"; and (4) "Safety and protection of the lives of American citizens abroad"; see also OSD, *Conduct of the Persian Gulf War (Public Law 102-25)*.

52. See also Edward C. Mann, *Thunder and Lightning: Desert Storm and the Airpower Debates*, vol. 2 of a two-volume series (Maxwell AFB, Ala.: Air University Press, 1995); and see also Richard T. Reynolds, *Heart of the Storm: The Genesis of the Air Campaign against Iraq*, vol. 1 of a two-volume series (Maxwell AFB, Ala.: Air University Press, 1995).

53. Secretary of State Warren Christopher illuminated issues regarding continued NATO credibility in February 1993 but to no avail. In his own words, "this rhetoric proved to be well ahead of our policy," as seen in Christopher, *In the Stream of History: Shaping Foreign Policy for a New Era.*

54. Holbrooke reports that Vice President Al Gore was very aware of this connection and that on 22 November 1995 in a meeting at the White House Gore said, "'I want to make an important practical point regarding the JCS and the Pentagon,' he said, looking directly at the Defense representatives in the room. 'I've had lots of conversations with the Congress. They have told me that our military representatives on the Hill usually leave their audience more comfortable than when they arrived. I'm not saying they are trying to undercut our policy, but they are losing us votes up there.' " Holbrooke, *To End a War*, 316.

55. Intelligence Community official.

56. Defense Department official.

57. State Department official.

58. National Security Interagency Policy-making official. In this case, the "cheat sheet" refers to the verbiage needed to ensure higher-ranking State Department officials would "buy" the proposal and adopt it as their own.

59. Intelligence Community official.

60. Defense Department official.

61. This simultaneously creates the fissure between the Washington decision makers and the field commander or ambassador who feel Washington

is out of touch with the realities of the context on the ground. For another perspective, see also Allotey, *Planning and Execution of Conflict Termination,* Historical Evaluation Research Organization (HERO), *Conventional Attrition and Battle Termination Criteria: A Study of War Termination* (Dunn Loring: HERO, 1982); and see also James E. Toth, "Foreign Policy Analysis: Conflict Termination in the Persian Gulf War" (Washington, D.C.: National Defense University, 1991).

62. State Department official.

63. See also, for example, Frank Aukofer and William P. Lawrence, *America's Team: The Odd Couple—A Report on the Relationship between the Media and the Military* (Nashville, Tenn.: The Freedom Forum First Amendment Center, 1995).

64. Initially, intensifying aerial bombardment in Yugoslavia did not separate the leader from the people; conversely, it drove them to his side, enhancing the political will of the government and its capacity to intensify ethnic cleansing. It appears that these decision makers failed to appreciate that armed intervention polarizes populations—there can be no neutrals once intervention occurs. See Michael Dobbs, "U.S. Starts Process of Army Aid; Some Allies Resist Bosnian Project," *The Washington Post,* 21 December 1995, A35.

65. See also John A. Warden III, *The Air Campaign: Planning for Combat* (McLean, Va.: Pergamon-Brassey's International Defense Publishers, Inc., 1989).

66. As of 1999, the military's civil affairs capability existed as part of USACAPOC (US Army Civil Affairs and Psychological Operations Command), not the "mainstream war fighting military" structure. The active Army provides "only 4 percent of the US Army's Civil Affairs resources. The remaining 96 percent come from other units in the reserve component." See USACAPOC, *U.S. Army Civil Affairs and Psychological Operations Command,* US Army, on-line, Internet, 2 April 1999, available from http://www.geocity. com/Pentagon/1012/psyop.html. As a result, war fighters have not incorporated civil affairs units into planning and execution as they are outside the combatant's primary mission and expertise. This practice is changing quite rapidly. It is also an outgrowth of the realization that these separate civil affairs activities (e.g., those performed nongovernmental organizations as well as the Army Reserve Civil Affairs units) require a coordinating function to fulfill their missions effectively.

67. Again, crisis analysis played a crucial role in this since many, Scowcroft in particular, viewed Iraq as an effective counterbalance to Iran. See also Bush and Scowcroft, *A World Transformed.*

68. Recall again that these conditions included the: (1) parties' adherence to the military requirements of the peace agreement (especially the absence of violations or unauthorized military activities); (2) parties' demonstration of a commitment to continued negotiations to resolve differences; (3) the creation of civil structures to assume responsibility and monitor compliance with the peace agreement; and (4) the establishment of conditions for ongoing nation-building activities.

69. Defense Department official.

70. National Security Interagency Policy-making official.

71. One study participant noted that the principal could in fact be "the expert" but claimed this is extremely rare. From this individual's perspective, the top leaders usually have little specific knowledge of any particular crisis. The data revealed his perspective remained consistent across the government.

72. Interestingly, Terrence Hopmann and Daniel Druckman make the same arguments concerning Henry Kissinger's shuttle diplomacy in the Middle East. See P. Terrence Hopmann and Daniel Druckman, "Henry Kissinger as Strategist and Tactician in the Middle East Negotiations," in *Dynamics of Third Party Intervention: Kissinger in the Middle East*, ed. Jeffrey Z. Rubin (New York: Praeger Publishers, 1981), 197–225.

73. Defense Department official.

74. It is important to acknowledge here that the literature linking strategy to conflict termination is expanding the classics. See, for example, Allotey et al., *Planning and Execution of Conflict Termination;* Stephen J. Cimbala, "C2 and War Termination," *Signal* 43 (1988): 73–78; see also Cimbala, "The Endgame and War"; see also Stephen J. Cimbala, ed., *Strategic War Termination* (New York: Praeger Publishers, 1986); see also Stephen J. Cimbala and Sidney R. Waldman, ed., *Controlling and Ending Conflict: Issues before and after the Cold War* (New York: Greenwood Press, 1992); see also Stephen J. Cimbala and Keith A. Dunn, eds., *Conflict Termination and Military Strategy: Coercion, Persuasion, and War* (Boulder.: Westview Press, 1987); see also Carl von Clausewitz, *On War*, ed. Michael Howard and Peter Paret, trans. Michael Howard (Princeton, N.J.: Princeton University Press, 1976); Lewis A. Coser, "The Termination of Conflict," *Conflict Resolution* 5, no. 4 (1961): 347–53; see also James E. Dornan Jr., et al., *War Termination Concepts and Political, Economic and Military Targeting* (Arlington, Va.: SRI International, Strategic Studies Center, 1978); Keith A. Dunn, "The Missing Link in Conflict Termination Thought: Strategy," in *Conflict Termination and Military Strategy*, ed. S. J. Cimbala and K. A. Dunn, 175–93; see also Joseph A. Engelbrecht Jr., "War Termination: Why Does a State Decide to Stop Fighting?" (World War II, Anglo-Boer War, Japan, Great Britain) (PhD diss., Columbia University, 1992); see also Gilpin, *Exit Strategy: The New Dimension in Operational Planning;* see also US House, "Crisis in the Persian Gulf" (Washington, D.C.: GPO, 1990); see also Herman Kahn, William Pfaff, and Edmund Stillman, *War Termination Issues and Concepts: Final Report* (Croton-on-Hudson, N.Y.: Hudson Institute, 1968); Paul Kecskemeti, "Political Rationality in Ending War," *American Academy of Political and Social Science Annals* 392 (1970): 105–15; see also Paul Kecskemeti, *Strategic Surrender: The Politics of Victory and Defeat* (New York: Atheneum, 1964); see also William J. Lademan, *War Termination: The Confluence of Strategy and Policy* (Newport, R.I.: US Naval War College, 1988); see also Roy R. Pinette, *Operational Considerations for War Termination* (Newport, R.I.: US Naval War College, 1994); see also Vicki J. Rast, "Conflict Termination in the Persian Gulf War: Policy Failure Sustains Conflict," in *Soldier, Scientist, Diplomat,*

Mediator: The Multi-Disciplinary Context of Conflict Resolution, ed. L. E. Hancock et al. (Fairfax, Va.: Graduate Students in Conflict Studies, Institute for Conflict Analysis and Resolution, George Mason University, 1999); see also Leon H. Rios, *Seeking a Final Victory: Creating Conditions for Conflict Resolution* (Carlisle Barracks, Pa.: US Army War College, 1993); see also Ricki Lynn Sullivan, *The Operational Planner and War Termination* (Newport, R.I.: US Naval War College, 1993); Harry G. Summers, "War: Deter, Fight, Terminate," *Naval War College Review* 39 (1986): 18–29; see also James E. Toth, *Conflict Termination: Considerations for Development of National Strategy* (Maxwell AFB, Ala.: Air War College, 1978); and see also Department of Corresponding Studies, *Conflict Termination and Military Operations Other Than War* (Carlisle Barracks, Pa.: US Army War College, 1997).

75. As one example, throughout the research process individuals within Defense remarked that before the appointment of William Cohen as secretary of defense, the three-star (uniformed) director of operations (J-3) signed troop deployment orders *upon the direction of* the secretary of defense. During the Clinton administration, Secretary Cohen personally signed all deployment orders. Uniformed personnel perceive this as micromanagement and this leadership style created friction between OSD civilians and Joint Staff military officials.

76. See also US Air Force Academy, *Contrails*, vol. 30, *Air Force Academy Cadet Handbook* (Colorado Springs, Colo.: USAFA, 1984).

77. According to the policy officials interviewed throughout this research, this "handoff" remained pronounced during the Persian Gulf War as Secretary Baker faded into the background once the war started. He reemerged to play a more visible diplomatic role only after the cease-fire.

78. See also Donald M. Snow and Dennis M. Drew, *From Lexington to Desert Storm: War and Politics in the American Experience* (New York: M. E. Sharpe, 1994); and see also Russell Frank Weigley, *The American Way of War: A History of United States Military Strategy and Policy* (Bloomington, Ind.: Indiana University Press, 1973).

79. A Defense official provided an example of this concerning Haiti: "The military is more concerned about getting out. Haiti is a perfect example because we haven't figured out the strategy to get out. [We] need to establish a constabulary force. We've been trying to get out but the administration says to stay there for interagency plug-in." This Defense official did not define one of the military's roles as "interagency plug-in."

80. Defense Department official. The nature of the unresolved conflict in Kosovo demonstrates that the threat, and indeed application, of overwhelming force may not bring about conflict termination in all cases.

81. For a satirical presentation of such ideas, see also *A Cartoon History of United States Foreign Policy, 1776–1976* (New York: William Morrow and Co., Inc., 1975), published by editors of the Foreign Policy Association with an introduction by Daniel P. Moynihan; and see also Richard H. Minear, *Dr. Seuss Goes to War: The World War II Editorial Cartoons of Theodor Seuss Geisel* (New York: W. W. Norton & Co., Inc., 1999).

82. See also Raymond Tanter, *Rogue Regimes: Terrorism and Proliferation* (New York: St. Martin's Press, 1998).

83. See also Paul Seabury and Angelo Codevilla, *War: Ends and Means* (New York: Basic Books, 1989).

84. Defense Department official.

85. In an interview with *Frontline*, Richard Haass recounts a meeting wherein President Bush seemed concerned as much with Iraqi casualties as he was with those for the coalition. Frontline, "The Gulf War: The Decision-makers" (PBS), on-line, Internet, 5 May 1998, available from http://www. pbs.org/wgbh/pages/frontline/gulf/oral/decision.html.

86. State Department official.

87. Ibid.

88. National Security Interagency Policy-making official.

89. Ambassador April Glaspie's communication to Saddam Hussein regarding potential US reaction to what Hussein classified as economic war may have contributed to getting the United States into such a position.

90. See also Salinger and Laurent, *Secret Dossier: The Hidden Agenda behind the Gulf War*.

91. See also W. A. Reese, *The Principle of the Objective and Promoting National Interests: Desert Shield/Storm—A Case Study* (Washington, D.C.: Industrial College of the Armed Forces, 1993). See also A. E. Goodman and S. C. Bogart, eds., *Making Peace: The United States and Conflict Resolution* (Boulder: Westview Press, 1992), and see also Snow and Drew, *From Lexington to Desert Storm: War and Politics in the American Experience*.

92. A notable exception to this practice occurred on the Defense side as Checkmate (the Pentagon's offline think tank under the direction of Col John Warden) brought in outsiders from different disciplines and businesses around the world to discuss targeting effects. However, Defense made no effort to incorporate State as an "agency" in this process.

93. These four objectives were (1) "Immediate, complete, and unconditional withdrawal of all Iraqi forces from Kuwait"; (2) "Restoration of Kuwait's legitimate government"; (3) "Security and stability of Saudi Arabia and the Persian Gulf"; and (4) "Safety and protection of the lives of American citizens abroad." See also OSD, *Conduct of the Persian Gulf War (Public Law 102-25)*.

94. See also Gordon and Trainor, *The Generals' War*.

95. Defense Department official.

96. National Security Interagency Policy-making official.

97. See also Holbrooke, *To End a War*.

98. National Security Interagency Policy-making official.

99. Interagency official.

100. State Department official.

Chapter 10

Termination Policy Development within a Volatile Environment

The analysis presented through this work advanced a more accurate conception of USG conflict termination policy development. Policy outcomes generated through the interagency process create the conditions for cease-fire (i.e., war termination), but they cannot create the environment required to transform this cease-fire into a sustainable peace. This discussion addresses the three interrogatives that framed this study.[1] First, it presents the process and substance relationships to identify the factors that create, generate, or exacerbate interagency conflict. It then concludes that Allison's bureaucratic politics model remains durable nearly 30 years after its inception by demonstrating that USG policy makers produce decisions through interagency negotiation processes in which the identification of the decision makers, the construction of the rules of the game, and the generation of policy alternatives reflect that collective choice is made through a negotiated consensus-building process, not rational choice theory's utility-maximization approach. To address the third research question, this analysis illustrated ways that interagency conflict influences the government's capacity to develop termination policies for international conflicts. It illuminates the effects that the policy makers' crisis analysis processes, vision for the desired end state, termination criteria selection, and termination strategy development had upon conflict termination in the Persian Gulf and Bosnia. Synthesizing these findings, the chapter concludes by generating a framework for future research, a framework that identifies sources of interagency conflict that leaders can eliminate to close the gap between diplomats and war fighters to create the integrated planning process required to envisage policy outcomes capable of achieving more than cease-fire.

The Interagency Process:
Synthesizing Process and Substance

This research focused on the development of interagency conflict and its influence on the USG's creation of conflict termination policy. Using complementary quantitative and qualitative approaches, the research explored interagency relations to identify factors that exacerbate, intensify, or create interagency conflict within the USG during termination policy development.[2] The discussion that follows reiterates those findings (as presented in chaps. 5–8) by addressing the models supported through analyses of the signed digraph models, then discussing the qualitative emergent themes.

The quantitative analysis revealed that interagency conflict emanates primarily from (1) perceptions regarding others' interagency behaviors, (2) leadership style (in general), (3) intradepartmental leadership style's relationship to crisis analysis and interagency communication, and (4) perceptions regarding one's own and other's abilities to influence policy making as a consequence of relationships with members of the NSC system.

Interagency dynamics become competitive when actors perceive that departmental relations at the time of crisis definition are hostile or when an agency perceives that other agencies have a high level of self-interest regarding the crisis.[3] Similarly, when agencies perceive that others act competitively, they respond reciprocally with similar competitive behaviors.[4] This behavioral dynamic deteriorates further as those agencies that believe they possess a limited ability to influence policy tend to act competitively to protect their equities. As a result of these perceptions acting in concert with one another, these competitive behaviors in conjunction with the hierarchical structuration of the interagency process itself constrain open debate and therefore lead to less effective development of termination policy. The nature of the public debate and interagency communication also reflect leadership styles and decision-making approaches.

Leaders who manage their agencies autocratically establish rigid communication patterns and perceptions of high penalties for failure. Across hierarchically structured organizations that limit communication, actors compete as they attempt to protect institutional equities within parameters established by their respective principals. These factors establish conceptions of risk for these actors by (1) analyzing estimates of success, (2) examining perspectives regarding which agency should lead the policy development effort, (3) assessing the crisis "fit" with national interests, (4) determining the agency's priority for the crisis, and (5) exploring the agency's prior experience with similar cases. The quantitative data analysis revealed no statistically significant relationships across these dimensions of *Crisis Definition*, making it irrelevant in terms of creating interagency conflict as a separate core factor.[5] Rather, risk is framed in bureaucratic terms related to stepping outside the shared images of the organization and promoting policy that does not parallel that of the principal. Leaders' decision-making styles also play a role in developing interagency conflict as these styles shape agency decision-making profiles.

Originally conceptualized as agency's decision-making style, the data revealed it would be more appropriate to consider this core factor in terms of intradepartmental leadership style's relationship to (1) crisis analysis and (2) innovative solution generation. As part of this factor, decision-making preferences for mid- and upper-level executives must take into account the role decision-making styles—directive or consensus-building—play in developing interagency conflict. The case analyses indicated that a more autocratic decision-taking approach by a chief executive stifled interagency conflict as this leadership style limited interagency debate but did so in a way that circumscribed integrated planning. Alternatively, the more participative, consensus-building decision style, also by a chief executive, exacerbated and polarized interagency conflict in the absence of strategic leadership as actors felt the need to protect institutional equities. In this manner, the crisis analysis portion of this core factor must include perceptions of risk in terms of threats to both functional and resource-based institutional equities and shared images. Relatedly, because the qualitative data revealed their importance, this modified core factor must include estimates of success and perceptions of prior experience for future investigation. As an added dimension, relationships between an individual's ability and willingness to propose innovative solutions should be analyzed in light of the individual's personal relationship with the principals. Given the structure of the interagency process, relationships with the NSC Staff proved of paramount import.

Perceptions regarding one's own and others' abilities to influence policy shaped agency perceptions regarding the NSC Staff's role in the policy-making process. Together with perceptions of other's interagency tactics and an emergent theme involving personal relationships and networks, it is logical to conclude that those enjoying personal relationships with NSC members discount the salience of the formal process and rely instead upon their networks to influence policy development. In this manner, the NSC system remains the focal point for policy development, playing more than a coordinating role as this agency controls information flow and personal access to the president as the ultimate arbiter of interagency disputes.

These findings illuminate the factors that create or intensify interagency conflict among the decision makers within the national security policy-making process. Alone, they are noteworthy. In conjunction with the qualitative findings, they provide a basis for suggesting means of minimizing interagency conflict.

Dynamic Themes and Interagency Dynamics: Leadership, Decision Making as Negotiation, and Domestic Politics

Three emergent themes characterized ways in which interagency dynamics shaped the substance of the policy process. These three process-substance themes are leadership, decision making as negotiation, and domestic politics. In the first instance, leadership plays a critical role in two ways—(1) by establishing strategic vision and (2) by defining the rules of the game. Leaders, such as the president and assistant to the president for national security affairs, establish the vision for US foreign and security policy and thereby set the tone for interagency relations. When the executive articulates a strategic vision, decision makers experience less interagency conflict because the principals align their positions with the president's and prove intolerant of excursions beyond the shared images

316

they promote. This practice establishes one "rule of the game" for interagency dynamics. However, leaders establish rules of the game in another manner as well through their adaptation and use of decision-making styles.

The decision-making styles examined revealed that the decision-taking and consensus-based approaches of two presidential administrations each failed to energize the interagency process in positive ways. However, the first style discourages the development of interagency conflict because a small group of in-group advisors makes all decisions.[6] This establishes the rules of the game as a practice wherein lower-level actors continually pass issues upward and remain reluctant to make decisions at their level. In contrast, the second style promotes interagency conflict as individuals attempt to advance their agencies (and themselves) in the president's eyes. Coupled with the absence of an articulated strategic vision, this style establishes the rules of the game as a "free for all" wherein the "strength of personality" (e.g., Richard Holbrooke, Madeleine Albright, and Colin Powell) tends to overwhelm institutionalized aspects of the policy process.

Competing executive personalities also reflect dissimilar organizational cultures and disparate worldviews (especially in terms of ideology and philosophy regarding the use of force). They channel communication to meet their needs in terms of influencing policy outcomes to protect institutional equities (and for some, to enhance their egos) while simultaneously limiting debate and stifling innovative thinking. In the final analysis, breakthroughs in policy development emanate from personal relationships and networks that exist before crisis onset. These personal relationships come to the fore in an environment wherein actors make decisions through a process they frame as a negotiation.

USG officials make decisions regarding national security policy through an interagency negotiation process that occurs at three levels—principals, deputies, and the interagency working groups—and across multiple agencies—the White House, the NSC and NSC Staff, the State Department, the Defense Department, the CIA, and assorted others who play lesser roles. The personal relationships that exist across these agencies shape the nature of an individual's access and the magnitude of the influence this access has upon policy outcomes that emerge as political resultants of the negotiation process. Personal relationships are not alone in influencing this process-substance relationship; domestic politics plays a crucial role through its capacity to shape the nature of interagency relationships.

Domestic politics shapes interagency dynamics through its ability to mobilize public opinion and the Congress. The interagency's ranking decision makers are politicians—either publicly elected or politically appointed—who secure their posts through political networks. These individuals remain concerned with public opinion polls as a measure of their performance and an indicator of future political possibilities. These individuals also recognize the relationship between the public, especially if dissatisfied, and the Congress.

A dissatisfied public can mobilize the Congress to oppose presidential policies through both (1) media pressure—congressional appearances denouncing the administration's policy and (2) budgetary controls—withholding funding for force deployments. This congressional pressure increasingly takes the form of escalating partisan politics that compel the administration to dilute policy approaches to secure consensus across multiple parties with competing worldviews. It is important to recognize that the Congress is not an actor in the sense of being an official participant in the executive branch's interagency process— it has no official "seat at the table." Yet, congressional influence drives interagency dynamics and creates interagency conflict. This same precaution holds for the ambiguity of roles and missions and the media's influence, factors that bridge the gap between the dynamic themes—issues exacerbating interagency conflict—and contextual parameters—factors that shape interagency dynamics via the dynamic themes.

Crosscutting Effects: Roles and Missions and Media Influence

Although roles and missions appear well-defined in theory, in reality the practice of making policy includes a great deal of ambiguity within a policy-making structure that includes "purposeful interagency conflict." In the first instance, role ambiguity results from functional overlap and ill-defined lines of responsibility. This problem is complicated by a resistance on the part of the Defense Department to performing roles it considers outside its core competencies in the face of increasing pressure from the State Department for Defense to get more involved in such missions. Finally, roles and missions delineations are blurred further as the NSC Staff assumes a role beyond that of policy coordinator while simultaneously abdicating its responsibility for overseeing policy implementation. In this capacity, it performs more of the State Department's traditional foreign policy development role. Together, these factors create confusion regarding "who's in charge" and which agencies remain responsible for specific aspects of the policy process. Such ambiguity creates interagency conflict regarding policy making's process-substance features. Roles and missions likewise affect the substance-process elements of policy making, particularly with regard to interagency process structure.

The interagency process induces lower-level decision makers to frame their roles in terms of protecting institutional equities. Hence, substantive inputs to policy making negatively affect interagency dynamics since some decision makers hold their assets in reserve when others believe they should employ them to end the crisis. This purposeful interagency conflict combines with role ambiguity to intensify interagency conflict. Media influence plays a similar crosscutting role as it affects both process-substance and substance-process relationships.

Media shape interagency dynamics through their ability to influence the substantive inputs to the policy process. Media reports bolster images surrounding public and decision-maker understanding of the conflict, at times creating sentiment that the USG must act (or, alternatively, that it should resist involvement). The USG reinforces these images by framing the issues, providing a feedback loop to the Congress, and developing the "move it off the front page" phenomenon. The media likewise shape the process-substance aspects of policy making as interagency conflict emanates from the decision maker's concern with the media's ability to shape the substantive inputs to the policy process. These concerns include the "CNN factor," the capacity for press guidance to drive policy, the "use of leaks," and the ability of "the necessity to manage the media" factor to deplete the interagency process of its critical intellectual, emotional, and psychological capital.

Issues regarding roles and missions and media influence play a prominent role in shaping interagency dynamics in conjunction with the substantive inputs to the policy process. In this manner, these themes bridge the gap between interagency dynamics and substantive inputs to the policy process.

Contextual Parameters: "Strategic Vision and Planning Processes" and Institutional Equities

The assumptions, worldviews, prior experience, and core competencies each decision maker brings to the interagency negotiation shape the nature of interagency conflict and the policy outcome of that interaction. These substantive inputs emerged in the form of "strategic vision and planning processes" and institutional equities. Together with the previous themes, these substance-process relationships help frame the entire interagency dynamic. A brief review makes this connection apparent.

Actors engaged in crisis action planning believe they possess a great ability to influence policy outcomes, while those engaged in strategic planning believe their influence remained limited. These feelings resulted from the lack of strategic vision that characterizes US foreign policy, one that equates success with crisis management. This void manifests itself in a lack of political vision, the absence of interagency-shared images, and a tactical focus that dominates the policy process. Political vision serves as the coalescing goal around which decision makers unite. The absence of such a goal encourages disparate worldviews and role ambiguity to promote divergent perspectives regarding both national interests and the utility of armed intervention. The result of dissimilar shared images, these fissures come to dominate perspectives regarding crisis analysis and course of action development. This incongruence leads decision makers to focus on the more visible, easier-to-address issues, thereby generating a tactical-level focus rather than creating a strategic vision to address a conflict's broader issues. The lack of integrated planning mechanisms facilitates this tactical focus.

The absence of integrated planning mechanisms enables perspectives concerning agencies' core competencies to frame national interests and intervention criteria, perspectives shaped simultaneously by incongruent worldviews regarding the utility of armed intervention for crisis management. Since these decision makers have difficulty communicating with one another, and even greater problems understanding one another's perspectives, this chasm thwarts their ability to debate the issues openly in a manner that encourages the development of innovative solutions. As a result of circumscribed information exchange, independent planning approaches push ideas to the highest levels of policy development where those least knowledgeable with the contextual specifics synthesize discordant analyses that focus on mutually exclusive aspects of the crisis. In the end, the vacuum related to strategic vision and the independent planning approaches of each agency implicitly establish criteria for professional success in terms of that agency's capacity to respond to crises. One of the salient criteria for success is the decision maker's ability to protect institutional equities.

Defined as any asset that adds value to or is the defining characteristic of an agency, the perceived need to protect institutional equities creates interagency conflict as agencies remain willing to commit their resources only at the margins of conflict intervention. They remain involved but are not committed to creating conditions for sustainable peace. Resources include the tangible assets an agency possesses in concert with its functional expertise. In this manner, institutional equities include personnel and budgets together with functional expertise framed by perceptions of risk and accountability, as informed by prior experience. The need to protect the former, while minimizing the latter in light of this prior experience, creates conflict across agencies as they attempt to define the crisis and determine the roles they are willing to play during intervention.

Factors Creating
Interagency Conflict

The conclusions drawn from these complementary analyses demonstrate that perceptions play a crucial role in creating and exacerbating interagency conflict. These perceptions regarding others' competitive behaviors and perceptions of self-interest amplify stereotypes perpetuated by dissimilar organizational cultures and disparate worldviews. In the absence of an articulated strategic vision, nonintegrated planning processes advance the protection of institutional equities within an environment in which the ambiguity that surrounds roles and missions shapes the interagency negotiation designed to produce a policy outcome. The media influences this decision process, as do perceptions regarding domestic politics. In the end, leaders must set the tone for the decision-making process. They must do so by ensuring that national security decision makers focus on the problem under consideration, not on enhancing their respective agencies' political currency within the bureaucratic arena. This realization provides an appropriate segue into the second issue this research explored, that of the ways in which decision making by negotiation shapes policy choices within the bureaucratic arena.

Decision Making
by Negotiation

USG decision makers formulate conflict termination policy through an interagency negotiation process strongly influenced by the factors just discussed.[7] This conclusion confirms the potency of Allison's work, conclusions developed from analysis of Cuban missile crisis decision making. Reviewing the ways the interagency process identifies the players and establishes bureaucratic boundaries proves of utility as a precondition for integrating findings relating process to outcomes in terms of policy alternatives.[8]

Identifying the Players and Establishing
Rules of the Game

In contravention to the expectations of rational choice theory that demand the "right people be in the right place at the right time," the development of conflict termination policy does not occur through a process wherein decision makers function as a unitary actor. The nature of the policy process dictates that they rarely know their goals, possess limited and incomplete information, experience cognitive limitations, remain bound by resource constraints, and lack the capacity to quantify alternatives. During real-world national security policy-making efforts, the "right people" are determined initially by the interagency process's three-tiered structure—principals, deputies, and interagency working-group actors. More importantly, personal relationships and personality determine the influence official actors have within the structured policy process. These individuals come together to create a group that acts as a "less than rational actor" when judged according to the rational actor model's tenets. The structure of the decision-making process, the "stands" these decision makers take, and the power each exerts within the interagency process all indicate their inability to act as a unitary actor.

In the case of termination policy, the structure of the interagency process establishes what Allison describes as an "action channel" that preselects official players according to three hierarchical levels and thereby determines these actors' points of entry into the decision-making process. First, the principals serve at the highest level and are directly responsible to the statutory members of the NSC.[9] Second, the deputies comprising the next tier serve as the "heavy lifters" to refine and present options to the principals. Finally, the interagency working group serves as the lowest level and is composed of agency representatives who frame the issues and conduct preliminary analyses for the deputies. In addition to this action channel, quasi-official actors influence these decision makers, particularly the principals, through their respective advisory capacities. Collectively, these actors shape policy alternatives.

Policy Alternatives

This study regarding termination policy making supports Allison's precept that decision makers do not make choices as posited by the rational actor model's cost-benefit utility-maximization approach. Rather, the interagency negotiating process produces "political resultants." Decision makers select options in the face of collective value dissensus through a process of social interaction wherein organizational cultures shape choices. Together, these influences generate incongruous reference points and asymmetric perceptions of risk that, in turn, produce dissimilar preference orderings. These dissimilar preference orderings create the "impression" that these decision makers develop policy through a process of negotiation.[10]

The subjectivity of values produces goals that represent the desires and needs of the principal, and hence, by extension, the agency. These desires and needs reflect disparate world-views in the case of termination policy particularly regarding the use of force for crisis management. Such differences produce dissimilar interpretations concerning the nature of the crisis, framing it in terms of disparate interest- or value-laden issues. As this research demonstrated, divergent conceptions of the same problem within a group decision-making environment create interagency conflict over crisis analysis, end-state vision, termination criteria, and termination strategy. Through a negotiation process, the group makes decisions that remain highly dependent upon intra- and interagency interaction.

A product of process structure, the principals, deputies, and interagency working group members remain interdependent actors within the decision-making process. This analysis highlighted the differences in organizational culture that exacerbate unproductive interaction as the actors perpetuate negative stereotypes and misconceptions of core competencies. In this manner, organizational culture ordains the pattern for interaction across agencies by establishing organizational climate, shaping communication, and truncating innovative thinking. As the findings indicated, interaction extends beyond the formal interagency decision-making process to its environment, including relationships with the public, the media, and the Congress. In conjunction with collective value dissensus, these

relationships help define the issues for decision makers by establishing their reference points (i.e., Tversky and Kahneman's
anchoring points),[11] shaping their conceptions of risk, and prioritizing their preference orderings.

Theoretically, the act of framing a situation—both consciously and unconsciously—establishes the starting point for all
decision-making activities. Findings demonstrated that this
theory appears valid—defining the nature of a crisis remains
the most crucial step in conflict termination policy development. This said, crisis definition is influenced by differing reference points that are shaped by decision makers' conceptions
of risk. Simply put, decision makers do indeed treat gains and
losses differently. Defense tends to overvalue anticipated
losses in terms of its institutional equities relative to the comparable gains that others forecast as the most likely outcome
of armed intervention. Taken in conjunction with increased
doubt regarding intervention outcomes, Defense orders its
preferences to minimize anticipated risk. Conversely, State
and the NSC Staff order preferences to maximize potential
gains. The previously cited defects surrounding the interagency process prevent decision makers from integrating multiple frames into a group utility function. Instead, decision
makers' utility functions reflect institutionally defined reference points, perceptions of risk, and preference orderings that
remain salient throughout the negotiation process. These dissimilar factors apply an institutionally based form of rational
choice theory as agencies frame these three factors based
upon "where they sit" within the policy and intervention
processes. In light of these differences, the decision makers interviewed for this study contended they use a negotiating
process to build consensus toward a policy decision. The form
of "negotiation" they cite, however, fails to parallel traditional
conceptions of negotiation and bargaining.[12]

Returning to the original definition set forth in chapter 1, the
crucial difference between a classic negotiation and the interagency policy-making process is that the interagency policy
process does not involve the exchange of formal offers.[13]
Rather, actors explain their positions to other decision makers
by posturing to establish a policy position. As one interagency

participant noted, decision makers "deploy their positions" within an environment characterized by little debate and virtually no "give and take." While some measure of bargaining occurs, decision makers do not "trade" equities in a bargaining fashion. Instead, they agree to alter the commitment of their equities—increase troop deployment levels—with little or no expectation of reciprocal moves regarding others' equities. Through several iterations, the decision makers reach a consensus decision (i.e., a middle ground option—usually suboptimal in the form of a "lowest common denominator") to take to the president as the ultimate responsibility for foreign and security policy rests with the executive. In this manner, one individual can overturn any measure of negotiation that has taken place. While the potential for this to occur remains low, especially if the agencies reach consensus on some of the issues, the ability for one individual to make decisions by fiat ensures that while interagency decision makers view the policy process as a form of negotiation, it is in fact not a negotiation in the classic sense but is a social interaction designed to build consensus toward policy decisions. In this sense, this research supports Zartman's ideas regarding "negotiation as a joint decision-making process."[14]

Summary: Players, Process, and Policy Alternatives

The method by which the players become actors within the interagency process concerned with termination policy ensures that influence results from personal relationships and personalities, not expertise on the issues involved. While these personal relationships provide some actors with greater influence within the process, the structure of the interagency process ensures departmental representation at all policy-making levels. However, their respective institutional affiliations and the action channels through which they gain entry largely predetermine the stands decision makers take on issues. In this manner, decision makers reflect their respective organizational cultures as they attempt to protect their institutional equities. For some, the protection of institutional equities becomes the superordinate objective. Within an environment characterized

326

by increasing risk and uncertainty, the protection of these equities creates interagency conflict as decision makers frame national interests according to disparate worldviews and competing ideologies shaped by divergent perspectives on the employment of force. This collective value dissensus is expressed most clearly during an interagency negotiation process that attempts to reconcile dissimilar reference points, perceptions of asymmetric risk, and incongruent preference orderings.

In combination, these factors ensure that officials make collective choices through a negotiating process that does not follow the tenets of rational choice theory but rather those of the bureaucratic politics model. This necessitates developing policy through a consensus-based approach that generates "political resultants" rather than collective utility-maximizing outcomes.

Policy Outcomes: Interagency Conflict Leads to War Termination

The nature of the gap between diplomacy and war fighting ensures the interagency process develops policy to bring about *war termination* in the form of a cease-fire but fails to achieve *conflict termination* in the form of a sustainable peace. This policy outcome derives from interagency conflict that emanates from defects in leadership, the absence of strategic vision, dissimilar organization cultures, disparate worldviews (i.e., political ideologies and philosophies regarding the use of force), and the absence of an integrated interagency planning mechanism to conduct ongoing crisis analysis and option generation. Together, these factors impede the effective development of crisis analysis, end-state vision, termination criteria, and termination strategy.[15]

Noted earlier in the discussion of reference points, crisis analysis remains the most crucial aspect of policy development. Because decision makers lack strategic vision and focus on tactical-level issues, policy tends to address parts of the conflict system but not the problems engulfing the system as a whole. Further, because the interagency process lacks an integrated planning mechanism and because decision makers exclude issue-specific experts from crisis analysis processes, the policy process fails to address the underlying causes and conditions of conflict, promoting instead a temporary solution to the immediate crisis in the form of a cease-fire. The effects of interagency conflict on envisaging the end state exacerbate this problem further.

The ways in which decision makers frame crises hold great import for the development of the desired end state. By extension, their analysis frames the end-state vision. The "nature of the crisis" determines goals regarding the postintervention environment. Again, the tactical focus employed by the decision makers causes them to frame the end state largely in terms of containing the conflict to prevent spillover. This tactical focus likewise negates the decision maker's ability to envisage the integration of the diplomatic, economic, military, informational, and social/psychological instruments of power in a fashion to bring about long-term systemic change. Such a perspective promotes the development of conflict termination criteria that establish goals in terms of simply ending the fighting.

The focus on inducing or forcing a cease-fire prevents the decision makers from recognizing the relationship between termination criteria and the political objectives that shape the end-state vision. Consequently, the clarity of a cease-fire (in terms of organized hostilities) overshadows the development of other "less assessable" termination criteria. In conjunction with self-limited crisis analysis and the absence of an agreed-upon desired end state, over-reliance upon cease-fire as a verifiable criterion prompts decision makers to frame the remaining termination criteria in ways that fail to induce necessary systemic change but may bring about temporary improvements in a tactical sense. By extension, these factors act in concert to produce an intervention and termination strategy that employs courses of action aimed at ending the physical violence but stopping short of achieving positive systemic change toward sustainable peace.

History credits Yogi Berra with the aphorism, "If you don't know where you want to go, any road will take you there." The validity of this axiom applies in its entirety to termination strategy development. Even though decision makers may agree that something should be done, their inability to define the destination ensures that termination strategy development becomes an exercise in driving without a map (termination criteria) toward an unspecified location (end state) as a product of an incomplete conception of what needs to be done (crisis analysis). The inability to articulate those three elements of conflict termination policy produces an environment wherein development of the fourth—termination strategy—defaults to the lowest common denominator: the use of force to induce cease-fire by creating a hurting stalemate. The absence of an integrated interagency planning mechanism can produce strategy aimed only at creating this temporary cease-fire (war termination) but not sustainable conflict termination. As the Persian Gulf and Bosnia cases illustrate, the application of force cannot terminate conflict for the long-term. Domestic politics magnifies this problem as the American public remains unwilling to accept casualties. Further, the perceived need to demonize the enemy to mobilize public support prompts decision makers to develop strategies that promote conflict escalation through the application of overwhelming force so they can sustain domestic (and international) support for their actions. Coupled with the need to save face, this dynamic ensures decision makers become more psychologically entrapped as they frame prior expenditures of blood and treasure as investments toward future success.[16]

Working synergistically, these boundaries constrain the decision-maker's capacity to consider alternative courses of action, making the use of force to bring about cease-fire the most implementable option irrespective of both short- and long-term consequences of that strategy.

Improving Conflict Termination Policy Development

The most critical aspect of conflict termination policy development relates to the nature of the process-substance and substance-process relationships highlighted throughout this analysis. Simply put, leaders must make their *first priority* that of ensuring the interagency process (1) is allowed to work and

(2) remains energized throughout the life cycle of a crisis. The cases analyzed herein demonstrate that the leaders truncated the interagency process—neither Bush nor Clinton ensured the process worked according to its intended design; hence, neither energized the interagency process to maximize its beneficial properties. While personal relationships can never and should never prevent outside experts and other influential individuals from gaining access to the principals and the president, leaders must make every effort to balance this outside influence by providing access to those who have an institutional role to play in policy development—crisis analysis in particular. This is the first step in "allowing" the process to work; the second requires more vision on the part of the leader.

Leaders need to establish the strategic vision for US foreign and security policy, and hence, the interagency process. They must design this vision with great care, considering domestic politics, the international context, and US national interests. In the absence of such vision from the highest level, agencies will interact competitively in an effort to protect their institutional equities and enhance their political currency. Leaders must be aware of this tendency and must not tolerate such behaviors. This connects with the second aspect of leadership—the idea that leaders must ensure the interagency process *does work* as intended.

The responsibility for educating agencies regarding others' core competencies and limitations rests with the leaders of the agencies (the principals) and the president. Only through immersion in the realities that each agency faces can decision makers diminish the negative stereotypes they hold for one another while narrowing gaps between dissimilar organizational cultures in terms of their understanding of respective core competencies. Closing those gaps will help diminish interagency conflict's harmful effects as impediments to policy development while promoting innovative and integrated crisis analysis and strategy development. Through constructive debate, the interagency process will be empowered to develop conflict termination policy toward sustainable peace.

Envisaging a More
Useful Termination Framework

The realities of group decision making (as depicted by the factors outlined in fig. 3 found in chap. 1 on p. 9) emphasize that the USG does not conduct policy development as a unitary actor. Different decision makers make choices through a bureaucratic negotiation process that provides these actors a means of protecting their institutional equities. Driven by disparate conceptions of strategic vision and nonintegrated planning processes, leadership and domestic politics play a crucial role in framing conflict termination policy. Interagency conflict influences this policy in myriad ways, not the least of which is the development of policy incapable of bringing about a sustainable peace. This said, a new framework for understanding the effects of interagency conflict on conflict termination policy development is warranted.

This model (fig. 25) provides a framework from which it should be possible to derive estimates of the likelihood and degree of interagency conflict. Through future empirical investigation, ideas generated from this improved framework could provide the basis for broadening the decision maker's understanding of the sources and the likely detrimental effects of interagency conflict. Analysis will identify specific areas for process improvement; such improvements could generate conflict termination policy addressing the crisis on the ground, as opposed to its current tendency to address the dynamics within the interagency process itself.

Figure 25 reflects the integrated findings, interpretations, and conclusions generated through this multimethod research. Note that it has six "improved" core factors: leadership style, crisis analysis, interagency behaviors, strategic vision and planning processes, policy-making approach, and NSC's role in policy making. Using a hypothetico-deductive approach, researchers can use discriminate analysis to analyze the indicators within each core factor while estimates for each factor can be derived to determine the level of interagency conflict surrounding policy development. As a heuristic model, researchers and policy makers can develop operational hypotheses using these core factors (and

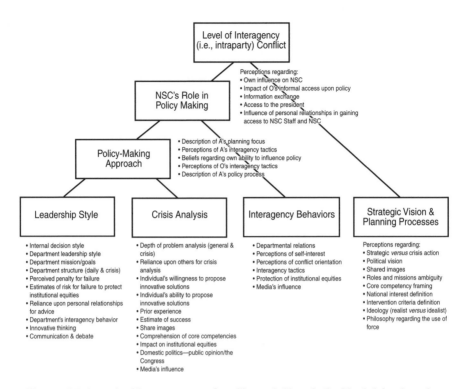

Figure 25. Level of Interagency Conflict—A Heuristic Model for Leaders

their respective indicators) to explore myriad conceptions of interagency conflict. In this manner, this model has utility beyond the US policy-making process as it addresses the organizational dynamics that affect all forms of group decision making, irrespective of organizational setting or issue specificity.

Implications of Relationships across Interagency Conflict

Leadership emerged as the most crucial factor affecting interagency dynamics and conflict termination policy development. Consequently, it serves as the cornerstone of this model. Originally conceived of in terms of dimensions from organizational communication and agency's decision-making profile, this core factor excludes those dimensions the quantitative and qualitative analyses identified as inconsequential (ideology and educational background) while incorporating dimensions that relate to a leader's ability to develop the agency's organizational culture (especially as it relates to intra- and interagency communication). In this manner, a few of the original indicators were retained (penalty for failure, mission/goals, leadership and decision-making styles, departmental structure, and department's interagency behavior). This new conception of leadership likewise includes dimensions related to communication and risk (i.e., communication and debate, innovative thinking, reliance upon personal relationships, and estimates of risk for failure to protect institutional equities). This enhanced core factor addresses the leader's role in developing interagency dynamics. These dimensions of leadership frame approaches to crisis analysis; hence, it becomes the second most influential core factor.

Crisis analysis serves as the second baseline factor of the model since this research revealed that it is a critical factor in crisis framing and developing a strategy to terminate and resolve conflict (see chap. 9). This enhanced approach to crisis analysis includes some of the original dimensions related to perceptions of risk for self (prior experience and estimate of success) but looks beyond those dimensions related to a consideration of the ways in which agencies conduct crisis analysis (depth of problem analysis, reliance upon others, willingness and ability to propose innovative solutions) and the factors that directly affect their crisis framing process (shared images, comprehension of core competencies, institutional equities, domestic politics, and media influence; see chaps. 6–8). Together, leadership and crisis analysis provide the lens through which agencies focus their policy-making approach.

Because this research operationalized two of the four statistically significant relationships supported by the data in the inverse direction and because the qualitative data revealed that stereotypes play a crucial role in developing interagency behaviors, policy-making approach as a core factor remains unchanged in the enhanced model. What becomes important in the new conceptualization, however, is its proximity to

NSC's role in policy making. The estimates derived for policy-making approach can be used in conjunction with those for interagency behaviors to establish an estimate for NSC's Role. Consequently, interagency behaviors emerges as the third baseline core factor.

The quantitative findings generated the conclusion that perceptions of other's self-interest and conflict orientation remained salient factors in developing departmental relations in terms of interagency tactics. Emergent findings from the qualitative analysis revealed that the protection of institutional equities and media influence likewise play a role in shaping interagency dynamics (see chaps. 6–8). Hence, taken in concert with the estimate for policy-making approach, the indicators framing interagency behaviors account for interagency conflict within the policy process leading to the coordinating role played by the NSC system. Note that this model implies a linear conception of the interagency process "leading to" the apex of the interagency process wherein the NSC Staff becomes involved. Obviously, this is not the case in reality as the NSC Staff remains involved throughout the policy process. Yet, figure 25 presents these core factors in this way for two reasons. First, this approach provides a method to operationalize parsimoniously the core factors for future research beyond a heuristic technique. Second, construction of the framework in this manner illuminates the pivotal role the NSC Staff plays in interagency dynamics (i.e., generating, managing, and mitigating interagency conflict; see chap. 8) and policy outcomes (i.e., through its policy coordination and oversight role on behalf of the executive office of the president). Based upon this perspective, let us now discuss the NSC's role.

As with the policy-making approach, the quantitative findings revealed that this research conceptualized two of the three statistically significant relationships related to NSC's Role in the inverse direction. Therefore, this enhanced core factor *retains* those dimensions (perceptions regarding one's own ability to influence NSC and perceptions regarding the impact of other's informal access upon policy). The qualitative findings necessitated expansion of this core factor to include perceptions regarding (1) information exchange, (2) access to the president, and (3) influence of personal relationships in gaining access to the NSC Staff and NSC (see chaps. 6–8). Through these added dimensions, an estimate for NSC's role addresses the perception issues related to interagency behaviors and policy process influence. These dimensions, together with those related to strategic vision and planning processes, determine the level of interagency conflict surrounding the development of conflict termination policy. A new core factor that emerged through the qualitative analysis serves as the final baseline factor in the model.

Through the qualitative analysis, strategic vision and planning processes emerged as the most important contextual parameter. The quantitative data revealed that conceptions of "strategic" versus "crisis action response" planning foci likewise shaped an agency's beliefs regarding its ability to influence policy outcomes. As a result, this core factor includes planning focus in conjunction with those dimensions the qualitative analysis revealed as crucial to the development of strategic vision and planning processes. These dimensions are political vision, shared images, roles and missions ambiguity, core competency framing, national interest and intervention criteria definition, and worldview perspectives—that is, political ideology and philosophy regarding the use of force.

In the final analysis, the level of interagency conflict framework (see fig. 25) integrates the most salient quantitative and qualitative findings that emerged as a result of this multimethod research designed to test hypotheses while providing an avenue for emergent themes to enrich our understanding of the effects of interagency conflict on conflict termination policy development. Through this framework, researchers and analysts can identify those factors that hamper policy development and implementation, irrespective of organizational setting or issue context. After all, while this research used USG decision makers as its unit of analysis, those individuals who comprise the interagency process necessarily reflect the attitudes, beliefs, and perceptions that individuals would reflect during any group decision-making process. Only future empirical research across multiple group decision-making contexts can validate the utility of this bureaucratic model of conflict termination policy.

Conclusion

This analysis developed a sophisticated model of conflict termination policy development. It explored the relationship between the bureaucratic decision-making process (i.e., decision making as negotiation), the US policy-making process (i.e., the interagency process), and conflict termination policy. In doing so, it rendered alternatives to bridge the gap between bureaucratic politics, decision theory, and conflict termination as a step toward conflict resolution.

The research found that the nature of the gap between diplomats and war fighters dominates an interagency process likely to produce a policy bringing about war termination in the form of a cease-fire. However, it almost inevitably fails to achieve conflict termination in the form of sustainable peace. This outcome results largely from interagency conflict that emanates from five key factors: (1) defects in leadership, (2) the absence of strategic vision, (3) dissimilar organization cultures, (4) disparate worldviews (i.e., divergent political ideologies and philosophies regarding the use of force), and (5) the absence of an integrated interagency planning mechanism to conduct ongoing crisis analysis and option generation. Working synergistically and in complex ways, these factors impede the effective development of crisis analysis, the desired end state, termination criteria, and termination strategy. Consequently, this approach ensures that conflict termination—viewed simply as a clear cessation of hostilities—cannot serve *alone* as the first step toward conflict resolution. A cease-fire creates only a temporary pause, not the cessation of organized violence for the long term. This finding holds import for future policy development and research, analyses that must explore further factors that create or intensify interagency conflict and methods by which such conflict can be resolved. Only then can decision makers develop conflict termination policy that addresses the underlying causes and conditions of conflict. Such progress can help the parties in conflict move toward a self-sustaining peace.

Notes

1. The three research questions were (1) What factors exacerbate, intensify, or create interagency conflict within the USG during the development of conflict termination policy? (2) How does "decision making by negotiation" shape policy choices within the USG crisis policy-making arena? and (3) In what ways does interagency conflict influence the USG's capacity to develop conflict termination policy for international conflicts?

2. The first research question framed this inquiry: What factors exacerbate, intensify, or create interagency conflict within the USG during the development of conflict termination policy?

3. Since this research question explores interagency conflict in terms of negative behaviors, the discussion that follows addresses negative competitive behaviors, not positive collaborative behaviors. In light of the conceptual framework undergirding these signed digraphs, reflecting upon the signed digraphs themselves will provide the counterarguments to those presented here.

4. This finding comports with the literature discussing reciprocity and "tit for tat" behaviors. See, for example, Elizabeth Heger Boyle and Edward J. Lawler, "Resolving Conflict through Explicit Bargaining," *Social Forces* 69, no. 4 (1991): 1183–204; see also J. P. Folger, M. S. Poole, and R. K. Stutman, *Working through Conflict: Strategies for Relationships, Groups, and Organizations*, 2d ed. (New York: HarperCollins, 1993); Tetsuo Kondo, "Some Notes on Rational Behavior, Normative Behavior, Moral Behavior, and Cooperation," *Journal of Conflict Resolution* 34, no. 3 (1990): 495–530; Fumie Kumagai and Murray A. Straus, "Conflict Resolution Tactics in Japan, India, and the USA," *Journal of Comparative Family Studies* 14, no. 3 (1983), 377–92; Deborah Welch Larson, "The Psychology of Reciprocity in International Relations," *Negotiation Journal* 4, no. 3 (1988): 281–301; Charles Osgood, "The Grit Strategy," *Bulletin of the Atomic Scientists* (1980): 58–60; Martin Patchen, "Testing Alternative Models of Reciprocity against Interaction During the Cold War," *Conflict Management and Peace Science* 14, no. 2 (1995): 163; see also M. E. Roloff, "Communication and Reciprocity within Intimate Relationships," in *Interpersonal Processes: New Directions in Communication Research*, ed. R. E. Roloff and G. R. Miller (Beverly Hills, Calif.: Sage, 1987); see also M. E. Roloff and D. E. Campion, "Conversational Profit-Seeking: Interaction as Social Exchange," in *Sequence and Pattern in Communicative Behavior*, ed. R. L. Street and J. N. Cappella (London: Edward Arnold, 1985); Benjamin Schneider, "Organizational Behavior," *Annual Review of Psychology* 36 (1985): 573–611; and James D. Westphal and Edward J. Zajac, "Defections from the Inner Circle: Social Exchange, Reciprocity, and the Diffusion of Board Independence in U.S. Corporations," *Administrative Science Quarterly* 42, no. 1 (1997): 161–83.

5. Note that the core factor represented in the original figure 19 subsumes some of these indicators. See figure 25 at the end of this chapter.

6. Some interagency conflict can be positive as it educates other decision makers regarding core competencies and option feasibility.

7. This discussion addresses research question number 2: How does "decision making by negotiation" shape policy choices within the USG crisis policy-making arena? For a more in-depth review of the process-substance factors shaping this decision-making process in terms of leadership, decision making as negotiation, and domestic politics, see chapter 6. Similarly, chapters 7 and 8 provide a broader discussion of the remaining substance-process factors—strategic vision and planning processes, institutional equities, roles and missions, and media influence.

8. The third research question is: In what ways does interagency conflict influence the USG's capacity to develop conflict termination policy for international conflicts?

9. Recall that the principals committee includes two of the four statutory members of the NSC—the secretaries of State and Defense—with the chairman of the Joint Chiefs and director of central intelligence serving in their statutory advisory capacities. The membership then expands via presidential prerogative, with the president and vice president serving as the final two statutory members of the NSC.

10. The decision to use armed forces in Bosnia as part of a NATO Implementation Force reflects this approach. Here, State and Defense officials interacted within a policy-making environment wherein these two agencies defined the crisis in very different ways based upon their dissimilar reference points and perceptions of risk (especially to troops on the ground in the case of Defense). Ultimately, the process of negotiation used to develop the policy generated an "end date" rather than a "desired end state," an outcome that parallels Allison's "political resultant."

11. Amos Tversky and Daniel Kahneman, "Judgment under Uncertainty: Heuristics and Biases," *Science* 185, no. 4157 (1974): 1124–31.

12. The literature on organizational and international bargaining and negotiation continues to enhance our understanding of the dynamics that characterize these social exchange processes. See, for example, Samuel B. Bacharach and Edward J. Lawler, *Power and Politics in Organizations: The Social Psychology of Conflict, Coalitions, and Bargaining* (San Francisco, Calif.: Jossey-Bass, 1980); Samuel B. Bacharach and Edward J. Lawler, "Power Dependence and Power Paradoxes in Bargaining," *Negotiation Journal* 2 (1986): 167–74; Nimet Beriker and Daniel Druckman, "Simulating the Lausanne Peace Negotiations, 1922–1923: Power Asymmetries in Bargaining," *Simulation and Gaming* 27, no. 2 (1996): 162–83; see also Jack Bilmes, "Negotiation and Compromise: A Microanalysis of a Discussion in the United States Federal Trade Commission" (Honolulu: University of Hawaii, 1994); see also Boyle and Lawler, "Resolving Conflict through Explicit Bargaining"; see also J. William Breslin and Jeffrey Z. Rubin, eds., *Negotiation Theory and Practice*, 2d ed. (Cambridge, Mass.: The Program on Negotiation at Harvard Law School, 1993); see also Raymond Cohen, *International Politics: The Rules of the Game* (London: Longman, 1981); John G. Cross, "Negotiation as a Learning Process," in *The Negotiation Process: Theories and Applications*, ed. I. William Zartman (Beverly Hills and London: Sage Publications, 1978),

29–54; Daniel Druckman, "Determinants of Compromising Behavior in Negotiation: A Meta-Analysis," *Journal of Conflict Resolution* 38, no. 3 (1994): 507–56; see also Daniel Druckman, "Dogmatism, Prenegotiation Experience, and Simulated Group Representation as Determinants of Dyadic Behavior in a Bargaining Situation" (PhD, diss., Northwestern University, 1966); Daniel Druckman, "Situational Levers of Position Change: Further Explorations," *Annals of the American Academy of Political and Social Science* 542 (November 1995): 61–80; Daniel Druckman, "Social Psychology and International Negotiations: Processes and Influences," in *Advances in Applied Social Psychology*, ed. Robert F. Kidd and Michael J. Saks (Hillsdale, N.J.: Lawrence Erlbaum Associates, Publishers, 1983): 51–81; Daniel Druckman, "Stages, Turning Points, and Crises: Negotiating Military Base Rights, Spain and the United States," *Journal of Conflict Resolution* 30, no. 2 (1986): 327–60; Daniel Druckman, B. J. Broome, and S. H. Korper, "Value Differences and Conflict Resolution: Facilitation or Delinking?" *Journal of Conflict Resolution* 32, no. 4 (1988): 489–510; Daniel Druckman and Justin Green, "Playing Two Games: Internal Negotiations in the Philippines," in *Elusive Peace: Negotiating an End to Civil Wars*, ed. I. William Zartman (Washington, D.C.: The Brookings Institution, 1995), 55–67; see also Daniel Druckman and P. Terrence Hopmann, "Behavioral Aspects of Negotiations on Mutual Security," in *Behavior, Society, and Nuclear War*, ed. P. E. Tetlock et al. (New York: Oxford University Press, 1989); Daniel Druckman, Jo L. Husbands, and Karin Johnston, "Turning Points in the INF Negotiations," *Negotiation Journal* (1991): 55–67; Daniel Druckman and Robert Mahoney, "Processes and Consequences of International Negotiations," *Journal of Social Issues* 33, no. 1 (1977): 60–87; Christophe Dupont, "Negotiation as Coalition Building," *International Negotiation* 1, no. 1 (1996): 47–64; Ole Elgstrom, "Norms, Culture, and Cognitive Patterns in Foreign Aid Negotiations," *Negotiation Journal* 6, no. 2 (1990): 147–59; M. I. Friedman and W. E. Jacka, "The Negative Effect of Group Cohesiveness on Intergroup Negotiation," *Journal of Social Issues* 225 (1975): 181–94; Paul F. Gerhart, "Determinants of Bargaining Outcomes in Local Government Labor Negotiations," *Industrial and Labor Relations Review* 29, no. 3 (1976): 331–51; P. Terrence Hopmann, "Two Paradigms of Negotiation: Bargaining and Problem Solving," *The Annals of the American Academy of Political and Social Science* 542 (1995): 24–47; Robert Jervis, "Political Implications of Loss Aversion, Special Issue: Prospect Theory and Political Psychology," *Political Psychology* 13 (1992):187–204; see also Peter G. Keen and Michael S. Scott Morton, *Decision Support Systems: An Organizational Perspective* (Reading, Mass.: Addison-Wesley Publishing Co., 1978); Patricia A. Keenan and Peter J. D. Carnevale, "Positive Effects of within-Group Cooperation on between-Group Negotiation," *Journal of Applied Social Psychology* 19, no. 12 (1989): 977–92; Roderick M. Kramer, Pamela Pommerenke, and Elizabeth Newton, "The Social Context of Negotiation: Effects of Social Identity and Interpersonal Accountability on Negotiator Decision Making," *Journal of Conflict Resolution* 37, no. 4 (1993): 633–54; see also Larson, "The Psychology of Reciprocity in

339

International Relations"; Jack S. Levy, "Prospect Theory, Rational Choice, and International Relations," *International Studies Quarterly* 41, no. 1 (1997): 87–112; Zvi Levy, "Negotiating Positive Identity in a Group Care Community: Reclaiming Uprooted Youth," *Child and Youth Services* 16, no. 2 (1993): xv–123; I. E. Morley, J. Webb, and G. M. Stephenson, "Bargaining and Arbitration in the Resolution of Conflict," in *The Social Psychology of Intergroup Conflict*, ed. W. Stroebe et al. (Berlin: Springer-Verlag, 1988), 117–34; Ian E. Morley, "Intra-Organizational Bargaining," in *Employment Relations: The Psychology of Influence and Control at Work*, ed. Jean F. Hartley and Geoffrey M. Stephenson (Oxford: Blackwell, 1992), 203–24; Paul Charles Nutt, "Some Guides for the Selection of a Decision-Making Strategy," *Technological Forecasting and Social Change* 19, no. 2 (1981): 133–45; Jeffrey T. Polzer, "Intergroup Negotiations: The Effects of Negotiating Teams," *Journal of Conflict Resolution* 40, no. 4 (1996): 678–98; see also Dean Pruitt, *Negotiation Behavior* (New York: Academic Press, 1981); see also Dean G. Pruitt and Peter J. Carnevale, *Negotiation in Social Conflict*, ed. Tony Manstead, *Mapping Social Psychology Series* (Pacific Grove: Brooks/Cole Publishing, 1993); Alvin E. Roth, "An Economic Approach to the Study of Bargaining," in *Research on Negotiation in Organizations*, ed. Max H. Bazerman, Roy J. Lewicki, and Blair H. Sheppard, *Handbook of Negotiation Research* (Greenwich & London: JAI Press, Inc., 1991), 35–67; Jeffrey Z. Rubin and I. William Zartman, "Asymmetrical Negotiations: Some Survey Results That May Surprise," *Negotiation Journal* 11, no. 4 (1995): 349–64; John Scanzoni and Deborah D. Godwin, "Negotiation Effectiveness and Acceptable Outcomes," *Social Psychology Quarterly* 53, no. 3 (1990): 234–52; Leigh Thompson, Erika Peterson, and Susan E. Brodt, "Team Negotiation: An Examination of Integrative and Distributive Bargaining," *Journal of Personality and Social Psychology* 70, no. 1 (1996): 66–78; see also Pamela S. Tolbert, "Negotiations in Organizations: A Sociological Perspective," in *Research on Negotiations in Organizations: A Research Annual*; see also James A. Wall, *Negotiation, Theory and Practice* (Glenview, Ill: Scott, Foresman, 1985); see also Richard E. Walton and Robert B. McKersie, *A Behavioral Theory of Labor Negotiations* (New York: McGraw-Hill Book Co., 1965); and I. William Zartman, "Negotiation as a Joint Decision-Making Process," *Journal of Conflict Resolution* 21, no. 4 (1977): 619–38.

13. That is, negotiation can be seen as "a form of conflict behavior" or a process "seeking to resolve the divergence of interest by means of some form of interaction (typically the verbal exchange of offers) between parties." See also Jeffrey Z. Rubin, Dean G. Pruitt, and Sung Hee Kim, *Social Conflict: Escalation, Stalemate, and Settlement*, 2d ed. (New York: McGraw-Hill, Inc., 1994).

14. See also Zartman, "Negotiation as a Joint Decision-Making Process."

15. This discussion applies to research question number 3: In what ways does interagency conflict influence the USG's capacity to develop conflict termination policy for international conflicts? Chapter 9 provides the discus-

sion and analysis of this question, particularly as it applies to termination policy development for the Persian Gulf and Bosnia.

16. For a rich literature on "entrapment," see J. Brockner, "The Escalation of Commitment to a Failing Course of Action: Toward Theoretical Progress," *Academy of Management Review* 17 (1992): 39–61; see also J. Brockner and Jeffrey Z. Rubin, *Entrapment in Escalating Conflicts: A Social Psychological Analysis* (New York: Springer-Verlag, 1985); J. Brockner, M. C. Shaw, and Jeffrey Z. Rubin, "Factors Affecting Withdrawal from an Escalating Conflict: Quitting before It's Too Late," *Journal of Experimental Social Psychology* 15 (1979): 492–503; Tatsuya Kameda and Shinkichi Sugimori, "Psychological Entrapment in Group Decision Making: An Assigned Decision Rule and a Groupthink Phenomenon," *Journal of Personality and Social Psychology* 65, no. 2 (1993): 282–92; C. R. Mitchell, "Classifying Conflicts: Asymmetry and Resolution," *Annals of the American Academy of Political and Social Science* 518 (November 1991): 23–38; Jeffrey Z. Rubin et al., "Factors Affecting Entry into Psychological Traps," *Journal of Conflict Resolution* 24, no. 3 (1980): 405–26; Barry M. Staw, "The Escalation of Commitment to a Course of Action," *Academy of Management Review* 6 (1981): 577–87; Barry M. Staw, "Knee-Deep in the Big Muddy: A Study of Escalating Commitment to a Chosen Course of Action," *Organizational Behavior and Human Performance* 16 (1976): 27–44; see also Barry M. Staw, ed., *Research in Organizational Behavior*, vol. 9 (Greenwich, Conn.: JAI Press, 1987); see also Alan I. Teger, *Too Much Invested to Quit: The Psychology of the Escalation of Conflict* (New York: Pergamon Press, 1980); and Donald Wittman, "How a War Ends: A Rational Approach," *Journal of Conflict Resolution* 23 (1979): 743–63.

Appendix

Participants

I remain indebted to each person who selflessly shared his or her time and expertise. These are the people whose perspectives shaped this work: Absent these professionals, this research would have proven impossible. Through this abridged biographical overview, I have located their expertise within the context of the research (1990–99). Each individual listed below gave explicit, written permission during my initial research to include his or her name and biographic information. To protect their privacy, the individuals named herein have not been specifically identified by quotation within the text.

Institutional affiliations are listed for identification purposes only—the views contained herein do not reflect the official positions of these institutions; rather, the views reflect the perspectives of the individuals.

Morton I. Abramowitz, Advisor, The Rambouillet Talks (1999); Senior Fellow, Council on Foreign Relations (1998–) and The Century Foundation (1998–); President of the Carnegie Endowment for International Peace (1997); Acting President of the International Crisis Group (1997); US Ambassador to Turkey (1989–91); Assistant Secretary of State for Intelligence and Research, US Department of State (1985–89); US Ambassador to the Mutual and Balanced Force Reduction Negotiations in Vienna (1983–84); and US Ambassador to Thailand (1978–81); Deputy Assistant Secretary of Defense for Inter-American, East-Asian, and Pacific Affairs, Office of the Secretary of Defense, US Department of Defense (1974–78)

Graham T. Allison, Douglas Dillon Professor of Government and Director, Belfer Center for Science and International Affairs, Harvard University (1995–); and Assistant Secretary of Defense for Policy and Plans, Office of the Secretary of Defense, US Department of Defense (1993–94)

Edward G. Anderson III, Director for Strategic Plans and Policy, The Joint Staff, US Department of Defense (1998–)

345

Timothy D. Andrews, Deputy Director for Peace Implementation in Bosnia and Herzegovina, US Department of State (1998–)

Anthony N. Banbury, Senior Policy Advisor, Office of the Under Secretary for Policy, Bosnia Task Force, US Department of Defense (1997–); and Political Affairs Official, UN/DPKO (1988–97)

Robert N. Bentley, Analyst—Arabian Peninsula, Office of Near East and South Asia, Bureau of Intelligence and Research, US Department of State

Sheila G. Berry, Special Assistant, Office of War Crimes, US Department of State (1997–); Advisor, Office of the High Representative (1996–97); Special Assistant to the Prosecutor, International Criminal Tribunal for Yugoslavia (1994–96); and International Relations Officer, Office of UN Political Affairs (1992–94)

Hans Binnendijk, Director, Institute for National Strategic Studies, National Defense University; and Principal Deputy Director of the Policy Planning Staff, US Department of State (1993–94)

Ronald M. Bonesteel, Pol-Mil Planner, J-5, The Joint Staff, US Department of Defense

Joseph F. Bouchard, Director for Defense Policy, National Security Council (1997–)

Charles G. Boyd, Director, National Security Studies Group; Deputy Commander in Chief, US European Command, Stuttgart-Vaihingen, Germany (1992–95); and Assistant Deputy Chief of Staff for Plans and Operations, Headquarters US Air Force (1989–90)

Esther D. Brimmer, Senior Associate, Carnegie Commission on Preventing Deadly Conflict (1995–); Special Assistant to the Under Secretary of State for Political Affairs, US Department of State (1993–95); and Foreign Affairs and Defense Analyst, Democratic Study Group, US House of Representatives (1991–93)

George B. Brown III, Chief of Staff, Marine Corps Base, Quantico, US Department of Defense (1995–); and Emergency Action Officer, Counterterrorism Branch, Special Operations

Division, Operations Division, The Joint Staff, US Department of Defense (1988–91)

Keirn C. Brown, Director, European Affairs, National Security Council; Military Assistant to the Under Secretary of Defense for Policy; and US Representative for the Supreme Allied Commander Europe (SACEUR), United States European Command, Belgium

Michael P. C. Carns, President and Executive Director, Center for International Political Economy; Vice Chief of Staff, US Air Force, US Department of Defense (1991–94); and Director, The Joint Staff, US Department of Defense (1989–91)

George W. Casey Jr., Deputy Director for Politico-Military Affairs, J-5, The Joint Staff, US Department of Defense (1997–); and Congressional Program Coordinator, Office of the Chief of Legislative Liaison (1988–89)

Richard B. Cheney, Secretary of Defense, US Department of Defense (1989–93)

David S. C. Chu, Assistant Secretary of Defense for Program Analysis and Evaluation, Office of the Secretary of Defense, US Department of Defense (1988–93)

Vern Clark, Director, The Joint Staff, US Department of Defense (1998–); Director of Operations, The Joint Staff, US Department of Defense (1997–98); and Director, The Joint Staff Crisis Action Team, US Department of Defense (1990–91)

Maria J. E. Copson-Niecko, Balkan Analyst, INR/EUR, US Department of State (1998–); and Senior Policy Advisor, Office of the Under Secretary for Policy, Bosnia Task Force, US Department of Defense (1995–97)

Jock Covey, Distinguished Visiting Fellow, Institute for National Strategic Studies, National Defense University (1998–); Special Assistant to the President for Implementation of the Dayton Peace Accords, National Security Council, The White House (1997–98); and Deputy High Representative, Office of the High Representative, Sarajevo (1995–97)

Barry W. Craigen, Chief, Systems Sustainment Branch, United States Air Force (1998–); and Chief, Senior Officer Management, Air Force/REPS, US Department of Defense (1994–97)

Ivo Daalder, Visiting Fellow, Foreign Policy Studies Program, Brookings Institution; Director, European Affairs, National Security Council (1995–96)

William C. Danvers, Washington Representative for the Organization for Economic Cooperation and Development (1997–99); Special Assistant to the President for National Security Affairs and Senior Director for Legislative Affairs for the National Security Council, The White House (1994–97); Senior Advisor to Strobe Talbott, Ambassador-at-Large and Senior Advisor to the Secretary of State for the New Independent States, US Department of State (1993–94); and Legislative Assistant, US Senate (1989–93)

Richard G. Davis, United States Air Force Historian (1980–)

William K. Davis, Deputy Head of Center for Public Affairs, Organization for Economic Cooperation and Development, Washington Center (1998–); Legislative Management Officer and Senior Advisor, Bureau of Legislative Affairs, US Department of State (1998); and Director/Acting Senior Director for Legislative Affairs, National Security Council, The White House (1995–97)

Terry Deibel, Professor of National Strategy, Department of National Security Policy, National War College, National Defense University (1978–)

J. Nicholas Dowling, Director for European Affairs, National Security Council, The White House (1996–98); and Staff Officer for Bosnian Issues, Office of the Secretary of Defense, US Department of Defense (1993–96)

Nancy Bearg Dyke, Executive Director, International Peace and Security Program, The Aspen Institute (1995–); Director of International Programs and Public Diplomacy, National Security Council, The White House (1998–93); Assistant to the Vice President for National Security Affairs, National Security Council, The White House 1981–82); Principal Deputy Assistant Secretary of the Air Force for Manpower and Personnel, Office of the Secretary of Defense, US Department of Defense (1979–81); Program and Budget Analyst, Congressional Budget Office (1975–77); and Research Assistant and Professional Staff Member, Senate Armed Services Committee (1971–75)

Lawrence S. Eagleburger, Senior Foreign Policy Advisor, Baker, Donelson, Bearman & Caldwell (1993–); Secretary of State, US Department of State (1992–93); and Deputy Secretary of State, US Department of State (1989–92)

Robert W. Farrand, Supervisor of Brcko, Bosnia-Herzegovina; Ambassador Extraordinary and Plenipotentiary, Papua New Guinea, Solomon Islands, and Vanuatu

Joseph N. Flanz, Senior Intelligence Officer, Office of the Under Secretary for Policy, Bosnia Task Force, US Department of Defense (1997–); and Senior Intelligence Officer, Defense Intelligence Agency (1992–97)

Michele A. Flournoy, Distinguished Research Professor, National Defense University (1998–); and Principal Deputy Assistant Secretary of Defense for Strategy and Threat Reduction, Office of the Secretary of Defense, US Department of Defense (1993–98)

Ronald R. Fogleman, Chief of Staff, Headquarters United States Air Force, US Department of Defense (1994–97); CINCUSTRANSCOM, Commander, Air Mobility Command (1992–94); Commander, 7th Air Force, Deputy Command in Chief, United Nations Command; Deputy Commander, US Forces Korea; and Commander, Republic of Korea/US Air Component Command, Combined Forces Command (1990–92)

James H. Fraser, Senior Political/Military Advisor, Office of the Undersecretary of Defense for Policy (1998–), US Department of Defense; and SFOR Headquarters, United Nations Stabilization Force, Zagreb, Croatia (1997)

Charles W. Freeman Jr., Chairman, Projects International, Inc. (1995–); Assistant Secretary of Defense for International Security Affairs, Office of the Secretary of Defense, US Department of Defense (1993–94); US Ambassador to the Kingdom of Saudi Arabia (1989–92); and Principal Deputy Assistant Secretary of State, African Affairs, US Department of State (1986–89)

Peter W. Galbraith, United States Ambassador to the Republic of Croatia (1993–98); Co-Mediator and Architect of the Basic Agreement on Eastern Slavonia, Baranja, and Western Sirmium—the Erdut Agreement (1995); Co-Chairman,

Croatia Peace Negotiations (1994–95); Member, US Negotiating Team for Bosnia-Herzegovina Peace Negotiations—the Dayton Negotiations (1995); and Senior Advisor, Senate Foreign Relations Committee (Near East and South Asia and the Foreign Relations Authorizations Legislation), United States Congress (1979–93)

Robert L. Gallucci, Dean, Georgetown University School of Foreign Service (1996–); Special Assistant to the President and Ambassador at Large, US Department of State (1994–98); Assistant Secretary of State for Political-Military Affairs, US Department of State (1992–94); and Deputy Executive Chairman of the UN Special Commission overseeing the disarmament of Iraq (1991–92)

Georgie Anne Geyer, Syndicated Columnist, *Universal Press Syndicate* (1981–)

Raffi Gregorian, Executive Assistant and Senior Advisor to the US Special Representative for Military Stabilization in the Balkans, US Department of State (1998–)

Stephen Grummon, Director, Office of Near East and South Asian Affairs, INR, US Department of State; and Policy Planning Staff, US Department of State (1991)

Rick Gutwald, Assistant Deputy Director, Pol-Mil Affairs (Europe/Africa), J-5, The Joint Staff, US Department of Defense

Michael J. Habib, Professor, Political Science and Elements of National Power, Industrial College of the Armed Forces, National Defense University; and Director, Eastern European and Yugoslav Affairs, US Department of State (1991–93)

Morton H. Halperin, Director, Policy Planning Staff, US Department of State (1998–); Senior Fellow, Council on Foreign Relations (1996–98); Special Assistant to the President and Senior Director for Democracy, National Security Council, The White House (1994–96); and Consultant to the Secretary of Defense and the Under Secretary of Defense for Democracy and Peacekeeping, US Department of Defense (1993)

Bernard E. Harvey, Strategic Air Campaign Planner, US Department of Defense (1990–91)

John C. Harvey Jr., Assistant to the Under Secretary of Defense for Policy, Office of the Secretary of Defense, US Department of Defense (1998–)

Mark A. Haselton, Strategic Planner, J-5, The Joint Staff, US Department of Defense (1995–)

Leonard R. Hawley, Director, Multilateral Affairs, National Security Council, The White House (1997–)

Donald F. Herr, Senior Research Fellow, Institute for National Strategic Studies (1998–); and Office of NATO Policy, Office of Secretary of Defense, US Department of Defense

Jane E. Holl Lute, Executive Director, Carnegie Commission on Preventing Deadly Conflict, Carnegie Corporation of New York (1994–); and Director for European Affairs, National Security Council, The White House (1991–94)

Fred Charles Iklé, Distinguished Scholar, Center for Strategic and International Studies (1988–); Under Secretary of Defense, Office of the Secretary of Defense, US Department of Defense (1980–88); and Director, Arms Control and Disarmament Agency (1973–77)

Karl Jackson, Professor and Director of Southeast Asian Studies, The School of Advanced International Studies, Johns Hopkins University (1995–); Senior Fellow for International Affairs, Hudson Institute (1993–95); Assistant to the Vice President for National Security Affairs (1991–92); Special Assistant to the President and Senior Director for Asia, National Security Council, The White House (1989–91); and Deputy Assistant Secretary of Defense for East Asia and Pacific, US Department of Defense (1986–89)

Charles J. Jefferson, Senior Policy Advisor, Bureau of Political-Military Affairs, Office of International Security and Peacekeeping, Bureau of Political-Military Affairs, US Department of State (1998–); and Director, Office of Political-Military Analysis, Bureau of Intelligence and Research, US Department of State (1987–95)

David E. Jeremiah, Partner and President, Technology Strategies & Alliances Corporation (1994–); and Vice Chairman, Joint Chiefs of Staff, US Department of Defense (1990–94)

George Joulwan, Supreme Allied Commander, Europe, Supreme Headquarters, Allied Powers Europe/Commander in Chief, United States European Command, Belgium (1993–97)

Greg Kaufmann, Chief of Staff, Office of Secretary of Defense Balkan Task Force (1997–)

James M. Keagle, Professor, Institute for National Strategic Studies, National Defense University (1997–); Senior Strategist, Office of the Secretary of Defense Inter-American Region, US Department of Defense (1996–97); and Acting Director, Office of the Secretary of Defense Bosnia Task Force, US Department of Defense (1994–96)

Zalmay Khalilzad, Program Director, Strategy and Doctrine Program, Project AIR FORCE, RAND (1994–); and Assistant Under Secretary of Defense for Policy Planning, Office of the Secretary of Defense, US Department of Defense (1990–93)

Robert M. Kimmitt, Partner, Wilmer, Cutler & Pickering (1998–); US Ambassador to Germany (1991–93); and Under Secretary of State for Political Affairs, US Department of State (1989–91)

L. Erik Kjonnerod, Senior Fellow and Chief of the Politico-Military Branch, War Gaming and Simulation Center, National Defense University

Jacques Paul Klein, Principal Deputy High Representative, Office of the High Representative in Bosnia and Herzegovina, The Hague (1997–)

Susan J. Koch, Deputy Assistant Secretary of Defense for Threat Reduction Policy, US Department of Defense (1993–); and Assistant Director of the Arms Control and Disarmament Agency for Strategic and Nuclear Affairs (1990–91)

Franklin D. Kramer, Assistant Secretary of Defense for International Security Affairs, Office of the Secretary of Defense, US Department of Defense (1996–); and Deputy Assistant Secretary of Defense for European and NATO Affairs, Office of the Secretary of Defense, US Department of Defense (1996)

Philip G. Laidlaw, Bosnia Desk Officer, US Department of State (1998–); and Political/Military Affairs Officer, Office of European Political and Security Affairs, US Department of State (1997–98)

Ellen Laipson, Vice Chairman, National Intelligence Council (1997–); Special Assistant to the US Ambassador to the United Nations; National Security Council, the White House (1993–95); and National Intelligence Officer, Near East and South Asian Affairs, Central Intelligence Agency (1990–93)

Anthony Lake, Distinguished Professor in the Practice of Diplomacy, The School of Foreign Service, Georgetown University (1997–); and Assistant to the President for National Security Affairs, National Security Council, The White House (1993–97)

J. Michael Lekson, Deputy to the Special Representative of the President and the Secretary of State for Implementation of the Dayton Peace Accords, US Department of State (1998–); Deputy Chief of the United States Mission to the Organization for Security and Cooperation in Europe (1995–98); and Director for Strategic Affairs of European Security and Political Affairs (1991–93)

Jan M. Lodal, Principal Deputy Under Secretary of Defense for Policy, Office of the Secretary of Defense, US Department of Defense (1994–98)

Thomas K. Longstreth, Deputy Under Secretary for Readiness, Office of the Secretary of Defense, US Department of Defense (1998–); Director, Bosnia Task Force, Office of the Secretary of Defense, US Department of Defense (1995–97); and Strategic Planner, The Joint Staff, US Department of Defense (1990–93)

James W. Lucas, Professor of National Security Policy, National War College and Defense Intelligence Agency Executive Representative to the National Defense University, National Defense University (1996–)

David L. Mack, Vice President, The Middle East Institute; Deputy Assistant Secretary of State for Near East Affairs, US Department of State (1990–93); and Ambassador to the United Arab Emirates, US Department of State (1986)

Ronald A. Marks, Special Assistant to the Associate Director of Central Intelligence for Military Support, Central Intelligence Agency

M. Lee McClenny, Director, Press Office, US Department of State (1998–)

Bernd McConnell, Director, Bosnia Task Force, Office of the Under Secretary of Defense for Policy, US Department of Defense (1996–99); and Director, Humanitarian Assistance to the Former Yugoslavia, US Department of Defense (1992–93)

Suzanne M. McCormick, Political Analyst, Office of Near East and South Asia, Bureau of Intelligence and Research, US Department of State

Steven E. Meyer, Professor of Political Science, Industrial College of the Armed Forces, National Defense University; Chief, Director of Central Intelligence Balkan Task Force, Central Intelligence Agency (1995–97)

Mark E. Miller, Chief, Director of Central Intelligence Balkan Task Force, Central Intelligence Agency (1997–)

T. Michael Moseley, Deputy Director Politico-Military Affairs for Asia/Pacific and Middle East, The Joint Staff, US Department of Defense (1997–)

John T. Nelsen II, Chief, Strategy Division, J-5, The Joint Staff, US Department of Defense (1996–)

David A. Nelson, Executive Assistant to the Director, Strategic Plans and Policy, The Joint Staff, US Department of Defense (1998–); and Technology Transfer Planner, Weapons Technology Control Division, Deputy Directorate for International Negotiations, Director for Strategic Plans and Policy (J-5), The Joint Staff, US Department of Defense (1996–98)

Joseph S. Nye Jr., Dean, John F. Kennedy School of Government, Harvard University (1995–); and Assistant Secretary of Defense for International Security Affairs, Office of the Secretary of Defense, US Department of Defense (1994–95)

Robert B. Oakley, Director, Public Security Project and Distinguished Visiting Fellow, the Institute for National

Strategic Studies, National Defense University; Assistant to Vice President for Middle East and South Asia; National Security Council Staff; Deputy Assistant Secretary of State for East Asia Affairs; Special Envoy to Somalia; and Ambassador to Pakistan, US Department of State (1988)

Roberts B. Owen, Presiding Arbitrator for the Brcko Arbitral Tribunal, Bosnia-Herzegovina (1996–99); Arbitrator, Federation of Bosnia and Herzegovina (1995–); and Senior Advisor to the Secretary of State for the Former Yugoslavia (Member of and Legal Advisor to the Holbrooke Negotiating Team, 1995)

James Pardew Jr., Special Representative for Kosovo Implementation and Military Stabilization in the Balkans, US Department of State (1996–)

Robert H. Pelletreau, Assistant Secretary of State for Near Eastern Affairs, US Department of State (1994–97); and Ambassador to Egypt and Member, US delegation to the Madrid Middle East Peace Conference (1991)

David Petraeus, Executive Assistant to the Chairman, Joint Chiefs of Staff (1997–)

Kenneth M. Pollack, Senior Research Professor, Institute for National Strategic Studies, National Defense University (1998–); and Persian Gulf Military Analyst, Central Intelligence Agency and Directorate of Near East and South Asian Affairs, National Security Council

Roman Popadiuk, Deputy Assistant to the President and Deputy Press Secretary for Foreign Affairs, The White House (1989–92)

Diane T. Putney, United States Air Force Historian (1989–)

Steven R. Rader, Senior Analyst, Strategy and Policy Analysis Division, Science Applications International Corporation (1994–); and Coordinator, SHAPE Crisis Response Group, NATO (1992–94)

George E. Rector Jr., Head, Interagency Policy Branch, Policy Division (J-5), The Joint Staff, US Department of Defense (1997–)

John Scott Redd, Director, Strategic Plans and Policy, The Joint Staff, US Department of Defense (1996–98);

355

Commander, Fifth Fleet, US Central Command (1994–96); and Assistant to the Under Secretary of Defense for Policy, Office of the Secretary of Defense, US Department of Defense (1989–91)

Jeffrey C. Remington, Chief, J-5 Policy Division, US Department of Defense (1998–)

Julie M. Reside, Deputy Director, Press Office, US Department of State (1997–)

Condoleeza Rice, Provost, Stanford University (1993–); Director/ Senior Director, Soviet and East European Affairs and Special Assistant to the President for National Security Affairs, National Security Council, The White House (1989–91); and International Affairs Fellow of the Council on Foreign Relations and Special Assistant to the Director of the Joint Chiefs of Staff, The Joint Staff, US Department of Defense (1986)

Edward A. Rice Jr., Deputy Executive Secretary, National Security Council (1997–)

Anne C. Richard, Deputy Chief Financial Officer, The Peace Corps (1997–); Senior Advisor, Secretary's Office of Resources, Plans, and Policy and Advisor, Deputy Secretary's Office of Policy and Resources, US Department of State (1990–97); and Budget Examiner, Office of Management and Budget, Executive Office of the President, The White House (1986–90)

Stephen S. Rosenfeld, Deputy Editorial Page Editor and Columnist, *The Washington Post* (1962–)

Richard Saunders, Deputy National Security Advisor, Office of the Vice President, The White House (1997–); Office of the Vice President, The White House (1993–96)

Kori Schake, Senior Research Professor, Institute for National Strategic Studies, National Defense University (1998–); and Special Assistant to the Assistant Secretary of Defense for Strategy and Requirements (1994–95)

Yvonne E. Schilz, Strategic Planner, J-5, The Joint Staff, US Department of Defense (1996–)

Norman Schindler, Executive Assistant to the Deputy Director for Central Intelligence, Central Intelligence Agency

(1997–); and Chief, Director for Central Intelligence Interagency Balkan Task Force (1994–97)

Gregory L. Schulte, Special Assistant to the President and Director for Implementation of the Dayton Accords, National Security Council, The White House (1998–); and Director, Crisis Management and Operations and Director, Bosnia Task Force, NATO International Staff, Brussels, Belgium (1992–98)

Aric Schwan, Public Affairs Advisor, Bureau of European and Canadian Affairs, US Department of State (1997–)

H. Norman Schwarzkopf, Commander in Chief, United States Central Command, US Department of Defense (1988–91)

Brent Scowcroft, Founder and President, The Forum for International Policy (1994–); and Assistant to the President for National Security Affairs, National Security Council, The White House (1989–92)

Stuart M. Seldowitz, Staff member, Office of the Special Representative of the President and Secretary of State for Implementation of the Dayton Peace Accords, US Department of State (1997–); and Action Officer for the Crisis in the Former Yugoslavia, US Mission to the United Nations (1991)

Sarah Sewall, Deputy Assistant Secretary of Defense for Peacekeeping and Humanitarian Assistance, US Department of Defense (1993–96)

John M. Shalikashvili, Chairman of the Joint Chiefs of Staff, US Department of Defense (1993–97); Supreme Allied Commander, Europe, Supreme Headquarters, Allied Powers Europe/Commander in Chief, United States European Command, Belgium (1992–93); Assistant to the Chairman, Joint Chiefs of Staff, The Joint Staff, US Department of Defense (1991–92)

John A. Shaud, Executive Director, Air Force Association, Washington, D.C. (1995–); and Chief of Staff, Supreme Headquarters Allied Powers Europe (1988–91)

Michael A. Sheehan, Coordinator for Counterterrorism, US Department of State (1998); Deputy Assistant Secretary, Bureau of International Organization Affairs, US Department of State (1997–98); Director of International

Organizations and Peacekeeping, National Security
Council, The White House (1995–97); Director of Political
Military Affairs and Special Counselor to Ambassador
Madeleine Albright, US Mission to the United Nations
(1993–95); and Director for International Programs,
National Security Council, The White House (1989–93)

Robert F. Simmons Jr., Senior Advisor to the Assistant
Secretary of State for European Affairs, the 1999 NATO
Summit, and European Nuclear, Arms Control, and Non-
proliferation Issues, US Department of State (1998–);
Deputy Director, Office of Regional Political and Security
Issues, Bureau of European and Canadian Affairs, US
Department of State (1995–98); and Deputy Political
Advisor, US Mission to NATO and US Representative to
the NATO Political Committee, US Department of State
(1989–93)

Charles R. Snyder, Director, Office of African Regional Affairs,
African Affairs Bureau, US Department of State (1995–);
and National Intelligence Officer for Africa, US Central
Intelligence Agency (1992–95)

Greg Steele, Executive Assistant, Director for Strategic Plans
and Policy, The Joint Staff, US Department of Defense
(1997–)

James W. Swigert, Director, Office of North Central European
Affairs, US Department of State (1998–)

Charles Thompson, Chief, Politico-Military Affairs Division
(Middle East), US Department of Defense

Wayne Thompson, Persian Gulf War "Checkmate" Planning
Cell Historian, US Department of Defense (1989–90); and
United States Air Force Historian (1975–)

Gwenyth E. Todd, Director for Near East and South Asian Affairs
(1997–); and Special Assistant to the Deputy Under
Secretary of Defense for Policy, Office of the Secretary of
Defense, US Department of Defense (1996–97)

Alan E. Van Egmond, Senior Policy Advisor, Office of the Under
Secretary of Defense for Policy Balkan Task Force, US
Department of Defense (1996–)

Roderick K. von Lipsey, Director, Defense Policy, National
Security Council, The White House (1997–); and Aide to

the Chairman of the Joint Chiefs of Staff, The Joint Staff, US Department of Defense (1991–93)

Peter K. Walsh, J-2 Deputy Chief, Director of Central Intelligence Interagency Balkan Task Force (1998–)

John A. Warden III, Strategic Air Campaign Planner, US Department of Defense (1990–91)

Edward L. Warner III, Assistant Secretary of Defense for Strategy and Threat Reduction, Office of the Secretary of Defense, US Department of Defense (1993–)

Kenneth C. Westbrook, Deputy Chief, DCI Interagency Balkan Task Force (1998–)

Alan G. Whittaker, Professor of Political Science, Industrial College of the Armed Forces, National Defense University (1990–); and Intelligence Officer, Office of the Director for Central Intelligence, Central Intelligence Agency (1983–90)

Thomas J. Wilson III, Chief, Pacific Command Division, Current Operations Directorate, The Joint Staff, US Department of Defense (1998–)

Richard H. Witherspoon, Senior Analyst, Strategy and Policy Analysis Division, Science Applications International Corporation (1995–); and Chief, SHAPE Liaison Office, US Department of Defense (1992–95); Army Member, Chairman's Staff Group, The Joint Staff, US Department of Defense (1990–92)

Paul Wolfowitz, Dean, The Paul H. Nitze School of Advanced International Studies, Johns Hopkins University (1994–); Under Secretary of Defense for Policy, Office of the Secretary of Defense, US Department of Defense (1989–93); US Ambassador to the Republic of Indonesia (1986–89); and Assistant Secretary of State for East Asian and Pacific Affairs, US Department of State (1982–86)

Susan L. Woodward, Senior Fellow, Brookings Institution (1990–); Professorial Lecturer, School for Advanced International Studies, Johns Hopkins University (1997–99); and Head, Analysis and Assessment Unit, Office of the Special Representative of the Secretary General, United Nations Protection Forces, Zagreb, Croatia (1994)

Judith S. Yaphe, Officer-in-Residence, Center for the Study of Intelligence, Central Intelligence Agency (1997–); Senior Analyst, Near East and South Asian Analysis (1993–95); and Senior Analyst, Persian Gulf Division, Central Intelligence Agency (1989–95)

Warren Zimmermann, Kathryn and Shelby Cullom Davis Professor in the Practice of International Diplomacy, School of International and Public Affairs, Columbia University (1997–); Director, Bureau of Refugee Programs, US Department of State (1992–94); Ambassador to Yugoslavia, US Department of State (1989–92)

Acronyms

ACDA	Arms Control and Disarmament Agency
AFIS	American Forces Information Service
APNSA	Assistant to the President for NSA
CAP	Combat Air Patrols
CIA	Central Intelligence Agency
CINC	Commander in Chief
CJCS	Chairman of the Joint Chiefs of Staff
COA	Course of Action
CS	Chief of Staff (White House, unless otherwise indicated)
DC	Deputies Committee (of the NSC, NSC/DC)
DCI	Director of Central Intelligence
DCI/IABTF	Director of Central Intelligence Interagency Balkan Task Force
DIA	Defense Intelligence Agency
DOD	Department of Defense
DOS	Department of State
ENO	Enticing Opportunity Model
ENT	Entrapment Model
EOP	Executive Office of the President
FOIA	Freedom of Information Act
GAO	Government Accounting Office
HERO	Historical Evaluation Research Organization
HS	Hurting Stalemate
IFOR	Implementation Force
IMC	Imminent Mutual Catastrophe
INR	State's Bureau of Intelligence and Research
JCS	Joint Chiefs of Staff
NAC	North Atlantic Council
NEA	Bureaus of Near East Affairs
NEC	National Economic Council
NEO	Noncombatant Evacuation Operation
NRO	National Reconnaissance Office
NSA	National Security Agency

NSC	National Security Council
OSD	Office of the Secretary of Defense
PC	Principals Committee (of the NSC, NSC/PC)
PCC	Policy Coordinating Committees (of the NSC; NSC/PCC)
PDD	Presidential Decision Directive
PMA	Political Military Affairs
SECDEF	Secretary of Defense
SECST	Secretary of State
SP	Strategic Planning
SVTC	Secure Video Teleconferencing System
USACAPOCUS	Army Civil Affairs and Psychological Operations Command
USAF	United States Air Force
USG	United States Government
USIA	United States Information Agency
VP	Vice President

Bibliography

Abelson, R. P. "Script Processing in Attitude Formation and Decision-Making." In *Cognition and Social Behavior.* J. S. Carroll and J. W. Payne, eds. Hillsdale, N.J.: Erlbaum Assoc., 1976.

Abelson, R. P., and A. Levi. "Decision Making and Decision Theory." In *Handbook of Social Psychology.* G. Lindzey and E. Aronson, eds. New York: Random House, 1985.

Abt, Clark C. "The Termination of General War." PhD diss., Massachusetts Institute of Technology, 1965.

Abt, Frederic E. *The Operational End State: Cornerstone of the Operational Level of War.* Fort Leavenworth, Kans.: US Army Command and General Staff College, 1988.

Affisco, John F., and Michael N. Chanin. "An Empirical Investigation of Integrated Multicriteria Group Decision Models in a Simulation/Gaming Context." *Simulation & Gaming* 21, no. 1 (1990): 27–47.

AFIS/OASD-PA, American Forces Information Service. *Early Bird.* Washington, D.C.: Current News Service, The Pentagon, 1998.

AFSC, Armed Forces Staff College. *AFSC Pub 1: The Joint Staff Officer's Guide.* Washington, D.C.: Government Printing Office (GPO), 1993.

Air Force Doctrine Document (AFDD) 2. *Organization and Employment of Aerospace Power,* HQ AFDC/DR (Lt Col D. Robert Poynor, ed.), Maxwell AFB, Ala.: Headquarters Air Force Doctrine Center, 17 February 2000.

Ajami, Fouad. "The Summer of Arab Discontent." *Foreign Affairs* 69 (winter 1990–91): 1–20.

————. "Strangers in Araby." *U.S. News & World Report,* 23 February 1998, 7.

Ajdukovic, Marina. "Psychosocial Aspects of Nonviolent Resolution of Conflicts; Psihosocijalni Aspekti Nenasilnog Rjesavanja Sukoba." *Drustvena Istrazivanja* 4, no. 1 (1995): 49–55.

Albert, Stuart, and Edward C. Luck, eds., *On the Endings of War.* Port Washington, N.Y.: Kennikat Press, 1980.

Ali, Yousef G., and Katherine Meyer. "Kuwait: Adaptation and Change." Columbus, Ohio: Dept. of Sociology, Ohio State University, 1994.

Allard, Kenneth. *Somalia Operations: Lessons Learned.* Washington, D.C.: National Defense University Press, 1995.

Allison, Graham T. *Essence of Decision: Explaining the Cuban Missile Crisis.* Boston: Little, Brown and Co., 1971.

———. "Conceptual Models and the Cuban Missile Crisis." In *International Relations: Contemporary Theory and Practice.* G. A. Lopez and M. S. Stohl, eds. Washington, D.C.: CQ Press, 1989, 107–32.

Allison, Scott T.; Anna Marie R. Jordan; and Carole E. Yeatts. "A Cluster-Analytic Approach toward Identifying the Structure and Content of Human Decision-Making." *Human Relations* 45, no. 1 (1992): 49–72.

Allison, Scott T.; Leila T. Worth; and Melissa W. Campbell King. "Group Decisions as Social Inference Heuristics." *Journal of Personality and Social Psychology* 58, no. 5 (1990): 801–11.

Allotey, Sam, et al. *Planning and Execution of Conflict Termination.* Maxwell Air Force Base, Ala.: Air Command and Staff College, 1995.

Allport, Gordon W. *The Nature of Prejudice.* New York: Anchor Books, 1958.

Anderson, Alan B. "The Changing Situation of Ethnolinguistic Minorities Along the Yugoslavian Frontier." *Canadian Review of Studies in Nationalism/Revue Canadienne des Etudes sur le Nationalisme* 16, no. 1–2 (1989): 263–75.

Anderson, James E. *Public Policy-Making.* New York: Praeger, 1975.

Anderson, James H. "End State Pitfalls: A Strategic Perspective." *Military Review* 77, no. 5 (1997): 93–95.

Andrews, Katherine Zoe. "Strategic Decision Making: It's All in the Process." *Harvard Business Review* 73, no. 5 (1995): 10–11.

Andriole, Stephen J. "Decision Process Models and the Needs of Policy-Makers: Thoughts on the Foreign Policy Interface." *Policy Sciences* 11, no. 1 (1979): 19–37.

Apprey, Maurice. "Heuristic Steps for Negotiating Ethno-National Conflicts: Vignettes from Estonia." *New Literary History* 27, no. 2 (1996): 199–212.

Argyris, Chris, and M. D. Cohen. "Single-Loop and Double-Loop Models in Research on Decision Making." *Administrative Science Quarterly* 21, no. 3 (1976): 363–75.

Arrow, Kenneth J. "Risk Perception in Psychology and Economics." *Economic Inquiry* 20 (1982): 1–9.

———. "Rationality of Self and Others in an Economic System." In *Decision Making: Alternatives to Rational Choice Models*, Ed. Mary Zey. Newbury Park, Calif.: Sage Publications, 1992.

Asch, Solomon E. "Effects of Group Pressure Upon the Modification and Distortion of Judgments." In *Classic Readings in Organizational Behavior*, ed. J. S. Ott. Pacific Grove, Calif.: Brooks/Cole Publishing Co., 1989.

Atkinson, Rick. *Crusade: The Untold Story of the Persian Gulf War.* New York: Houghton Mifflin, 1993.

Aukofer, Frank, and William P. Lawrence. *America's Team: The Odd Couple—A Report on the Relationship between the Media and the Military.* Nashville, Tenn.: The Freedom Forum First Amendment Center, 1995.

Avital, Eytan, and Eva Jablonka. "Social Learning and the Evolution of Behaviour." *Animal Behaviour* 48, no. 5 (1994): 1195–99.

Babbie, Earl. *The Practice of Social Research.* 5th ed. Belmont, Calif.: Wadsworth Publishing Co., 1989.

———. *Survey Research Methods.* 2d ed. Belmont, Calif.: Wadsworth Publishing Co., 1990.

Babbitt, Eileen F. "Gulf War Mediation Efforts Offered Too Little, Too Late." *Negotiation Journal* 8, no. 1 (1992): 37–39.

Bacharach, Samuel B., and Edward J. Lawler. *Power and Politics in Organizations: The Social Psychology of Conflict, Coalitions, and Bargaining.* San Francisco, Calif.: Jossey-Bass, 1980.

———. "Power Dependence and Power Paradoxes in Bargaining." *Negotiation Journal* 2 (1986): 167–74.

Bade, Bruce C. *War Termination: Why Don't We Plan for It?* Washington, D.C.: National War College, 1994.

Bahramzadeh, Mohammad Ali. "The US Foreign Policy in the Persian Gulf, 1968–1988: From Regional Surrogate to Direct Military Involvement." PhD diss., University of Arizona, 1993.

Bair, Andrew. "Which End-Game in Bosnia?" *Strategic Forum*, no. 16 (1995).

Baker, James A., III. *The Politics of Diplomacy: Revolution, War, and Peace, 1989–1992.* New York: G. P. Putnam's Sons, 1995.

Baker, Sally Hillsman, et al. "Tolerance for Bureaucratic Structure: Theory and Measurement." *Human Relations* 26, no. 6 (1973): 775–86.

Banac, Ivo. "The Destruction of Yugoslavia: Tracking the Break-up, 1980–92." *Foreign Policy*, no. 93 (winter 1993–1994): 76–90.

Banks, Michael. "Four Conceptions of Peace." In *Conflict Management and Problem Solving: Interpersonal to International Applications.* Dennis J. D. Sandole and Ingrid Sandole-Staroste, eds. New York: New York University Press, 1987, 259–74.

Bantel, Karen A. "Comprehensiveness of Strategic Planning: The Importance of Heterogeneity of a Top Team." *Psychological Reports* 73, no. 1 (1993): 35–49.

Barnard, Chester. *The Functions of the Executive* Cambridge, Mass.: Harvard University Press, 1938.

Barnett, Jeffery R. "Exclusion as National Security Policy." *Parameters* 24, no. 1 (1994): 51–65.

Barringer, Richard E., with the collaboration of Robert K. Ramers. *War: Patterns of Conflict.* Cambridge, Mass.: MIT Press, 1972.

Barry, Charles. "After IFOR: Maintaining a Fragile Peace in the Balkans." *Strategic Forum*, no. 62 (1996).

Bartos, Otomar. "Negotiation as Friendship Formation." *International Negotiations* 1, no. 1 (1996): 29–46.

Bateson, G. *Steps to an Ecology of Mind.* San Francisco, Calif.: Chandler, 1972.

Beach, Lee Roy. "Broadening the Definition of Decision Making: The Role of Pre-choice Screening of Options." *Psychological Science* 4, no. 4 (1993): 215–20.

Beach, L. R., and T. R. Mitchell. "A Contingency Model for the Selection of Decision Strategies." *Academy of Management Review* 3 (1978): 439–44.

Beach, Lee Roy, et al. "Image Theory: Decision Framing and Decision Liberation." In *Decision-Making and Leadership.* Frank Heller, ed. Cambridge: Cambridge University Press, 1992, 172–88.

Beamish, Thomas D.; Harvey Molotch; and Richard Flacks. "Who Supports the Troops? Vietnam, the Gulf War, and the Making of Collective Memory." *Social Problems* 42, no. 3 (1995): 344–60.

Beatty, Michael J. "Group Members' Decision Rule Orientations and Consensus." *Human Communication Research* 16, no. 2 (1989): 279–96.

Beer, Francis A., and Thomas F. Mayer. "Why Wars End: Some Hypotheses." *Review of International Studies* 12 (1986): 95–106.

Belk, Russell W. "It's the Thought That Counts: A Signed Digraph Analysis of Gift-Giving." *Journal of Consumer Research* 3, no. 3 (1976): 155–62.

Belliveau, Lorraine M., and John F. Stolte. "The Structure of Third Party Intervention." *Journal of Social Psychology* 103, no. 2 (1977): 243–50.

Ben Zvi, Abraham. "The Outbreak and Termination of the Pacific War: A Juxtaposition of American Preconceptions." *Journal of Peace Research* 15, no. 1 (1978): 33–49.

Bendor, J., and T. H. Hammond. "Rethinking Allison's Models." *American Political Science Review* 86 (1992): 301–22.

Bennett, Peter, and Steve Cropper. "Uncertainty and Conflict: Combining Conflict Analysis and Strategic Choice." *Journal of Behavioral Decision-Making* 3, no. 1 (1990): 29–45.

Berger, Samuel R., National Security Affairs. Address. "The Road Forward in Bosnia." Washington, D.C.: Georgetown University Press, 23 September 1997.

Beriker, Nimet, and Daniel Druckman. "Models of Responsiveness: The Lausanne Peace Negotiations (1922–1923)." *Journal of Social Psychology* 131, no. 2 (1991): 297–300.

———. "Simulating the Lausanne Peace Negotiations, 1922–1923: Power Asymmetries in Bargaining." *Simulation and Gaming* 27, no. 2 (1996): 162–83.

Berkeley Campus Peace Committee, University of California. "Gulf War: Questions and Answers." University of California, Berkeley, 1991.

Berk, Jonathan B.; Eric Hughson; and Kirk Vandezande. "The Price Is Right, but Are the Bids? An Investigation of Rational Decision Theory." *American Economic Review* 86, no. 4 (1996): 954–70.

Berry, F. S. *Impact of the 1973 War Powers Resolution on the Military*. Carlisle Barracks, Pa.: US Army War College, 1989.

Bettenhausen, Kenneth, and J. Keith Murnighan. "The Emergence of Norms in Competitive Decision-Making Groups." *Administrative Science Quarterly* 30, no. 3 (1985): 350–72.

Beveridge, Reid K. "End of Pan Arabism." *National Guard* 45 (1991): 14–15.

Bilmes, Jack. "Negotiation and Compromise: A Microanalysis of a Discussion in the United States Federal Trade Commission." In A. Firth, ed. *The Discourse of Negotiation: Studies of Language in the Workplace*. New York: Pergamon Press, 1995.

Bin Sultan, Khaled. *Desert Warrior: A Personal View of the Gulf War by the Joint Forces Commander*. New York: HarperCollins Publishers, 1995.

Black, Jerome H. "The Probability-Choice Perspective in Voter Decision Making Models." *Public Choice* 35, no. 5 (1980): 565–74.

Black, Max. "Making Intelligent Choices: How Useful Is Decision Theory?" *Dialectica* 39, no. 1 (1985): 19–34.

Blainey, Geoffrey. "Past and Future Wars." In *International Conflict Resolution*, ed. Ramesh Thakur. Boulder: Westview Press, 1989, 91–104.

Bloomfield, Lincoln P. *The Foreign Policy Process: A Modern Primer*. Englewood Cliffs, N.J.: Prentice-Hall, Inc., 1982.

Blumer, H. *Symbolic Interaction.* Englewood Cliffs, N.J.: Prentice-Hall, 1969.

Bonham, G. Matthew; Michael J. Shapiro; and George J. Nozicka. "A Cognitive Process Model of Foreign Policy Decision-Making." *Simulation and Games* 7, no. 2 (1976): 123–52.

Boone, Larry W. "An Assessment of Organizational Decision-Making for Simple and Complex Problems." PhD diss., University of Pittsburgh, 1987.

Bornstein, Gary; Danny Mingelgrin; and Christel Rutte. "The Effects of Within-Group Communication on Group Decision and Individual Choice in the Assurance and Chicken Team Games." *Journal of Conflict Resolution* 40, no. 3 (1996): 486–501.

Bornstein, Gary, et al. "Within- and Between-Group Communication in Intergroup Competition for Public Goods." *Journal of Experimental Social Psychology* 25 (1989): 422–36.

Boschi, Renato Raul, and Eli Diniz Cerqueira. "The Bureaucracy, Its Clientele and Power Relations: A Theoretical Model." *Dados* 17 (1978): 97–116.

Bostick, Wallace E. "Selected Factors Involved in War Termination." Carlisle Barracks, Pa.: US Army War College, 1975.

Boulding, Kenneth E. "Peace Research." *International Social Science Journal* 29, no. 4 (1977): 601–14.

Boutros-Ghali, Boutros. "Leadership and Conflict." In *Essays on Leadership: Perspectives on Prevention.* New York: Carnegie Corp. of New York, 1998.

Boutros-Ghali, Boutros, et al. *Essays on Leadership: Perspectives on Prevention.* New York: Carnegie Corp. of New York, 1998.

Bowden, Mark. *Black Hawk Down: A Story of Modern War.* New York: Atlantic Monthly Press, 1999.

Bowen, Elinor R. "The Pressman-Wildavsky Paradox: Four Addenda or Why Models Based on Probability Theory Can Predict Implementation Success and Suggest Useful Tactical Advice for Implementers." *Journal of Public Policy* 2, no. 1 (1982): 1–21.

Bower, Joseph L. "The Role of Conflict in Economic Decision Making Groups: Some Empirical Results." *The Quarterly Journal of Economics* 79, no. 2 (1965): 263–77.

Bowey, Angela M. "Approaches to Organization Theory." *Social Science Information/Information sur les Sciences Sociales* 11, no. 6 (1972): 109–28.

Boyle, Brett A., and F. Robert Dwyer. "Power, Bureaucracy, Influence, and Performance: Their Relationships in Industrial Distribution Channels." *Journal of Business Research* 32 (1995): 189–200.

Boyle, Elizabeth Heger, and Edward J. Lawler. "Resolving Conflict through Explicit Bargaining." *Social Forces* 69, no. 4 (1991): 1183–204.

Bremer, Stuart A., and Thomas R. Cusack, eds. *The Process of War: Advancing the Scientific Study of War*. Luxembourg: Gordon and Breach Publishers, 1995.

Brennan, Geoffrey. "What Might Rationality Fail to Do?" In *Decision Making: Alternatives to Rational Choice Models*, ed. Mary Zey. Newbury Park, Calif.: Sage Publications, 1992.

Brennan, Timothy J. "Talking to One's Selves: The Social Science of Jon Elster—Ulysses and the Sirens: Studies in Rationality and Irrationality by Jon Elster/Sour Grapes by Jon Elster/the Cement of Society by Jon Elster/and Others." *Journal of Communication* 44, no. 1 (1994): 73.

Breslin, J. William, and Jeffrey Z. Rubin, eds. *Negotiation Theory and Practice*. 2d ed. Cambridge, Mass.: The Program on Negotiation at Harvard Law School, 1993.

Brewer, Thomas L. "Issue and Context Variations in Foreign Policy: Effects on American Elite Behavior." *Journal of Conflict Resolution* 17, no. 1 (1973): 89–114.

Brockner, J. "The Escalation of Commitment to a Failing Course of Action: Toward Theoretical Progress." *Academy of Management Review* 17 (1992): 39–61.

Brockner, J., and Jeffrey Z. Rubin. *Entrapment in Escalating Conflicts: A Social Psychological Analysis*. New York: Springer-Verlag, 1985.

Brockner, J., M. C. Shaw, and Jeffrey Z. Rubin. "Factors Affecting Withdrawal from an Escalating Conflict: Quitting before

It's Too Late." *Journal of Experimental Social Psychology* 15 (1979): 492–503.

Brown, Gordon S. *Coalition, Coercion, & Compromise: Diplomacy of the Gulf Crisis, 1990–91.* Washington, D.C.: The Institute for the Study of Diplomacy, Georgetown University, 1997.

Brune, Lester H. *America and the Iraqi Crisis, 1990–1992: Origins and Aftermath.* Claremont, Calif.: Regina Books, 1993.

Bruszt, Laszlo, and George K. Horvath. "1989: The Negotiated Revolution in Hungary." *Social Research* 57, no. 2 (1990): 365–87.

Brzezinski, Zbigniew, and Brent Scowcroft. *Differentiated Containment: U.S. Policy toward Iran and Iraq.* On-line. Council on Foreign Relations, 1997. Internet (cited 26 March 1999). Available from http://www.foreignrelations.org/studies/transcripts/contain.html.

Bueno de Mesquita, Bruce. *The War Trap.* New Haven, Conn.: Yale University Press, 1981.

———. "The Costs of War: A Rational Expectations Approach." *The American Political Science Review* 77 (1983): 347–57.

———. "The War Trap Revisited: A Revised Expected Utility Model." *The American Political Science Review* 79 (1985): 156–77.

Bunn, D. W. "Policy Analytic Implications for a Theory of Prediction and Decision." *Policy Sciences* 8, no. 2 (1977): 125–34.

Burns, James MacGregor. *Leadership.* New York: Harper & Row, 1978.

Bush, George. *Address before a Joint Session of the Congress on the State of the Union.* 29 January 1991. On-line. Internet (cited 1 December 1998). Available from http://www.csdl.tamu.edu/bushlib/papers/1991/91012902.html.

———. "Against Aggression in the Persian Gulf." *US Department of State Dispatch* 1, no. 1 (1990).

———. "America's Role in the World." *US Department of State Dispatch* 4, no. 2 (1993).

———. "America's Stand against Aggression." *US Department of State Dispatch* 1, no. 1 (1990).

———. "American Leadership and the Prevention of Deadly Conflict." In *Essays on Leadership: Perspectives on Prevention.* New York: Carnegie Corporation of New York, 1998.

———. "The Arabian Peninsula: US Principles." *US Department of State Dispatch* 1, no. 1 (1990).

———. "A Collective Effort to Reverse Iraqi Aggression." *US Department of State Dispatch* 1, no. 2 (1990).

———. "Crisis in the Gulf." *US Department of State Dispatch* 2, no. 2 (1991).

———. "Crisis in the Persian Gulf." *US Department of State Dispatch* 1, no. 17 (1990).

———. *Gulf War.* On-line. The George Bush Presidential Library, 1999. Internet (cited 3 April 1999). Available from http://www.csdl.tamu.edu/bushlibrary/library/research/research.html.

———. "The Gulf: A World United against Aggression." *US Department of State Dispatch* 1, no. 14 (1990).

———. "Iraq Responsible for US Hostages." *US Department of State Dispatch* 1, no. 2 (1990).

———. "Letter Saddam Hussein." *US Department of State Dispatch* 2, no. 2 (1991).

———. "Letter to Congress." *US Department of State Dispatch* 2, no. 2 (1991).

———. "Liberation of Kuwait." *US Department of State Dispatch* 2, no. 3 (1991).

———. "Opening Session of Middle East Peace Conference." *US Department of State Dispatch* 3, no. 2 (1992): 8–9.

———. "Operation Desert Storm Is Working." *US Department of State Dispatch* 2, no. 4 (1991).

———. "Operation Desert Storm Launched." *US Department of State Dispatch* 2, no. 3 (1991).

———. "Persian Gulf Crisis: Going the Extra Mile for Peace." *US Department of State Dispatch* 2, no. 1 (1991).

———. "Persian Gulf War: Supporting a Noble Cause." *US Department of State Dispatch* 2, no. 5 (1991).

———. "Radio Address to the Nation." *US Department of State Dispatch* 2, no. 1 (1991).

———. "The State Department: On the Front Lines of US Interests Abroad." *US Department of State Dispatch* 2, no. 13 (1991).

———. "State of the Union Address." *US Department of State Dispatch* 2, no. 5 (1991).

———. "Statement from Baghdad: A Cruel Hoax." *US Department of State Dispatch* 2, no. 7 (1991).

———. "Statement on Resolution 687." *US Department of State Dispatch* 2, no. 14 (1991).

———. *Statement on the United Nations Security Council Resolution Authorizing the Use of Force against Iraq.* On-line. The George Bush Presidential Library, 1990. Internet (cited 3 April 1999). Available from http://www.csdl.tamu.edu/bushlibrary/library/research/research.html.

———. "Taped Address to the Iraqi People." *US Department of State Dispatch* 1, no. 4 (1990).

———. "Thanksgiving Day Address to US Forces in Saudi Arabia." *US Department of State Dispatch* 1, no. 13 (1990).

———. "US Action in the Gulf: A Matter of Principle." *US Department of State Dispatch* 1, no. 5 (1990).

———. "The World after the Persian Gulf War." *US Department of State Dispatch Supplement* 3, no. 2 (1992): 1–3.]

Bush, George, and Brent Scowcroft. *A World Transformed.* New York: Alfred A. Knopf, 1998.

Calahan, Harold A. *What Makes a War End?* New York: Vanguard Press, 1944.

Caldwell, Dan. "Bureaucratic Foreign Policy-Making." *American Behavioral Scientist* 21 (1977): 87–110.

Camerer, C. F. "Individual Decision Making." In *The Handbook of Experimental Economics.* J. H. Kagel and A. E. Roth, eds. Princeton, N.J.: Princeton University Press, 1995, 587–703.

Campbell, David. "Washed in Shades of Grey: The Persian Gulf War in Context." In *The Gulf War: Critical Perspectives.* M. McKinley, ed. Canberra ACT, Australia: Australian National University, 1994.

Caplan, Nathan. "Social Research and National Policy: What Gets Used, by Whom, for What Purposes, and with What

Effects?" *International Social Science Journal* 28, no. 1 (1976): 187–94.

CARDI (Committee Against Repression and for Democratic Rights in Iraq). *Saddam's Iraq: Revolution or Reaction?* London: Zed Books, 1986.

Carlisle, Johan, et al. "Symposium—Special Gulf War Forum." *Propaganda Review*, no. 7 (1990): 5–34.

Carnevale, Peter J., and Patricia A. Keenan. "The Resolution of Conflict: Negotiation and Third Party Intervention." In *Employment Relations: The Psychology of Influence and Control at Work.* Jean F. Hartley and Geoffrey M. Stephenson, eds. Oxford and Cambridge: Blackwell, 1992, 225–45.

Carpenter, Ted Galen. *Holbrooke Horror: The U.S. Peace Plan for Bosnia.* Cato Foreign Policy Briefing No. 37. Cato Institute, 1995.

Carroll, Berenice A. "How Wars End: An Analysis of Some Current Hypotheses." *Journal of Peace Research* 6, no. 4 (1969): 295–321.

———. "War Termination and Conflict Theory: Value Premises, Theories, and Policies." *The Annals of the American Academy of Political and Social Science* 392 (1970): 14–29.

Carroll, John S., and John W. Payne. "An Information Processing Approach to Two-Party Negotiations." In *Research on Negotiation in Organizations.* Max H. Bazerman, Roy J. Lewicki, and Blair H. Sheppard, eds. Greenwich & London: JAI Press, Inc., 1991, 3–34.

Carter, Jimmy. "Searching for Peace." *Essays on Leadership: Perspectives on Prevention.* New York: Carnegie Corp. of New York, 1998.

Cassirer, Ernst. "Implications of the New Theory of the State." *The Prince: A New Translation, Backgrounds, Interpretations.* Robert M. Adams, ed. New York: Norton, 1977.

CCPDC (Carnegie Commission on Preventing Deadly Conflict). *Preventing Deadly Conflict: Final Report.* Washington, D.C.: CCPDC, 1997.

———. *Preventing Deadly Conflict: Executive Summary of the Final Report (Pre-Publication Draft).* Washington, D.C.: Carnegie Corp. of New York, 1997.

Challener, Richard D. *Admirals, Generals, and American Foreign Policy, 1989–1914.* Princeton: Princeton University Press, 1973.

Chan, Steve. "Rationality, Bureaucratic Politics and Belief System: Explaining the Chinese Policy Debate, 1964–66." *Journal of Peace Research* 16, no. 4 (1979): 333–47.

Chang, Noh-Soon. "Bargaining During Interstate Wars: A Game-Theoretic Approach toward War Termination." PhD diss., Florida State University, 1994.

Chartrand, Gary; Linda Lesniak; and Mehdi Behzad. *Graphs & Digraphs.* Monterey, Calif.: Wadsworth & Brooks/Cole Advanced Books & Software, 1986.

Chatman, Jennifer A., and Sigal G. Barsade. "Personality, Organizational Culture, and Cooperation: Evidence from a Business Simulation." *Administrative Science Quarterly* 40 (1995): 423–43.

Chaudhry, Kiren Aziz. "On the Way to Market: Economic Liberalization and Iraq's Invasion of Kuwait." *Middle East Report* 21, no. 3 (1991): 14–23.

Chaves, Mark, and James D. Montgomery. "Rationality and the Framing of Religious Choices." *Journal for the Scientific Study of Religion* 35, no. 2 (1996): 128–44.

Chomsky, Noam. *The Fateful Triangle: Israel, the United States, and the Palestinians.* Boston: South End Press, 1983.

———. "On the Gulf War." *Philosophy and Social Action* 17, no. 1–2 (1991): 9–23.

———. "Twentieth Century American Propaganda." *Propaganda Review* 8 (fall 1991): 8–11, 37–44.

Christopher, Warren. *In the Stream of History: Shaping Foreign Policy for a New Era.* Stanford, Calif.: Stanford University Press, 1998.

Cimbala, Stephen J., ed. *Strategic War Termination.* New York: Praeger Publishers, 1986.

———. "The Endgame and War." In *Conflict Termination and Military Strategy: Coercion, Persuasion, and War,* ed. S. J. Cimbala. Boulder: Westview Press, 1987, 1–12.

———. "C^2 and War Termination." *Signal* 43 (1988): 73–78.

Cimbala, Stephen J., and Sidney R. Waldman, eds. *Controlling and Ending Conflict: Issues before and after the Cold War.* New York: Greenwood Press, 1992.

Cimbala, Stephen J. *U.S. Military Strategy and the Cold War Endgame.* Ilford, Essex, England: F. Cass, 1995.

Cimbala, Stephen J., and Keith A. Dunn. *Conflict Termination and Military Strategy: Coercion, Persuasion, and War.* Boulder: Westview Press, 1987.

Clarke, Bruce B. G. *Conflict Termination: A Rational Model.* Carlisle Barracks, Pa.: US Army War College, 1992.

———. "Conflict Termination: What Does It Mean to Win?" *Military Review* 72 (1992): 85-86.

Clausewitz, Carl von. *On War.* Translated by Michael Howard. Michael Howard and Peter Paret, eds. Princeton, N.J.: Princeton University Press, 1976.

Clawson, Patrick. "Iran: Torn by Domestic Disputes." *Strategic Forum,* no. 124 (1997).

Clinton, William J. "America Must Continue to Bear the Responsibility of World Leadership." *Dispatch* 6, no. 42 (1995): 731–36.

———. "Letter to Congress on Iraqi Compliance with UN Security Council Resolutions." *US Department of State Dispatch* 4, no. 40 (1993): 675–76.

———. "Status Report on Iraq's Non-Compliance with UN Resolutions." *US Department of State Dispatch* 4, no. 49 (1993): 851–52.

Cohan, Roger. "Taming the Bullies of Bosnia: Frenetic as Usual, Richard Holbrooke Shouted, Whispered and Threatened, Even to Excess. The Balkan Blood Rivals Came Around. His Critics Are Another Story." *The New York Times Magazine,* 17 December 1995, 58.

Cohen, Lenard J. "Whose Bosnia? The Politics of Nation Building." *Current History: A Journal of Contemporary World Affairs* (March 1998): 103–12.

Cohen, Raymond. *International Politics: The Rules of the Game.* London: Longman, 1981.

Cohen, Robin. *Endgame in South Africa?: The Changing Structures and Ideology of Apartheid.* Trenton, N.J.: Africa World Press, 1988.

Cohen, Saul B. "The Geopolitical Aftermath of the Gulf War." *FOCUS on Geography* 41, no. 2 (1991): 23–26.

Cohen, William S. *Statement of Secretary of Defense William S. Cohen before the House Appropriations Committee Subcommittee on National Security, in Connections with the FY 1998 Department of Defense Budget.* Washington, D.C.: House Appropriations Committee, 1997.

Coker, Christopher. "How Wars End." In *War Endings: Reasons, Strategies, and Implications.* Sanja Carolina and Per Hammarlund, eds. Cambridge, Mass.: MIT Press, 1997, 615–29.

Coleman, James S. "Introducing Social Structure into Economic Analysis." In *Decision Making: Alternatives to Rational Choice Models.* Mary Zey, ed. Newbury Park, Calif.: Sage Publications, 1992.

Coleman, T. L. *News Media: Should They Play a Role in Crisis Management.* Carlisle Barracks, Pa.: US Army War College, 1989.

Converse, Jean M., and Stanley Presser. *Survey Questions: Handcrafting the Standardized Questionnaire.* Newbury Park, Calif.: Sage Publications, 1986.

Cooley, J. K. "Pre-War Gulf Diplomacy." *Survival* 33, no. 2 (1991): 126.

Coplin, William D. *Introduction to International Politics.* Columbus, Ohio: Charles E. Merrill, 1971.

Corman, Steven R. "A Model of Perceived Communication in Collective Networks." *Human Communication Research* 16, no. 4 (1990): 582–602.

Coser, Lewis. *The Functions of Social Conflict.* New York: The Free Press, 1956.

Coser, Lewis A. "The Termination of Conflict." *Conflict Resolution* 5, no. 4 (1961): 347–53.

Coser, Rose Laub; Murray Hausknecht; and Irving Howe. "Thoughts after the War." *Dissent* 38, no. 3 (1991): 321–25.

Cottam, Martha L. *Foreign Policy Decision Making: The Influence of Cognition.* Boulder: Westview Press, 1986.

Craig, Gordon Alexander, and Alexander L. George. *Force and Statecraft: Diplomatic Problems of Our Time.* New York: Oxford University Press, 1990.

Creswell, John W. *Research Design: Qualitative and Qualitative Approaches.* Thousand Oaks, Calif.: Sage Publishers, 1994.

Croft, Stuart, ed. *The Conventional Armed Forces in Europe Treaty: The Cold War Endgame.* Brookfield, Vt.: Dartmouth Publishing Co., 1994.

Cross, John G. "Negotiation as a Learning Process." In *The Negotiation Process: Theories and Applications.* I. William Zartman, ed. Beverly Hills and London: Sage Publications, 1978, 29–54.

Curtiss, Richard H. "Who Caused the War in the Gulf? Five Versions of History." *Washington Report on Middle East Affairs* 9 (1991): 10–11.

Cusimano, Maryann Kathleen. "Committing the Troops: New Perspectives on United States Military Deployments." PhD diss., Johns Hopkins University, 1993.

Cyert, Richard, and James March. *A Behavioral Theory of the Firm.* Englewood Cliffs, N.J.: Prentice-Hall, 1963.

Cyert, Richard M., and James G. March. "A Behavioral Theory of Organizational Objectives." In *Classics in Organization Theory.* J. M. Shafritz and J. S. Ott, eds. Pacific Grove, Calif.: Brooks/Cole Publishing Co., 1987.

————. *A Behavioral Theory of the Firm.* 2d ed. Cambridge, Mass.: Blackwell Publishers, 1992.

Cyert, R. M.; H. A. Simon; and D. B. Trow. "Observation of a Business Decision." *The Journal of Business* 29 (1956): 237–48.

Dalbey, Steven W. *The March to Baghdad: Did We Stop Too Soon?* Carlisle Barracks, Pa.: US Army War College, 1997.

Daly, Joseph P. "The Effects of Anger on Negotiations over Mergers and Acquisitions." *Negotiation Journal* 7 (1991): 31–39.

Dandeker, Christopher. "Public Opinion, the Media, and the Gulf War." *Armed Forces and Society* 22, no. 2 (1995): 297–302.

Davis, Benjamin O., Jr. *American: An Autobiography.* Washington, D.C.: Smithsonian Institution Press, 1991.

Davis, Paul K., and John Arquilla. *Deterring or Coercing Opponents in Crisis: Lessons from the War with Saddam Hussein.* Santa Monica, Calif.: RAND, 1991.

Davis, Richard G. *Roots of Conflict: A Military Perspective on the Middle East and the Persian Gulf Crisis.* Washington, D.C.: Center for Air Force History, 1993.

Davison, W. Phillips. "News Media and International Negotiation." *Public Opinion Quarterly* 38, no. 2 (1974): 174–91.

DeMarzo, Peter M. "Majority Voting and Corporate Control: The Rule of the Dominant Shareholder." *Review of Economic Studies* 60, no. 3 (1993): 713–24.

Dennis, Michael F. H. "The Policy Basis of General Purpose Forces: A Model for Quantitative Analysis." *Journal of Conflict Resolution* 18, no. 1 (1974): 3–36.

Deshong, Howard Cooper, III. "Resolution and Disillusion: Bureaucratic Politics and the Reagan Administration's Counterterrorism Policy, 1982–1986." PhD diss., Tufts University, 1996.

Destler, I. M.; Leslie H. Gelb; and Anthony Lake. *Our Own Worst Enemy: The Unmaking of American Foreign Policy.* New York: Simon and Schuster, 1984.

Diamond, Louise, and John McDonald. *Multi-Track Diplomacy: A Systems Approach to Peace.* 3d ed. West Hartford, Conn.: Kumarian Press, Inc., 1996.

Dickey, Christopher. "Why We Can't Seem to Understand the Arabs." *Newsweek*, 7 January 1991, 26–27.

Dobbs, Michael. "U.S. May Have Picked Wrong Milosevic." *The Washington Post*, 3 April 1999, A9.

———. "U.S. Starts Process of Army Aid; Some Allies Resist Bosnian Project." *The Washington Post*, 21 December 1995, A35.

"U.S. May Have Picked Wrong Milosevic." *The Washington Post*, 3 April 1999, A9.

Docherty, Jayne S. "When the Parties Bring Their Gods to the Table: Learning Lessons from Waco." PhD diss., George Mason University, 1998.

DOD, The Special Assistant to the Secretary and Deputy Secretary of Defense. *White Paper—Department of Defense and*

Congress. Washington, D.C.: US Department of Defense, 1989.

Donohue, William A., et al. "Crisis Bargaining in Intense Conflict Situations." *International Journal of Group Tensions* 21, no. 2 (1991): 133–53.

Doreian, Patrick, and Andrej Mrvar. "A Partitioning Approach to Structural Balance." *Social Networks* 18, no. 2 (1996): 149–68.

Dornan, James E., Jr., et al. *War Termination Concepts and Political, Economic and Military Targeting.* Arlington, Va.: SRI International, Strategic Studies Center, 1978.

Dowd, Ann Reilly. "How Bush Decided." *Fortune,* 11 February 1991, 45–46.

Dower, John W. *Embracing Defeat: Japan in the Wake of World War II.* New York: W. W. Norton & Co./New Press, 1999.

Drew, Dennis M., and Donald M. Snow. *Making Strategy: An Introduction to National Security Processes and Problems.* Maxwell Air Force Base, Ala.: Air University Press, 1988.

Drew, Elizabeth. "Letter from Washington." *The New Yorker,* 3 December 1990, 174–80.

———. "Letter from Washington." *The New Yorker,* 20 December 1990, 87–92.

———. "Letter from Washington." *The New Yorker,* 4 February 1991, 82–90.

Drew, S. Nelson, ed. *NSC-68: Forging the Strategy of Containment, with Analyses by Paul H. Nitze.* Washington, D.C.: Institute for National Strategic Studies, 1996.

Druckman, D., and P. C. Stern. "Evaluating Peacekeeping Missions." Washington, D.C.: National Research Council, 1997.

Druckman, Dan, and K. Zechmeister. "Conflict of Interest and Value Dissensus: Propositions in the Sociology of Conflict." *Human Relations* 26 (1973): 449–66.

Druckman, Daniel. "Determinants of Compromising Behavior in Negotiation: A Meta-Analysis." *Journal of Conflict Resolution* 38, no. 3 (1994): 507–56.

———. "Dogmatism, Prenegotiation Experience, and Simulated Group Representation as Determinants of Dyadic Behavior in a Bargaining Situation." *Journal of Personality and Social Psychology* 6, no. 3 (1967): 279–90.

———. "Dogmatism, Prenegotiation Experience, and Simulated Group Representation as Determinants of Dyadic Behavior in a Bargaining Situation." PhD diss., Northwestern University, 1966.

———. "Group Processes and Changes in Foreign Policy." Paper presented to the Mershon Center conference on "Changes in Foreign Policy," Ohio State University, February 1989.

———. "Organizational Culture." In *Enhancing Organizational Performance*. Daniel Druckman, Jerome E. Singer, and Harold Van Cott, eds. Washington, D.C.: National Academy Press, 1997, 65–96.

———. "Situational Levers of Position Change: Further Explorations." *Annals of the American Academy of Political and Social Science* 542 (November 1995): 61–80.

———. "Social Psychology and International Negotiations: Processes and Influences." In *Advances in Applied Social Psychology*. Robert F. Kidd and Michael J. Saks, eds. Hillsdale, N.J.: Lawrence Erlbaum Associates, Publishers, 1983, 51–81.

———. "Stages, Turning Points, and Crises: Negotiating Military Base Rights, Spain and the United States." *Journal of Conflict Resolution* 30, no. 2 (1986): 327–60.

Druckman, Daniel, and Benjamin J. Broome. "Value Differences and Conflict Resolution: Familiarity or Liking?" *Journal of Conflict Resolution* 35, no. 4 (1991): 571–93.

Druckman, Daniel; B. J. Broome; and S. H. Korper. "Value Differences and Conflict Resolution: Facilitation or Delinking?" *Journal of Conflict Resolution* 32, no. 4 (1988): 489–510.

Druckman, Daniel; Jo L. Husbands; and Karin Johnston. "Turning Points in the INF Negotiations." *Negotiation Journal* 6 (1991): 55–67.

Druckman, Daniel, and Justin Green. "Playing Two Games: Internal Negotiations in the Philippines." In *Elusive Peace: Negotiating an End to Civil Wars*, ed. I. William Zartman. Washington, D.C.: Brookings Institution, 1995, 299–331.

———. *Political Stability in the Philippines: Framework and Analysis.* Karen A. Feste, ed. Vol. 22, Book 3, *Monograph Series in World Affairs.* Taiwan, ROC: University of Denver, 1986.

Druckman, Daniel, and P. Terrence Hopmann. "Behavioral Aspects of Negotiations on Mutual Security." In *Behavior, Society, and Nuclear War,* ed. P. E. Tetlock et al. New York: Oxford University Press, 1989.

Druckman, Daniel, and Robert Mahoney. "Processes and Consequences of International Negotiations." *Journal of Social Issues* 33, no. 1 (1977): 60–87.

Dunn, Keith A. "The Missing Link in Conflict Termination Thought: Strategy." In *Conflict Termination and Military Strategy: Coercion, Persuasion, and War.* S. J. Cimbala and K. A. Dunn, eds. Boulder: Westview Press, 1987, 175–93.

Dupont, Christophe. "Negotiation as Coalition Building." *International Negotiation* 1, no. 1 (1996): 47–64.

Eden, Colin. "Strategy Development as a Social Process." *Journal of Management Studies* 29, no. 6 (1992): 799–811.

Ederington, L. Benjamin, and Michael J. Mazarr, eds. *Turning Point: The Gulf War and U.S. Military Strategy.* Boulder: Westview Press, 1994.

Ehrlich, Matthew C. "Taken by Storm: The Media, Public Opinion, and US Foreign Policy in the Gulf War." *Journalism and Mass Communication Quarterly* 72, no. 1 (1995): 251–52.

Einstein, Albert. *Relativity: The Special and the General Theory.* Reprint ed. New York: Crown Publication, 1995.

Elgstrom, Ole. "National Culture and International Negotiations." *Cooperation and Conflict* 29, no. 3 (1994): 289–301.

———. "Norms, Culture, and Cognitive Patterns in Foreign Aid Negotiations." *Negotiation Journal* 6, no. 2 (1990): 147–59.

Ellingwood, Susan. "The Dayton Game: A Casualty of Peace." *The New Republic* 217, no. 2–3 (1997): 16–17.

Elliott, David R. "Prospect Theory and Crisis Decision-Making in the Middle East." MA thesis, Dalhousie University (Canada), 1994.

Elliott, Steven R., and Michael McKee. "Collective Risk Decisions in the Presence of Many Risks." *KYKLOS* 48, no. 4 (1995): 541–45.

Elster, Jon. *The Multiple Self*. Cambridge, England: Cambridge University Press, 1987.

———. *Sour Grapes*. Cambridge: Cambridge University Press, 1983.

———. *Ulysses and the Sirens*. Cambridge: Cambridge University Press, 1979.

Engelbrecht, Joseph A., Jr. "War Termination: Why Does a State Decide to Stop Fighting? (World War II, Anglo-Boer War, Japan, Great Britain)." PhD diss., Columbia University, 1992.

Estes, Ernest F. *Conflict Termination in Crisis Management*. Maxwell Air Force Base, Ala.: US Air Command and Staff College, 1973.

Etzioni, Amitai. "The Crisis of Modernity: Deviation or Demise?" *Journal of Human Relations* 21, no. 4 (1973): 370–94.

———. "Normative-Affective Factors: Toward a New Decision-Making Model." In *Decision Making: Alternatives to Rational Choice Models*. Mary Zey, ed. Newbury Park: Sage Publications, 1992.

Eveland, William P., Jr.; Douglas M. McLeod; and Nancy Signorielli. "Actual and Perceived U.S. Public Opinion: The Spiral of Silence During the Persian Gulf War." *International Journal of Public Opinion Research* 7, no. 2 (1995): 91–109.

Farkas, Andrew. "Evolutionary Models in Foreign Policy Analysis." *International Studies Quarterly* 40, no. 3 (1996): 343–61.

Fast, Larissa A., with V. Rast, J. Golden, V. Perry, and L. Peterson, eds. *Intervention Design in Conflict Analysis and Resolution: Theory, Practice, and Research*. Fairfax, Va.: Institute for Conflict Analysis and Resolution, 1998.

Fearon, James D. "Domestic Political Audiences and the Escalation of International Disputes." *The American Political Science Review* 88, no. 3 (1994): 577–92.

Feaver, Peter D., and Richard H. Kohn. "Project on the Gap between the Military and Civilian Society: Digest of Findings and Studies." Research Project Summary. Chapel Hill, N.C.: Triangle Institute for Security Studies, 1999.

Felman, Marc D. *The Military/Media Clash and the New Principle of War: Media Spin.* Maxwell AFB, Ala.: Air University Press, 1993.

Ferejohn, J., and D. Satz. "Unification, Universalism, and Rational Choice Theory." *Critical Review* 9 (1995): 71–84.

Festinger, Leon. "The Motivating Effect of Cognitive Dissonance." In *Classic Readings in Organizational Behavior.* J. S. Ott, ed. Pacific Grove, Calif.: Brooks/Cole Publishing Co., 1989, 74–84.

———. *A Theory of Cognitive Dissonance.* Stanford: Stanford University Press, 1957.

Fiedler, Fred E. "The Contingency Model: A Theory of Leadership Effectiveness." In *Problems in Social Psychology.* C. W. Backman and P. F. Secord, eds. New York: McGraw-Hill, 1966, 278–89.

———. "Style or Circumstance: The Leadership Enigma." *Psychology Today* 2, no. 10 (1969): 38–43.

Fiedler, Fred E., and M. M. Chemers. *Leadership Style and Effective Management.* Glenview, Ill.: Scott, Foresman, and Co., 1974.

———. *Improving Leadership Effectiveness: The Leader Match Concept.* New York: John Wiley, 1976.

Fischhoff, Baruch; Bernard Goitein; and Zur Shapira. "Subjective Expected Utility: A Model of Decision Making." In *Decision Making under Uncertainty: Cognitive Decision Research, Social Interaction, and Development and Epistemology.* R. W. Scholz, ed. North-Holland: Elsevier Science Publishers B. V., 1983, 183–207.

Fishel, John T. *Liberation, Occupation, and Rescue: War Termination and Desert Storm.* Carlisle Barracks, Pa.: Strategic Studies Institute, US Army War College, 1994.

Fisher, Louis. *Presidential War Power.* Lawrence, Kans.: University Press of Kansas, 1995.

Fisher, Roger. "'Quick-Fix' Solutions Are Not the Answer." *Negotiation Journal* 8, no. 1 (1992): 15–20.

Fleishman, Jeffrey. "U.S. Peacekeepers: Changing Role Ahead?" *Philadelphia Inquirer*, 31 January 2001, 1.

Fleming, Paula. "Capabilities and Objectives in the Gulf Crisis." *International Journal of Politics, Culture, and Society* 5, no. 1 (1991): 95–110.

Folger, J. P.; M. S. Poole; and R. K. Stutman. *Working through Conflict: Strategies for Relationships, Groups, and Organizations*. 2d ed. New York: HarperCollins, 1993.

Follert, Vincent. "Risk Analysis: Its Application to Argumentation and Decision-Making." *Journal of the American Forensic Association* 18, no. 2 (1981): 99–108.

Foreign Policy Association, with an introduction by Daniel P. Moynihan, ed. *A Cartoon History of United States Foreign Policy, 1776–1976*. New York: William Morrow and Co., Inc., 1975.

Forester, John. "Bounded Rationality and the Politics of Muddling Through." *Public Administration Review* 44, no. 1 (1984): 23–31.

Foster, James L., and Garry D. Brewer. "And the Clocks Were Striking Thirteen: The Termination of War." *Policy Sciences* 7, no. 2 (1976): 225–43.

———. *And the Clocks Were Striking Thirteen: The Termination of War*. Santa Monica, Calif.: Rand Corporation, 1976.

Fotion, Nicholas G. "The Gulf War: Cleanly Fought." *Bulletin of the Atomic Scientists* 47, no. 7 (1991): 24–29.

Fox, William T. R. "The Causes of Peace and Conditions of War." *The Annals of the American Academy of Political and Social Science* 392 (1970): 1–13.

Foyle, Douglas C. "Public Opinion and Foreign Policy: Elite Beliefs as a Mediating Variable." *International Studies Quarterly* 41 (1997): 141–69.

Foyle, Douglas Charles. "The Influence of Public Opinion on American Foreign Policy Decision-Making: Context, Beliefs, and Process." PhD diss., Duke University, 1996.

Frankfort-Nachmias, Chava, and David Nachmias. *Research Methods in the Social Sciences*. 4th ed. New York: St. Martin's Press, 1992.

Freedman, Lawrence, and Efraim Karsh. *The Gulf Conflict, 1990–1991: Diplomacy and War in the New World Order.* Princeton, N.J.: Princeton University Press, 1993.

Freeman, Charles W., Jr. *Arts of Power: Statecraft and Diplomacy.* Washington, D.C.: United States Institute of Peace, 1997.

———. *The Diplomat's Dictionary.* Revised edition. Washington, D.C.: United States Institute of Peace, 1997.

Freij, Hanna Yousif. "Perceptions and Behavior in U.S. Foreign Relations Towards the Republic of Iraq." PhD diss., University of Pittsburgh, 1992.

Frensley, Nathalie Julia. "Domestic Politics and International Conflict Termination: The Dynamic Group Theory of Conflict Processes with Northern Ireland as a Test Case." PhD diss., University of Texas at Austin, 1996.

Friedman, Jeffrey, ed. *The Rational Choice Controversy.* New Haven, Conn.: Yale University Press, 1996.

Friedman, M. I., and W. E. Jacka. "The Negative Effect of Group Cohesiveness on Intergroup Negotiation." *Journal of Social Issues* 225 (1975): 181–94.

Friedman, Raymond A. "Hard Thoughts on the Gulf War." *Negotiation Journal* 8, no. 1 (1992): 11–14.

Frontline. "Ambush in Mogadishu." On-line. PBS, 1999. Internet (cited 27 March 2002). Available from http://www.pbs.org/wgbh/pages/frontline/ shows/ambush/etc/synopsis.html.

———. "The Gulf War: The Decisionmakers." On-line. PBS, 1998. Internet (cited 5 May 1998). Available from http://www.pbs.org/wgbh/pages/frontline/gulf/oral/decision.html.

Fuller, Graham. "The Next Ideology." *Foreign Policy* 98 (1995): 145–58.

Gallhofer, Irmtraud N. *Foreign Policy Decision-Making: A Qualitative and Quantitative Analysis of Political Argumentation.* Westport, Conn.: Praeger, 1996.

Galtung, Johan. "A Structural Theory of Aggression." *Journal of Peace Research* 1, no. 2 (1964): 95–119.

———. "Violence, Peace, and Peace Research." *Journal of Peace Research* 6, no. 3 (1969): 167–91.

GAO. *Military Personnel: Perspectives of Surveyed Members in Retention Critical Specialties (Briefing Report, 08/16/1999, Gao/Nsiad-99-197br)*. On-line. GAO, 1999. Internet (cited 02/01/2001). Available from http://www.ala-national.org/Legis/GAORetention.html.

Garamone, Jim. *Operations Tempo Remains Retention Challenge*. American Forces Press Service. On-line. 1999. Internet (cited 02/01/2001). Available from http://www.af.mil/news/Aug1999/n19990819_991549.html.

Garborg, Arne. "Garborg's Heart'n Home Collection: Leadership." Bloomington, Minn.: Garborg's, Inc., 1993.

Garrett, Banning Nicholas. "The "China Card" and Its Origins: US Bureaucratic Politics and the Strategic Triangle (United States)." PhD diss., Brandeis University, 1984.

Gelb, Leslie H., and Richard K. Betts. *The Irony of Vietnam: The System Worked*. Washington, D.C.: Brookings Institution, 1979.

Gellman, Barton. "Iraqi Work toward A-Bomb Reported: U.S. Was Told of 'Implosion Devices'." *Washington Post*, 30 September 1998, A01.

George, Alexander L. *Bridging the Gap: Theory and Practice in Foreign Policy*. Washington, D.C.: United States Institute of Peace Press, 1993.

———. "Case Studies and Theory Development: The Method of Structured, Focused Comparison." In *Diplomacy: New Approaches in History, Theory, and Policy*, Paul Gordon Lauren, ed. New York: Free Press, 1979, 43–68.

———. *Deterrence in American Foreign Policy: Theory and Practice*. New York: Columbia University Press, 1974.

———. "The 'Operational Code': A Neglected Approach to the Study of Political Leaders and Decision Making." *International Studies Quarterly* 13 (1969): 190–222.

Gerhart, Paul F. "Determinants of Bargaining Outcomes in Local Government Labor Negotiations." *Industrial and Labor Relations Review* 29, no. 3 (1976): 331–51.

Gerstenzang, James, and Richard E. Meyer. "An Angry Man." *The Wichita Eagle*, 9 December 1990, 8B.

Gettys, C. F., et al. "An Evaluation of Human Act Generation Performance." *Organizational Behavior and Human Decision Processes* 39 (1987): 23–51.

Gibson, Martha Liebler. "Weapons of Influence: The Legislative Veto, American Foreign Policy and the Irony of Reform." PhD diss., University of Colorado at Boulder, 1991.

Gigot, Paul A. "A Great American Screw-Up. The U.S. and Iraq, 1980–1990." *The National Interest*, no. 22 (1991): 3–10.

Gilbert, Jason. "The Changing Face of Peacekeeping: Termination or Prolongation?" *Peacekeeping & International Relations* 25, no. 3 (1996): 13.

Gilpin, Michael D. *Exit Strategy: The New Dimension in Operational Planning.* Carlisle Barracks, Pa.: US Army War College, 1997.

Gitlin, Todd, et al. "The Gulf War-Taking Positions." *Dissent* 38, no. 2 (1991): 153–57.

Glaser, Barney G., and Anselm L. Strauss. *The Discovery of Grounded Theory: Strategies for Qualitative Research.* Chicago: Aldine Publishing Co., 1967.

Glaser, Charles L., and John C. Matthews III. "Current Gains and Future Outcomes." *International Security* 21, no. 4 (1997): 186–97.

Goffman, Erving. *Frame Analysis.* Cambridge, Mass.: Harvard University Press, 1974.

———. *Interaction Ritual.* New York: Doubleday, 1967.

Golich, Vicki L. "A Multilateral Negotiations Challenge: International Management of the Communications Commons." *Journal of Applied Behavioral Science* 27, no. 2 (1991): 228–50.

Gompert, David C. "The United States and Yugoslavia's Wars." In *The World and Yugoslavia's Wars.* Richard H. Ullman, ed. New York: Council on Foreign Relations, 1996.

Goodman, A. E., and S. C. Bogart, eds. *Making Peace: The United States and Conflict Resolution.* Boulder: Westview Press, 1992.

Goodman, Allan E. *The Diplomatic Record 1992–1993.* Boulder: Westview Press, 1995.

Gorbachev, Mikhail. "On Nonviolent Leadership." In *Essays on Leadership: Perspectives on Prevention*. New York: Carnegie Corp. of New York, 1998.

Gordon, Michael R. "Cracking the Whip." *New York Times Magazine*, 27 January 1991, 16.

Gordon, Michael R., and Bernard E. Trainor. *The Generals' War: The Inside Story of the Conflict in the Gulf*. Boston: Little, Brown and Company, 1995.

Gore, W. J. *Administrative Decision Making: A Heuristic Model*. New York: Wiley, 1964.

Goren, Dina. "The News and Foreign Policy: An Examination of the Impact of the News Media on the Making of Foreign Policy." *Research in Social Movements, Conflicts and Change* 3 (1980): 119–41.

Gortner, Harold F.; Julianne Mahler; and Jeanne Bell Nicholson. *Organization Theory: A Public Perspective*. Pacific Grove, Calif.: Brooks/Cole Publishing Company, 1989.

———. *Organization Theory: A Public Perspective*. 2d ed. Fort Worth: Harcourt Brace College Publishers, 1997.

Gow, James. *Triumph of the Lack of Will: International Diplomacy and the Yugoslav War*. New York: Columbia University Press, 1997.

Goyal, Sanjeev, and Maarten Janssen. "Can We Rationally Learn to Coordinate?" *Theory and Decision* 40, no. 1 (1996): 29–49.

Green, Donald P., and Ian Shapiro. *Pathologies of Rational Choice Theory: A Critique of Applications in Political Science*. New Haven, Conn.: Yale University Press, 1994.

Greene, Aleza S., et al. "Attitudes About War: Implications of the War with Iraq." *Contemporary Social Psychology* 15 (1991).

Greer, Edward. "The Hidden History of the Iraq War." *Monthly Review* 43 (1991): 1–14.

Gregorian, Hrach. *Congressional-Executive Relations and Foreign Policymaking in the Post–Vietnam Period: Case Studies of Congressional Influence*. Brandeis University, Dept. of Politics: UMI, 1980.

Grether, D. M., and C. R. Plott. "Economic Theory of Choice and the Preference Reversal Phenomenon." *American Economic Review* 69 (1979): 623–38.

Griffith, Michael C. *War Termination: Theory, Doctrine, and Practice*. Fort Leavenworth, Kans.: School of Advanced Military Studies, US Army Command and General Staff College, 1992.

Grusec, Joan E. "Social Learning Theory and Developmental Psychology: The Legacies of Robert Sears and Albert Bandura." *Developmental Psychology* 28, no. 5 (1992): 776–86.

Guetzkow, Harold. "Relations among Organizations." In *Studies on Behavior in Organizations*. R. V. Bowers, ed. Athens, Ga.: University of Georgia Press, 1966, 13-44.

Gulliver, P. H. "The Process of Negotiation." *Disputes and Negotiation: A Cross Cultural Perspective*. New York: Academic Press, 1979.

GWAPS. *Gulf War Air Power Survey*. Washington, D.C.: Government Printing Office, 1992.

Haass, Peter M. "Introduction: Epistemic Communities and International Policy Coordination." *International Organization* 46 (1992): 1–35.

Hallion, Richard P. *Storm over Iraq: Air Power and the Gulf War*. Washington & London: Smithsonian Institution Press, 1992.

Halperin, Morton H. "War Termination as a Problem in Civil-Military Relations." *American Academy of Political and Social Science Annals* 392 (1970): 86–95.

Halperin, Morton H., and Graham T. Allison. "Bureaucratic Politics: A Paradigm and Some Policy Implications." In *Theory and Policy in International Relations*. Raymond Tanter and Richard H. Ullman, eds. Princeton: Princeton University Press, 1974.

Halperin, Morton H., with the assistance of Priscila Clapp and Arnold Kanter. *Bureaucratic Politics and Foreign Policy*. Washington, D.C.: Brookings Institution, 1974.

Handel, Michael. "The Study of War Termination." *Journal of Strategic Studies* 1 (1978): 51–75.

———. "The Yom Kippur War and the Inevitability of Surprise." *International Studies Quarterly* 21 (1977): 461–502.

Handel, Michael I. *War Termination—A Critical Survey*. Jerusalem: The Hebrew University Press, 1978.

Harrison, J. Richard, and Paul McIntosh. "Using Social Learning Theory to Manage Organizational Performance." *Journal of Managerial Issues* 4, no. 1 (1992): 84–105.

Harrison, Michael I., and Bruce Phillips. "Strategic Decision Making: An Integrative Explanation." *Research in the Sociology of Organizations* 9 (1991): 319–58.

Harrison, Thomas. "A Cold Peace in Bosnia." *New Politics (New Series)* 5, no. 4(20) (1996): 8–18.

Hastie, R. "Schematic Principles of Human Memory." In *Social Cognition: The Ontario Symposium.* E. T. Higgins, C. A. Herman, and M. P. Zanna, eds. Hillsdale, N.J.: Erlbaum, 1981.

Head, William, and Earl H. Tilford Jr., eds. *The Eagle in the Desert: Looking Back on U.S. Involvement in the Persian Gulf War.* Westport, Conn.: Praeger, 1996.

Heckscher, Charles. "Multilateral Negotiation and the Future of American Labor." *Negotiation Journal* 2, no. 2 (1986): 141–54.

Herek, Gregory M.; Irving L. Janis; and Paul Huth. "Decision Making During International Crisis: Is Quality of Process Related to Outcome?" *Journal of Conflict Resolution* 31, no. 2 (1987): 203–26.

Herman, Margaret G. "Leaders, Leadership, and Flexibility: Influences on Heads of Government as Negotiators and Mediators." *The Annals of the American Academy of Political and Social Science* 542 (1995): 148–67.

Hermann, Charles F. "The Knowledge Gap: The Exchange of Information between the Academic and the Foreign Policy Communities." Paper presented at the Annual Political Science Association Meeting. Chicago, Ill., 7–11 September 1971.

Hicks, D. Bruce. "Internal Competition over Foreign Policy-Making: The Case of U.S. Arms Sales to Iran." *Policy Studies Review* 9, no. 3 (1990): 471–84.

Hickson, David J. "Decision-Making at the Top of Organizations." *Annual Review of Sociology* 13 (1987): 165–92.

Higgins, Rosalyn. "The New United States and Former Yugoslavia." *International Affairs* 69, no. 3 (1993): 465–83.

Hilsman, Roger. "Congressional-Executive Relations and the Foreign Policy Consensus." *American Political Science Review* (1958).

———. "The Foreign-Policy Consensus: An Interim Research Report." *Journal of Conflict Resolution* 3, no. 4 (1959).

———. *George Bush vs. Saddam Hussein: Military Success! Political Failure?* Novato, Calif.: Lyford Books, 1992.

———. *To Move a Nation: The Politics of Foreign Policy in the Administration of John F. Kennedy.* New York: Doubleday, 1967.

———. *The Politics of Policy Making in Defense and Foreign Affairs.* New York: Harper and Row, 1971.

———. *The Politics of Policy Making in Defense and Foreign Affairs: Conceptual Models and Bureaucratic Politics.* New York: Prentice-Hall, 1987.

Hirokawa, Randy Y., and Dierdre D. Johnston. "Toward a General Theory of Group Decision Making: Development of an Integrated Model." *Small Group Behavior* 20, no. 4 (1989): 500–523.

Hirsh, Michael, and John Barry. "How We Stumbled into War." *Newsweek*, 12 April 1999, 38–40.

Historical Evaluation Research Organization (HERO). *Conventional Attrition and Battle Termination Criteria: A Study of War Termination.* Dunn Loring: HERO, 1982.

Hitchens, Christopher. "Why We Are Stuck in the Sand—Realpolitik in the Gulf: A Game Gone Tilt." *Harper's Magazine*, January 1991, 70–76.

Hoffman, P. J. "The Paramorphic Representation of Clinical Judgement." *Psychological Bulletin* 47 (1960): 116–31.

Hoffman, Stanley. *The State of War.* New York: Praeger, 1965.

Holbrooke, Richard C. *To End a War.* New York: Random House, 1998.

Holl, Jayne Ellen Kyrstyn. "From the Streets of Washington to the Roofs of Saigon: Domestic Politics and the Termination of the Vietnam War." PhD diss., Stanford University, 1989.

Hollenbeck, John R., et al. "Multilevel Theory of Team Decision Making: Decision Performance in Teams Incorporating Distributed Expertise." *Journal of Applied Psychology* 80, no. 2 (1995): 292–316.

Hollis, Martin. *The Philosophy of Social Science: An Introduction.* Cambridge: Cambridge University Press, 1994.

Holsti, K. J. "Resolving International Conflicts: A Taxonomy of Behavior and Some Figures on Procedures." *Journal of Conflict Resolution* 10, no. 3 (1966): 272–96.

Holsti, Ole. "Foreign Policy Formation Viewed Cognitively." In *Structure of Decision: The Cognitive Maps of Political Elites.* Robert Axelrod, ed. Princeton: Princeton University Press, 1976.

Homans, George. *Social Behavior.* New York: Harcourt & Brace, 1974.

Hoos, Ida R. *Systems Analysis in Public Policy: A Critique.* 2d ed. Berkeley, Calif.: University of California Press, 1974.

Hopmann, P. Terrence. "Two Paradigms of Negotiation: Bargaining and Problem Solving." *The Annals of the American Academy of Political and Social Science* 542 (1995): 24–47.

Hopmann, P. Terrence, and Daniel Druckman. "Henry Kissinger as Strategist and Tactician in the Middle East Negotiations." In *Dynamics of Third Party Intervention: Kissinger in the Middle East.* Jeffrey Z. Rubin, ed. New York: Praeger Publishers, 1981, 197–225.

Hubbard, Charles M. *The Burden of Confederate Diplomacy.* Knoxville: University of Tennessee Press, 1998.

Huber, George P. "Decision Support Systems: Their Present Nature and Future Applications." In *Decision Making: An Interdisciplinary Inquiry.* G. R. Ungson and D. N. Braunstein, eds. Boston, Mass.: Kent Publishing Co., 1982, 249–62.

Hunt, E. B. *Artificial Intelligence.* New York: Academic Press, 1975.

Huntington, Samuel P. *The Soldier and the State: The Theory and Politics of Civil-Military Relations.* Cambridge: The Belknap Press of Harvard University Press, 1957.

Hybel, Alex Roberto. *Power over Rationality: The Bush Administration and the Gulf Crisis.* New York: State University of New York Press, 1993.

Hybel, Alex R. "Power, War, and Decision-Making Aptitudes." In *Power over Rationality: The Bush Administration and the Gulf Crisis.* New York: State University of New York Press, 1993, 1–27.

Iklé, Fred Charles. *Every War Must End.* New York: Columbia University Press, 1991.

———. *How Nations Negotiate.* New York: Harper, 1964.

Insko, Chester A., et al. "The Role of Communication in Interindividual-Intergroup Discontinuity." *Journal of Conflict Resolution* 37, no. 1 (1993): 108–38.

Irwin, Dana, et al. "Group Versus Individual Decision Making in the Commons Problem." *The Journal of Social Psychology* 129, no. 4 (1989): 551–53.

Institute for Foreign Policy Analysis, Inc. "Strategic War Termination: Political-Military-Diplomatic Dimensions." Speech. Madison Hotel, Washington, D.C., 2–3 April 1986.

Iyengar, Shanto. *Is Anyone Responsible? How Television Frames Political Issues.* Chicago: University of Chicago Press, 1991.

Iyengar, Shanto, and Adam Simon. "News Coverage of the Gulf Crisis and Public Opinion: A Study of Agenda-Setting, Priming, and Framing." *Communication Research* 20, no. 3 (1993): 365–83.

Jaber, N. "Saudi Arabia Dampens Arab Peace Bids." *Middle East International* (1990): 3–4.

Jacobson, Dan. "Intraparty Dissensus and Interparty Conflict Resolution: A Laboratory Experiment in the Context of the Middle East Conflict." *Journal of Conflict Resolution* 25, no. 3 (1981): 471–94.

Jain, R. B. "Politicization of Bureaucracy: A Framework for Measurement." *Res Publica* 16, no. 2 (1974): 279–302.

James, Patrick, and John R. O'Neal. "The Influence of Domestic and International Politics on the President's Use of Force." *Journal of Conflict Resolution* 35, no. 2 (1991): 307–32.

Janis, Irving L. *Crucial Decisions: Leadership in Policymaking and Crisis Management.* New York: Free Press, 1989.

———. "Groupthink: The Desperate Drive for Consensus at Any Cost." In *Classic Readings in Organizational Behavior*, ed. J.

Steven Ott. Pacific Grove, Calif.: Brooks/Cole Publishing Co., 1989, 223–32.

Janis, Irving L., and Leon Mann. "Coping with Decisional Conflict." *American Scientist* 64, no. 6 (1976): 657–67.

———. *Decision Making: A Psychological Analysis of Conflict, Choice, and Commitment*. New York: Free Press, 1977.

Janosik, Robert J. "Rethinking the Culture-Negotiation Link." *Negotiation Journal* 3, no. 4 (1987): 385–95.

Jervis, Robert. "Hypotheses on Misperception." In *International Relations: Contemporary Theory and Practice*. G. A. Lopez and M. S. Stohl, eds. Washington, D.C.: CQ Press, 1989, 75–82.

———. "Political Implications of Loss Aversion. Special Issue: Prospect Theory and Political Psychology." *Political Psychology* 13 (1992): 187–204.

Jervis, Robert; Richard Ned Lebow; and Janice Gross Stein. *Psychology and Deterrence*. Baltimore, Md.: Johns Hopkins University Press, 1989.

Jhally, Sut; Justin Lewis; and Michael Morgan. "The Gulf War: A Study of the Media, Public Opinion and Public Knowledge." *Propaganda Review* 8 (fall 1991): 14–15, 50–52.

Johnsen, W. T. *Insights into the Balkan Enigma*. Carlisle Barracks, Pa.: US Army War College Strategic Studies Institute, 1993.

Johnson, David E. *Modern US Civil-Military Relations: Wielding the Terrible Swift Sword*. Washington, D.C.: Institute for National Strategic Studies, National Defense University, 1997.

Johnson, D. V. *Impact of the Media on National Security Policy Decision Making*. Carlisle Barracks, Pa.: US Army War College, Strategic Studies Institute, 1994.

Johnson, Garey Antony. "US Arms Shipments to the Kingdom of Saudi Arabia During the Ronald Reagan Administration: In Search of a Policy Paradigm." D.P.A. diss., University of Southern California, 1992.

Johnson, Leah D. "Non-Rational Considerations Towards Conflict Termination." Newport, R.I.: US Naval War College, 1994.

Joulwan, George A., and Christopher C. Shoemaker. *Civilian-Military Cooperation in the Prevention of Deadly Conflict: Implementing Agreements in Bosnia and Beyond.* New York: Carnegie Corp. of New York, 1998.

Jungermann, Helmut. "The Two Camps on Rationality." In *Decision Making under Uncertainty: Cognitive Decision Research, Social Interaction, and Development and Epistemology.* R. W. Scholz, ed. North-Holland: Elsevier Science Publishers B. V., 1983, 63–86.

Kachigan, Sam Kash. *Statistical Analysis: An Interdisciplinary Introduction to Univariate and Multivariate Methods.* New York: Radius Press, 1986.

Kahn, Herman; William Pfaff; and Edmund Stillman. *War Termination Issues and Concepts: Final Report.* Croton-on-Hudson, New York: Hudson Institute, 1968.

Kahneman, Daniel. "Judgment and Decision Making: A Personal View." *Psychological Science* 2, no. 3 (1991): 142–45.

Kahneman, Daniel; Paul Slovic; and Amos Tversky, eds. *Judgement under Uncertainty: Heuristics and Biases.* Cambridge: Cambridge University Press, 1982.

Kahneman, Daniel, and Amos Tversky. "On the Psychology of Prediction." *Psychological Review* 80 (1973): 237–51.

———. "Prospect Theory: An Analysis of Decision under Risk." *Econometrica* 47 (1979): 263–91.

Kameda, T., and J. H. Davis. "The Function of the Reference Point in Individual and Group Risk Decision Making." *Organizational Behavior and Human Decision Processes* 46 (1990): 55–76.

Kameda, Tatsuya, and Shinkichi Sugimori. "Psychological Entrapment in Group Decision Making: An Assigned Decision Rule and a Groupthink Phenomenon." *Journal of Personality and Social Psychology* 65, no. 2 (1993): 282–92.

Kanjirathinkal, Mathew, and Joseph V. Hickey. "Media Framing and Myth: The Media's Portrayal of the Gulf War." *Critical Sociology* 19, no. 1 (1992): 103–12.

Kaplan, Robert D. "The Coming Anarchy." *The Atlantic Monthly.* February 1994.

Karsh, Efraim, and Inari Rautsi. *Saddam Hussein: A Political Biography.* New York: Free Press, 1991.

Katz, Andrew W. "Public Opinion, Congress, President Nixon, and the Termination of the Vietnam War." PhD diss., Johns Hopkins University, 1987.

Katz, Elihu, et al. "Symposium: Journalism in Crisis and Change." *Journal of Communication* 42, no. 3 (1992): 5–107.

Kaufmann, Johan. "The Middle East Peace Process: A New Case of Conference Diplomacy." *Peace and Change* 18, no. 3 (1993): 290–306.

Kecskemeti, Paul. "Political Rationality in Ending War." *American Academy of Political and Social Science Annals* 392 (1970): 105–15.

———. *Strategic Surrender: The Politics of Victory and Defeat.* New York: Atheneum, 1964.

———. "Utilization of Social Research in Shaping Policy Decisions." Santa Monica, Calif.: RAND Corp., 1961.

Keen, Peter G., and Michael S. Scott Morton. *Decision Support Systems: An Organizational Perspective.* Reading, Mass.: Addison-Wesley Publishing Co., 1978.

Keenan, Patricia A., and Peter J. D. Carnevale. "Positive Effects of within-Group Cooperation on between-Group Negotiation." *Journal of Applied Social Psychology* 19, no. 12 (1989): 977–92.

Keller, L. R., and J. L. Ho. "Decision Problem Structuring: Generating Options." Vol. 18. *IEEE Transactions on Systems, Man, and Cybernetics.* Irvine, Calif: California University, 1988, 715–28.

Kellerman, Barbara, ed. *Leadership: Multidisciplinary Perspectives.* Englewood Cliffs, N.J.: Prentice-Hall, 1984.

Kellerman, Barbara, and Jeffrey Z. Rubin, eds. *Leadership and Negotiation in the Middle East.* New York: Praeger Publisher, 1988.

Kelley, Harold H. "The Processes of Causal Attribution." *American Psychologist* 28, no. 2 (1973): 107–28.

Kelly, John, and Caroline Kelly. "Industrial Action." In *Employment Relations: The Psychology of Influence and Control at*

Work, Jean F. Hartley and Geoffrey M. Stephenson, eds. Oxford: Blackwell, 1992, 246–68.

Kelly, Janice R.; Jay W. Jackson; and Sarah L. Hutson-Comeaux. "The Effects of Time Pressure and Task Differences on Influence Modes and Accuracy in Decision-Making Groups." *Personality & Social Psychology Bulletin* 23, no. 1 (1997): 10–22.

Khanum, Saeeda. "Inside Iraq." *New Statesman and Society* 4, no. 152 (1991): 12–16.

Kim, Hyun. "Rationality, Bureaucratic Politics, and Cognitive Processes in Foreign Policy Decision-Making: An Analysis of the United States Policy Decisions Towards Japan, 1948–1954." PhD diss., City University of New York, 1996.

Kissinger, Henry A. "Doing Injury to History." *Newsweek*, 5 April 1999, 38–39.

Kleiboer, Marieke, and Paul Hart. "Time to Talk? Multiple Perspectives on Timing of International Mediation." *Cooperation and Conflict* 30, no. 4 (1995): 307–48.

Kohut, Andrew, and Robert C. Toth. "Arms and the People." *Foreign Affairs* 73, no. 6 (1994): 47–61.

Kondo, Tetsuo. "Some Notes on Rational Behavior, Normative Behavior, Moral Behavior, and Cooperation." *Journal of Conflict Resolution* 34, no. 3 (1990): 495–530.

Koopman, Paul, and Jeroen Pool. "Organizational Decision Making: Models, Contingencies and Strategies." In *Distributed Decision Making: Cognitive Models for Cooperative Work*. Jens Rasmussen, Berndt Brehmer, and Jacques Leplat, eds. Chichester, England: John Wiley & Sons, 1991.

Korbani, Agnes Gerges. "Presidential Working-System Style, Cognition, and Foreign Policy: A Comparative Study of U.S. Decisions to Intervene Militarily in Lebanon in 1958 and 1982." PhD diss., Northwestern University, 1989.

Kowert, Paul Andrew. "Between Reason and Passion: A Systems Theory of Foreign Policy Learning." PhD diss., Cornell University, 1992.

Kozak, David C., and James M. Keagle, eds. *Bureaucratic Politics and National Security: Theory and Practice*. Boulder & London: Lynne Rienner Publishers, 1988.

Kramer, Michael. "Toward a New Kuwait." *Time*, May 1990, 26–33.

Kramer, Roderick M.; Pamela Pommerenke; and Elizabeth Newton. "The Social Context of Negotiation: Effects of Social Identity and Interpersonal Accountability on Negotiator Decision Making." *Journal of Conflict Resolution* 37, no. 4 (1993): 633–54.

Kriesberg, Louis. *International Conflict Resolution: The US-USSR and Middle East Cases.* New Haven, Conn.: Yale University Press, 1992.

———. *Social Conflicts.* 2d ed. Englewood Cliffs, N.J.: Prentice-Hall, Inc., 1982.

Krippendorff, Klaus. *Content Analysis: An Introduction to Its Methodology.* Beverly Hills, Calif.: Sage, 1980.

Krosnick, Jon A., and Laura A. Brannon. "The Media and the Foundations of Presidential Support: George Bush and the Persian Gulf Conflict." *Journal of Social Issues* 49, no. 4 (1993): 167–82.

Kull, Steven, and I. M. Destler. *Misreading the Public: The Myth of a New Isolationism.* Washington, D.C.: Brookings Institution Press, 1999.

Kumagai, Fumie, and Murray A. Straus. "Conflict Resolution Tactics in Japan, India, and the USA." *Journal of Comparative Family Studies* 14, no. 3 (1983): 377–92.

Kuniholm, Bruce R. "Retrospect and Prospect: Forty Years of U.S. Middle East Policy." *MEJ* 41 (1987): 7–25.

Lademan, William J. *War Termination: The Confluence of Strategy and Policy.* Newport, R.I.: US Naval War College, 1988.

Lagemann, Ellen Condliffe. *The Politics of Knowledge: The Carnegie Corporation, Philanthropy, and Public Policy.* Middletown, Conn.: Wesleyan University Press, 1989.

Lake, Anthony. "Bosnia after Dayton." On-line. Washington, D.C.: The White House. Internet, 21 September 1998. Available from: http://www.whitehouse.gov/WH/EOP/NSC/html/speeches/tlgtown.html.

Larson, Deborah Welch. "The Psychology of Reciprocity in International Relations." *Negotiation Journal* 4, no. 3 (1988): 281–301.

Larson, James R., Jr.; Pennie G. Foster-Fishman; and Christopher B. Keys. "Discussion of Shared and Unshared Information in Decision-Making Groups." *Journal of Personality and Social Psychology* 67, no. 3 (1994): 446–61.

Lasswell, Harold D. *The Decision Process: Seven Categories of Functional Analysis.* College Park, Md.: Bureau of Governmental Research, 1956.

Last, D. M. "The Challenge of Interagency Cooperation in International Peace Operations: A Conference Report." *Peacekeeping & International Relations* 24, no. 1 (1995): 5.

Lazarus, Arnold A. "Theory, Subjectivity and Bias: Can There Be a Future?" *Psychotherapy* 30, no. 4 (1993): 674–77.

Lebow, Richard Ned. *Between Peace and War: The Nature of International Crisis.* Baltimore and London: Johns Hopkins University Press, 1981.

Lee, Paul. *War Termination in a Low-Intensity Conflict.* Carlisle Barracks, Pa.: US Army War College, 1988.

Leff, Walli F. "Groupthink." *Omni* 3 (1981): 26–27.

Levi, Ariel S., and Glen Whyte. "A Cross-Cultural Exploration of the Reference Dependence of Crucial Group Decisions under Risk: Japan's 1941 Decision for War." *Journal of Conflict Resolution* 41, no. 6 (1997): 792–813.

Levy, Jack S. "Prospect Theory and International Relations: Theoretical Applications and Analytical Problems. Special Issue: Prospect Theory and Political Psychology." *Political Psychology* 13, no. 2 (1992): 283–310.

———. "Prospect Theory, Rational Choice, and International Relations." *International Studies Quarterly* 41, no. 1 (1997): 87–112.

Levy, Zvi. "Negotiating Positive Identity in a Group Care Community: Reclaiming Uprooted Youth." *Child and Youth Services* 16, no. 2 (1993): xv–123.

Lian, Bradley, and John R. O'Neal. "Presidents, the Use of Military Force, and Public Opinion." *Journal of Conflict Resolution* 37, no. 2 (1993): 277–300.

Liddell Hart, Sir Basil Henry. *Strategy.* New York: Praeger, 1954.

Lief, Louise. "Battling for the Arab Mind." *U.S. News & World Report*, 21 January 1991, 22–24.

Lijphart, Arend. "Comparative Politics and the Comparative Method." *American Political Science Review* 65 (1971): 682–93.

Lindblom, Charles E. "Initiating Change: Modes of Social Inquiry." *American Behavioral Scientist* 40, no. 3 (1997): 264–76.

———. "The Science of 'Muddling through'." *Public Administration Review* 19 (1959): 79–88.

Lippman, Thomas W. "U.S. Diplomacy Behind the Times, Studies Say." *The Washington Post*, 28 October 1998, A17.

Lo, Ven Hwei. "Media Use, Involvement, and Knowledge of the Gulf War." *Journalism Quarterly* 71, no. 1 (1994): 43–54.

Lopez, George A. "The Gulf War: Not So Clean." *Bulletin of the Atomic Scientists* 77, no. 7 (1991): 30–35.

Lowenthal, M. M. "The Persian Gulf War: Preliminary Foreign Policy 'Lessons' and Perceptions." Edited by Congressional Research Service. Washington, D.C.: Library of Congress, Report to Congress No. 91-260 RCO, 1991.

Lynn, Laurence E., Jr. "Policy Analysis in the Bureaucracy: How New? How Effective?" *Journal of Policy Analysis and Management* 8, no. 3 (1989): 373–77.

Machan, Tibor R. "Rational Choice and Public Affairs." *Theory and Decision* 12, no. 3 (1980): 229–58.

Macintosh, James. "Confidence-Building Measures—A Conceptual Exploration." In *Confidence Building Measures and International Security*. R. B. Byers et al., eds. New York: Institute for East-West Security Studies, 1986, 9–29.

Mack, Raymond W., and Richard C. Snyder. "The Analysis of Social Conflict—Toward an Overview and Synthesis." *Journal of Conflict Resolution* 1, no. 1 (1957): 231.

Mahler, Julianne G. "Structured Decision Making in Public Organizations." *Public Administration Review* 47, no. 4 (1987): 336–42.

Maki, Cynthia Siemsen, and Walter L. Goldfrank. "Lessons from the Gulf Wars: Hegemonic Decline, Semiperipheral Turbulence, and the Role of the Rentier State." In *A New World Order? Global Transformations in the Late Twentieth Cen-*

tury. David A. Smith and Jozsef Borocz, eds. Westport, Conn.: Praeger Publishers, 1995, 57–70.

Manchester, William. *American Caesar: Douglas MacArthur, 1880–1964*. New York: Dell Publishing, 1978.

Mann, Edward C. *Thunder and Lightning: Desert Storm and the Airpower Debates*. Vol. 2. Maxwell Air Force Base, Ala.: Air University Press, 1995.

Mansfield, Edwin. *Applied Microeconomics*. New York: W. W. Norton & Co., 1994.

Maoz, Zeev. "Framing the National Interest: The Manipulation of Foreign Policy Decisions in Group Settings." *World Politics* 43, no. 1 (1990): 77–100.

March, James G., and Zur Shapira. "Behavioral Decision Theory and Organizational Decision Theory." In *Decision Making: Alternatives to Rational Choice Models*. Mary Zey, ed. Newbury Park, Calif.: Sage Publications, 1992.

March, James G., and Herbert A. Simon. *Organizations*. New York: John Wiley, 1958.

———. "Theories of Bureaucracy." In *Classics of Organization Theory*. Jay M. Shafritz and J. Steven Ott, eds. Pacific Grove, Calif.: Brooks/Cole Publishing Co., 1978, 146–54.

Marr, Phebe A. "Iraq: Troubles and Tension." *Strategic Forum*, no. 123 (1997).

Marzul, Julius V. "Termination of Conflict: Then What?" Carlisle Barracks, Pa.: US Army War College, 1975.

Mason, Richard O. *Challenging Strategic Planning Assumptions: Theory, Cases, and Techniques*. New York: Wiley, 1981.

Massoud, Tansa George. "The Termination of Wars." PhD diss., New York University, 1992.

———. "War Termination." *Journal of Peace Research* 33, no. 4 (1996): 491–96.

Mastanduno, Michael. "Preserving the Unipolar Moment: Realist Theories and US Grand Strategy after the Cold War." *International Security* 21, no. 4 (1997): 49–88.

Mathews, Tom. "The Road to War: A Behind-the-Scenes Account of Gross Errors and Deft Maneuvers." *Newsweek*, 28 January 1991, 54–65.

———. "A Soldier of Conscience: Stormin' Norman Becomes the Hero the Country Has Longed for since Vietnam." *Newsweek*, 11 March 1991, 32–34.

Maurer, Todd J., and Robert G. Lord. "An Exploration of Cognitive Demands in Group Interaction as a Moderator of Information Processing Variables in Perceptions of Leadership." *Journal of Applied Social Psychology* 21, no. 10 (1991): 821–39.

Maynes, Charles William. "Bottom-up Foreign Policy." *Foreign Policy* 104 (fall 1996): 35–53.

McCauley, Clark. "The Nature of Social Influence in Groupthink: Compliance and Internalization." *Journal of Personality and Social Psychology* 57, no. 2 (1989): 250–60.

McDonald, John M. "Ten Missed Opportunities for Peace in the Gulf." Paper presented at *War in the Gulf V: The Persian Gulf War and Peace Communication.* Symposium conducted at the 75th annual meeting of the Speech Communication Association, Atlanta, Ga., November 1991.

McGlynn, Richard P., Darla D. Tubbs, and Kurt G. Holzhausen. "Hypothesis Generation in Groups Constrained by Evidence." *Journal of Experimental Social Psychology* 31, no. 1 (1995): 64–81.

McGowan, Eleanor Farrar. "Rational Fantasies." *Policy Sciences* 7, no. 4 (1976): 439–54.

Mearsheimer, John J. "Will Iraq Fight or Fold Its Tent?" *New York Times*, 8 February 1991, A15.

Meernik, James David. "Presidential Decision-Making and the Political Use of Military Force." PhD diss., Michigan State University, 1992.

Meier, Kenneth J., and Jeffrey L. Brudney. *Applied Statistics for Public Administration.* 3d ed. Belmont, Calif.: Wadsworth Publishing Co., 1993.

Merton, Robert K. "Bureaucratic Structure and Personality." In *Classic Readings in Organizational Behavior.* J. S. Ott, ed. Pacific Grove, Calif.: Brooks/Cole Publishing Co., 1989.

Mestrovic, Stjepan G., ed. *The Conceit of Innocence: Losing the Conscience of the West in the War against Bosnia.* College Station, Tex.: Texas A&M University Press, 1997.

Michaelson, Larry K., et al. "Group Decision Making: How You Frame the Question Determines What You Find." *Journal of Applied Psychology* 77, no. 1 (1992): 106–8.

Midlarsky, Manus I., ed. *Handbook of War Studies.* Boston: Unwin Hyman, 1989.

Millennium: Journal of International Studies. "War Endings: Reasons, Strategies, and Implications. Special Issue: Journal of International Studies." Sanja Carolina and Per Hammarlund, eds. Cambridge, Mass.: MIT Press, 1997.

Miller, Benjamin. "The Great Powers and Regional Conflicts: Eastern Europe and the Balkans from the Post–Napoleonic Era to the Post–Cold War Era." *International Studies Quarterly* 41 (1997): 51–85.

———. *When Opponents Cooperate: Great Power Conflict and Collaboration in World Politics.* Ann Arbor, Mich.: University of Michigan Press, 1995.

Miller, Judith, and Laurie Mylroil. *Saddam Hussein and the Crisis in the Gulf.* New York: Times Books, 1990.

Miller, Paul David. *The Interagency Process: Engaging America's Full National Security Capabilities.* Cambridge: Institute for Foreign Policy Analysis, 1993.

Minear, Richard H. *Dr. Seuss Goes to War: The World War II Editorial Cartoons of Theodor Seuss Geisel.* New York: W. W. Norton & Co., Inc., 1999.

Minsky, M. *Semantic Information Processing.* Cambridge, Mass.: MIT Press, 1968.

Mintz, Alex. "The Decision to Attack Iraq: A Noncompensatory Theory of Decision Making." *Journal of Conflict Resolution* 37, no. 4 (1993): 595–618.

Mintzberg, Henry. "The Five Basic Parts of the Organization." In *Classics in Organization Theory.* J. M. Shafritz and J. S. Ott, eds. Pacific Grove, Calif.: Brooks/Grove Publishing Co., 1987.

———. "The Power Game and the Players." In *Classics in Organization Theory.* J. M. Shafritz and J. S. Ott, eds. Pacific Grove, Calif.: Brooks/Cole Publishing Co., 1987.

———. *The Structuring of Organizations: A Synthesis of the Research.* Englewood Cliffs, N.J.: Prentice-Hall, 1979.

Mintzberg, Henry; Duru Raisinghani; and Andre Theoret. "The Structure of 'Unstructured' Decision Processes." *Administrative Science Quarterly* 21 (1976): 246–75.

Mintzberg, Henry, et al. "Studying Deciding: An Ex-change of Views between Mintzberg and Waters, Pettigrew, and Butler." *Organization Studies* 11, no. 1 (1990): 1–16.

Mitchell, Christopher R. "Classifying Conflicts: Asymmetry and Resolution." *Annals of the American Academy of Political and Social Science* 518 (November 1991): 23–38.

———. *Cutting Losses: Reflections on Appropriate Timing, ICAR Working Paper no. 9.* Fairfax, Va.: George Mason University, 1996.

———. "Ending Conflicts and Wars: Judgement, Rationality and Entrapment." *International Social Science Journal* 43, no. 1 (1991): 35–55.

———. "Necessitous Man and Conflict Resolution: More Basic Questions About Basic Human Needs Theory." In *Conflict: Basic Human Needs Theory.* John Burton, ed. New York: St. Martin's Press, 1990, 149–76.

———. "The Right Moment: Notes on Four Models of 'Ripeness'." *Paradigms* 9, no. 2 (1995): 38–52.

———. *The Structure of International Conflict.* New York: St. Martin's Press, 1981.

Mitchell, Christopher R., and Michael Nicholson. "Rational Models and the Ending of Wars." *Journal of Conflict Resolution* 27 (1983): 495–520.

Mnookin, Robert H., and Richard Birke. "Saddam's Folly: Playing Chicken with George Bush." *Negotiation Journal* 8, no. 1 (1992): 41–47.

Molnar, Joseph J. "Comparative Organizational Properties and Interorganizational Interdependence." *Sociology and Social Research* 63, no. 1 (1978): 24–48.

Monroe, K. R., ed. *The Economic Approach to Politics: A Critical Reassessment of the Theory of Rational Action.* New York: HarperCollins, 1991.

Moore, C. W. *The Mediation Process: Practical Strategies for Resolving Conflict.* San Francisco, Calif.: Jossey-Bass Publishers, 1986.

Moore, John Norton, ed. *Crisis in the Gulf: Enforcing the Rule of Law*. New York: Oceana Publications, 1992.

Moore, Raymond A. "The Case for the War." In *The Presidency and the Persian Gulf War*. Marcia Lynn Whicker, James P. Pfiffner, and Raymond A. Moore, eds. Westport, Conn.: Praeger, 1993.

Moore, William H., III. "Why Internal Wars End: The Decision to Fight, Negotiate, or Surrender." PhD diss., University of Colorado, 1991.

Moose, Richard M. "Initiative to Reform U.S. International Affairs Programs." *Dispatch* 5, no. 10 (1994): 120–22.

Moreno, Dario. "Ideology and United States Central American Policy under Carter and Reagan." PhD diss., University of Southern California, 1987.

Morgan, Gareth. *Images of Organization*. London: Sage, 1986.

Morley, Ian E. "Intra-Organizational Bargaining." In *Employment Relations: The Psychology of Influence and Control at Work*. Jean F. Hartley and Geoffrey M. Stephenson, eds. Oxford: Blackwell, 1992, 203–24.

Morley, I. E.; J. Webb; and G. M. Stephenson. "Bargaining and Arbitration in the Resolution of Conflict." In *The Social Psychology of Intergroup Conflict*. W. Stroebe, A. W. Kruglanski, D. Bar-Tal, and M. Hewstone, eds. Berlin: Springer-Verlag, 1988, 117–34.

Morrill, Calvin. "The Management of Managers: Disputing in an Executive Hierarchy." *Sociological Forum* 4, no. 3 (1989): 387–407.

Morrow, Frank Spurgeon, Jr. "The U.S. Power Structure and the Mass Media." PhD diss., The University of Texas at Austin, 1984.

Mortimer, Edward. "The Thief of Bagdad." *The New York Review*, 27 September 1990.

Munro, Alan. *An Embassy at War: Politics and Diplomacy Behind the Gulf War*. London: Brassey's, 1996.

Nakazawa, Jun, et al. "From Social Learning Theory to Social Cognitive Theory: Recent Advances in Bandura's Theory and Related Research." *Japanese Psychological Review* 31, no. 2 (1988): 229–51.

Nan, Susan H. Allen. "Interactive Effects of Multiple Conflict Resolution Activities in Eurasian Sovereignty Conflict: The Cases of Georgian-Abkhazian, Georgian-South Ossetian, and Moldovan-Transdniestrian Conflict." PhD diss., George Mason University, 1997.

National Defense University (NDU) Interagency Transformation, Education, and After Action Review (ITEA). *Defense Is from Mars, State Is from Venus: Improving Communications and Promoting National Security.* On-line. National Defense University, 2001. Internet (cited 01/31/2001 & 11/25/2003). Available from http://www.theinteragency.org/index.cfm?state=resource.2.

National Public Radio (NPR). "The All Things Considered Persian Gulf Book List." Washington, D.C.: NPR, 1991.

Neck, Christopher P., and Charles C. Manz. "From Groupthink to Teamthink: Toward the Creation of Constructive Thought Patterns in Self-Managing Work Teams." *Human Relations* 47, no. 8 (1994): 929–52.

Neme, Laurel Abrams. "The Power of a Few: Bureaucratic Decision-Making in the Okavango Delta." *The Journal of Modern African Studies* 35, no. 1 (1997): 37–51.

Neumann, Ronald. "Overview of US Policy toward Iraq." *US Department of State Dispatch* 5, no. 7 (1994): 66–68.

Neustadt, Richard. *Alliance Politics.* New York: Wiley, 1980.

Neustadt, Richard E. *Presidential Power—the Politics of Leadership.* New York: John Wiley, 1960.

Newhouse, John. "The Diplomatic Round: Building a Cage." *The New Yorker,* 8 October 1990, 102–5.

Newman, Richard J. "Stalking Saddam: A 'Pinprick' Is out, but 'Getting' the Iraqi Leader Would Take 200,000 Troops." *U.S. News & World Report,* 23 February 1998, 18–26.

Nicholson, Michael. "Negotiation, Agreement and Conflict Resolution: The Role of Rational Approaches and Their Criticism." In *New Directions in Conflict Theory: Conflict Resolution and Conflict Transformation.* Raimo Vayrynen, ed. Newbury Park, Calif.: Sage Publications, Inc., 1991, 57–78.

Ning, Lu. *The Dynamics of Foreign-Policy Decisionmaking in China.* Boulder: Westview Press, 1997.

Nonneman, Gerd. *Iraq, the Gulf States, & the War: A Changing Relationship 1980–1986 and Beyond.* Atlantic Highlands, N.J.: Ithaca Press, 1986.

North, Robert C., et al. *Content Analysis: A Handbook with Applications for the Study of International Crisis.* Mich.: Northwestern University Press, 1963.

Nowlin, David van. "War as an Instrument of Policy: A Comparative Analysis of South Africa in Angola and the United States in the Persian Gulf War." D.P.A. diss., University of Southern California, 1994.

Nudler, Oscar. "On Conflicts and Metaphors: Toward an Extended Rationality." In *Conflict: Human Needs Theory.* J. Burton, ed. New York: St. Martin's Press, 1990, 178–87.

Nutt, Paul Charles. "Some Guides for the Selection of a Decision-Making Strategy." *Technological Forecasting and Social Change* 19, no. 2 (1981): 133–45.

Oberst, David J. *Why Wars End: An Expected Utility War Termination Model.* Carlisle Barracks, Pa.: US Army War College, 1992.

Odom, William E. *Yugoslavia: Quagmire or Strategic Challenge?* Indianapolis, Ind.: Hudson Institute, 1992.

Office of the Director of Central Intelligence (ODCI). *Central Intelligence Agency.* On-line. 15 June 1998. Internet (cited 21 Sep 1998). Available from http://www.odci.gov/ic/cia.html.

———. *Agencies of the U.S. Intelligence Community: Department of Energy.* On-line. 15 June 1998. Internet (cited 6 February 1999). Available from http://www.odci.gov/ic/icagen2.htm.

———. *Agencies of the U.S. Intelligence Community: Defense Intelligence Agency.* On-line. 15 June 1998. Internet (cited 6 February 1999). Available from http://www.odci.gov/ic/icagen2.htm.

———. *Agencies of the U.S. Intelligence Community: Department of State—Bureau of Intelligence and Research.* On-line. 15 June 1998. Internet (cited 6 February 1999). Available from http://www.odci.gov/ic/icagen2.htm.

———. *Agencies of the U.S. Intelligence Community: Federal Bureau of Investigation.* On-line. 15 June 1998. Internet (cited 6 February 1999). Available from http://www.odci. gov/ic/icagen2.htm.

————. *Agencies of the U.S. Intelligence Community: National Intelligence Council.* On-line. 15 June 1998. Internet (cited 6 February 1999). Available from http://www.odci.gov/ic/ icagen2.htm.

————. *Agencies of the U.S. Intelligence Community: National Reconnaissance Office.* On-line. 15 June 1998. Internet (cited 6 February 1999). Available from http://www.odci. gov/ic/icagen2.htm.

————. *Agencies of the U.S. Intelligence Community: National Security Agency.* On-line. 15 June 1998. Internet (cited 6 February 1999). Available from http://www.odci.gov/ic/ icagen2.htm.

————. *Agencies of the U.S. Intelligence Community: The Treasury Department—Office of Intelligence Support.* On-line. 15 June 1998. Internet (cited 6 February 1999). Available from http://www.odci.gov/ic/icagen2.htm.

————. *United States Intelligence Community.* On-line. 15 June 1998. Internet (cited 6 February 1999). Available from http://www.odci. gov/ic/index.html.

————. *U.S. Intelligence Community—Who We Are and What We Do.* On-line. 15 June 1998. Internet (cited 21 Sep 1998). Available from http://www.odci.gov/ic/functions.html.

Office of the United States Secretary of Defense (OSD). *Conduct of the Persian Gulf War, Final Report to Congress Pursuant to Title V of the Persian Gulf Conflict Supplemental Authorization and Personnel Benefits Act of 1991 (Public Law 102-25).* Washington, D.C.: GPO, 1992.

Okey, Jeffrey L. "Human Aggression: The Etiology of Individual Differences." *Journal of Humanistic Psychology* 32, no. 1 (1992): 51–64.

O'Loughlin, Michael G. "What Is Bureaucratic Accountability and How Can We Measure It?" *Administration and Society* 22, no. 3 (1990): 275–302.

O'Neill, John. "Cost-Benefit Analysis, Rationality and the Plurality of Values." *The Ecologist* 26, no. 3 (1996): 98–103.

Orbovich, Cynthia Biddle. "Cognitive Style and Foreign Policy Decisionmaking: An Examination of Eisenhower's National Security Organization." PhD diss., Ohio State University, 1986.

Osgood, Charles. "The Grit Strategy." *Bulletin of the Atomic Scientists* (1980): 58–60.

Osgood, John. *The Persian Gulf War—Was It Legal and Moral?* On-line. 26 April 1998. Internet (cited 11 February 1999). Available from http://pw2.netcom.com/~jrosgood/w15.htm.

Ott, J. Steven. *The Organizational Culture Perspective*. Chicago: Dorsey Press, 1989.

Ott, J. Steven, ed. *Classic Readings in Organizational Behavior*. Pacific Grove, Calif.: Brooks/Cole Publishing Co., 1989.

Pagnucco, Ron. "The Political Psychology of the Gulf War: Leaders, Publics, and the Process of Conflict." *Contemporary Sociology* 23, no. 3 (1994): 385–87.

Pamir, Peri. "Peace-Building Scenarios after the Gulf War." *Third World Quarterly* 13, no. 2 (1992): 283–300.

Pan, Zhongdang, and Gerald M. Kosicki. "'Voters' Reasoning Processes and Media Influences During the Persian Gulf War." *Political Behavior* 16, no. 1 (1994): 117–56.

Papacosma, S. Victor. "NATO in the Post–Cold War Balkans." *Journal of Political and Military Sociology* 24, no. 2 (1996): 233–52.

Papayoanou, Paul A. "Intra-Alliance Bargaining and US Bosnia Policy." *Journal of Conflict Resolution* 41, no. 1 (1997): 91–116.

Papp, Daniel S. "The Gulf War Coalition: The Politics and Economics of a Most Unusual Alliance." *The Eagle in the Desert: Looking Back on U.S. Involvement in the Persian Gulf War.* William Head and Earl H. Tilford Jr., eds. Westport, Conn.: Praeger, 1996.

Park, Byeong Chul. "Generational Problems and Their Effect on Foreign Policy." New York: Dept. of Sociology, Syracuse University, 1991.

Parker, Jay Morgan. "Understanding Intervention: The Utility of Decision-Making Theory." PhD diss., Columbia University, 1991.

Parker, Suzanne L. "Toward an Understanding of 'Rally' Effects: Public Opinion in the Persian Gulf War." *Public Opinion Quarterly* 59, no. 4 (1995): 526–46.

Parnell, John A., and Edward D. Bell. "The Propensity for Participative Decision Making Scale: A Measure of Managerial Propensity for Participative Decision Making." *Administration & Society* 25, no. 4 (1994): 518–30.

Parnell, John A., and Ben L. Kedia. "The Impact of National Culture on Negotiating Behaviors across Borders." *International Journal of Value Based Management* 9, no. 1 (1996): 45–61.

Parry, Robert. "The Peace Feeler That Was: Did Saddam Want a Deal?" *The Nation*, 15 April 1991, 480–82.

Patchen, Martin. "Attitudes and Behaviors toward Ethnic Outgroups: How Are They Linked?" *International Journal of Group Tensions* 25, no. 2 (1995): 169.

———. "Contact between Ethnic Groups: When and How Does It Lead to More Positive Relations?" *International Journal of Group Tensions* 25, no. 4 (1995): 271.

———. "Ethnic Group Loyalties and Societal Strife." *International Journal of Group Tensions* 25, no. 3 (1995): 227.

———. "Reciprocity of Coercion and Cooperation between Individuals and Nations." Richard B. Felson and James T. Tedeschi, eds. *Aggression and Violence: Social and Internationalist Perspectives*. Washington, D.C., 1993.

———. "Testing Alternative Models of Reciprocity against Interaction during the Cold War." *Conflict Management and Peace Science* 14 no. 2 (1995): 163.

Pavitt, Charles. "Another View of Group Polarizing: The 'Reasons for' One-Sided Oral Argumentation." *Communication Research* 21, no. 5 (1994): 625–42.

Payne, J. W. "Contingent Decision Behavior." *Psychological Bulletin* 92 (1982): 382–402.

Pescosolido, Bernice A. "Beyond Rational Choice: The Social Dynamics of How People Seek Help." *The American Journal of Sociology* 97, no. 4 (1992): 1096–138.

Pettigrew, Andrew. "On Studying Organizational Cultures." *Administrative Science Quarterly* 24, no. 4 (1979): 570–81.

———. *The Politics of Organisational Decision Making.* London: Tavistock, 1973.

Pfeffer, Jeffrey. "Understanding the Role of Power in Decision Making." In *Classics in Organization Theory.* J. M. Shafritz and J. S. Ott, eds. Pacific Grove, Calif.: Brooks/Cole Publishing Co., 1987.

Pfeffer, Jeffrey; Gerald R. Salancik; and Huseyin Leblebici. "The Effect of Uncertainty on the Use of Social Influence in Organizational Decision Making." *Administrative Science Quarterly* 21, no. 2 (1976): 227–45.

Pfiffner, James P. "Presidential Policy-Making and the Gulf War." *The Presidency and the Persian Gulf War.* Marcia Lynn Whicker, James P. Pfiffner, and Raymond A. Moore, eds. Westport, Conn.: Praeger, 1993, 3–23.

Pfiffner, James P., and R. Gordon Hoxie, eds. *The Presidency in Transition.* Vol. 6, no. 1. New York: Center for the Study of the Presidency, 1989.

Pickus, Robert, and Robert Woito. *To End War: An Introduction to the Ideas, Organizations and Current Books.* New York: Harper & Row Publishers, 1970.

Pillar, Paul R. *Negotiating Peace: War Termination as a Bargaining Process.* Princeton, N.J.: Princeton University Press, 1983.

Pinette, Roy R. *Operational Considerations for War Termination.* Newport, R.I.: US Naval War College, 1994.

Plesch, Daniel T. "A Military Tragedy." *The New York Times,* 8 February 1991.

Plummer, Anne. *GAO: Military Support to Civil Missions Does Not Impact Retention.* On-line. Inside The Pentagon, 2001. Internet (cited 02/01/2001). Available from http://ebird.dtic.mil/Feb2001/s20010201gao.htm.

Polzer, Jeffrey T. "Intergroup Negotiations: The Effects of Negotiating Teams." *Journal of Conflict Resolution* 40, no. 4 (1996): 678–98.

Poole, Marshall Scott, and Jonelle Roth. "Decision Development in Small Groups IV: A Typology of Group Decision Paths." *Human Communication Research* 15, no. 3 (1989): 323–56.

———. "Decision Development in Small Groups V: Test of a Contingency Model." *Human Communication Research* 15, no. 4 (1989): 549–89.

Posen, Barry R., and Andrew L. Ross. "Competing Visions for US Grand Strategy." *International Security* 21, no. 3 (1996): 5–53.

Potter, W. James. "Examining Cultivation from a Psychological Perspective: Component Subprocesses." *Communication Research* 18, no. 1 (1991): 77–102.

Powell, Colin L. "The NSC System in the Last Two Years of the Reagan Administration." In *The Presidency in Transition.* Edited by James P. Pfiffner, R. Gordon Hoxie, with Peri E. Arnold, Gerald R. Ford and Center for Study of the Presidency. New York: Center for the Study of the Presidency, 1989, 204–18.

Powell, Colin L., and Joseph E. Persico. *My American Journey.* New York: Random House, 1995.

Powlick, Philip J. "The Attitudinal Bases for Responsiveness to Public Opinion among American Foreign Policy Officials." *Journal of Conflict Resolution* 35, no. 4 (1991): 611–41.

———. "The American Foreign Policy Process and the Public." PhD diss., University of Pittsburgh, 1990.

Prados, John. *Keepers of the Keys: A History of the National Security Council from Truman to Bush.* New York: William Morrow and Co., Inc., 1991.

Preston, John Thomas. "The President and His Inner Circle: Leadership Style and the Advisory Process in Foreign Policy-Making." PhD diss., Ohio State University, 1996.

Prohaska, Charles R., and Ellen J. Frank. "Using Simulations to Investigate Management Decision Making." *Simulation & Gaming* 21, no. 1 (1990): 48–58.

Pruitt, Dean. *Negotiation Behavior.* New York: Academic Press, 1981.

—————. "Strategy in Negotiation." In *International Negotiation: Analysis, Approaches, Issues.* V. Kremenyuk, ed. San Francisco, Calif.: Jossey-Bass, 1991.

Pruitt, Dean G., and Peter J. Carnevale. *Negotiation in Social Conflict.* In *Mapping Social Psychology Series,* Tony Manstead, ed. Pacific Grove, Calif.: Brooks/Cole Publishing Co., 1993.

Pugliaresi, Lucian, and Diane T. Berliner. "Policy Analysis at the Department of State: The Policy Planning Staff." *Journal of Policy Analysis and Management* 8, no. 3 (1989): 379–94.

Putnam, Robert D. "Diplomacy and Domestic Politics: The Logic of Two-Level Games." *International Organization* 42, no. 3 (1988): 427–60.

Qin, Zhining; David W. Johnson; and Roger T. Johnson. "Cooperative Versus Competitive Efforts and Problem Solving." *Review of Educational Research* 65, no. 2 (1995): 129–43.

Quade, E. S., ed. *Analysis for Military Decisions.* Chicago: RAND McNally, 1964.

Quester, George H. "Wars Prolonged by Misunderstood Signals." *The Annals of the American Academy of Political and Social Science* 392 (1970): 30–39.

Rabbie, J. M. "The Effects of Intergroup Competition and Cooperation on Intragroup and Intergroup Relationship." In *Cooperation and Helping Behavior: Theories and Research.* V. J. Derlega and J. Grezlak, eds. New York: Academic Press, 1982.

Rampy, Michael R. "Endgame: Conflict Termination and Post–Conflict Activities." *Military Review* 72 (1992): 42–54.

Ramsdell, Penny Smith. "Staff Participation in Organizational Decision-Making: An Empirical Study." *Administration in Social Work* 18, no. 4 (1994): 51–71.

Randle, Robert. "The Domestic Origins of Peace." *The Annals of the American Academy of Political and Social Science* 392 (1970): 76–85.

Rapoport, Anatol. *Fights, Games, and Debates.* Binghamton, New York: Vail-Ballou Press, 1960.

Rast, Vicki J. "Conflict Termination in the Persian Gulf War: Policy Failure Sustains Conflict." In *Soldier, Scientist, Diplomat, Mediator: The Multi-Disciplinary Context of Conflict Resolu-*

tion. Edited by L. E. Hancock and et al. Fairfax, Va.: Graduate Students in Conflict Studies, Institute for Conflict Analysis and Resolution, George Mason University, 1999.

———. "Group Decision-Making: A Critique of Rational Choice Theory Reveals the Bureaucratic Politics Model's Descriptive Value." Fairfax, Va.: Institute for Conflict Analysis and Resolution, 1998.

———. "Interagency Conflict and U.S. Intervention: Toward a Bureaucratic Model of Conflict Termination." PhD diss., George Mason University, 1999.

———. "The Iraq-Kuwait Crisis: Structural Deprivation Leads to Revolution." In *Intervention Design in Conflict Analysis and Resolution: Theory, Practice, and Research.* Edited by L. A. Fast with V. J. Rast et al. Fairfax, Va.: Institute for Conflict Analysis and Resolution, George Mason University, 1998.

Rast, Vicki J., and Bruce R. Sturk. "Coalitions: The Challenge of Effective Command and Control in Support of the Air Campaign." In *Theater Air Campaign Studies.* Pat Battles, ed. Maxwell AFB, Ala.: Air Command and Staff College, 1995.

Raymond, Gregory A. "Democracies, Disputes, and Third-Party Intermediaries." *Journal of Conflict Resolution* 38, no. 1 (1994): 24–42.

Reese, W. A. *The Principle of the Objective and Promoting National Interests: Desert Shield/Storm—A Case Study.* Washington, D.C.: Industrial College of the Armed Forces, 1993.

Reich, Bernard. *The United States and Israel: Influence in the Special Relationship.* New York: Praeger, 1984.

Reynolds, Richard T. *Heart of the Storm: The Genesis of the Air Campaign against Iraq.* Vol. 1. Maxwell Air Force Base, Ala.: Air University Press, 1995.

Richards, Diana. "Is Strategic Decision Making Chaotic?" *Behavioral Science* 35, no. 3 (1990): 219–32.

Richman, Sheldon L. "Washington's Interventionist Record in the Middle East." In *America Entangled.* Ted Galen Carpenter, ed. Washington, D.C.: The Cato Institute, 1991.

Rios, Leon H. *Seeking a Final Victory: Creating Conditions for Conflict Resolution.* Carlisle Barracks, Pa.: US Army War College, 1993.

Riscassi, Robert W. "Principles for Coalition Warfare." *Joint Forces Quarterly* (1993): 58–71.

Rivas, J. P. *Petroleum Status of the Western Persian Gulf.* CRS, ed. Report to Congress No. 90-378 SPR. Washington, D.C.: The Library of Congress, 1990.

Rizer, Kenneth R., Major, USAF. *Military Resistance to Humanitarian War in Kosovo and Beyond: An Ideological Explanation, The Fairchild Papers.* Maxwell Air Force Base, Ala.: Air University Press, 2000.

Robins, Barbara J. "Policy Outputs and Bureaucracy: The Roles of Need, Demand, and Agency Structure." *Urban Affairs Quarterly* 18, no. 4 (1983): 485–509.

Robinson, J. P. Perry. "The Negotiations on Chemical-Warfare Arms Control." *Arms Control* 1, no. 1 (1980): 30–52.

Robson, Colin. *Real World Research: A Resource for Social Scientists and Practitioner-Researchers.* Oxford, United Kingdom: Blackwell, 1993.

Rockman, Burt A. *The Leadership Question.* Pittsburgh, Pa.: University of Pittsburgh Press, 1986.

Rogers, David L., and Joseph Molnar. "Organizational Antecedents of Role Conflict and Ambiguity in Top-Level Administrators." *Administrative Science Quarterly* 21 (1976): 598–610.

Rogers, Thomas L. "The Good War Revisited: Two Instant Histories of the Persian Gulf Conflict." *Military Sociology Reviews* 19, no. 1 (1991): 175–76.

———. "Secret Dossier: The Hidden Agenda Behind the Gulf War." *Journal of Political and Military Sociology* 19, no. 1 (1991): 175–76.

Rohde, David. *Endgame: The Betrayal and Fall of Srebrenica, Europe's Worst Massacre since World War II.* New York: Farrar, Straus, and Giroux, 1997.

Roloff, M. E. "Communication and Reciprocity within Intimate Relationships." In *Interpersonal Processes: New Directions in Communication Research.* R. E. Roloff and G. R. Miller, eds. Beverly Hills, Calif.: Sage, 1987.

Roloff, M. E., and D. E. Campion. "Conversational Profit-Seeking: Interaction as Social Exchange." In *Sequence and Pattern in*

Communicative Behavior. R. L. Street and J. N. Cappella, eds. London: Edward Arnold, 1985.

Rosati, Jerel A. "The Power of Human Cognition in the Study of World Politics." *International Studies Review* 2, no. 3 (2000): 45–75.

Rosenthal, Uriel, and Alexander Kousmin. "Crisis and Crisis Management: Toward Comprehensive Government Decision Making." *Journal of Public Administration Research and Theory* 7, no. 2 (1997): 277–304.

Rosner, Jeremy D. "NATO Enlargement's American Hurdle: The Perils of Misjudging Our Political Will." *Foreign Affairs* 75, no. 4 (1996): 9–16.

Roth, Alvin E. "An Economic Approach to the Study of Bargaining." In *Research on Negotiation in Organizations.* Max H. Bazerman, Roy J. Lewicki, and Blair H. Sheppard, eds. Greenwich & London: JAI Press, Inc., 1991, 35–67.

———. "Introduction to Experimental Economics." In *The Handbook of Experimental Economics.* J. H. Kagel and A. E. Roth, eds. Princeton, N.J.: Princeton University Press, 1995, 3–109.

Rothstein, Robert. "Domestic Politics and Peacemaking: Reconciling Incompatible Imperatives." *The Annals of the American Academy of Political and Social Science* 392 (1970).

———. *Planning, Prediction, and Policymaking in Foreign Affairs: Theory and Practice.* Boston, Mass.: Little, Brown and Co., 1972.

Rourke, Francis E. *Bureaucracy, Politics, and Public Policy.* Boston, Mass.: Little, Brown and Co., 1976.

Rourke, Francis E., and Paul R. Schulman. "Adhocracy in Policy Development." *Social Science Journal* 26 (1989): 131–42.

Rubenstein, Richard E. *On Taking Sides: Lessons of the Persian Gulf War.* Fairfax, Va.: George Mason University, 1993.

Rubin, Jeffrey Z., et al. "Factors Affecting Entry into Psychological Traps." *Journal of Conflict Resolution* 24, no. 3 (1980): 405–26.

Rubin, Jeffrey Z.; Dean G. Pruitt; and Sung Hee Kim. *Social Conflict: Escalation, Stalemate, and Settlement.* 2d ed. New York: McGraw-Hill, Inc., 1994.

Rubin, Jeffrey Z., and I. William Zartman. "Asymmetrical Negotiations: Some Survey Results That May Surprise." *Negotiation Journal* 11, no. 4 (1995): 349–64.

Russett, Bruce, and Thomas W. Graham. "Public Opinion and National Security Policy: Relationships and Impacts." In *Handbook of War Studies.* Manus I. Midlarsky, ed. Boston: Unwin Hyman, 1989, 239–57.

Russett, Bruce M. "Refining Deterrence Theory: The Japanese Attack on Pearl Harbor." In *Theory and Research on the Causes of War.* D. G. Pruitt and R. C. Snyder, eds. Englewood Cliffs, N.J.: Prentice-Hall, 1969.

Sabrosky, Alan Ned; James Clay Thompson; and Karen A. McPherson. "Organized Anarchies: Military Bureaucracy in the 1980s." *Journal of Applied Behavioral Science* 18, no. 2 (1982): 137–53.

Said, Edward W., and Barbara Harlow. "The Intellectuals and the War." *Middle East Report* 21, no. 4 (1991): 15–20.

Salant, Priscilla, and Don A. Dillman. *How to Conduct Your Own Survey.* New York: John Wiley & Sons, Inc., 1994.

Salazar, Abran J., et al. "In Search of True Causes: Examination of the Effect of Group Potential and Group Interaction on Decision Performance." *Human Communication Research* 20, no. 4 (1994): 529–59.

Salinger, Pierre, and Eric Laurent. *Secret Dossier: The Hidden Agenda Behind the Gulf War.* New York: Penguin Books, 1991.

Salmon, Trevor C. "Testing Times for European Political Cooperation: The Gulf and Yugoslavia, 1990–1992." *International Affairs* 68, no. 2 (1992): 233–53.

Samuelson, Larry. "Bounded Rationality and Game Theory." *The Quarterly Review of Economics and Finance* 36 (1996): 17–35.

Sanders, Jerry W. "The Gulf War and Bush's Folly." *Peace Review* 3, no. 2 (1991): 27–35.

Sandole, Dennis J. D. "Ethnic Conflict Resolution in the New Europe: A Case for an Integrated Systems Approach." In *Peace Research for the 1990s.* J. Balasz and H. Wiberg, eds. Budapest, Hungary: Hungarian Academy of Sciences, 1993.

———. "Paradigms, Theories, and Metaphors in Conflict Resolution: Coherence or Confusion." In *Conflict Resolution Theory and Practice: Integration and Application*. Dennis J. D. Sandole and H. van der Merwe, eds. Manchester & New York: Manchester University Press, 1993.

Sandole, Dennis J. D., and Hugo van der Merwe. *Conflict Resolution Theory and Practice: Integration and Application*. Manchester & New York: Manchester University Press, 1993.

Sandven, Tore. "Intentional Action and Pure Causality: A Critical Discussion of Some Central Conceptual Distinctions in the Work of Jon Elster." *Philosophy of the Social Sciences* 25, no. 3 (1995): 286.

Sarkesian, Sam C. *U.S. National Security: Policymakers, Processes, and Politics*. 2d ed. Boulder & London: Lynne Rienner Publishers, 1995.

Sawyer, Jack, and Harold Guetzkow. *Bargaining and Negotiation in International Relations*. In *International Behavior*. Herbert C. Kolman, ed. New York: Holt, Rinehart, and Winston, 1965.

Scanzoni, John, and Deborah D. Godwin. "Negotiation Effectiveness and Acceptable Outcomes." *Social Psychology Quarterly* 53, no. 3 (1990): 239–52.

Schein, Edgar H. "Defining Organizational Culture." In *Classics of Organization Theory*. J. M. Shafritz and J. S. Ott, eds. Pacific Grove, Calif.: Brooks/Cole Publishing Co., 1987.

———. "Group and Intergroup Relationships." In *Classic Readings in Organizational Behavior*. J. S. Ott, ed. Pacific Grove, Calif.: Brooks/Cole Publishing Co., 1989.

———. *Organizational Culture and Leadership*. San Francisco: Jossey-Bass, 1992.

Schelling, Thomas C. *The Strategy of Conflict*. Cambridge, Mass.: Harvard University Press, 1963.

———. *Choice and Consequence*. Cambridge: Harvard University Press, 1984.

Schneider, Barry. "Terminating Strategic Exchanges: Requirements and Prerequisites." In *Conflict Termination and Military Strategy: Coercion, Persuasion, and War*. S. J. Cimbala and K. A. Dunn, eds.. Boulder: Westview Press, 1987, 109–19.

Schneider, Benjamin. "Organizational Behavior." *Annual Review of Psychology* 36 (1985): 573–611.

Scholz, Roland W., ed. *Decision Making under Uncertainty: Cognitive Decision Research, Social Interaction, and Development and Epistemology.* G. E. Stelmach and P. A. Vroon, eds. *Advances in Psychology.* Vol. 16. North-Holland: Elsevier Science Publishers B. V., 1983.

———. "Introduction" to *Decision Making under Uncertainty: Cognitive Decision Research, Social Interaction, and Development and Epistemology.* North-Holland: Elsevier Science Publishers B. V., 1983, 3–18.

Schön, Donald A., and Martin Rein. *Frame Reflection: Toward the Resolution of Intractable Policy Controversies.* New York: Basic Books, 1994.

Schwarzkopf, H. Norman, and with Peter Petre. *General H. Norman Schwarzkopf: The Autobiography: It Doesn't Take a Hero.* New York: Bantam Books, 1992.

Sclove, Richard. "Decision-Making in a Democracy." *Bulletin of the Atomic Scientists* 38 (1982): 44–48.

Scott, Patrick G. "Assessing Determinants of Bureaucratic Discretion: An Experiment in Street-Level Decision Making." *Journal of Public Administration Research and Theory* 7, no. 1 (1997): 35–57.

Seabury, Paul, and Angelo Codevilla. *War: Ends and Means.* New York: Basic Books, 1989.

Serwer, Daniel. "Bosnia: Peace by Piece." *Strategic Forum,* no. 81 (1996).

Sethi, Amarjit S. "Developing Excellence through Imaginative Organizational Culture: A Strategic Systems Approach." Ontario, Canada: University of Ottawa, 1994.

Shafritz, Jay M., and J. Steven Ott, eds. *Classics of Organization Theory.* 2d, Revised and Expanded edition. Chicago: Dorsey Press, 1987.

Shaheen, Jack G., et al. "Media Coverage of the Middle East: Perception and Foreign Policy." *Annals of the American*

Academy of Political and Social Science 482 (November 1985): 160–73.

Shapiro, M. J., and G. M. Bonham. "Cognitive Process and Foreign Policy Decision-Making." *International Studies Quarterly* 17 (1973): 147–74.

Sheehan, Neil. *A Bright Shining Lie: John Paul Vann and America in Vietnam.* New York: Random House, 1988.

Shoemaker, Christopher. *The NSC Staff: Counseling the Council.* Boulder: Westview Press, 1991.

———. *Structure, Function and the NSC Staff: An Officers' [Sic] Guide to the National Security Council.* Carlisle Barracks, Pa.: Strategic Studies Institute, US Army War College, 1989.

Shoup, Paul. *The Bosnian Crisis of 1992.* Washington, D.C.: The National Council for Soviet and East European Research, 1992.

Sidrow, Michael Robert. "Politics and Military Weapons Acquisition: The Limits of Bureaucratic Political Theory." PhD diss., University of California, Riverside, 1983.

Siegel, Sidney, and N. John Castellan Jr. *Nonparametric Statistics for the Behavioral Sciences.* New York: McGraw-Hill, Inc., 1988.

Sigal, Leon V. *Disarming Strangers: Nuclear Diplomacy with North Korea.* Princeton: Princeton University Press, 1998.

———. *Fighting to a Finish: The Politics of War Termination in the United States and Japan, 1945.* Ithaca & London: Cornell University Press, 1988.

Simon, Herbert A. *Administrative Behavior: A Study of Decision-Making Processes in Administrative Organizations.* New York: Free Press, 1976.

———. "A Behavioral Model of Rational Choice." *Quarterly Journal of Economics,* vol. 69 (February 1955): 99–118.

———. "Human Nature in Politics: The Dialogue of Psychology and Political Science." *American Political Science Review* 79 (1985): 293–305.

———. "Motivational and Emotional Controls of Cognition." *Psychological Review* 74 (1967): 29–39.

———. "Rational Decision Making in Business Organizations." *American Economic Review* 64, no. 4 (1979): 493–513.

———. *The Sciences of the Artificial.* Cambridge, Mass.: MIT Press, 1969.

Simon, Herbert A., and Associates. "Decision Making and Problem Solving." In *Decision Making: Alternatives to Rational Choice Models.* Mary Zey, ed. Newbury Park, Calif.: Sage Publications, 1992.

Simon, Jeffrey. "Sources of Balkan Insecurity: The Need for a Comprehensive Strategy." *Strategic Forum*, no. 150 (1998).

Sjoberg, Gideon, and Roger Nett. *A Methodology for Social Research.* New York: Harper & Row, 1968.

Slovic, Paul. "The Construction of Preference." *The American Psychologist* 50, no. 5 (1995): 364–71.

Slovic, Paul, and Sarah Lichtenstein. "Preference Reversals: A Broader Perspective." *American Economic Review* 73 (1983): 596–605.

Smith, James A. *The Idea Brokers: Think Tanks and the Rise of the New Policy Elite.* New York: Free Press, 1991.

Smith, James D. D. *Stopping Wars: Defining the Obstacles to Cease-Fire.* Boulder: Westview Press, 1995.

Smoler, Fredric. "What Does History Have to Say About the Persian Gulf?" *American Heritage* 41 (1990): 100–107.

Snow, Donald M. *National Security: Enduring Problems in a Changing Defense Environment.* 2d ed. New York: St. Martin's Press, 1991.

Snow, Donald M., and Eugene Brown. *Puzzle Palaces and Foggy Bottom: US Foreign and Defense Policy-Making in the 1990s.* New York: St. Martin's Press, 1994.

Snow, Donald M., and Dennis M. Drew. *From Lexington to Desert Storm: War and Politics in the American Experience.* New York: M. E. Sharpe, 1994.

Snyder, Richard; H. W. Bruck; and Burton Sapin. *Foreign Policy Decision-Making.* New York: Free Press, 1962.

Snyder, William P. *Making US National Security Policies.* Carlisle Barracks, Pa.: US Army War College, 1976.

———. *Strategy: Defining It, Understanding It, and Making It.* Maxwell AFB, Ala.: Air War College, 1 June 1991: 11–21.

Sorenson, James R. "Group Member Traits, Group Process, and Group Performance." *Human Relations* 26, no. 5 (1973): 639–55.

Spanier, John, and Eric M. Uslaner. *How American Foreign Policy Is Made.* New York & Washington: Praeger, 1974.

Spector, Bertram I. "Creativity Heuristics for Impasse Resolution: Reframing Intractable Negotiations." *The Annals of the American Academy of Political and Social Science* 542 (1995): 81–99.

———. "Metaphors of International Negotiation." *International Negotiation* 1, no. 1 (1996): 1–9.

Springer, J. Fred. "Policy Analysis and Organizational Decisions: Toward a Conceptual Revision." *Administration & Society* 16, no. 4 (1985): 475–508.

SPSS Base 8.0 Applications Guide. Chicago, Ill.: SPSS Inc., 1998.

St. Amand, Gerard A. *Clausewitz and the Gulf War: The Political-Military Dynamics in Balance.* Washington, D.C.: National Defense University, 1994.

Stallaerts, Robert. "Forging War. The Media in Serbia, Croatia and Bosnia-Hercegovina." *Tijdschrift voor Sociale Wetenschappen* 40, no. 1 (1995): 102.

Staudenmaier, William O. "Conflict Termination in the Third World: Theory and Practice." In *The Lessons of Recent War in the Third World.* Stephanie G. Neuman and Robert E. Harkavy, eds. Lexington: D. C. Heath and Co., 1987.

Staw, Barry. "The Escalation of Commitment to a Course of Action." *Academy of Management Review* 6 (1981): 577–87.

———. "Knee-Deep in the Big Muddy: A Study of Escalating Commitment to a Chosen Course of Action." *Organizational Behavior and Human Performance* 16 (1976): 27–44.

———. "Motivation from the Bottom Up." In *Psychological Foundations of Organizational Behavior.* B. Staw, ed. Santa Monica, Calif.: Goodyear, 1977.

———. *Psychological Foundations of Organizational Behavior.* Santa Monica, Calif.: Goodyear, 1977.

Staw, Barry M., ed. *Research in Organizational Behavior.* Vol. 9. Greenwich, Conn.: JAI Press, 1987.

Staw, Barry M., and J. Ross. "Behavior in Escalation Situations: Antecedents, Prototypes, and Situation." In *Research in Organizational Behavior.* B. M. Staw, ed. Greenwich, Conn.: JAI Press, 1987, 39–78.

Sterner, Michael. "Navigating the Gulf." *Foreign Policy*, no. 81 (winter 1990–1991): 39–52.

Stoessinger, John D. *Crusaders and Pragmatists: Movers of American Foreign Policy.* New York: Norton, 1979.

Strauch, Ralph E. "Winners and Losers: A Conceptual Barrier in Our Strategic Thinking." Santa Monica, Calif.: RAND Corp., 1972.

Strauss, Anselm. "Summary, Implications, and Debate." *Negotiations: Varieties, Contexts, Processes, and Social Order.* San Francisco: Jossey-Bass, 1978.

Strauss, Anselm, and Juliet Corbin. *Basics of Qualitative Research: Grounded Theory Procedures and Techniques.* Newbury Park. Calif.: Sage Publications, 1990.

———. "Grounded Theory Methodology: An Overview." In *Handbook of Qualitative Research.* Norman K. Denzin and Yvonna S. Lincoln, eds. Thousand Oaks, Calif.: Sage Publications, 1994.

Strednansky, Susan E. *Balancing the Trinity: The Fine Art of Conflict Termination.* Maxwell Air Force Base, Ala.: Air University Press, 1996.

Sullivan, Peter. "Iraq's Enduring Proliferation Threat." *Strategic Forum*, no. 95 (1996).

Sullivan, Ricki Lynn. *The Operational Planner and War Termination.* Newport, R.I.: US Naval War College, 1993.

Summers, Harry G. *A Critical Analysis of the Gulf War.* New York: Dell, 1992.

———. "War: Deter, Fight, Terminate." *Naval War College Review* 39 (1986): 18–29.

Sutherland, M. A., and H. M. Lommer. *1234 Modern End-Game Studies with Appendix Containing 24 Additional Studies.* New York: Dover Publications, 1968.

Tack, Werner H. "Conditions of Violating Individual Rationality." In *Decision Making under Uncertainty: Cognitive Decision Research, Social Interaction, and Development and Episte-*

mology. R. W. Scholz, ed. North-Holland: Elsevier Science Publishers B.V., 1983.

Tajfel, Henri; M. G. Billig; and R. P. Bundy. "Social Categorization and Intergroup Behavior." *European Journal of Social Psychology* 1 (1971): 149–77.

Talbott, Strobe. *Endgame: The Inside Story of Salt II.* New York: Harper & Row, 1979.

Tan, Qingshan. "U.S.-China Policy: A Function of Strategy or Process?" PhD diss., Emory University, 1989.

Tanter, Raymond. *Rogue Regimes: Terrorism and Proliferation.* New York: St. Martin's Press, 1998.

Tarver, Heidi. "Words of War: The Persian Gulf Crisis and American Public Discourse." PhD diss., University of California, Berkeley, 1997.

Teger, Alan I. *Too Much Invested to Quit: The Psychology of the Escalation of Conflict.* New York: Pergamon Press, 1980.

Terssac, Gilbert de, and Nicole Lompre. "Autonomy as a Principle of Organization: Relationships between Organizational Models and Technology." 1994.

Thalos, Mariam. "Self-Interest, Autonomy, and the Presuppositions of Decision Theory." *American Philosophical Quarterly* 34, no. 2 (1997): 287–300.

Thomas, Craig W. "Public Management as Interagency Cooperation: Testing Epistemic Community Theory as the Domestic Level." *Journal of Public Administration Research and Theory* 7, no. 2 (1997): 221–46.

Thomas, Norman C. "The Presidency and Policy Studies." *Policy Studies Journal* 9, no. 7 (1981): 1072–82.

Thomas, Pierre. "Interagency FBI-CIA Tensions Defy Decades of Efforts to Resolve Them." *Washington Post*, 3 May 1994, A4.

Thompson, Earl A., and Roger L. Faith. "Social Interaction under Truly Perfect Information." *Journal of Mathematical Sociology* 7, no. 2 (1980): 181–97.

Thompson, James D. "Organizations in Action." In *Classics of Organization Theory.* J. M. Shafritz and J. S. Ott, eds. Pacific Grove, Calif.: Brooks/Cole Publishing Co., 1987.

———. *Organizations in Action: Social Science Bases of Administrative Theory.* New York: McGraw-Hill, 1967.

Thompson, James R. *Empirical Model Building.* New York: Wiley, 1989.

———. *Nonparametric Function Estimation, Modeling, and Simulation.* Philadelphia: Society for Industrial and Applied Mathematics, 1990.

Thompson, Leigh; Erika Peterson; and Susan E. Brodt. "Team Negotiation: An Examination of Integrative and Distributive Bargaining." *Journal of Personality and Social Psychology* 70, no. 1 (1996): 66–78.

Thompson, Richard K. "Another Pizza, Another Policy: Decision-Making in the Clinton White House." *Contemporary Review* 267, no. 1557 (1995): 188–92.

Tims, Albert R., and M. Mark Miller. "Determinants of Attitudes toward Foreign Countries." *International Journal of Intercultural Relations* 10, no. 4 (1986): 471–84.

Tindale, R. Scott, and James R. Larson Jr. "It's Not How You Frame the Question, It's How You Interpret the Results." *Journal of Applied Psychology* 77, no. 1 (1992): 109–10.

Tolbert, Pamela S. "Negotiations in Organizations: A Sociological Perspective." In *Research on Negotiations in Organizations: A Research Annual.* Max H. Bazerman, Roy J. Lewicki, and Blair H. Sheppard, eds. Greenwich, Conn.: JAI Press, 1991, 99–117.

Toth, James. *Conflict Termination: Considerations for Development of National Strategy.* Maxwell Air Force Base, Ala.: Air War College, 1978.

———. "Demonizing Saddam Hussein: Manipulating Racism as a Prelude to War." *New Political Science* 21–22 (spring–summer 1992): 5–39.

———. "Foreign Policy Analysis: Conflict Termination in the Persian Gulf War." Washington, D.C.: National Defense University, 1991.

Tucker, Robert C. *Politics as Leadership.* Columbia: University of Missouri Press, 1981.

Turner, Ralph H. "Unanswered Questions in the Convergence between Structuralist and Interactionist Role Theories." Los Angeles: University of California, 1982.

Tutu, Desmond. "Leadership." *Essays on Leadership: Perspectives on Prevention.* New York: Carnegie Corp. of New York, 1998.

Tversky, Amos, and Daniel Kahneman. "The Framing of Decisions and the Psychology of Choice." *Science* 211 (1981): 453–58.

———. "Judgment under Uncertainty: Heuristics and Biases." *Science* 185, no. 4157 (1974): 1124–31.

———. "Loss Aversion in Riskless Choice: A Reference Dependent Model." *Quarterly Journal of Economics* 41 (1991): 1039–61.

———. "Rational Choice and the Framing of Decisions." *Journal of Business* 59, no. 4, 2 (1986): S251–S78.

Tversky, Amos; Paul Slovic; and Daniel Kahneman. "The Causes of Preference Reversal." *American Economic Review* 80 (1990): 204–17.

Tversky, Amos, and Peter Wakker. "Risk Attitudes and Decision Weights." *Econometrica* 63, no. 6 (1995): 1255–80.

Tyler, Tom, and Reid Hastie. "The Social Consequences of Cognitive Illusions." In *Research on Negotiation in Organizations.* Max H. Bazerman, Roy J. Lewicki, and Blair H. Sheppard, eds. Greenwich & London: JAI Press, 1991, 69–98.

Ugalde, Antonio. "A Decision Model for the Study of Public Bureaucracies." *Policy Sciences* 4, no. 1 (1973): 75–84.

Ulen, Thomas S. "The Theory of Rational Choice, Its Shortcomings, and the Implications for Public Policy Decision Making." *Knowledge: Creation, Diffusion, Utilization* 12, no. 2 (1990): 170–98.

United Nations High Commissioner on Refugees (UNHCR). "Refugee Crisis." *The Washington Post*, 2 April 1999, A22.

United Nations. *Resolutions of the United Nations Security Council and Statements by Its President Concerning the Situation between Iraq and Kuwait.* New York: United Nations Department of Public Information, 1994.

United States Institute of Peace (USIP). *The Military Balance in Bosnia and Its Effect on the Prospects for Peace.* Washington, D.C.: USIP, 1995.

US *The Declaration of Independence and the Constitution of the United States of America, with an Introduction by Richard G. Stevens.* Washington, D.C.: GPO, 1995.

US Air Force Academy (USAFA). *Contrails.* Vol. 30, *Air Force Academy Cadet Handbook.* Boulder, Colo.: USAFA, 1984.

US Army Civil Affairs and Psychological Operations Command (USACAPOC). On-line. US Army, 1999. Internet (cited 2 April 1999). Available from http://www.geocity.com/Pentagon/1012/psyop.html.

US Army, Headquarters, Department of the Army. "Information Operations and Battlefield Simulation/Digitization." *Military Review* 75, no. 6 (1995).

US Army War College, Dept. of Corresponding Studies. *Conflict Termination and Military Operations Other Than War.* Carlisle Barracks, Pa.: US Army War College, 1997.

US Congress. "National Security Act of 1947." House, Committee on Armed Services, DOD Reorganization Act of 1958. Report, 85th Cong., 2d sess.: 26 July 1958.

———. "Persian Gulf Crisis." Washington, D.C.: GPO, 1990.

———. "Postwar Economic Recovery in the Persian Gulf." Washington, D.C.: GPO, 1991.

US Department of Defense (DOD). *Office of the Secretary of Defense Organization and Functions Book.* Washington, D.C.: Office of the Secretary of Defense, 1996.

US Department of Defense (DOD) Joint Chiefs of Staff (JCS). "National Military Strategy: Shape, Respond, Prepare Now: A Military Strategy for a New Era." Washington, D.C.: The Joint Staff, 1997.

———. Joint Pub 3-0, *Doctrine for Joint Operations.* 1995.

———. Joint Pub 3-07, *Joint Doctrine for Military Operations Other Than War.* 1995.

———. Joint Pub 3-08, *Interagency Coordination During Joint Operations.* Vol. 1. 1996.

US Department of Defense (DOD) Joint Warfighting Center (JWC). *Joint Task Force Commander's Handbook for Peace Operations.* Fort Monroe, Va.: Joint Warfighting Center, 1995.

US Department of State (DOS). *ACDA: U.S. Arms Control and Disarmament Agency.* On-line. 1997. Internet (cited 6 February 1999). Available from http://www.state.gov/www/publications/statemag/statemag_sep–oct/feature2.html.

———. "Advancing U.S. Interests in Europe." *Dispatch* 6, no. 12 (1995).

———. *Albright Newscon with Croatia President Tudjman.* On-line. US Department of State, 1998. Internet (cited 21 September 1998). Available from http://secretary.state.gov/www/statements/1998/980830c.html.

———. "American Leadership and the New Europe: Implementing the Dayton Peace Agreement." *Dispatch* 6, nos. 50, 51, 52 (1995): 917–20.

———. "American Leadership at Stake." *Dispatch* 6, no. 21 (1995): 411–16.

———. "American Leadership in the Middle East: Supporting the Friends and Opposing the Enemies of Peace." *Dispatch* 6, no. 15 (1995): 292–95.

———. "American Power and American Diplomacy." *Dispatch* 5, no. 46 (1994): 766–69.

———. "The Americas in the 21st Century: Defining U.S. Interests." *Dispatch* 7, nos. 1, 2, 3 (1996): 4–7.

———. "Bosnia: An Acid Test of U.S. Leadership." *Dispatch* 6, no. 48 (1995): 870–72.

———. "Bosnians Agree to Implement Cease-Fire." *Dispatch* 6, no. 42 (1995): 736.

———. "Building the Structures of Peace and Prosperity in the New Middle East." *Dispatch* 5, no. 45 (1994): 733–34.

———. "Casablanca Declaration." *Dispatch* 5, no. 45 (1994): 735–37.

———. "Combating Threats to Peace in the Middle East." *Dispatch* 5, no. 43 (1994): 712–15.

———. "Contact Group Meeting on Bosnia-Herzegovina." *Dispatch* 5, no. 51 (1994): 836–38.

———. "Contact Group Ministers Urge Strengthening of Unprofor." *Dispatch* 6, no. 23 (1995): 476–77.

———. *Duties of the Secretary of State*. On-line. 1997. Internet (cited 6 February 1999). Available from http://www.state.gov/www/albright/.

———. "Establishing a Basis for Peace in Bosnia-Herzegovina." *Dispatch* 6, no. 37 (1995).

———. "Fact Sheet: Structure and Organization." Edited by Bureau of Public Affairs Office of Public Communication. Washington, D.C.: US Department of State, 1995.

———. "Fifth Report on War Crimes in the Former Yugoslavia." *Dispatch* 4, no. 6 (1993): 75–79.

———. "Focus on Diplomacy: The State Department at Work." On-line. Internet. Available from http://www.state.gov./www/about_state/diplomacy.html. 1996.

———. "The Foreign Affairs Budget: Our Foreign Policy Cannot Be Supported on the Cheap." *Dispatch* 6, no. 15 (1995): 285–91.

———. "Foreign Policy: Year-End Review and Goals for 1995." *Dispatch* 6, no. 1 (1995): 1–2.

———. "Implementing the Dayton Agreements: New Partnerships." *Dispatch* 7, no. 7 (1996): 33–38.

———. "The Importance of Civilian Implementation." In *Dispatch*. Washington, D.C.: US Department of State, 1996.

———. "The International Conference on Bosnia: Now We Must Act." *Dispatch* 6, no. 30 (1995).

———. "The Last Best Chance for Peace in Bosnia-Herzegovina." *Dispatch* 6, no. 45 (1995): 807–13.

———. "Maintaining the Momentum for Peace in the Middle East." *Dispatch* 5, no. 43 (1994): 709–11.

———. "Measuring Successes and Continuing Negotiations in the Middle East." *Dispatch* 7, no. 7 (1996): 38–40.

———. "The New Geopolitics: Defending Democracy in the Post–Cold War Era." *Dispatch* 5, no. 46 (1994): 761–65.

———. "The OSCE in Bosnia." *Dispatch* 6, nos. 50, 51, 52 (1995): 921–22.

———. "The OSCE's Role in Building an Undivided Europe." *Dispatch* 6, nos. 50, 51, 52 (1995): 920–21.

———. "Peace in Bosnia: A Dividend of American Leadership." *Dispatch* 6, nos. 50, 51, 52 (1995): 901.

———. "Peace-Keeping and Multilateral Relations in U.S. Foreign Policy." *Dispatch* 5, no. 49 (1994): 808–10.

———. "Policy and Principles: The Clinton Administration's Approach." *Dispatch* 7, no. 6 (1996): 26–29.

———. "Political Reform in the Middle East: America's Stake." *Dispatch* 6, no. 44 (1995): 800–802.

———. "Prospects of Peace with Justice in Bosnia." *Dispatch* 7, no. 8 (1996): 53–57.

———. *Reorganization Plan and Report: Submitted by President Clinton to the Congress on December 30, 1998, Pursuant to Section 1601 of the Foreign Affairs Reform and Restructuring Act of 1998, as Contained in Public Law 105-277.* On-line. 30 December 1998. Internet (cited 6 February 1999). Available from http://www.state.gov/www/publications/state mag/statemag_nov-dec97.featxt2.html.

———. "A Review of Developments in the Middle East." *Dispatch* 5, no. 41 (1994): 681–86.

———. "Tribute to U.S. Peace Delegation to Bosnia-Herzegovina." *Dispatch* 6, no. 36 (1995).

———. "Turning from the Horror of War to the Promise of Peace in the Balkans." *Dispatch* 6, nos. 50, 51, 52 (1995): 899–900.

———. *USIA: On Meeting the Public Diplomacy Challenge.* On-line. 1997. Internet (cited 6 February 1999). Available from http://www.state.gov/www/publications/statemag/state mag_nov-dec97.featxt2.html.

———. "The United States Must Continue to Lead in Bosnia." *Dispatch* 6, no. 43 (1995): 755–56.

———. "U.S. Leadership and the Balkan Challenge: Deputy Secretary Talbott Remarks at the National Press Club." *Dispatch* 6, no. 47 (1995): 859–61.

———. "U.S. Policy on Bosnia and Assistance to Unprofor." *Dispatch* 6, no. 26 (1995): 531–32.

———. "The U.S. and Saudi Arabia: Working Together for Security, Stability, and Peace in the Middle East." *Dispatch* 6, no. 46 (1995): 831–32.

———. "U.S. Support for Implementing the Bosnian Peace Agreement." *Dispatch* 6, no. 48 (1995): 867–69.

———. "U.S. Support for UN Security Council Resolutions Concerning Bosnia." *Dispatch* 5, no. 47 (1994): 778–79.

———. "U.S. Troops Meet the Challenge of Maintaining Peace in Bosnia." *Dispatch* 6, no. 49 (1995): 889–90.

US General Accounting Office (GAO). *Operation Desert Storm: Evaluation of the Air Campaign.* Washington, D.C.: GPO, 1997.

US House. "Briefing on Operation Desert Shield: Costs and Contributions." Washington, D.C.: GPO, 1991.

———. "Congress and Foreign Policy, 1991." Washington, D.C.: GPO, 1992.

———. "Congress, the President and the War Powers," edited by Committee on Foreign Affairs. Washington, D.C.: GPO, 1970.

———. "Consideration of Draft Legislation on the Situation in the Persian Gulf." Washington, D.C.: GPO, 1991.

———. "Crisis in the Persian Gulf." Washington, D.C.: GPO, 1990.

———. "Crisis in the Persian Gulf: Sanctions, Diplomacy and War." Washington, D.C.: GPO, 1990.

———. "Current Developments in the United Nations System." Washington, D.C.: GPO, 1990.

———. "Department of Defense Appropriations for 1992, Part 7." Washington, D.C.: GPO, 1991.

———. "Developments in Europe, October 1990." Washington, D.C.: GPO, 1990.

———. "Developments in the Middle East." Washington, D.C.: GPO, 1991.

———. "Developments in the Middle East." Washington, D.C.: GPO, 1992.

———. "Economic Impact of the Persian Gulf Crisis." Washington, D.C.: GPO, 1990.

———. "Energy Impact of the Persian Gulf Crisis." Washington, D.C.: GPO, 1991.

———. "Europe and the U.S.: Competition and Cooperation in the 1990s." Washington, D.C.: GPO, 1992.

———. "Foreign Contributions to the Costs of the Persian Gulf War." Washington, D.C.: GPO, 1991.

———. "Future of U.S. Foreign Policy in the Post–Cold War Era." Washington, D.C.: GPO, 1992.

———. "Hearings on National Defense Authorization Act for FY98: H.R. 1119 and Oversight of Previously Authorized Programs. Title I: Procurement." Washington, D.C.: GPO, 1997.

———. "Hearings on the Decision-Making Processes and Interagency Cooperation of the National Marine Fisheries Service Northwest Region." Washington, D.C.: GPO, 1998.

———. "Human Rights and Democracy in Kuwait." Washington, D.C.: GPO, 1991.

———. "Humanitarian Crisis in Iraq: Challenge for U.S. Policy." Washington, D.C.: GPO, 1991.

———. "Humanitarian Dilemma in Iraq." Washington, D.C.: GPO, 1991.

———. "National Defense Authorization Act for FY91." Washington, D.C.: GPO, 1990.

———. "Options for Dealing with Iraq." Washington, D.C.: GPO, 1992.

———. "Persian Gulf Crisis." Washington, D.C.: GPO, 1990.

———. "Persian Gulf Crisis." Washington, D.C.: GPO, 1991.

———. "Post–War Policy Issues in the Persian Gulf." Washington, D.C.: GPO, 1991.

———. "Regional Threats and Defense Options for the 1990s." Washington, D.C.: GPO, 1992.

———. "Risk/Benefit Analysis in the Legislative Process." Washington, D.C.: GPO, 1979.

———. "U.N. Role in the Persian Gulf and Iraqi Compliance with U.N. Resolutions." Washington, D.C.: GPO, 1991.

———. "U.N. Role in the Persian Gulf and Iraqi Compliance with U.N. Resolutions." Washington, D.C.: GPO, 1992.

———. "U.S. Policy in the Persian Gulf." Washington, D.C.: GPO, 1996.

———. "U.S. Policy toward Iraq." Washington, D.C.: GPO, 1996.

———. "Update on the Situation in the Persian Gulf." Washington, D.C.: GPO, 1990.

———. "U. S. Economic and Energy Security Interests in the Persian Gulf." Washington, D.C.: GPO, 1990.

———. "U.S. Policy toward the Middle East and Persian Gulf."
Washington, D.C.: GPO, 1991.

US Senate. "Changes in the European Security Environment."
Washington, D.C.: GPO, 1991.

———. "Crisis in the Persian Gulf Region: U.S. Policy Options
and Implications." Washington, D.C.: GPO, 1990.

———. "Department of Defense Appropriations, FY92, Part 1."
Washington, D.C.: GPO, 1991.

———. "Department of Defense Authorization for Appropriations
for FY92–FY93, Part 1." Washington, D.C.: GPO, 1991.

———. "Desert Storm, the Budget and Other Issues: The State of
the U.S. Government Two Years after the Bush Transition."
Washington, D.C.: GPO, 1991.

———. "Implementation of Lessons Learned from the Persian
Gulf Conflict." Washington, D.C.: GPO, 1994.

———. "Implications of the Middle Eastern Crisis for near-Term
and Mid-Term Oil Supply." Washington, D.C.: GPO, 1990.

———. "Middle East." Washington, D.C.: GPO, 1991.

———. *National Security Act.* 80th Cong., 1st sess., 1948.

———. "National Security Council." Washington, D.C.: GPO,
1970.

———. *Organizing for National Security. Final Statement of Senator Henry M. Jackson.* 87th Cong., 1st sess., 1961.

———. *Organizing for National Security: The Bureau of the Budget and the Budgetary Process.* 87th Cong., 1st sess., 1961.

———. *Organizing for National Security: The National Security
Council.* 86th Cong. 2d sess., 1960.

———. "Pentagon Rules on Media Access to the Persian Gulf
War." Washington, D.C.: GPO, 1991.

———. "Refugee Crisis in the Persian Gulf." Washington, D.C.:
GPO, 1991.

———. "U.S. Policy in the Persian Gulf." Washington, D.C.: GPO,
1990.

———. "U.S. Policy in the Persian Gulf." Washington, D.C.: GPO,
1991.

———. "U.S. Policy in the Persian Gulf, Part 1." Washington,
D.C.: GPO, 1990.

————. "U.S. Policy in the Persian Gulf, Part 2." Washington, D.C.: GPO, 1990.

van de Vall, Mark. "Utilization and Methodology of Applied Social Research: Four Complementary Models." *Journal of Applied Behavioral Science* 11, no. 1 (1975): 14–38.

Van Evera, Stephen. "Hypotheses on Nationalism and War." *International Security* 18, no. 4 (1994): 5–39.

Vayrynen, Raimo, ed. *New Directions in Conflict Theory: Conflict Resolution and Conflict Transformation.* Newbury Park, Calif.: Sage Publications, Inc., 1991.

Verstandig, Toni G. "Principal Elements of US Policy in the Persian Gulf." *US Department of State Dispatch* 5, no. 14 (1994): 198–200.

Vliert, Evert van de, and Martin C. Euwema. "Managing Conflict with a Subordinate or a Superior: Effectiveness of Conglomerated Behavior." *Journal of Applied Psychology* 80, no. 2 (1995): 271–81.

von Neumann, John, and Oskar Morgenstern. *Theory of Games and Economic Behavior.* Princeton, N.J.: Princeton University Press, 1944.

Vroom, C. W. "Routine Decision-Making: The Future of Bureaucracy." *Organization Studies* 1, no. 4 (1980): 380–81.

Vroom, Victor H., and P. W. Yetton. *Leadership and Decision Making.* Pittsburgh, Pa.: University of Pittsburgh Press, 1973.

Walczak, Lee, and John Rossant. "Kosovo: A Bad Beginning and No Good Ending." *Business Week,* 12 April 1999, 58.

Wall, James A. *Negotiation, Theory and Practice.* Glenview, Ill.: Scott, Foresman, 1985.

Wallace, Michael D.; Peter Suedfeld; and Kimberley Thachuk. "Political Rhetoric of Leaders under Stress in the Gulf Crisis." *Journal of Conflict Resolution* 37, no. 1 (1993): 94–107.

Wallensteen, Peter, and Margareta Sollenberg. "The End of International War? Armed Conflict 1989–95." *Journal of Peace Research* 33, no. 3 (1996): 353–70.

Walt, Stephen M. "The Hidden Nature of Systems." *The Atlantic Monthly* 282, no. 3 (1998): 130–34.

Walton, Richard E., and John M. Dutton. "The Management of Interdepartmental Conflict: A Model and Review." In *Classic*

Readings in Organizational Behavior. J. S. Ott, ed. Pacific Grove, Calif.: Brooks/Cole Publishing Co., 1989.

Walton, Richard E., and Robert B. McKersie. *A Behavioral Theory of Labor Negotiations.* New York: McGraw-Hill Book Company, 1965.

Waltz, Kenneth N. *Man, the State, and War: A Theoretical Analysis.* New York: Columbia University Press, 1959.

Warden, Col John A., III. *The Air Campaign: Planning for Combat.* McLean, Va.: Pergamon-Brassey's International Defense Publishers, Inc., 1989.

Watson, Warren, Larry K. Michaelsen, and Walt Sharp. "Member Competence, Group Interaction, and Group Decision Making: A Longitudinal Study." *Journal of Applied Psychology* 76, no. 6 (1991): 803–9.

Watzlawick, Paul; John H. Weakland; and Richard Fisch. *Change: Principles of Problem Formulation and Problem Resolution.* New York: W. W. Norton & Co., Inc., 1974.

Weaver, Brett H. *War Termination: A Theater CINC's Responsibility?* Washington, D.C.: National Defense University, 1997.

Weaver, Larry A., and Robert D. Pollock. "Campaign Planning for the 21st Century: An Effects-Based Approach to the Planning Process." In *War Theory.* M. Kwolek and G. Story, eds. Maxwell AFB, Ala.: Air Command and Staff College, 1995, 13–20.

Weber, Max. "Bureaucracy." In *Classics of Organization Theory.* J. M. Shafritz and J. S. Ott, eds. Pacific Grove, Calif.: Brooks/Cole Publishing Co., 1987, 81–86.

Weick, Karl E. "Rethinking Research on Decision Making." In *Decision Making: An Interdisciplinary Inquiry.* G. R. Ungson and D. N. Braunstein, eds. Boston, Mass.: Kent Publishing Co., 1982, 325–33.

Weigley, Russell Frank. *The American Way of War: A History of United States Military Strategy and Policy.* Bloomington, Ind.: Indiana University Press, 1973.

Weingart, Laurie R., Rebecca J. Bennett, and Jeanne M. Brett. "The Impact of Consideration of Issues and Motivational Orientation on Group Negotiation Process and Outcome." *Journal of Applied Psychology* 78, no. 3 (1993): 504–17.

Wentz, Larry, ed. *Lessons from Bosnia: The IFOR Experience.* Washington, D.C.: Institute for National Strategic Studies, 1997.

West, William F. "Searching for a Theory of Bureaucratic Structure." *Journal of Public Administration Research and Theory* 7, no. 4 (1997): 591–613.

Westphal, James D., and Edward J. Zajac. "Defections from the Inner Circle: Social Exchange, Reciprocity, and the Diffusion of Board Independence in U.S. Corporations." *Administrative Science Quarterly* 42, no. 1 (1997): 161–83.

Whicker, Marcia Lynn. "The Case against the War." In *The Presidency and the Persian Gulf War.* Marcia Lynn Whicker, James P. Pfiffner, and Raymond A. Moore, eds. Westport, Conn.: Praeger, 1993, 111–29.

Whicker, Marcia Lynn; James P. Pfiffner; and Raymond A. Moore, eds. *The Presidency and the Persian Gulf War.* Westport, Conn.: Praeger, 1993.

White House, The. *Fact Sheet: Reinventing State, ACDA, USIA, and AID.* On-line. Office of Press Secretary, 18 April 1997. Internet (cited 6 February 1999). Available from http://www.state.gov/www/global/general_foreign_policy/.

———. *A National Security Strategy for a New Century.* Washington, D.C.: GPO, 1998.

———. *A National Security Strategy for a New Century.* Washington, D.C.: GPO, 1999.

———. *A National Security Strategy of Engagement and Enlargement.* Washington, D.C.: GPO, 1994.

———. *National Security Strategy of the United States.* Washington, D.C.: GPO, 1991.

White, Ralph K. "Empathizing with Saddam Hussein." *International Society of Political Psychology* 12, no. 2 (1991): 291–308.

Whyte, Glen. "Diffusion of Responsibility: Effects on the Escalation Tendency." *Journal of Applied Psychology* 76, no. 3 (1991): 408–15.

Wijninga, Lt Col Peter W. W., Royal Netherlands Air Force, and Richard Szafranski. *Beyond Utility Targeting toward Axiological Air Operations.* On-line. Air University Chronicles,

2000. Internet (cited 25 January 2001). Available from http://www.airpower.maxwell.af.mil/airchronicles/apj/apj00/win00/szafranski.

Wilcken, Patrick. "The Intellectuals, the Media and the Gulf War." *Critique of Anthropology* 15, no. 1 (1995): 37–69.

Wilcox, Clyde; Aiji Tanaka; and Dee Allsop. "World Opinion in the Gulf Crisis." *Journal of Conflict Resolution* 37, no. 1 (1993): 69–93.

Willer, David. "Is Elementary Theory a Satisfactory Rational Choice Theory?" Presentation. American Sociological Association Meetings, Cincinnati, Ohio, 1991.

Wittman, Donald. "How a War Ends: A Rational Approach." *Journal of Conflict Resolution* 23 (1979): 743–63.

Wojdakowski, Walter. *Conflict Termination: Integrating the Elements of Power in Today's Changing World.* Carlisle Barracks, Pa.: US Army War College, 1993.

Woodward, Bob. *The Commanders.* New York: Simon and Schuster, 1991.

Woodward, Susan L. *Balkan Tragedy: Chaos and Dissolution after the Cold War.* Washington, D.C.: Brookings Institution, 1995.

Worth, Robert. "Clinton's Warriors: The Interventionists." *World Policy Journal* 15, no. 1 (1998): 43–48.

Wright, Quincy. "The Escalation of International Conflicts." *Journal of Conflict Resolution* 9, no. 4 (1965).

Wright, Quincy. "How Hostilities Have Ended: Peace Treaties and Alternatives." *The Annals of the American Academy of Political and Social Science* 392 (1970): 51–61.

Yap, Hian Poh. *Some Topics in Graph Theory.* Cambridge & New York: Cambridge University Press, 1986.

Yaphe, Judith S. "Saudi Arabia: Uncertain Stability." *Strategic Forum,* no. 125 (1997).

Yarmolinsky, Adam. "Professional Military Perspectives on War Termination." In *On the Endings of Wars.* Stuart Albert and Edward C. Luck, eds. Port Washington, N.Y.: Kennikat Press, 1980, 121–30.

Yergin, Daniel. *The Prize: The Epic Quest for Oil, Money, and Power.* New York: Simon and Schuster, 1990.

York, Reginald O. "Situational Decision Making: An Empirical Examination." *Journal of Applied Social Sciences* 15, no. 2 (1991): 207–19.

Young, Oran R. "Intermediaries: Additional Thoughts on Third Parties." *Conflict Resolution* 16, no. 1 (1972): 51–65.

———. "Intermediaries and Interventionists: Third Parties in the Middle East Crisis." *International Journal* 23 (1967): 52–73.

Zagumny, Matthew J. "Mentoring as a Tool for Change: A Social Learning Perspective." *Organization Development Journal* 11, no. 4 (1993): 43–48.

Zaller, John. "Information, Values, and Opinions." *American Political Science Review* 85 (1991): 1215–38.

———. *The Nature and Origins of Mass Opinion.* New York: Cambridge University Press, 1993.

Zartman, I. William. "Decision Support and Negotiation Research: A Researcher's Perspective." *Theory and Decision* 34 (1993): 345–51.

———. "Negotiation as a Joint Decision-Making Process." *Journal of Conflict Resolution* 21, no. 4 (1977): 619–38.

———. *Ripe for Resolution: Conflict and Intervention in Africa.* New York: Oxford University Press, 1989.

———. "The Structure of Negotiation." In *International Negotiation: Analysis, Approaches, Issues.* Viktor Aleksandrovich Kremeniuk, ed. San Francisco, Calif.: Jossey-Bass, 1991.

Zelikow, Philip. "Foreign Policy Engineering: From Theory to Practice and Back Again." *International Security* 18, no. 4 (1994): 143–71.

Zey, Mary. "Alternative Perspectives: Microemphasis on the Individual." In *Decision Making: Alternatives to Rational Choice Models*, ed. Mary Zey. Newbury Park, Calif.: Sage Publications, 1992.

———. "Criticisms of Rational Choice Models." In *Decision Making: Alternatives to Rational Choice Models.* Mary Zey, ed. Newbury Park, Calif.: Sage Publications, 1992.

———. "Introduction to Alternative Perspectives: Macroemphasis on Organizations and Institutions." In *Decision Making: Alternatives to Rational Choice Models.* Mary Zey, ed. Newbury Park, Calif.: Sage Publications, 1992.

Zey, Mary, ed. *Decision Making: Alternatives to Rational Choice Models.* Newbury Park, Calif.: Sage Publications, 1992.

Zimmerman, Warren. *Origins of a Catastrophe.* New York: Times Books, 1996.

Zox, Alan A. "A Heuristic Typology of Policy Formation within Institutions of Higher Education." New Brunswick, N.J.: Rutgers University, 1977.

Zuber, Johannes A., Helmut W. Crott, and Joachim Werner. "Choice Shift and Group Polarization: An Analysis of the Status of Arguments and Social Decision Schemes." *Journal of Personality and Social Psychology* 62, no. 1 (1992): 50–61.

Index

intentional leaks, 255. *See also* "leaks with intent"

interagency conflict, 4–5, 15–19, 22, 31, 74, 82, 93–94, 100, 121, 129–33, 135, 139, 146–48, 160–62, 170–72, 175–77, 181, 188, 195–97, 210, 215, 220, 223, 228–30, 235–36, 245–50, 256–58, 265, 267–68, 272, 284, 287, 296–99, 313–22, 324, 327–28, 330–32, 334–36

interagency dynamic(s), 257

interagency working group (IWG), 150, 154–55, 157, 172, 176, 180, 187, 197, 211, 297–98, 323–24

interdepartmental conflict, 287

Joint Chiefs of Staff (JCS), 96, 102, 228, 292

judgmental heuristics, 35, 37, 39

Kahneman, Daniel, 35

Kecskemeti, Paul, 111

Kuwait, 32, 195, 270–71, 279, 292

Lake, Anthony, 110, 113

"leaks with intent," 255–57. *See also* intentional leaks

Middle East, 113, 292

mutually hurting stalemate, 68

National Security Council (NSC), 8–9, 11–12, 68, 85, 87, 89, 91, 93–97, 99, 101, 103, 105–11, 113, 115, 117, 119, 121, 123, 125, 127, 131–32, 144–46, 150, 152–53, 156–59, 171–72, 175–76, 179, 181, 185, 187–89, 193–94, 210, 212–14, 216, 219–20, 223–24, 226, 228–30, 232–33, 245–50, 254–57, 267–68, 272, 277, 281–82, 286, 290–92, 294, 297, 314, 316–17, 319, 323, 325, 331, 334–358

Nicholson, Michael, 30, 79, 93

North Atlantic Council (NAC), 282

NSC Staff, 107–10, 113, 145, 159, 175, 179, 181, 189, 212, 216, 219, 223, 226, 245–46, 248–49, 254–55, 268, 277, 291, 297, 316–17, 319, 325, 334–35

NSC System, 8–9, 12, 188, 193–94, 314, 316, 334

Nudler, Oscar, 221

Office of the Director of Central Intelligence (ODCI), 153

Office of the Secretary of Defense (OSD), 97, 248, 254

partisan politics, 193, 195, 219, 236, 318

Perry, William, 172, 218

Persian Gulf War, 4, 18, 93, 111–12, 119, 129, 161, 238, 257–58, 265, 270, 278–79, 285, 290–91

president, 8–11, 87, 89, 96–100, 103–11, 113, 115–16, 169–73, 177, 186, 194, 196–97, 211, 213, 219, 226, 232–33, 245–46, 248, 253, 270–71, 273, 280, 284, 289, 291–92, 316–17, 326, 330, 334–35

Presidential Decision Directive (PDD), 56, 212
principals committee (PC), 150–51, 187, 211, 214, 230, 275

rational actor model, 7, 16–17, 28–31, 37–38, 41, 61–62, 66–70, 73–74, 76–80, 87, 91–92, 106, 191–92, 214, 323–24
rational choice theory, 17, 20, 27–35, 37–43, 45, 47–49, 51, 53, 55, 57, 59, 61, 66–67, 77, 79–80, 85–87, 90, 92, 121, 191–92, 234, 283, 313, 323, 325, 327
Realpolitik, 74, 101, 155, 299

Scowcroft, Brent, 232, 270
social learning, 43, 45
State Department, 94, 100–106, 108, 118, 152–53, 170, 172–73, 176–77, 179, 184–86, 189, 191, 193, 196, 210–13, 216, 218–24, 226–31, 233, 235, 245–49, 251–55, 257, 266, 273–74, 277, 281–82, 284–85, 299, 317, 319
Strategic Planning, 155, 212, 247, 320
subjective expected utility (SEU), 29, 31, 40
sustainable peace, 5, 16, 94, 295–96, 299, 313, 321, 327–28, 330–31, 336

termination criteria, 4, 15–16, 18, 27, 94, 111, 122, 135, 215, 251, 257, 265, 278, 281, 283–88, 293–94, 297–99, 313, 324, 327–29, 336
termination strategy, 6, 16, 18, 20, 27, 265, 286–91, 293–95, 298–99, 313, 324, 327–29, 336
"Train and Equip" plan, 281
Tversky, Amos, 35

United Nations (UN), 95, 97, 112, 195, 285, 293

War Powers Resolution, 10–11, 89, 95, 117, 193, 284
Weber, Max, 7
Weinberger Doctrine, 218, 289
World War II, 9, 99, 111, 117, 119

Zartman, I. William, 5, 68
Zey, Mary, 36, 42